YELLOWSTONE TREASURES

The Traveler's Companion to the National Park

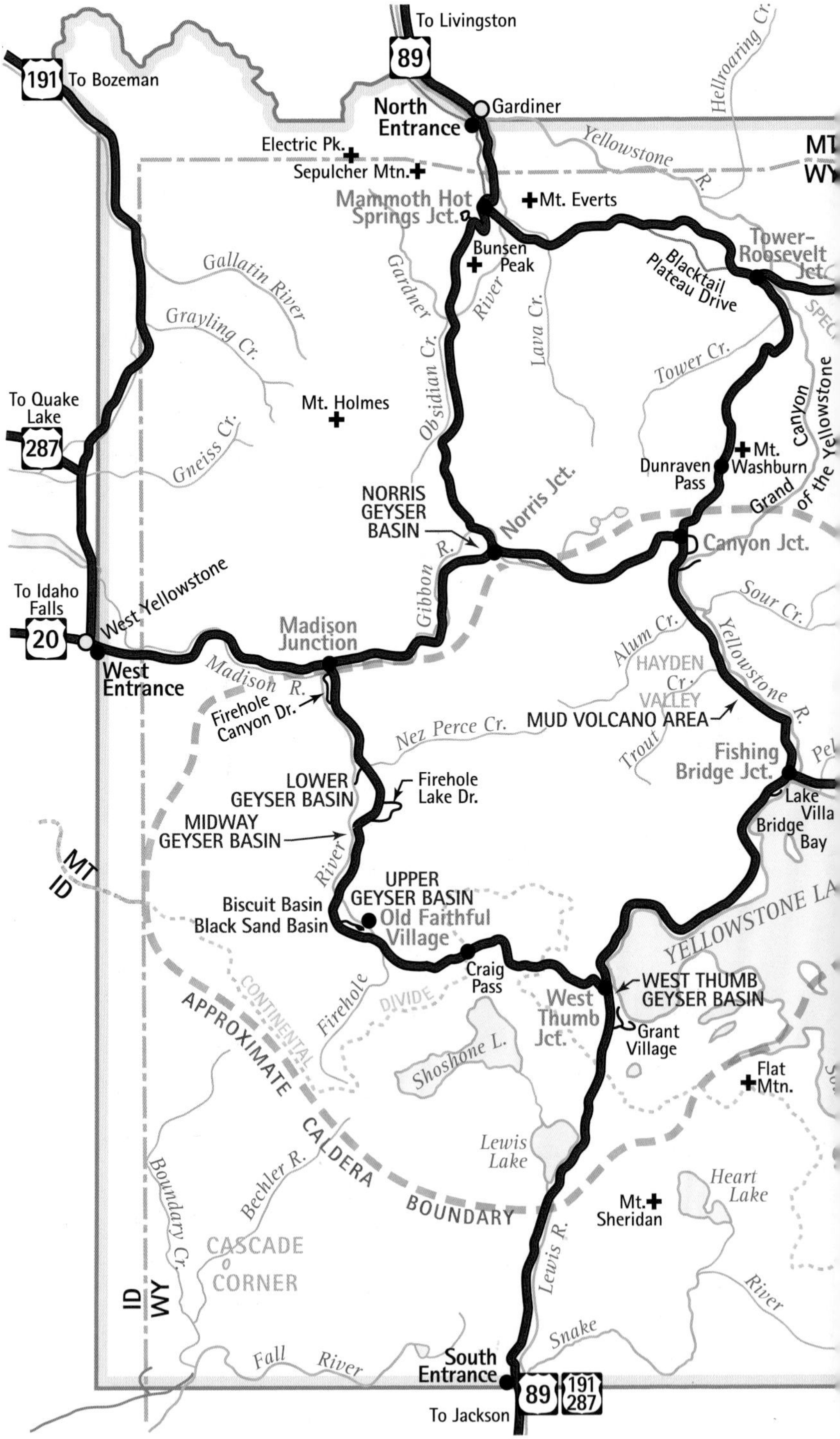
To Livingston
89
191
To Bozeman
Gardiner
North Entrance
Electric Pk.
Sepulcher Mtn.
Yellowstone R.
Hellroaring Cr.
MT
WY
Mammoth Hot Springs Jct.
Mt. Everts
Bunsen Peak
Tower-Roosevelt Jct.
Blacktail Plateau Drive
Gallatin River
Gardner River
Lava Cr.
Grayling Cr.
Tower Cr.
Obsidian Cr.
Mt. Holmes
To Quake Lake
287
Mt. Washburn
Dunraven Pass
Grand Canyon of the Yellowstone
Gneiss Cr.
NORRIS GEYSER BASIN
Norris Jct.
Canyon Jct.
Gibbon R.
To Idaho Falls
20
West Yellowstone
Madison Junction
Sour Cr.
Alum Cr.
HAYDEN VALLEY
Yellowstone R.
West Entrance
Madison R.
Firehole Canyon Dr.
Nez Perce Cr.
MUD VOLCANO AREA
Trout Cr.
Fishing Bridge Jct.
LOWER GEYSER BASIN
Firehole Lake Dr.
Lake Village
Bridge Bay
MIDWAY GEYSER BASIN
MT
ID
River
UPPER GEYSER BASIN
Biscuit Basin
Black Sand Basin
Old Faithful Village
YELLOWSTONE LAKE
Craig Pass
West Thumb Jct.
WEST THUMB GEYSER BASIN
Grant Village
CONTINENTAL DIVIDE
Firehole
APPROXIMATE CALDERA BOUNDARY
Shoshone L.
Flat Mtn.
Lewis Lake
Heart Lake
Boundary Cr.
Bechler R.
Mt. Sheridan
CASCADE CORNER
Lewis R.
River
ID
WY
Snake
Fall River
South Entrance
89
191
287
To Jackson

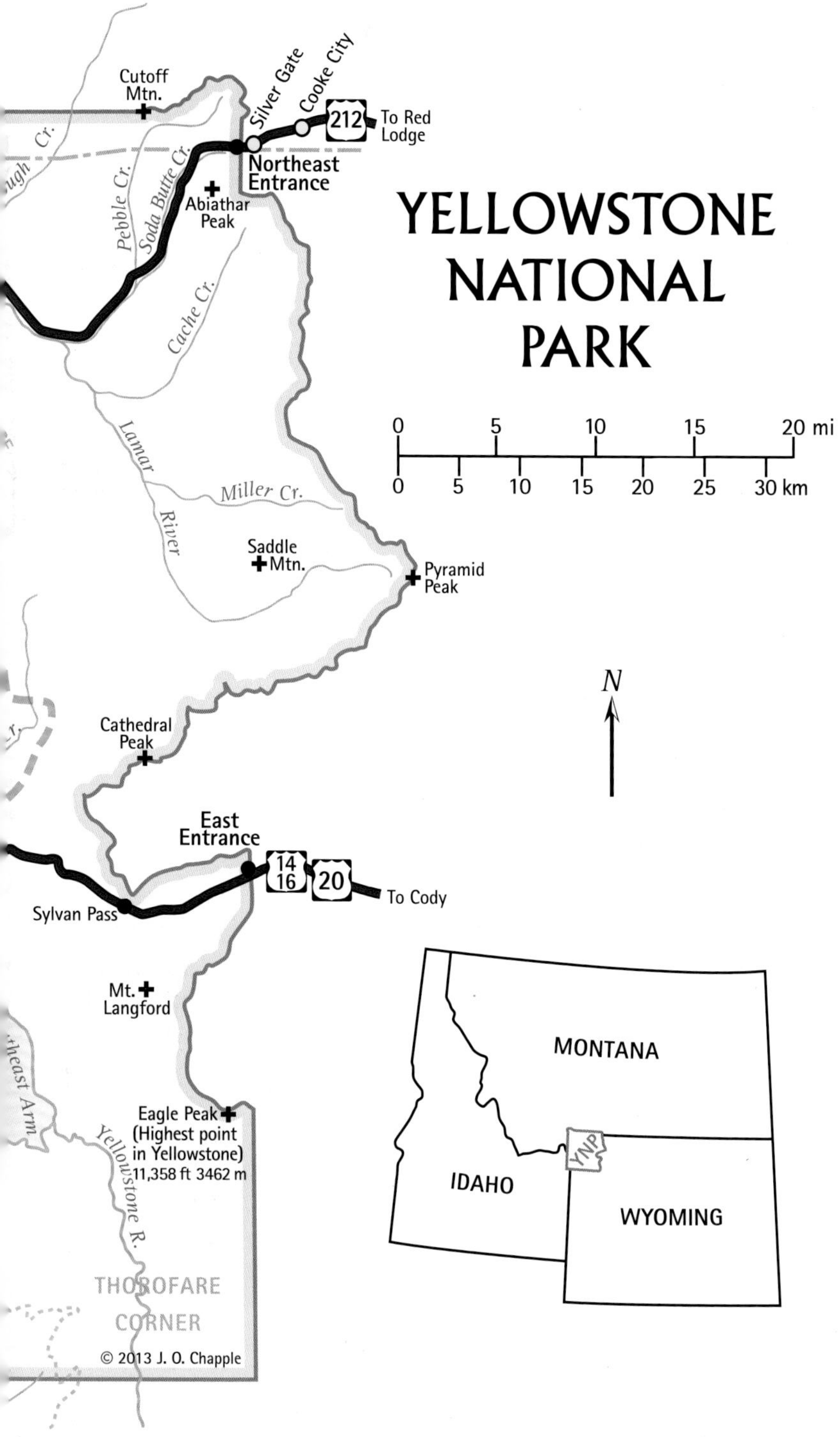
YELLOWSTONE NATIONAL PARK
0 5 10 15 20 mi
0 5 10 15 20 25 30 km
N
Cutoff Mtn.
Silver Gate
Cooke City
212
To Red Lodge
Northeast Entrance
Abiathar Peak
Pebble Cr.
Soda Butte Cr.
Cache Cr.
Lamar River
Miller Cr.
Saddle Mtn.
Pyramid Peak
Cathedral Peak
East Entrance
14 16
20
To Cody
Sylvan Pass
Mt. Langford
Eagle Peak (Highest point in Yellowstone) 11,358 ft 3462 m
Yellowstone R.
THOROFARE CORNER
MONTANA
IDAHO
WYOMING
YNP
© 2013 J. O. Chapple

YELLOWSTONE TREASURES

The Traveler's Companion to the National Park

JANET CHAPPLE

with geological text and advice by

Bruno J. Giletti

Professor Emeritus of Geological Sciences

Brown University

and

Jo-Ann Sherwin, PhD, P. G.

FOURTH EDITION

Granite Peak Publications, Oakland, California

To my sister, Joan Orvis,
whose love and encouragement
have always guided my life
(1931–2001)

16 15 14 13   1 2 3 4 5 6
ISBN 978-0-9706873-8-8

Publishers Cataloging-in-Publication

Chapple, Janet
Yellowstone treasures : the traveler's companion to the national park / Janet Chapple ; with geological text and advice by Bruno J. Giletti and Jo-Ann Sherwin.—
Updated 4th ed.
p. : cm.
Includes bibliographical references and index.
LCCN 2012946902
ISBN 978-0-9706873-8-8
ISBN 978-0-9706873-9-5
ISBN 978-0-9858182-0-3
ISBN 978-0-9858182-1-0

1. Yellowstone National Park—Guidebooks.
I. Giletti, Bruno J. II. Sherwin, Jo-Ann III. Title
F722.C458 2012   917.87'520434
QBI12-600182

Park Historian Lee H. Whittlesey reviewed this book for historical accuracy.
Editor: Beth Chapple
Book designer: Alice Merrill
Printed by C&C Offset Printing Co., Ltd.

Published by Granite Peak Publications, Oakland, CA
www.yellowstonetreasures.com

CONTENTS

ROAD LOGS AND DESTINATIONS

Maps

Geological Figures

ACKNOWLEDGMENTS

It was in 1995 that I began to research and write *Yellowstone Treasures*. So many people have helped me in so many ways along the way that I cannot be sure to acknowledge them all. If you are one of those, please forgive the omission of your name and know that your help was appreciated.

For initial and continuing help I must single out my husband, Bruno J. Giletti; editor and daughter Beth Chapple; the late Bob English, who had the original idea for this guide; and incomparable mapmaker Linton A. Brown. My thanks also goes to all the photographers and others credited on page 397.

The following list includes some of the many kind, patient, and dedicated park rangers and other National Park Service, Yellowstone Association, and Yellowstone Institute personnel, as well as friends and relations whose help and encouragement has been invaluable: Holly Bartlett, Vic Benson, Sarah Broadbent, Thomas and Kathie Brock, Scott Bryan, Ed and Judy Mulvaney Bunnell, Karen Chapple, Nancy Chapple, Vanessa Christopher, Eleanor Williams Clark, Pat Cole, Mike Condon, Carol Critelli, Niklas Dellby, Ann Deutch, Duncan Foley, Donald Forsyth, David Fountain, Alan Fox, Nathan Fox, Bob Fuhrmann, Laura Giletti, David Goldberg, Bob Greenburg, Steve Gryc, Aubrey Haines, Virgil Hall, Tamsen Hert, Karl Hoppe, Tom Hougham, Tim Hudson, Jeanne Johnson, Kay and Durwood Johnson, Laura Joss, Susan Kraft, Harmon Kredit, Kathryn Kirby, Ted Koel, Greg Kroll, Catherine Lentz, Marcia and Phil Lieberman, Doug Madsen, John Martin, Cheryl Matthews, Margie and Bob McCoy, Marlene Merrill, Judith Meyer, Lisa Morgan, Lisa Nelbach, Tom Olliff, Joan Orvis, Ted Parkinson, Jim Peaco, Bev Peterson, Wayne Phillips, Anna-Louise Reysenbach, Roberta Ryan, John Sacklin, Caryl and Henry Seidenberg, Sandy Snell-Dobert, Lynn Stephens, Brian Suderman, Mary Taber, Mary Van Buskirk, Andrew Washburn, Rachel Weinberger, Jennifer Whipple, Lee Whittlesey, Marylor Wilson, and Barbara Zafft. Libraries and organizations: Brown University's Science, Rockefeller, and John Hay; Providence Public; Yellowstone Heritage and Research Center, Yellowstone Library and Archives; Geyser Observation and Study Association. Additional third edition assistance came from M. A. Bellingham, Paul Doss, John King, Barbara Lasseter, Tim McDermott, Linda Miller, Pat Shanks, Kurt Strempel, and John Tebby; fourth edition assistance from Al Hofmann, William Leidenthal, Lois Oakes, and Jo-Ann Sherwin.

PREFACE

So she sat on, with closed eyes, and half believed herself in Wonderland,
though she knew she had but to open them again and
all would change to dull reality...
—Alice's Adventures in Wonderland,
Lewis Carroll, 1865

A late summer day begins at Yellowstone Lake.

Some people in our fast-paced age make Yellowstone just one stop on a whirlwind western tour. But if you can allow several days or a week or two to savor it, Yellowstone will reward you fully. This guide is intended for such relatively unhurried first-time visitors and for the many thousands of us who return to explore anew.

I am one of the fortunate few who have spent many summer months in the park, first as an impressionable small child, later as an adult who could never get enough of the Yellowstone country. My association with the park and its surrounding mountains goes back two generations to my maternal grandfather, Fred Inabnit, a Swiss native who organized hiking trips and popularized the idea of appreciating the mountains—particularly the Beartooths—by exploring them. He spent years constructing a relief map of the Yellowstone area, now at the Museum of the Beartooths, Columbus, Montana. After his death in 1928, a mountain was named for him not far from Montana's highest mountain, Granite Peak, which he just missed conquering.

For four idyllic summers of my childhood I lived near Old Faithful Inn, where my father was transportation agent. My sister Joan and I played countless games of Parcheesi while waiting for Great Fountain Geyser to erupt. Once my parents got us out of bed late at night to see Giant Geyser play. I played hide and seek with Joan when most of Old Faithful Inn's guests had left for the day's excursions and Mother was rehearsing music in the lobby with the Ladies' Ensemble. On rainy days, we read Frances Farnsworth's *Cubby in Wonderland* and *Cubby Returns*. Sometimes we left Daddy at his favorite hole above Firehole Cascades to catch a mess of trout for supper.

Yellowstone means many things to many people: bears and bison, geysers and colorful pools, hikes and horseback rides, distant vistas and the stillness of the backcountry. It can also mean clear dry western air, spectacular sunsets, and night skies so full of stars you think you're seeing to the end of the universe. Author Owen Wister said it for me back in 1891: "I have tested the power of the moon by consulting the second hand of my watch and reading a letter with rapid ease. But that's a poor mathematical way to talk or think about such magic. And all through the still air, the clean sharp odor of the sage. Not dusty, as it smells at noon, but cool, like something a fairy would give you to make you suddenly well. Nobody, nobody who lives on the Atlantic strip, has a notion of what sunrise and sunset and moonlight can be in their native land till they have come here to see."

Yellowstone Park was called Wonderland by many writers in the early days, traceable to the publication of *Alice's Adventures in Wonderland* shortly before the park was created. Since the first Hayden Survey in 1871, scientists and other curious people have learned much about the origin of the park's wonders and how they function, but there are still countless wonders to be explained.

Visitors to Yellowstone Park now span six generations, from the explorers who braved some danger and considerable discomfort, to today's backseat youngsters with their handheld electronic games. Like so many others, my parents and sister and I in the third and fourth of those generations came with a copy of the *Haynes Guide* in our hands. I have followed that guide's organizational plan, and I honor the memory of pioneers F. "Jay" and Jack E. Haynes, who, for more than 75 years, published their comprehensive guidebooks full of information about park features, animals, plants, and photography.

My loving gratitude goes to my three Chapple daughters, Nancy, Beth, and Karen, for the support they gave me toward initial publication of this book.

INTRODUCTION

Although the principal sights like Old Faithful Geyser and the Grand Canyon of the Yellowstone are notorious for crowds, you'll surely want to see them. But there are myriad other ways to enjoy Yellowstone. Imagine yourself walking a half mile (0.8 km) to a quiet, lily-covered lake—like Harlequin Lake near Madison Junction. Maybe you'd enjoy hiking or biking on a level road through untouched meadows to see an eruption of Lone Star Geyser, or waiting with other wildlife watchers for wolves to appear in Lamar Valley. Here are a few hints for maximizing your enjoyment of Yellowstone.

When to go and what to see

In June or September you'll find fewer people than in midsummer (see "When Is the Best Time to Visit?" for other seasonal information). If you can arrange your stroll around Upper Geyser Basin or the Mammoth Terraces for early morning or late evening, it may be yours to enjoy alone. Above all, what you need to truly enjoy the park is adequate time spent out of your vehicle, to observe and savor all the park's treasures. Choose among the numerous wonderful short hikes on pages 366–68. Check the Best Sights of Yellowstone later in this introduction to help you plan your visit. I also list less-known places I love, none more than one-half mile (0.8 km) from a road.

This road guide is designed for visitors traveling in their own or a rented vehicle or by bus, particularly during the warm months of the year, when all destinations are accessible. This is high mountain terrain, and most roads in Yellowstone are not plowed between early November and mid April. Travel in the winter season (mid December through mid March) is by snowmobile or snowcoach only and limited to a few sections of the park. Most accommodations are open from mid May or early June until mid September or early October.

You'll encounter the best weather in July and August, but also the most people. Weather in Yellowstone's summers is unpredictable, ranging from hot sun to rain and hail. Lightning storms are common, especially in late afternoons. It can snow or the temperature can drop to freezing any month of the year.

Safety and Hiking

Remember that you must not approach or feed any wildlife in the park. Park regulations tell you, "You must stay at least 100 yards (91 m) away from bears and wolves and at least 25 yards (23 m) away from bison, elk, bighorn sheep, deer, moose, and coyotes." For your safety and the animals' welfare, especially

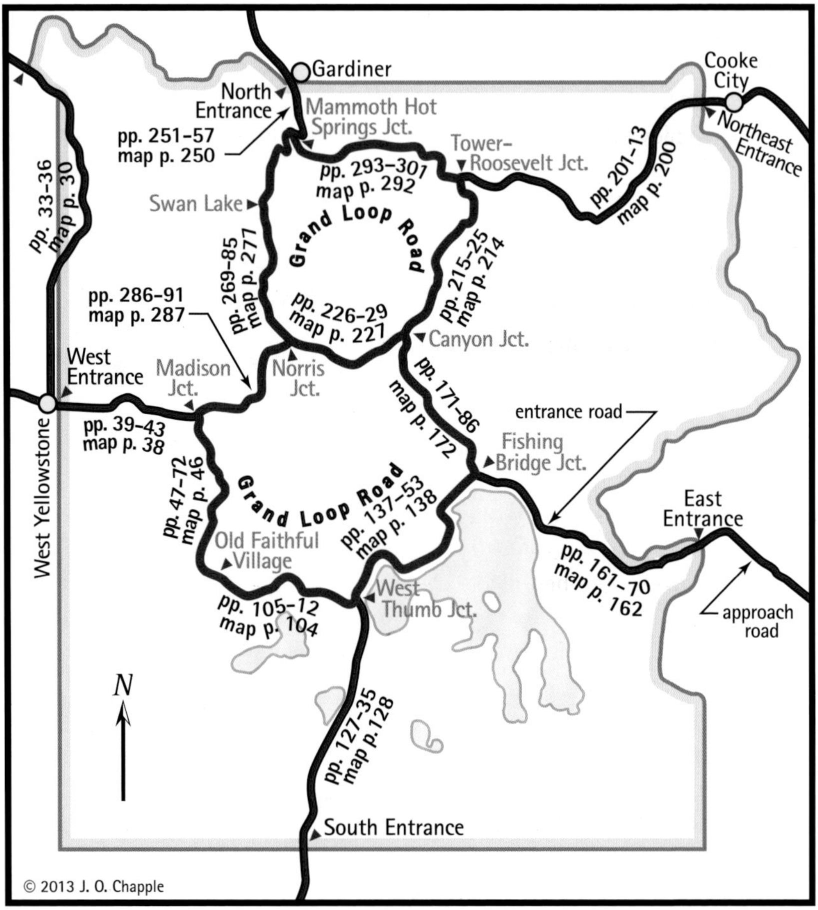

Key to the Park Roads

avoid all wildlife with young. Never hike alone. Make some noise so you won't surprise an animal, and carry bear spray on backcountry hikes.

When Is the Best Time to Visit?

Spring—May, June

When the snow has melted from the lowlands and the red bison calves are trailing after their mothers, you know springtime has come to Yellowstone.
TEMPERATURES: 50s–60s °F (teens °C) by day; 30s °F (0–4°C) at night
PROS: Baby animals numerous, wildflowers (at lower elevations), waterfalls at their peak

CONS: Some mountain passes closed, biting insects common, rain common, meadows flooded, streams very high

Summer—July, August

A time to enjoy hikes in the high country, long vigils in the geyser basins, and picnics along the riversides.

TEMPERATURES: 70s–low 80s °F (20s °C) by day; 40s °F or below (below 9°C) at night

PROS: Wildflowers everywhere; drier trails in mid July and August; ripening berries in August; clear, starlit nights; fishing best in late July into September

CONS: Visitor numbers at their peak, late afternoon thunderstorms, potential fire danger or hordes of grasshoppers in dry years

Thimbleberries may be found along some park trails in late summer.

Autumn—September, early October

Brisk nights, cool but pleasant days, and great light for photography are some of the joys of this season.

TEMPERATURES: 40s–60s °F (5–20°C) by day; freezing and below at night

PROS: Fewer visitors, elk gather and bugle, aspen turn golden, few mosquitoes

CONS: Cold nights, greater chance of rain and snow

Winter—mid October through April

A snowcoach can take you to Old Faithful or Canyon (December to March), where you'll marvel at the beauty of steamy pools and frozen waterfalls.

TEMPERATURES: Well below freezing to a few degrees above by day; usually freezing, often below 0°F (-18°C) at night

PROS: Cross-country skiing, ice-encrusted "ghost" trees, animals near roads

CONS: Extreme cold, heavy snows and severe storms, most roads closed to cars

Traveling with children

Some places are dangerous for small children, and there are no playgrounds, no wading pools, no television, and very few radio stations that can be heard in the park. Be especially vigilant around the geyser basins. Stay well away from the animals—they are all wild.

Before you go to the park with children let them know how different it will be, and read books and watch videos about the park. While visiting, be sure to stop frequently for short hikes and to observe anything that interests them, from moss and insects to rocks and birds.

Children between the ages of 5 and 12 can become Junior Rangers. A special newspaper, available at visitor centers, guides them through the requirements, such as jotting down the animals they see and attending ranger talks and walks. In addition, three Young Scientist programs appropriate for ages 5–14 and up are available at Old Faithful and Canyon Visitor Centers (see www.nps.gov/yell/forteachers/youngscientist.htm).

What to expect and what Yellowstone is not

Yellowstone is a wonderful vacation spot for able-bodied adults and children over about five years of age. However, only a relatively small part of the developed area is accessible to wheelchairs. See "Accessibility" in the Travel Tips for details about what facilities and features are accessible in Yellowstone.

A woman touring Yellowstone in 1912 complained to visitor L. Louise Elliott: "There is such a sameness to it all. . . . Now, I supposed I should be seeing something different and interesting constantly without all the long, dusty rides between places. I thought the park fairly teemed with graceful fawn and antelope and other animals, and truly, I see more animals right at home in our city park, you know."

Reflecting on this complaint, Elliott wrote:

> I understand now as I never did before why so many people are disappointed when they come here. It is because of the fact that it is called a park and they come with the expectation of seeing a man-made park, similar to those of the cities, only on a much larger and vastly grander scale; with the curiosities all conveniently grouped, and the animals collected in large numbers in enclosed corrals. They forget that it is merely a district controlled by the Government and preserved as far as possible in its wild and natural state, and that the wild animals, native to this territory, are permitted to roam at will over miles and miles of country, and that the greater part of them come down to the mainly traveled districts only when forced to do so by hunger, when the snow gets deep and the grazing poor.
>
> —from Elliott, *Six Weeks on Horseback through Yellowstone Park*, 1913

How this guidebook is organized

The five Road Logs start with the gateway communities and sights outside the park, and then follow the approach roads and then the entrance roads onto the Grand Loop Road. Consult the maps called Key to the Park Roads, page

14, and Key to the Approach Roads, page 24. The latter map is color-coded to match the tops of the pages in the Road Log chapters. In the Road Logs, pairs of mileage indications show the distance in miles from an entrance station or major junction, as well as the distance from the other direction. Mileage figures are general guidelines; park road improvements sometimes change distances. Metric equivalents for the distances are provided in the introduction to each road segment and on the maps.

Destinations you encounter along the way are described in detail as you come to them. In the hydrothermal areas, I describe only the most readily visible, historically interesting, and fascinating geysers and hot springs. Since geysers are notoriously changeable, eruption details are kept somewhat general. While no one can predict where to see wild animals, you'll find hints for finding them on some of the maps and in the Living Things chapter. Also note that you won't necessarily find a certain animal or plant near a feature bearing its name.

After the Road Logs come chapters on Yellowstone's geologic past, its human history, and its flora and fauna. Practical help for planning your trip is found in the Travel Tips chapter and in the facilities and campgrounds charts. Before the index you'll find a suggested reading list, a chart of 56 recommended short walks, and a glossary of terms.

New to the fourth edition: This update of *Yellowstone Treasures* more thoroughly reflects my lifelong interest in geology. The truly remarkable geology of Yellowstone is the foundation of all the phenomena you see and experience, from the black glassy sand underfoot to the towering lodgepole pines above.

Best Sights of Yellowstone

We all have our own reasons for loving the park, and rating natural phenomena is subjective. Still, for the first-time visitor I've arranged some of the outstanding features by type, and, within each type, in order of appearance in the Road Logs.

I've only included predictable geysers, although this excludes many thrilling ones. All geysers in the list below are in Upper Geyser Basin except Great Fountain Geyser, which is on Firehole Lake Drive in Lower Geyser Basin.

Ratings: ★★ Don't miss!
★ Worth making time for or taking a detour

Geyser eruptions

Rangers at Old Faithful post predictions for these six geysers. Riverside, Castle, and Daisy Geysers are accessible by wheelchair or bicycle.

Great Fountain Geyser,★★ tall, exciting eruptions safe to witness at close range, page 60

Old Faithful Geyser,★★ world famous and easily accessible, page 78
Grand Geyser,★★ a favorite of many experienced geyser watchers, page 90
Riverside Geyser,★★ graceful, unique, and very predictable eruption over the Firehole River, page 93
Castle Geyser,★ unusual for its formation and roaring steam phase, page 99
Daisy Geyser,★ with oblique and frequent eruptions, page 101

Other thermal areas and features

Fountain Paint Pot,★ a loop trail that includes hot springs, fumaroles, and geysers as well as colored mud pots, page 56
Firehole Lake Drive,★ a short loop that includes Great Fountain Geyser, page 59
Midway Geyser Basin Loop Walk,★★ with the largest hot features in the park: Excelsior Geyser (now dormant) and Grand Prismatic Spring, page 63
Black Sand Basin,★ short trail to lovely hot springs, page 70
Crested Pool,★ superheated and beautifully formed pool near Castle Geyser, page 100
Punch Bowl Spring★ and Black Sand Pool,★ on an extension of the trail beyond Daisy Geyser, page 102
West Thumb Geyser Basin,★ a beautifully situated area with brilliantly colored hot springs, page 140
Mud Volcano★ and Dragon's Mouth,★ best thermal features in the Mud Volcano thermal area, pages 174 and 175
Norris Geyser Basin,★ hottest and most acidic basin, page 230
Porcelain Basin vista,★ hot treeless plain with colorful pools, page 243
Mammoth Hot Springs Lower and Upper Terraces,★ a mountain of travertine terraces with ever-changing hot springs, pages 263–67 and 271–74

Drives and vistas

Firehole Canyon Drive,★ falls and cascades in an interesting geological setting, page 49
View in front of Lake Hotel,★ beautiful lake and mountain panorama, pages 150–51
Grand View,★ best view of Canyon colors along North Rim Drive, page 185
Inspiration Point,★★ outstanding view of Canyon colors, page 186
Dunraven Pass★ and its trails, outstanding mountain pass for wildflowers and panoramas, north of Canyon Junction, page 223

Waterfalls

Artist Point,★★ short walk to an incomparable view of the Lower Falls and the Grand Canyon of the Yellowstone River, page 182

Tower Fall,★ high waterfall in a dramatic rocky setting, page 219

Buildings

Old Faithful Inn,★★ immense hundred-year-old log inn that rivals its namesake geyser in beauty and interest, page 75

Lake Hotel,★ the oldest and most comfortable lodgings in the park in an unparalleled setting, page 152

LESS WELL-KNOWN YET BEAUTIFUL PLACES

Apollinaris Spring, a verdant spot graced with historic stonework north of Norris Junction, page 281

Brink of Lower Falls, a strenuous but rewarding walk to the very top of the thunderous falls, page 184 (picture, page 185)

Firehole River behind Old Faithful Geyser, where a wooden bridge crosses the stream, creating a serene spot barely away from the crowds around the geyser, page 84 (picture, page 81)

Floating Island Lake, a pleasant site for bird-watching west of Tower-Roosevelt Junction, page 299

Lake Butte, an extensive view encompassing much of Yellowstone Lake and its surrounding mountains, page 166

Lamar Valley near the Buffalo Ranch area, unusually beautiful in evening light, page 208 (picture, page 207)

Moose Falls, a small waterfall and tranquil site near the South Entrance, page 129

Nez Perce picnic area, by the Firehole River, convenient to Lower Geyser Basin, page 52

Yellowstone River from Chittenden Bridge, quietly flowing water just above the tumult, page 180

DRIVING DISTANCES

	Alpine, WY	Ashton	Big Sky	Billings	Bozeman	Canyon Junction	Cody	Dubois	East Entrance	Fishing Bridge
Ashton, ID	98									
Big Sky, MT	207	109								
Billings, MT	319	272	186							
Bozeman, MT	245	153	44	142						
Canyon Junction	152	95	92	177	119					
Cody, WY	216	189	186	103	211	94				
Dubois, WY	124	159	214	309	242	140	204			
East Entrance	163	136	133	156	160	41	53	151		
Fishing Bridge	137	110	107	182	134	15	79	125	26	
Gardiner /N. Entrance	189	109	106	169	80	38	132	178	79	53
Idaho Falls, ID	73	56	165	328	203	151	245	177	192	166
Jackson, WY	37	72	189	282	217	115	179	87	126	100
Livingston, MT	244	164	70	116	26	93	187	233	134	108
Madison Junction	149	70	67	202	105	25	119	137	66	40
Mammoth Junction	184	104	101	176	86	33	127	173	74	48
Moran Junction	68	103	158	255	186	84	148	56	95	69
Norris Junction	162	83	80	189	107	12	106	152	53	27
Northeast Entrance	199	142	139	130	133	47	81	187	88	62
Old Faithful Village	135	87	84	219	122	42	119	123	66	40
Red Lodge, MT	269	212	183	60	149	117	62	257	115	132
South Entrance	95	130	121	224	159	57	121	83	68	42
Tower Junction	171	113	110	159	104	18	113	158	60	34
West Entrance	154	56	53	216	92	39	133	151	80	54
West Thumb Jct.	116	103	100	203	138	36	100	104	47	21

Chart shows shortest distances in miles on fully paved roads.
Information about park roads: (307) 344-2117
Wyoming roads: 511 in WY or (888) 996-7623
Montana roads: 511 in MT or (800) 226-7623
Idaho roads: 511 in ID or (888) 432-7623

Gardiner/N.Entrance	Idaho Falls	Jackson	Livingston	Madison Junction	Mammoth Junction	Moran Junction	Norris Junction	Northeast Entrance	Old Faithful Village	Red Lodge	South Entrance	Tower Junction	West Entrance
165													
151	90												
54	229	206											
40	126	112	94										
5	160	146	60	34									
121	121	31	175	81	115								
26	139	125	81	13	21	94							
52	198	163	107	72	47	132	59						
57	143	98	111	17	51	67	30	89					
122	268	233	123	142	117	202	129	70	159				
94	148	58	148	54	88	27	67	105	40	175			
23	169	134	78	43	18	103	30	29	60	99	76		
53	112	126	108	14	48	95	27	86	31	156	68	57	
73	159	79	127	33	69	48	46	83	19	153	21	54	47

KEY TO SYMBOLS

- Amphitheater
- Bicycling trail
- Bird-watching spot
- Boat launch site
- Campground
- Clinic
- Commercial airport
- Fishing (selected good spots)
- Horse corral
- Horsepacking trail
- Information station / bookstore
- Inn, hotel, or cabins
- Parking
- **(n)** Picnic area (number of tables)
- Post office
- Public telephone
- Recommended short walk or part of walk
- Recommended short walk with pamphlet available
- Restaurant, cafeteria, or lunch counter
- Restroom
- Self-guiding trail with Yellowstone Association pamphlet available
- Service station
- Store
- Trailhead
- Visitor center, entrance station, or ranger station
- Wheelchair access

Blue line bordering text points out historical information from the human history of the park before about 1960.

On maps, sets of parallel blue lines indicate waterfalls.

On geyser basin maps, parallel black lines indicate steps.

• Red dots indicate thermal features.

[GEO.1] through **[GEO.26]**: Points of geological interest explained in the Geological History chapter

★★ Don't miss!

★ Worth making time for

See the glossary just before the index for the definitions of *words in italics*.

Sidebar Topic Colors

Pale yellow: geology and geography

Green: natural history

Blue: human history

Beige: park information

THE FIVE APPROACHES TO YELLOWSTONE NATIONAL PARK

Yellowstone National Park is situated between 44 and 45 degrees north latitude and 109.5 and 111 degrees west longitude. Most of the park lies in the state of Wyoming, but a small portion in the north is in Montana and a strip on the west side is in Idaho. The park covers an area of 3472 square miles (8992 sq km), most of which is undeveloped mountain and forest. In spite of this huge size, almost all of the most interesting sights are available to visitors along or close to the more than 300 miles (483 km) of roads. Because there's so much to see and do and so many people who want to use the limited housing and camping facilities, advance planning is essential.

Your first decision will be which way to enter. The approach roads to the five entrances are shown on the map on page 24 and described below, along with an idea of the scenery you'll encounter and the available activities and facilities.

Arriving by Air

If you plan to start your trip by commercial airplane, consider flying to Billings, Montana, the largest city in the vicinity of the park, with the most connecting flights. You can rent a car there to drive conveniently to any entrance except the South Entrance.

Closest airport options other than Billings are: Jackson, Wyoming, the closest commercial airport to the South Entrance; Cody, Wyoming, for the East Entrance; Bozeman, Montana, for the north or west; and West Yellowstone, Montana, for the West Entrance. These are also good options for private planes, and all have car rentals available. Additional general aviation airports are at Gardiner, Livingston, and Red Lodge, Montana, as well as Dubois, Wyoming.

If you want to begin in Idaho Falls, Idaho, several airlines can serve you. Many people begin a western trip from Salt Lake City, Utah, which is a much longer drive but is especially well served by airlines and is relatively convenient to Grand Teton National Park and the South Entrance of Yellowstone.

WEST ENTRANCE Page 31

There are several good reasons to approach Yellowstone along U.S. Highway 191 to its West Entrance. First, you'll find ample tourist accommodations in Bozeman, in the Big Sky area, and in West Yellowstone, Montana. Second, the scenery through the Gallatin River canyon, though not the most spectacular of the approaches, can be a delightful introduction to the Rocky Mountains.

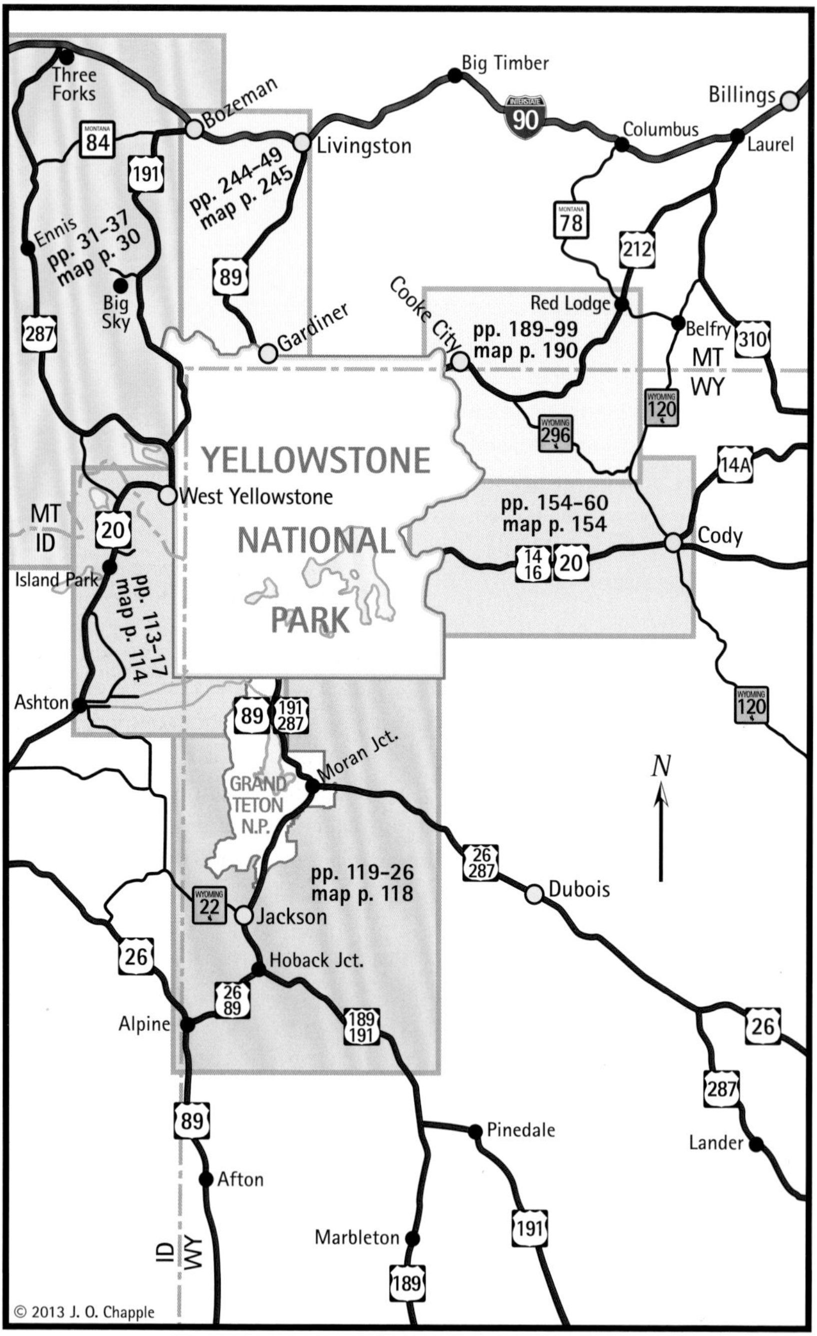

Key to the Approach Roads

The third advantage of coming this way is that the Gallatin River and Gallatin National Forest abound in opportunities for camping, hiking, fishing, kayaking, and float trips, while guest ranches provide horseback trips and offer western hospitality. One caveat: U.S. 191 is a two-lane road used by many heavy trucks.

The Gallatin Canyon opens out a few miles north of the park boundary.

This entrance gives geyser enthusiasts the closest access to the unique geysers and hot springs in the western half of the park. It's about 90 miles (145 km) from Bozeman to the West Entrance; then 30 miles (48 km) farther to Upper Geyser Basin in Old Faithful Village, or 27 miles (43 km) to Norris Geyser Basin.

Besides U.S. 191 from Bozeman, you can reach the West Entrance from the northwest (on U.S. 287) and from the southwest (on U.S. 20 and Interstate 15). Montana towns northwest of the park include two where vacationers might want to linger, Ennis and Virginia City. Ennis is a center for trout fishing, and Virginia City and Alder Gulch were famous for gold mining in the nineteenth century. In Virginia City, the capital of the Territory of Montana from 1865 to 1876, you can visit several restored historical buildings. The town boasts two small museums and performances all summer in an opera house and a former brewery.

A little known but beautiful area that is easily reached from West Yellowstone or from Ashton, Idaho, stretches from Big Springs, Idaho, down U.S. Highway 20 and Idaho 47 to the two Mesa waterfalls and into the water-rich Bechler Region. These sights are described on pages 113–17.

Idaho towns somewhat farther from Yellowstone but with lodgings and other visitor facilities include Rexburg and St. Anthony on U.S. 20, and Idaho Falls and Pocatello on Interstate 15. While the latter two are served by major airlines and car rental companies and have many accommodations, both of these towns of more than 50,000 people exceed 100 miles (160 km) from Yellowstone's West Entrance.

SOUTH ENTRANCE Page 119

Mountain lovers and backcountry hikers would do well to choose the South Entrance. The entire southern section of the park, about one-quarter of the

The Tetons are some of the most strikingly beautiful mountains in the world.

whole, is remote mountain country of undeveloped high meadow and forest. The southeast section of the park, together with large areas outside park borders, comprises a vast wilderness, probably the largest area in the contiguous United States without roads. If your main goal is canoeing or fishing on Lewis and Shoshone lakes, the South Entrance is for you. This is also one of the two closest ways to reach Yellowstone Lake.

Each corner of Jackson's central square is adorned with elk antlers.

Within a half-day's drive outside the park's South Entrance are wonderful examples of the beautiful scenery for which Wyoming is famous. The mountains and lakes of Grand Teton National Park are visited annually by one million more people than visit Yellowstone.

The largest town in the area is Jackson, serving visitors summer and winter and located about 58 miles (93 km) south of Yellowstone. Smaller Wyoming towns somewhat farther from Yellowstone but with less expensive tourist facilities are Dubois to the southeast and Alpine on the Idaho/Wyoming state line. Dubois is 83 miles (134 km) from the South Entrance; Alpine is 37 miles (60 km) south of Jackson.

EAST ENTRANCE Page 154

The East Entrance will be your first choice as a way to enter Yellowstone if you're interested in Native American Indian lore or western museums (in Cody), or horseback riding and guest ranches. It's relatively close to Yellowstone Lake for boating or fishing.

Rock formations called hoodoos along the road from Cody to the East Entrance.

Between Cody and the park, you can indulge in every sort of outdoor activity, from golf and fishing to backpacking and windsurfing. Attractions include the Buffalo Bill Dam, with its visitor center and 10 square miles (26 sq km) of reservoir, and Buffalo Bill State Park, which borders the reservoir and provides places to camp, picnic, or launch boats. The Buffalo Bill Cody Scenic Byway (U.S. Highways 14/16/20) passes through several areas of hoodoos visible from the road. It's 53 miles (85 km) from Cody to the East Entrance.

NORTHEAST ENTRANCE Page 189

The Northeast Entrance is the closest one to Billings, Montana, yet the fastest route to the park from Billings is via the North Entrance, described below. Two high, spectacular mountain roads approach Yellowstone from the northeast.

The most popular road, the Beartooth Scenic Byway (U.S. 212), crosses the Beartooth Plateau on a series of switchbacks between Red Lodge and Cooke City. The late CBS news correspondent Charles Kuralt asserted in his 1979 book, Dateline America, that "the most beautiful road in America is U.S. 212, which leaves Red Lodge, climbs to Beartooth Pass at eleven thousand feet, and drops down into the northeast entrance of Yellowstone Park." Most visitors agree with him when they see the tremendous panoramas and exquisitely colored wildflowers, especially above timberline. The distance from Billings to the Northeast

Little Bear Creek runs through a field of flowers below Beartooth Butte.

Entrance this way is about 130 miles (209 km). Allow about four hours to enjoy it. Note, however, that the Beartooth Highway is open only from Memorial Day weekend (end of May) to early October.

An alternative if you're coming from east of the park is the Chief Joseph Scenic Byway (Wyoming 296), which crosses the Absaroka Range. It affords breathtaking views of the surrounding countryside and access to Sunlight Basin, with its ranches and summer homes. The Chief Joseph Highway joins U.S. 212 a few miles east of Cooke City. The distance from Billings to the Northeast Entrance this way is about 150 miles (240 km); from Cody, about 80 miles (130 km). Because its summit is lower than that of the Beartooth Highway, this road is open earlier in spring and later in fall.

Visitors suffering from a fear of heights should be forewarned that there are several switchbacks on these roads with long views to the valleys far below.

The Northeast Entrance was the last to be opened, in 1936, and still has the fewest cars passing through it. Cooke City and Silver Gate just outside the park have tourist accommodations, as does Red Lodge.

NORTH ENTRANCE

Page 244

The North Entrance was the first, and for years the most popular, way to enter Yellowstone. Lower in elevation than any of the others, this entrance has always been the most accessible by road (and formerly by rail) from Montana towns such as Helena, Butte, Billings, or Bozeman.

The Yellowstone River is popular for rafting, kayaking, and fishing.

You reach the North Entrance via Interstate 90 to Livingston, turning south on U.S. 89. Following the north-flowing Yellowstone River, you pass through serene Paradise Valley, now famous as a resort area for movie stars and other high-profile Americans.

The distance from Livingston to Gardiner, the small town at the park's northern boundary, is 54 miles (87 km). The section of park road from Gardiner to Cooke City is the only park road kept open to motor vehicles all winter.

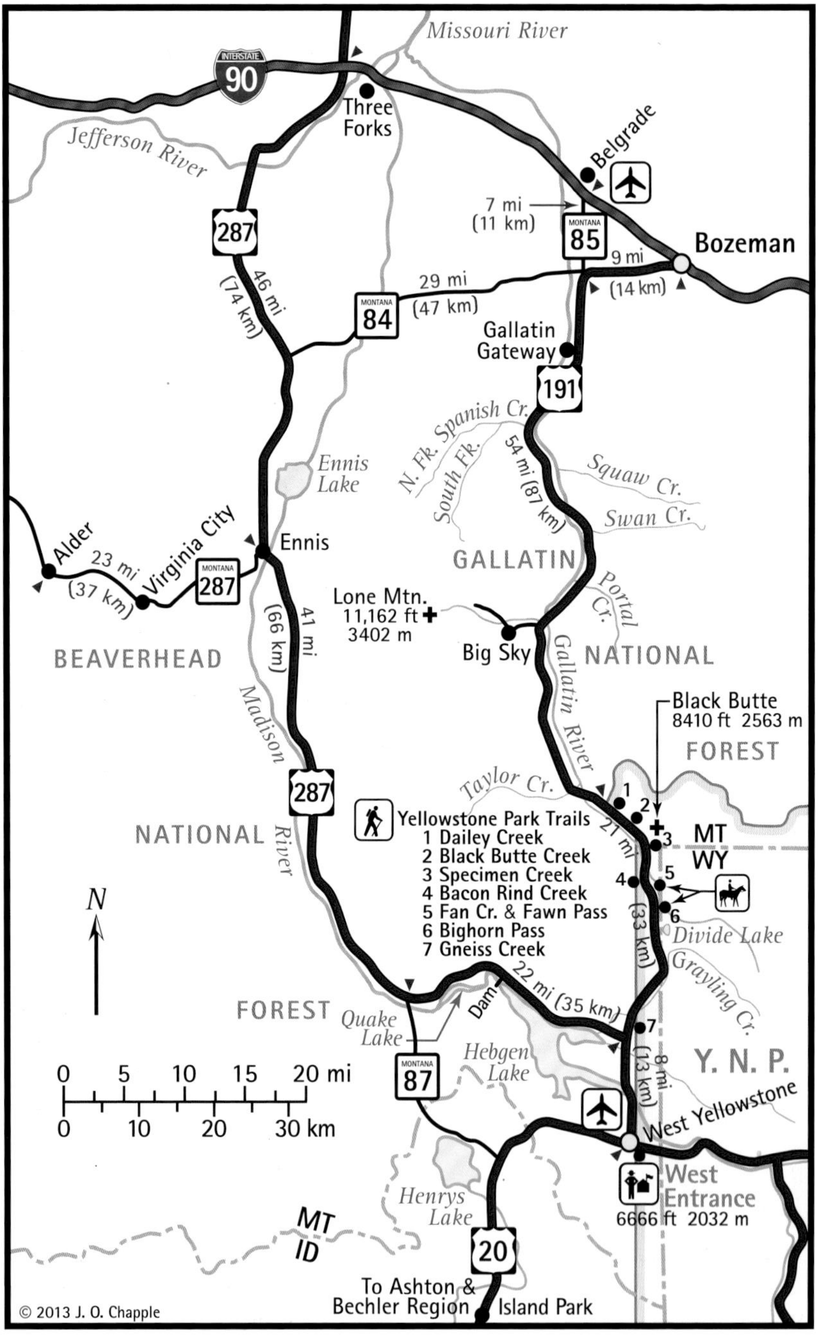

Approaches to the West Entrance

Road Logs and Destinations

I. NORTHWESTERN SECTION

Each road log section begins at a gateway community and continues into the park to a junction on the Grand Loop Road. The exception is section II, "The Bechler Region," whose roads do not connect with interior park roads.

Approaches to the West Entrance

From Bozeman, Montana, driving south on U.S. Highway 191 through the Gallatin Canyon, you traverse pleasant mountain scenery without crossing any high mountain passes. On this route, you can find all types of accommodations. About halfway along the 90-plus miles (145 km) from Bozeman to West Yellowstone is the road to the famous ski resort of Big Sky. Further south, more than 20 miles (32 km) of U.S. 191 pass inside the western edge of Yellowstone.

If you're approaching from the west or south, there are two other good roads you might take. They are U.S. 287 and the road from Pocatello, Idaho Falls, and Ashton, Idaho (Interstate 15, then U.S. 20). The Ashton to West Yellowstone drive is described in the other direction on pages 113–15.

Bozeman, Montana — **Bozeman Yellowstone International Airport**

Population (2010): 37,300 — *8 mi. (13 km) NW*

Bozeman is a rapidly growing town and one of Montana's oldest, established in 1864. The former agricultural college, now Montana State University, is the home of the **Museum of the Rockies**, with a planetarium and excellent dinosaur and geology exhibits.

FROM BOZEMAN TO THE WEST ENTRANCE

You'll need about two hours' driving time to cover the distance to West Yellowstone. The road follows the Gallatin River up its beautiful mountain-bound canyon. Take Interstate 90 west to Montana Highway 85, which leads to U.S. 191, or take U.S. 191 due west out out of town and then follow it south.

The village of Gallatin Gateway is 15 miles (24 km) from Bozeman, just off the highway. As you pass near it, you'll see the restored **Gallatin Gateway Inn**, built as the terminus of the Chicago, Milwaukee, St. Paul, and Pacific Railroad (nicknamed the Milwaukee Road), which operated a branch line to this inn from 1927 to 1961. In those years, park visitors arriving by train were met at the inn by the classic yellow park concessionaire's buses.

Soon you'll be following the canyon of the **Gallatin River**, flowing north out of the park and long famous for its trout. Fishing scenes in the movie *A River Runs Through It* were filmed here in the 1990s. Guest ranches and private vacation cabins are numerous in the canyon.

There are several Gallatin National Forest campgrounds and trailheads along the highway. Forty-three miles (69 km) from Bozeman is the turnoff to **Big Sky**. Motels and eating establishments are plentiful, and you'll find a small chapel near the turnoff. Since TV journalist Chet Huntley began it in the early 1970s, Big Sky has become a major vacation resort and skiing center. Before that, this part of the Gallatin Valley was fertile farmland; it was known for its lettuce and provided oats and hay for Yellowstone Park horses in the very early years.

Above Big Sky stands the pyramid of **Lone Mountain**, a *glacial horn* carved by the action of glaciers.

About 12 miles (20 km) south of the Big Sky Junction you begin to see eroded gray and yellow rock formations made of welded *tephra,* that is, particles

Lone Mountain from the Big Sky road.

erupted from a volcano. This tephra also tops Crown and Lava Buttes just inside the park.

As Black Butte appears in the distance, you pass a big turnout on the road's west side and then a lovely small cascade that enters the Gallatin River. Just beyond the cascade, look to the east side of the road (1.1 mile north of the Y.N.P. entrance sign), and you'll see Gorilla Rock, a jutting rock formation resembling a gorilla.

Along U.S. 191 in the Park

Approximately 60 miles (96 km) from Bozeman, Highway 191 enters the northwestern corner of Yellowstone, elevation about 6,700 ft (2,040 m), and continues inside the park for about 20 miles (32 km), crossing in and out of Wyoming and Montana. There are no campgrounds, picnic areas, or restrooms along this stretch of road, but there is access to several trails into the backcountry, both in the park and in Gallatin National Forest. This road was first built in 1910–11 and now passes through land that was added to the park in 1929.

Road Log

0.0/20.5 Yellowstone National Park boundary. Just a large sign marks the edge of the park here; there's no entrance fee to pay until you reach the West Entrance station.

This short stretch of U.S. 191 is the only road within the park where the speed limit is 55 miles per hour rather than 45. The only park road used by large trucks, it's open year round.

The mountains northeast of the road (to your left as you enter the park) are **Crown Butte** (elevation 8,051 ft / 2,454 m) and **Lava Butte** (7,904 ft / 2,409 m). Crown Butte resembles a crown when seen from the south. Geologists tell us that both Crown Butte and Lava Butte (a mile or two farther along) are topped with *Huckleberry Ridge tuff*, the 2-million-year-old welded tephra that can be seen in several localities in the park. Here the tuff overlies *shale*, a *sedimentary rock* rich in clays. Shale weathers and erodes easily, producing landslides that sometimes encroach upon the road.

Entering park territory, you are greeted by Black Butte.

0.9/19.6 **Dailey Creek Trailhead**. Small parking area and Dailey Creek crossing. Dailey Creek was named for one of the first families to winter in the valley on the other side of the Gallatin Range. The family arrived in 1866 and still had a ranch there in the 1930s.

Lodgepole Creek joins the Gallatin

opposite Dailey Creek. Note that locals pronounce the word creek like CRICK, to rhyme with trick.

All trails in this part of the park are long, steep ones that lead into the Gallatin Range. Dailey, Black Butte, and Specimen Creek trails all join with the Sky Rim Trail 5 miles or more away and 3,000 feet up (about 8 km away and 900 m up). The Sky Rim Trail affords spectacular mountain views to the very hardy climber or horseback rider. Also, some stumps of petrified wood are preserved there, but they are harder to reach and less interesting than those on Specimen Ridge in the Lamar River Valley. Both grizzlies and black bears live in this northwest corner of Yellowstone.

Along the far side of the river, you'll see red-tipped white stakes marking the park boundary.

2.6/17.9 **Black Butte Creek Trailhead**; parking area on the west, trail on the east. This is the shortest but steepest of the trails that connect to the Sky Rim Trail.

3.0/17.5 The almost perfect cone shape of **Black Butte** looms over the road to the east. Unlike most *buttes*, this is not a flat-topped mountain. Geologists call Black Butte an *igneous intrusion*. This means that it's made of rock that rose as a molten mass from deep within the earth, but stopped and crystallized before reaching the earth's surface. Since the overlying rocks eroded away, we can now see the intrusion. Black Butte's rock is about 50 million years old.

3.9/16.6 There's a tiny stream called **Wickiup Creek** here. A wickiup was a temporary shelter used by nomadic tribes of Native American Indians. A group of these hunting lodges stood near the stream here in the park's early days.

4.6/15.9 **Specimen Creek Trailhead**. This trail connects to the Sky Rim, High Lake, and Sportsman Lake trails. In spite of its name, this is not the best route to take to see petrified wood specimens. A ranger or local resident can best advise you on how to reach them. Remember that no samples may be removed from the park. Two easier ways to see petrified trees are by hiking from Yellowstone's northern approach road north of Gardiner, Montana, and at Petrified Tree near Tower-Roosevelt Junction.

To the east is **Lightning Hill**, so named when rangers from the now-razed ranger station near Wickiup Creek used to climb it to check for lightning-caused fires.

5.3/15.2 Road crosses the 45th parallel of latitude.

5.8/14.7 To the west, **Snowslide Creek** cascades into the Gallatin River in an area that's marshy except when the creek dries up in late summer. On the far side of the river along here, you can see remnants of the original road through Gallatin Canyon.

6.4/14.1 Terminal Monument Creek crossing. The strange name of this creek stems from a wooden post placed up the hill to the northeast that marks the northwest corner of the state of Wyoming.

7.5/13.0 Gallatin River Bridge.

8.8/11.7 **Bacon Rind Creek Trail** begins 0.3 mile (0.5 km) up the side road to the west. After the first 2.5 miles (4 km), the trail continues out of the park into the Lee Metcalf Wilderness. The century-old name Bacon Rind Creek may have reflected breakfast around the campfire or baiting bears by hanging bacon rind in a tree.

As you travel south, you begin to see the *snags*, standing burned trees left from the Fan fire of 1988.

9.1/11.4 **Fan Creek** and **Fawn Pass Trailheads**. Fan Creek flows into the Gallatin from the northeast through a valley that nineteenth-century geologists thought looked like a large fan, because of its radiating minor valleys. Both trails take hikers and riders into the southern expanses of the Gallatin Range.

To see an undisturbed, beautiful mountain valley, you might follow the start of the Fan Creek Trail for about 2 miles (3 km), turning northeast at the trail junction.

10.5/10.0 From this point south, we no longer follow the Gallatin River. The river flows west from its source, then turns north here and meanders through the flat floodplain that you've just traversed if traveling southward. This is also the Montana/Wyoming state line.

10.9/9.6 **Bighorn Pass Trailhead.** The sign indicates a short side road primarily for unloading horse trailers. The Bighorn Pass Trail follows the Gallatin River almost to its source at Gallatin Lake some 12 miles (19 km) away and 2,000 feet (610 m) up. Both the Bighorn Pass and Fawn Pass trails continue across the high mountains and all the way to the Grand Loop Road between Mammoth and Norris. Looking east up the Gallatin River here, you see Bannock Peak (10,332 ft / 3,149 m), with Quadrant Mountain (10,213 ft / 3,113 m) behind it.

In the 1920s, citizens and Milwaukee Road officials were eyeing the Bighorn Pass Trail route as an attractive place to build a road or a railroad. We must thank the first director of the National Park Service (NPS), Stephen Mather, and Yellowstone Park Superintendent Horace Albright for their foresight in objecting to these plans. Long before designated wilderness areas were thought of, Mather wrote to Albright: "We must keep a large area of Yellowstone in a state of untouched wildness if we are to be faithful to our trust as protectors of the wild life with which the park abounds." The road was not built, nor was the railroad company even allowed to conduct a survey.

12.0/8.5 Divide Lake, at an elevation of about 7,250 feet (2,210 m), takes its name from the fact that water flows from this vicinity into two different watersheds. To the north all streams flow to the Gallatin River, while to the south they flow to the Madison River. These rivers (along with the Jefferson River) join to form the Missouri River, and their waters eventually flow to the Atlantic Ocean.

14.0/6.5 Pass Creek and **Grayling Creek** join here. U.S. 191 parallels Grayling Creek until that creek's southern exit from the park, crossing it three or four times. The old road crossed the creek even more times, to avoid having to excavate the sidehills.

The road skirts a severely burned area at the northwestern reach of the 1988 North Fork fire.

20.3/0.2 Tepee Creek crossing.

20.5/0.0 Yellowstone National Park boundary. Here U.S. 191 leaves the park.

From Outside the Park Boundary to West Yellowstone

From here U.S. 191 descends into the valley of the Madison River and reaches the town of West Yellowstone and the West Entrance in about 11 miles (18 km). Off to the west and southwest, you may see parts of the Snowcrest, Centennial, and Henry's Lake Ranges beyond Hebgen Lake. To the east is the high but relatively flat and tree-covered Yellowstone Plateau.

At 1.4 miles (2.3 km) outside the park boundary and about 9.5 miles (15 km) north of West Yellowstone is the parking area for the **Gneiss Creek Trailhead**, next to the private Fir Ridge Cemetery road. This long trail is described from the other end at mile 7.6/6.3 on the West Entrance Road.

At the nearby junction with U.S. 287, you can take a side trip of less than 20 miles (32 km) to visit Hebgen Lake and Quake Lake, where you can see a remarkable landslide and learn about the devastating earthquake of 1959. In 8 miles (13 km) more on U.S. 191, you pass entrances to two Forest Service campgrounds and a private one, Yellowstone Airport, and a ranger station before entering West Yellowstone.

Quake Lake

If you're entering or leaving the park via the West Entrance, it's worthwhile to allow time for a visit to Earthquake Lake (often shortened to Quake Lake), northwest of West Yellowstone on U.S. 287. This is the site of the devastating August 17, 1959, earthquake and huge landslide that killed 28 people, most of them campers in a now-buried campground.

Quake Lake was created by a huge landslide.

The landslide, caused by an earthquake of Richter magnitude 7.3, dammed the Madison River, forming the lake. This earthquake affected Yellowstone's Upper and Lower Geyser Basins more than 35 miles away.

Start your visit at the

Forest Service visitor center, where you'll find exhibits and information about the earthquake and how a potential Madison River flood was avoided. Hebgen Dam, completed in 1915, cracked but did not give way in the quake.

WEST YELLOWSTONE, MONTANA

YELLOWSTONE AIRPORT

Population: 1,270

1.2 mi. (1.8 km) N

Motel and hotel accommodations and other tourist facilities are available throughout the year in the town of West Yellowstone. It's possible to travel by public bus between West Yellowstone and Bozeman, the only regularly scheduled public bus connection between one of the gateway communities and a larger city.

Snowcoaches provide a warm alternative to snowmobiles for winter visits.

In winter, you can arrange snowcoach transportation from West Yellowstone to Old Faithful Village through the park concessionaire and several other companies. A snowcoach can carry 10 to 12 people in relative comfort over unplowed roads. In addition to serving as a starting point for snowcoaches, West Yellowstone is a major center for snowmobile rental.

West Yellowstone's first post office was established as Riverside in 1908, but the town soon changed its name to Yellowstone, Montana. This proved confusing, so in 1920 the name became West Yellowstone; locals now simply call it West.

Before 1908 the Union Pacific Railroad reached only to Idaho Falls, and visitors to the park traveled a day or more by stagecoach to reach the West Entrance. From that year until 1961, the U.P.'s Oregon Short Line served the town and this entrance to Yellowstone.

The former railroad station is now **The Museum of the Yellowstone**, featuring railroad history and exhibits about wildlife, the Hebgen Lake earthquake, and the 1988 fires. Another West Yellowstone attraction is the nonprofit **Grizzly Discovery Center**, currently home to nine grizzlies and eight gray wolves. These attractions are on or close to Yellowstone Avenue, the town's main street leading into the park, and both host park ranger programs in the summer. Also just outside the park entrance is the **West Yellowstone Visitor Information Center**.

Riverside Trail (primarily a ski trail) enters the park from the eastern edge of town.

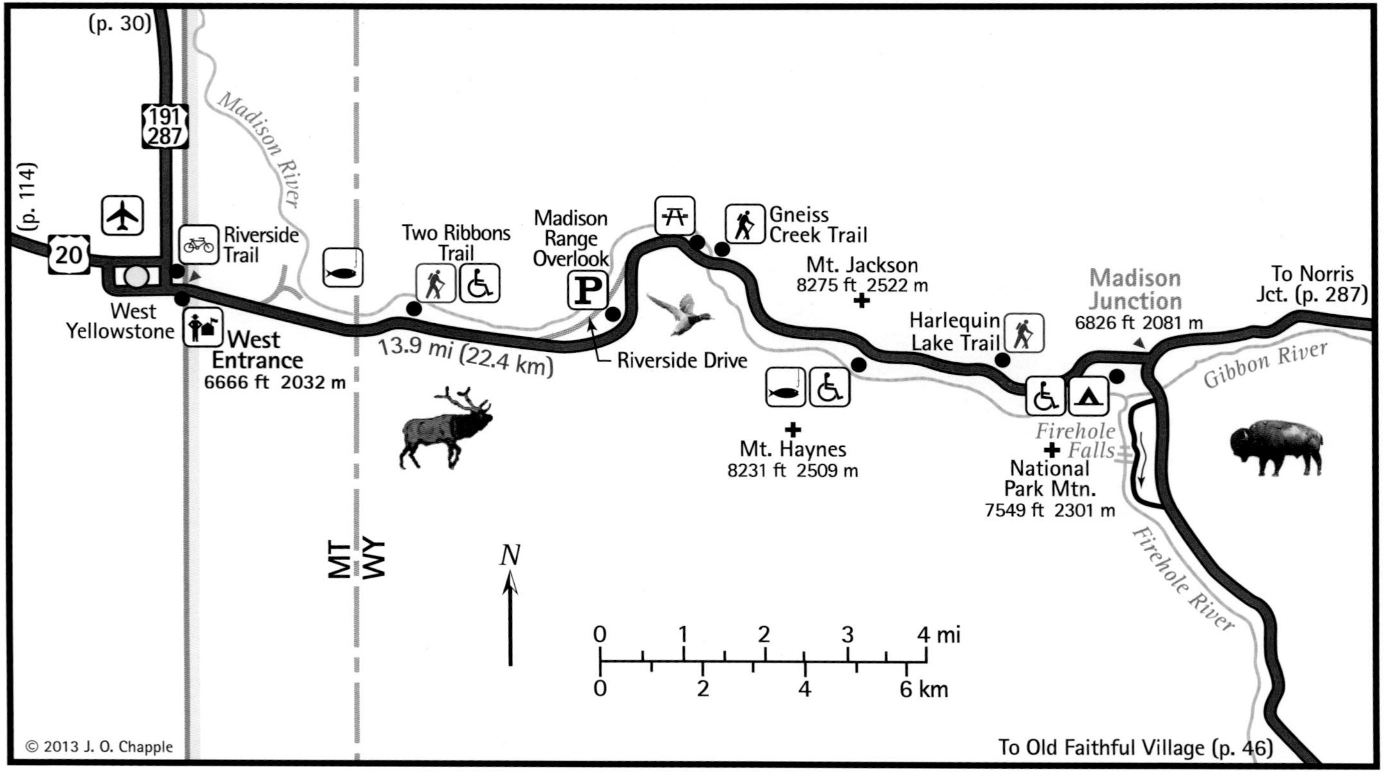
(p. 30)
(p. 114)
20
191
287
Madison River
Riverside Trail
West Yellowstone
West Entrance
6666 ft 2032 m
MT
WY
Two Ribbons Trail
Madison Range Overlook
13.9 mi (22.4 km)
Riverside Drive
Gneiss Creek Trail
Mt. Jackson
8275 ft 2522 m
Mt. Haynes
8231 ft 2509 m
Harlequin Lake Trail
Madison Junction
6826 ft 2081 m
To Norris Jct. (p. 287)
Gibbon River
Firehole Falls
National Park Mtn.
7549 ft 2301 m
Firehole River
N
0 1 2 3 4 mi
0 2 4 6 km
© 2013 J. O. Chapple
To Old Faithful Village (p. 46)

West Entrance to Madison Junction

From the West Entrance to Madison Junction

The West Entrance is the most popular way to enter Yellowstone, welcoming over 3,000 visitors each day in the summer months. In fact, it's second only to Grand Canyon National Park's South Rim as a busy national park entrance.

From West Yellowstone, this entrance road passes through stands of lodgepole pine, burned in the devastating 1988 North Fork fire but now largely regrown. The Madison River is tepid all winter from geothermal runoff, which prevents ice from forming and provides habitat for the rare and beautiful trumpeter swan, which you may see here, especially in winter. There's also a strong possibility of seeing elk or bison.

The route you follow by taking this entrance road approximates that used by early-day trappers, Native American Indians, and some would-be gold miners. No gold in minable quantities was ever discovered within what is now the park. Stagecoach lines used this route to bring visitors into the new national park from 1880 until 1917, when buses and cars replaced stagecoaches completely.

It's about 14 miles (22 km) from the West Entrance to Madison Junction and the Grand Loop Road.

Road Log

NOTE: There are several very short side roads along this entrance road. The mileage for such roads is given at approximately the midpoint between the two ways to enter the loop.

0.0/13.9 Yellowstone National Park boundary.

0.1/13.8 West Entrance station, built in 2008. Stop here to pay the entrance fee (see the Travel Tips for fee information). To the south is a new regional ranger headquarters. The restroom is just outside the entrance station.

This area housed the offices and warehouses of Hamilton Stores until 2003, when Delaware North Companies took them over while becoming the retail concessionaire. Charles A. Hamilton purchased his first store at Upper Geyser Basin in 1915 and expanded his business to 14 stores, the longest-lasting concession in the national park system.

0.7/13.2 Unmarked gravel road to the north leads to Madison River fishing access about 1.3 miles (2 km) away; fly fishing only. Over the years, this large meadow has been called Riverside and the Barns (for extensive horse barns here in the early years, later used by park buses). Stagecoach drivers one hundred years ago dubbed this area Christmas Tree Park, because a very old forest fire burn had been overgrown by a new forest of uniform lodgepoles.

The Madison River

A world-famous trout fishing stream, the Madison is extremely rich in the calcium bicarbonate needed for abundant plant growth, which furnishes hiding places for insects and trout. The river flows westward out of the park through Hebgen and Quake lakes, then turns north, and eventually joins the Gallatin and Jefferson to form the Missouri River near Three Forks, Montana. Members of the Lewis and Clark Expedition of 1803–6 named the three rivers but did not follow any of them into what is now park territory, since their mission was to reach the Pacific Ocean by the most direct route possible.

The three rivers were named for Thomas Jefferson, the visionary third U.S. president, who conceived and authorized the Lewis and Clark Expedition; James Madison, Jefferson's secretary of state, who became the fourth U.S. president in 1809; and Albert Gallatin, secretary of the treasury under Jefferson.

Along the river was the site of one of the Wylie Camping Company's lunch stations. Beginning in the 1890s and into the 1940s, William W. Wylie and his successors provided stagecoach passengers and then motorists with low-cost tent camps and lunch stops.

1.7/12.2 Paved road for river access.

2.2/11.7 Montana/Wyoming state line. A small portion of the park is in Montana, even less in Idaho, because the original Yellowstone boundaries were set in relation to their distance from natural landmarks, before the states' boundaries had been established. As one example, in 1872 Congress set the western boundary of the park to run "fifteen miles west of the most western point of Madison Lake" (present-day Shoshone Lake).

3.0/10.9 🚶 ♿ Unmarked side road to the north leads to the western end of an accessible boardwalk, the **Two Ribbons Nature Trail**. Interpretive displays at both ends of the trail explain the fire phenomena encountered. This is a three-quarter mile (1.2 km) loop walk that splits in two, with one branch near the river, the other slightly away from it.

Between here and the east end of the Two Ribbons Trail is a stand of lodgepole pines that burned in the 1988 fire. The snags don't have deep roots and can easily topple over, but park officials only remove trees when they're obstructing roads or trails. As of 2012, however, most snags had fallen and some new pines reach 10 feet tall.

There were definitely some positive aftereffects of the fires. Fifty-five kinds of birds and 24 kinds of mammals use these snags for nesting, perching, and food.

Such trees also help prevent soil erosion and provide nutrients to fungi, young trees, and other plants. Wildflowers were especially abundant in the first few years after the fire. And far from spoiling the vista, the fire has opened up views of the Madison River and the distant Gallatin and Madison Ranges.

3.5/10.4 East end of Two Ribbons Trail.

4.1/9.8 Near here was the Riverside mail station and later a soldier station in the earliest years of the park, when small groups of U.S. Cavalry troops were sent on patrol to outlying areas. A steep mail route, called the Madison Plateau Road by Supt. Norris but the Norris Slide by others, climbed the plateau to descend at Fountain Flats.

Twenty years after the 1988 fires, tall lodgepoles again cover burned areas.

4.9/9.0 Riverside Drive (west end) parallels the river for a little more than a mile.

5.6/8.3 Mountain overlook. This turnout has particularly good views of the Madison Range to the northwest (outside of the park) and the Gallatin Range (partly inside, partly outside of the park) to the north.

6.1/7.8 Riverside Drive (east end).

7.5/6.4 **(9)** Madison River picnic area in a pleasant shady spot.

7.6/6.3 Madison River Bridge, often called the Seven-Mile Bridge, is about that far from the West Entrance station.

Parking for **Gneiss Creek Trailhead** is on the east side of the bridge. This nearly level 14-mile (23 km) trail traverses the Madison Valley, where moose, grouse, grizzly bears, and biting flies abound. The trail meets U.S. Highway 191 a short distance outside the western park boundary. Gneiss (pronounced NICE) Creek gets its name from the outcrops of *Precambrian gneiss*, a very old granite-like rock found in the mountains near the creek's headwaters.

7.8/6.1 Interpretive display about the historical use of this entrance road and about nesting trumpeter swans.

8.6/5.3 West end of Madison Canyon.

9.7/4.2 **P** River access road and informational sign about *talus* (pronounced TAY-luhs), the geological name for the steeply sloping mass of rock debris across the river. To fishermen this is the Madison Notch.

Immediately north of the road is a good example of columnar jointing in volcanic rock on **Mount Jackson**. Look for the regular columns of rock several yards (or meters) high near the top of

A Tale of Two Photographers

William H. Jackson (1843–1942), for whom Mount Jackson was named, was the photographer who took some of the first photographs of Yellowstone. He accompanied the 1871 Hayden Survey around what was soon to become the world's first national park, and his photographs contributed to its formation. Also a painter, Jackson created four murals for the Department of Interior building in Washington, D.C. at the age of 92 and continued to visit Yellowstone until the age of 97.

Mammoth Terraces and Hotel in the late 19th century. W. H. Jackson climbed to unusual vantage points for his photographs.

The skiing party of F. J. Haynes passes Obsidian Cliff in winter 1886–87.

It's fitting that Mount Haynes and Mount Jackson should be located near each other (about half a mile apart). Mount Haynes was named for Yellowstone photographer and concessionaire, **Frank Jay Haynes** (1853–1921), official Park Photographer starting in 1883. Haynes published early road guides to the park, operated stagecoach lines, and ran the Haynes Picture Shops. His shops were popular small stores that sold photographs and postcards in the days when few people had cameras of their own.

the mountain. (See the explanation of columnar jointing, "Lava Columns," on pages 217–18.)

10.3/3.6 Interpretive display about brown and rainbow trout. To the south across the river is the cliff face of **Mount Haynes**.

12.1/1.8 The side road here is a convenient place to park for the **Harlequin Lake Trailhead**, which is on the opposite side of the main road and slightly to the east. This is an easy half-mile (0.8 km) trail through burned lodgepoles to a delightful lily pad pond. The name Harlequin is for a type of duck found during the summer in the park, primarily along the Yellowstone River.

Beaver lodge in Harlequin Lake.

Near here the entrance road skirts the edge of the Yellowstone Caldera (see the explanation on the next page). Although numerous calderas have been discovered in the Rockies in the past few decades, Yellowstone's is the largest. In fact, it's one of the largest in the world.

12.5/1.4 Interpretive sign about fire in lodgepole forests.

12.8/1.1 An interpretive sign shows the Madison elk herd's summer and winter ranges.

13.7/0.2 Entrance to **Madison Campground**; wheelchair-accessible restroom and three campsites on Loop A. This campground, opened in 1961, is one of the largest in the park. Some of the more than 250 reservable sites overlook the Madison River. Nearby is an amphitheater for the park rangers' evening lectures.

13.9/0.0 Madison Junction. To the northeast about 13 miles (21 km) away are Norris Junction and Norris Geyser Basin. Upper Geyser Basin and Old Faithful Village are 17 miles (27 km) to the south.

At the Edge of the Yellowstone Caldera

The road approaching Madison Junction from the west enters one of the major geological features of Yellowstone Park, the Yellowstone Caldera or huge crater that formed 639,000 years ago. (Figure 6 in the Geological History chapter shows how *calderas* form.) The caldera no longer looks like a vast crater but rather is part of the large Yellowstone Plateau. The location of the crater's rim is determined by the difference in the rocks on either side of it rather than by the elevation of those rocks. At the time of the formation of the Yellowstone Caldera, a vast volcanic explosion occurred, which blew out at least 1,000 times as much rock as the Mount St. Helens eruption in Washington state did in 1980. The molten rock from a huge underground chamber was blown high into the air and then settled as tephra (now called the *Lava Creek tuff*). The chamber extended from here east beyond the present-day Canyon Village and Fishing Bridge Junction areas and south almost to the edge of the park. Its boundary is shown by the dashed line on the map given to park visitors and on the map on page 302.

The tephra settled out partly within the caldera itself but mostly over the nearby land and was also carried to most of the southern Rockies, eastward to the Great Plains as far as Iowa, and southeast to the Gulf of Mexico. So much rock was expelled, along with *superheated* water and other gases at high pressure, that the roof of this partly emptied chamber collapsed, leaving a large hole, the caldera.

The volcanic activity did not cease after the ground collapsed inward. More molten rock rose into the chamber, forcing large volumes of thick, tacky *lava* out onto the caldera floor. The lava flows continued intermittently over the course of a few hundred thousand years, partly filling the caldera and building up a large, high flat area. This explains why today the caldera no longer appears like a hole or crater.

The cliffs you can see across the river from the entrance road west of Madison Junction are a good example of these lava flows. Here they form the northern edge of the Madison Plateau, which reaches southwest approximately to the Idaho line, occupying 250 square miles (650 sq km). You can see good examples of its lava close up along the drive through Firehole River Canyon just south of Madison Junction. The caldera is roughly oval, about 30 by 45 miles (48 by 72 km), and partly surrounded by cliffs, like a volcano's crater but far larger. Cliffs extend along the road for about 8 miles (13 km) eastward past Madison Junction to Gibbon Falls, forming the northern wall of the caldera.

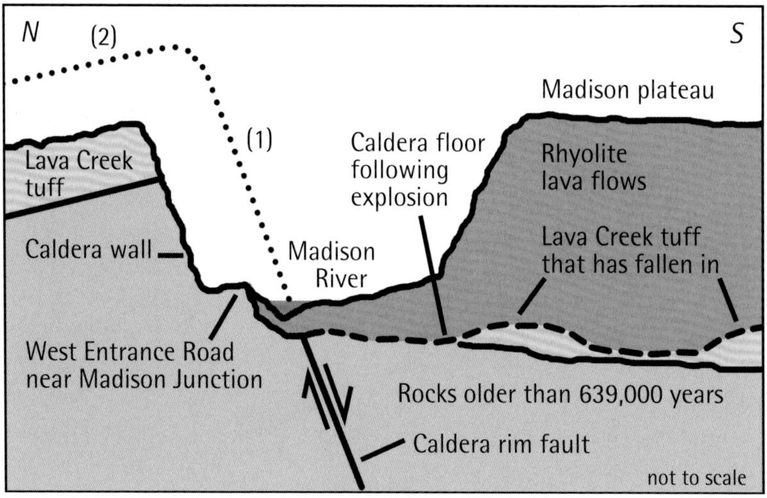

Figure 1. Cross section of the Yellowstone Caldera rim.
This north-to-south cross section shows the northern rim of the Yellowstone Caldera just west of Madison Junction. When the Lava Creek tuff erupted and covered the older rocks 639,000 years ago, the ground surface then collapsed into the space left by the erupted tuff and so created the caldera. Most of the tuff landed outside the caldera, forming thick layers of tephra; some fell back into the caldera and formed uneven and irregular mounds and blocks. The arrows show the relative motion of the *fault* at the edge of the collapsed part. *Rhyolite* lavas later flowed out and covered the caldera floor and sometimes also covered the caldera edge. The dotted lines show approximately: (1) where the original caldera edge at the fault surface was before erosion and (2) where the surface of the tuff was outside the caldera before erosion. The dashed line shows the caldera floor after the eruption with discontinuous blocks of Lava Creek tuff lying on top of older rocks.
—B.J.G./J.S.

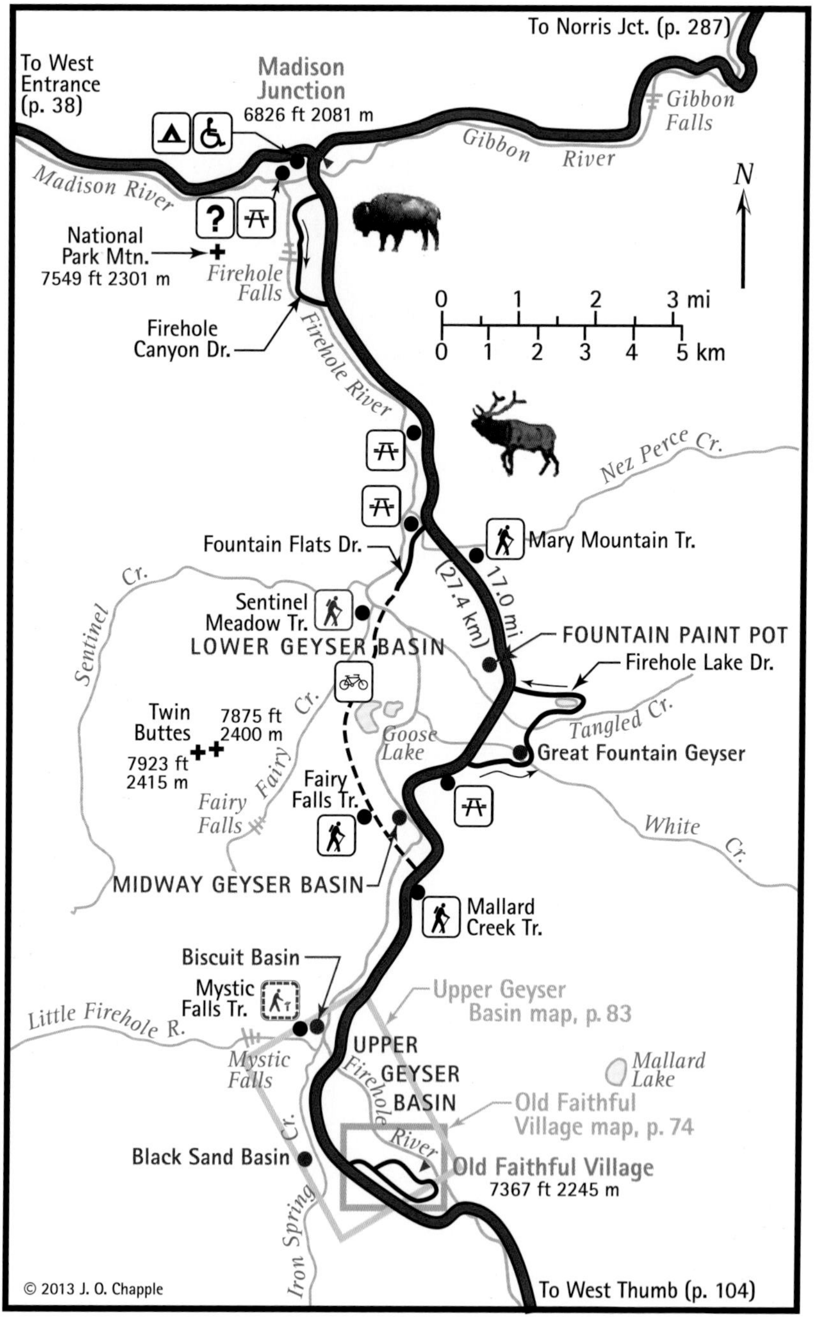
To Norris Jct. (p. 287)
To West Entrance (p. 38)
Madison Junction
6826 ft 2081 m
Gibbon Falls
Gibbon River
Madison River
N
National Park Mtn.
7549 ft 2301 m
Firehole Falls
0 1 2 3 mi
0 1 2 3 4 5 km
Firehole Canyon Dr.
Firehole River
Nez Perce Cr.
Fountain Flats Dr.
Mary Mountain Tr.
Sentinel Cr.
(27.4 km) 17.0 mi
Sentinel Meadow Tr.
LOWER GEYSER BASIN
FOUNTAIN PAINT POT
Firehole Lake Dr.
Twin Buttes
7875 ft 2400 m
7923 ft 2415 m
Fairy Cr.
Goose Lake
Tangled Cr.
Great Fountain Geyser
Fairy Falls Tr.
Fairy Falls
White Cr.
MIDWAY GEYSER BASIN
Mallard Creek Tr.
Biscuit Basin
Upper Geyser Basin map, p. 83
Mystic Falls Tr.
Little Firehole R.
Mystic Falls
UPPER GEYSER BASIN
Firehole River
Mallard Lake
Old Faithful Village map, p. 74
Black Sand Basin
Old Faithful Village
7367 ft 2245 m
Iron Spring Cr.
© 2013 J. O. Chapple
To West Thumb (p. 104)

Madison Junction to Old Faithful Village

From Madison Junction to Old Faithful Village

This section of the Grand Loop Road leads south to Upper Geyser Basin at Old Faithful Village, 17 miles (27 km) away. There are three side roads of interest. Firehole Canyon Drive closely parallels the canyon of the Firehole River and runs one way north to south. A few miles farther south, Fountain Flats Drive takes you to a walking or bicycle trail. The third side road is the Firehole Lake Drive—a one-way road (south to north) where you might catch an eruption of Great Fountain or White Dome Geysers or stroll around steaming Firehole Lake.

On the main road you'll find numerous turnouts for access to the Firehole River. Before you reach Old Faithful, you'll pass four thermal areas: the Fountain Paint Pot area and the geyser basins called Midway, Biscuit, and Black Sand.

Road Log

NOTE: Mileage in this road log goes to and from the Old Faithful Visitor Center.

0.0/17.0 Madison Junction intersects with the Grand Loop Road, the figure eight road that has taken visitors to the major features of the park for over one hundred years. Norris Junction and Norris Geyser Basin are to the northeast; Old Faithful Village is to the south.

0.1/16.9 (14) (2) ? Madison picnic area and information station/bookstore. Drinking water and flush toilets are available here, unlike at most picnic areas.

The information station has a park ranger on duty, small exhibits, a Yellowstone Association bookstore, and current geyser predictions for Upper Geyser Basin. For Old Faithful predictions you can call (307) 344-2751 on some cell phones. This is also headquarters for the free Junior Ranger Program.

This building, designed by architect Herbert Maier, was opened in 1929 as a museum of history and is one of the six National Historic Landmarks in Yellowstone. Just behind it are the amphitheater for evening lectures and a path to the Madison Campground. Attractive

Madison information station and National Park Mountain

plaques relate the long-accepted story of Yellowstone as the first national park and tell about Stephen Mather, the first NPS director.

The Gibbon and Firehole Rivers join here to form the Madison River, which flows west out of the park. The name Madison Junction, originally applied to the river junction, also applies to the road junction.

The prominent rise to the southwest beyond the rivers is **National Park Mountain**. Its cliffs form the edge of the Madison Plateau.

The National Park Idea

At the junction of the Gibbon and Firehole Rivers, members of the Washburn Expedition camped in September, 1870, after exploring much of what is now Yellowstone Park. In his reminiscences many years later, one of the expedition's leaders, Nathaniel P. Langford, credited fellow expedition member Cornelius Hedges with originating the national park idea at that time and upon this spot. For a few years in the middle of the twentieth century, an annual pageant was held at Madison to reenact the story of the National Park idea.

Historians now point out that Hedges was only one of several forward-thinking men (including Langford himself) who believed in preserving this area for the enjoyment of all future generations and preventing it from being divided up and commercially exploited. These men worked to persuade Congress and the American people to set aside this unique area as the first national park in the entire world. There is no proof that this campfire conversation did *not* take place, but neither is there any proof that it did. Perhaps we should preserve this creation story as part of Yellowstone's heritage.

0.4/16.6 Gibbon River Bridge. Look for bison (also called buffalo) in the wide meadow along the river, where a large herd often spends the summer.

Bison may seem placid but can be dangerous if approached too closely.

0.6/16.4 Firehole Canyon Drive begins. This narrow road is now one way north to south, but until it was damaged during the 1959 Hebgen Lake earthquake, it was part of the Grand Loop Road. It's about the same length as the newer main road and well worth taking.

Firehole Canyon Drive★

NOTE: The mileage from the beginning of this side loop is given in parentheses. Grand Loop Road mileage continues at 2.4 miles from Madison Junction, where Firehole Canyon Drive rejoins it.

(0.4) The small spring at the left was a favorite spot for refreshing oneself, but now Yellowstone's water cannot be guaranteed safe for drinking untreated.

Near here occurred the last of five stagecoach robberies in the park. In July of 1915, one highwayman stopped five coaches and robbed passengers of some $200. One of the victims happened to be Bernard Baruch, statesman and advisor to U.S. presidents for nearly half a century. According to Jack Haynes's booklet, *Yellowstone Stage Holdups*, Baruch later commented, "It was the best 50 dollars I ever spent!" The robber was never brought to justice.

Firehole Falls

(0.7) As the road climbs away from the river, look for a rhyolite flow to the left. Rhyolite lava, a rock rich in *silica*, is commonly found in Yellowstone in the form of tuff or *obsidian*, and occasionally as pumice.

(1.0) Firehole Falls and an interpretive display about the rhyolite flow around you. Before 1889, there were no fish occurring naturally in the Firehole River above the falls, but in that year the river was stocked with brook trout, and soon the upstream reach became a favorite with many park fishermen.

There are cascades in the river both above and below the falls. All are caused by the varying resistance that different rocks offer to river erosion.

Rhyolite and the Plateau of Fire

Lava is molten rock that reaches the earth's surface, and rhyolite is one type of lava. Rhyolite lava, which formed the rocks exposed along Firehole Canyon Drive, is very stiff and does not flow readily (that is, it's highly viscous), behaving much like asphalt or molasses. It's so stiff that a lot of force is required to push it out from within the earth. As it's being pushed out, it rips fragments from the rocks through which it's flowing and carries them to the surface.

If you stop at Firehole Falls, look closely at the rock face around the parking area. Portions of the rock consist of thin layers—a pencil thickness or less—that extend in the same direction as the original flow motion. This rock cooled very quickly. It didn't have time to form crystals throughout, but ended up consisting mostly of what geologists term *glass*. The very dark layers you can see are glass, and the light layers are mostly very tiny crystals of the minerals quartz and feldspar. Embedded in the rhyolite are rock fragments that have sharp, jagged edges. These were the bits of rock that the lava ripped out and carried along as it came toward the surface.

When it was flowing slowly, the lava's temperature would have been about 1,200°F (650°C). Where the moving surface cracked apart, it would have glowed a bright orange until cooled by the air.

The northern edge of the Madison Plateau is where Firehole Canyon Drive begins, but the plateau extends southwestward about 30 miles (50 km) to the Idaho boundary. Imagine the number of flows and the total amount of lava that must have flowed to create this massive plateau.

The slow movement of rhyolite to form the Madison Plateau contrasts sharply with the massive explosive eruptions that resulted in the Yellowstone Caldera. It was the caldera floor onto which the rhyolites later flowed.

(2.0) **(2)** Swimming area—one of two places near park roads where the water is really warm enough for swimming. (Read about the other on pages 255–56.) The water of the Firehole here is a pleasant temperature—about 75°F (24°C), neither warm nor cold. However, the Park Service keeps this area closed to swimming until the water is low enough to be safe, usually in July.

A stairway and a couple of rocky paths lead down to the water. There's no lifeguard on duty, but park rangers check the area periodically. If you choose to swim here, you should keep your head out of the water entirely, to avoid contact with harmful microorganisms. (See page 256 for details.) You will not be lonely: about 50 cars were parked along the road one recent warm July afternoon. The restrooms on the side of the road away from the river are large enough for changing clothes.

(2.2) Just before Firehole Canyon Drive rejoins the Grand Loop Road, a sign announces "Firehole Cascade." A blocked-off stretch of former highway provides a short walkway to the best of the cascades and to fishing access, for fly fishing only. Parking is along the side loop road.

Continuing on the Grand Loop Road

2.4/14.6 Note the "small, almond-shaped" island just above the Firehole Cascades, as mentioned in Harry J. Norton's 1873 guide, *Wonderland Illustrated*. Here, according to Norton, two members of his party camped for the night and returned in the morning "with glowing descriptions of the sighing and singing of the merry water-sprites who lulled them to sleep in their island couch. . . . "

This stretch of river abounds in rainbow trout, while further upriver, brook and brown trout are common.

From the point where the one-way Firehole Canyon Drive rejoins the Grand Loop Road, lodgepole pines grow directly out of some of the rocks in the Firehole River. Somehow, they find enough soil for their roots.

4.5/12.5 (12) Firehole River picnic area.

5.6/11.4 Fountain Flats Drive leads off to the south. This was the 1882 road to Upper Geyser Basin, later called the Fountain Freight Road. The present more scenic road section of the Grand Loop Road replaced it a few years later. Beyond the first mile (1.6 km), this flat loop road is closed to cars, with generous parking provided. It's recommended for bicycles, which may travel it in either direction for about 5 miles (8 km).

Fountain Flats Drive is the best approach to the Sentinel Meadow Trailhead, but there's a shorter way (at mile 11.3/5.7) to get to the Fairy Falls Trailhead or reach Imperial Geyser.

Fountain Flats was named for a major geyser in the Fountain Paint Pot area—Fountain Geyser, a spectacular performer from the 1870s into the 1930s and again in recent years.

NOTE: The area from Fountain Flats Drive to Biscuit Basin (mile 13.8/3.2) is closed for bear management from mid March to Memorial Day. (See page 133 about Bear Management Areas.)

The Firehole River

Contrary to what you might think, the Firehole River did not get its name from the fact that *hot springs* and geysers adorn its banks for many miles and pour their hot waters into the stream. In the early nineteenth century, hole was a word for a mountain-bound valley, and the Burnt Hole or Fire Hole was a burnt-over section of the Madison River Valley. Trappers (perhaps even the famous Jim Bridger) transferred the latter name to the river. Bridger is credited with having concocted the notion (not supported by scientists!) that the water flowed downhill here so fast that the rocks were heated by the friction.

Although the Firehole's name had another origin, in some places hot springs in the bed of the river *do* keep the rocks hot. Perhaps early trappers forded this river in their bare feet, since they needed to keep their boots or moccasins dry, as well as their powder. What is known for sure is that in 1870 Nathaniel Langford discovered a hot spring vent in the river while crossing it near Castle Geyser in Upper Geyser Basin. These facts certainly contribute to the aptness of the name.

The temperature of the Firehole is definitely influenced by the gallons of runoff water contributed by all the geothermal sources along the river and its tributaries. From Lone Star Geyser (the geyser that's farthest upstream) to just above the Lower Geyser Basin, the river's temperature rises a total of almost 29°F (18°C) in this meandering stretch of about 13 miles (21 km). Rainbow trout grow faster and spawn later in the season than their cousins in cool mountain streams.

Fountain Flats Drive and trail access

(15) After the bridge crosses the creek, a short dirt road leads to the Nez Perce picnic area. Nez Perce Creek and the Firehole River come together just to the north, creating one of the prettiest picnic spots in the park.

Beginning in 1880, guests stayed in a primitive hotel called Marshall House at this site. The 1884 Firehole Hotel here was abandoned after Fountain Hotel was built (in 1891), but stood until the 1930s. For a short time there was also a guardhouse here, built to incarcerate those who violated park laws but almost never used.

Beyond the picnic area you'll see steam rising to the left from **Hygeia Spring** (Hygeia was the Greek goddess of health). Though occupants of the Marshall House used the water of this spring for bathing and cooking, now it's lukewarm.

Near the river is **Maiden's Grave Spring**, named in memory of the wife of the winter hotel keeper at Marshall House. Her gravestone is between the present-day picnic area and the Firehole River's confluence with Nez Perce Creek.

As you continue on Fountain Flats Drive, you'll be in an area heavily burned

Ojo Caliente is the most accessible of the River Group of hot springs and small geysers.

by the North Fork fire of 1988. Until the mid 1990s, this road continued to a thermal area, two trailheads, and a pair of fishing lakes. The road was closed off in an effort to mitigate impact on the wetland area and to create an additional biking opportunity. You have the option of turning back at the turning circle or leaving your car to walk about a quarter mile (0.4 km) to Ojo Caliente Spring.

Bicyclists and hikers can continue on to rejoin the Grand Loop Road less than 4 miles (6.4 km) from here.

One of the two wheelchair-accessible campsites in Yellowstone is at Goose Lake, a little more than a mile (less than 2 km) from the turning circle and parking area.

Continuing south on foot (extension of Fountain Flats Drive)

Ojo Caliente Spring is a beautiful greenish blue to deep blue hot spring (its color depends on the time of day). Stay a safe distance away: the thin silica crust that overlies the superheated water can be dangerous. Ojo Caliente means "hot spring" in Spanish.

The area to the east of Ojo Caliente and the river, including the explosion crater called Pocket Basin, is too full of hazards to enter without a ranger or other knowledgeable person. Visitors have been severely burned in this area. One person died and two were seriously injured from falling into one of these hot springs in the summer of 2000.

An Explosion Crater: Pocket Basin

Geoscientists have found evidence that Pocket Basin is the crater left from a hydrothermal explosion (or steam explosion) some 10,000 years ago. As the region warmed, glaciers started to melt, and a glacial ice dam broke, suddenly lowering the lake level behind it and reducing pressure below the former lake. The pressure drop caused the hot water in the underlying rocks to flash into steam, blasting large rock fragments to the surface and leaving a hole. This is called an *explosion crater*.

The blasting happened because steam occupies about one thousand times the volume of the same amount of liquid water. Since the steam could not escape to the atmosphere fast enough, it created a huge explosion. The result of this violent event was an oval depression about a mile (1.6 km) across and a large assortment of very active *mud pots*.

Sentinel Meadow Trail goes west just across the bridge near Ojo Caliente Spring. It's about a 2.2-mile (3.5 km) walk to the Queens Laundry hot spring. On the way are several other springs and at least eight small *geysers* in the Sentinel Meadow Group of hot springs. Be aware that the whole area may be too wet for hiking before late July and that the trail provides no shade.

Sentinel Meadow was named in 1872 for the high *geyserite* mounds or cones that seem to guard it like sentinels. In the southwest corner of a large marshy area is the very hot spring called **Queens Laundry**. Here a two-room bathhouse was begun in 1881 by Superintendent Norris. The bathhouse was never completed, but the ruins are still there, now listed on the National Register of Historic Places.

Another trail to Sentinel Meadow leaves the former road (now only for walking and bicycling) about a mile (1.6 km) south of the bridge near Ojo Caliente. This trail forks to access the Fairy Meadows Group of hot springs to the northwest; on the southwest fork are the Fairy Creek Group, Imperial and Spray Geysers, and Fairy Falls.

Goose and Feather Lakes are slightly farther along the main trail on the left. Goose has some rainbow and brook trout.

In another mile or so, the main trail to Fairy Falls takes off to the west, described from the other end at mile 11.3/5.7.

~

Continuing on the Grand Loop Road

6.0/11.0 P "Chief Joseph Story" interpretive sign. The Nez Perce (pronounced nez-PURS) tribe passed through this part of the park in the summer of 1877. Their name means "pierced nose" in French, but tribal members had stopped piercing their noses by the 1830s.

6.1/10.9 Nez Perce Creek bridge. The road enters a broad meadow, Fountain Flats, where elk can often be seen.

Nez Perce Creek was first called the East Fork of the Firehole, but the name was changed to commemorate the tribe's passage eastward up this creek.

6.4/10.6 **Mary Mountain Trailhead** (also called Nez Perce Creek Trail). This was the stagecoach road from Fountain Flats to the Canyon area in the first years of the park. Near Mary Lake there's a stretch as steep as a stairway where stagecoach passengers were asked to walk so the horses could make the grade. Mary Mountain and Mary Lake were named for Mary Clark of Chicago, an 1873 visitor who crossed the park here and was said to have had a lovely singing voice.

At the start of the Mary Mountain Trail, the low hills of thermally cemented glacial gravel, called the Porcupine Hills, have some hot springs at their base. The trail passes through an extensively burned area and prime grizzly bear country. It is 11 miles (18 km) to Mary Lake (no fish there) and another 9 miles (14.5 km) or more to a point on the Grand Loop Road between Canyon and Fishing Bridge Junctions. No overnight camping is allowed anywhere on this trail.

7.4/9.6 Entering the Lower Geyser Basin area. These meadows may be carpeted with purple fringed gentians in August.

The Lower Geyser Basin is somewhat lower in altitude and downriver from the Upper Geyser Basin. The explorers who placed names on the land while passing through on horseback or on foot were much more aware of the topography than we are in our powerful cars and buses.

To the west about 4 miles (6.5 km) away are the small round mountains called the **Twin Buttes**. These buttes are mounds of debris left behind while the glaciers covered Lower Geyser Basin. The hot steam in this thermal area caused some of the ice to melt and release its load of rocks and gravel. As more ice moved over this area it melted, leaving more rocks and gravel. When the glacier retreated, hot vapors continued to rise from below, permeated the hills of debris, cooled, and precipitated out silica, which cemented the hills.

8.0/9.0 P (2) Entrance to Fountain Paint Pot parking for those traveling south. If you take this half-mile (0.8 km) walk, you can see all four principal types of hydrothermal discharge: geysers, hot springs, *fumaroles* (steam vents), and mud pots. At the start of the trail, an informative Yellowstone Association pamphlet is available.

Lower Geyser Basin

Seventeen hot spring groups covering about 5 square miles (13 sq km) nestle in the valley of Lower Geyser Basin. Not all are accessible by trail or boardwalk. The basin's most popular feature is Great Fountain Geyser, easy to reach on Firehole Lake Drive at mile 9.0/8.0. At Great Fountain expect to see some of the world's most exciting geyser eruptions.

Leather Pool provided hot water to the Fountain Hotel (Ely Cook photo).

Near the Fountain Hotel site (see below) is the Thud Group of thermal features—in an area closed to the public. Looking east from the road, you might see frequently erupting Kidney Spring and Thud Spring, notable for the 1948 cleaning-out it was given by ranger George Marler. He found an amazing hodgepodge of things in it, including a pitchfork, a 40-gallon metal drum, a tree, and a section of a 1913 guidebook!

Historical Fountain Hotel

The Fountain Hotel, located less than one-half mile (0.8 km) from the Fountain Paint Pot area, opened in 1891. It was an unusually elegant place for its remote location, having electric lights, steam heat, and hot spring water in the baths. It was the place where bears were first fed hotel garbage to entertain the tourists. In 1917, when motorization of park transportation made a hotel here unnecessary, Fountain Hotel was permanently closed.

Fountain Paint Pot Loop Walk★

NOTE: Visitors in wheelchairs should be aware that there are stairs at the point farthest from the parking lot.

Celestine Pool (probably from Latin *celestinus*, meaning "heavenly," or sky blue) is the large, quiet pool nearest the parking lot. A tragic event occurred here in 1981, when a young man tried to rescue his dog after it jumped into the pool. Both man and dog died as a result of contact with the scalding water.

Walking straight up the boardwalk, you come to **Silex Spring**, a large, pale blue pool that sometimes erupts as a geyser. Silex means "silica" in Latin. Although called a spring, Silex was known to erupt until 1979, reactivated in 2000, and continues to have periods of activity.

Fountain Paint Pot [GEO.22] is Yellowstone's largest easily accessible mud pot. These occur in areas of limited water supply, where gas bubbles of *carbon dioxide* and rotten-egg-smelling *hydrogen sulfide* rise and, helped by bacteria, form acids that break down the tephra into fine clay and silica. The *paint pot* is delicately tinted by oxides of iron, nickel, aluminum, and manganese. The fascinating bubbling activity depends upon the amount of groundwater available, usually decreasing as summer progresses. The boardwalk sometimes has to be moved as the paint pot grows.

A nineteenth-century visitor, Gen. John Gibbon, remarked that the paint pots are like "a group of politicians, each one trying to outdo the other"—and he said something about mudslinging in the same connection.

At the top of the hill, you can often hear a loud, high-pitched, and persistent hissing sound coming from a jumble of rocks next to bubbling mud. This is a

Fountain Paint Pot

fumarole, a vent where steam and other gases escape from deep underground.

Red Spouter formed in a grassy area soon after the 1959 Hebgen Lake earthquake. When the water table is high, its two large vents or pools are perpetual spouters. A *perpetual spouter* erupts continuously. When there's less water, Red Spouter's pools become noisy fumaroles. The gray crater sometimes sports bright red patches.

Leather Pool was named for the brown *bacteria* that used to line it. But after the 1959 Hebgen Lake earthquake, it became a clear blue pool. The brown color has returned to the rocks lining the pool, but the water remains fairly clear. A trace of the former pipeline to Fountain Hotel can still be seen.

At a slightly lower level, you'll pass **Fountain Geyser** (not the same as Great Fountain Geyser) to the north of the boardwalk. It and sometimes its neighbor **Morning Geyser** were major attractions for the hotel guests—rather like Old Faithful still is today for guests at Old Faithful Inn.

A Fountain Hotel guest of 1899 wrote a vivid description of an eruption of Morning Geyser. Guests were aroused about midnight one August night by gongs and bells and porters shouting, "The new geyser is playing!" Tourists rushed to the geyser basin in all states of dress and undress. "Upward into the black night shot a stupendous column of water three hundred feet high. The porters were the first to arrive and playing their red calcium lights on the wonderful body of falling water gave us a display of fire and water that must be seen to be appreciated. . . ."

When active, Fountain may erupt as high as 100 feet (30 m). Since both Fountain and Morning Geysers have years-long dormant periods, catching one or both erupting is a treat you can't count on. Yellowstone's geysers are notorious for changing their eruption patterns. In past summers Fountain erupted every five to seven hours, whereas in 2012 you were lucky to catch it once or twice a day.

The geysers of the Fountain Group are interdependent, exhibiting what scientists call *exchange of function*. This means that the underground plumbing of each influences the others a great deal. These geysers are consequently irregular and mostly unpredictable.

Geysers of two other groups, the Kaleidoscope and Sprinkler groups, can sometimes be seen erupting as you stand on the boardwalks above or near Fountain. There has been more activity in this area in the past few years than ever before, according to those who've been watching closely.

Twig Geyser, at the base of the steps, can be seen erupting a few feet high (a meter or two), related to Fountain's eruptions.

Jet Geyser built its formation from six vents along a long break in the sinter. It erupts every few minutes up to 20 feet (6 m) high when either Fountain or Morning geyser is active.

Spasm Geyser (near the bend in the boardwalk) plays about 3 feet high (1 m), often beginning to erupt two or three hours before Fountain. Spasm has a yellow-stained cone and pale green water. Its rocky edge is the result of a hydrothermal explosion this geyser experienced in 1963.

Clepsydra Geyser (pronounced CLEP-si-drah), farther from the boardwalk than Spasm Geyser, clearly exhibits the geysers' exchange of function. If Fountain Geyser is not active, Clepsydra rarely stops playing, but when Fountain is active, Clepsydra sometimes pauses. Before Fountain reactivated in the late 1990s, Clepsydra's spurts were as high as 45 feet (14 m); lately they have been lower.

Clepsydra is the ancient Greek word for water clock (literally, "to steal water"). The name was applied to this geyser in the 1870s, because at that time its eruptions could be expected regularly every three minutes. As you tour the park you'll find that early park explorers, officials, and guides drew on their classical education, choosing Greek and Latin names for many features.

Clepsydra Geyser erupts from two major jets and several minor ones. Spasm Geyser's two vents are in the foreground.

Jelly Spring (its official name, although it has sometimes erupted as a geyser) becomes lined with thick, jelly-like masses of cyanobacteria during its long dormant periods. Some scientists think that the microorganisms in Jelly Spring have helped it deposit its gelatinous geyserite.

Several more geysers, as well as many

Geyserite

As you tour the geyser basins of Yellowstone, you'll notice that a white or pale gray brittle rock surrounds the geysers and hot springs and forms gravelly areas. With a few exceptions (such as Terrace Springs and the Firehole Drive area) this rock is made of *hydrous silicon dioxide*. Other names for it are *siliceous sinter*, geyserite, or sometimes simply *sinter* or silica.

The volcanic rhyolite that underlies most of the park's thermal areas contains a lot of silica. When hot water percolates through the rhyolite, silica dissolves and is brought to the surface. There, the water cools and precipitates the silica as geyserite. In some places this process creates vast, nearly flat rocky areas, such as here at Fountain Flats.

Microorganisms that thrive in these hot waters can form microbial mats that sometimes act as templates, controlling the shapes that the geyserite takes. Sometimes the silica deposits build fantastic formations, such as those of Castle and Grotto Geysers at Upper Geyser Basin.

For information about microbes that live in very acidic water, see page 175.

hot springs, cover the flats between here and the river. You may catch sight of them erupting from the boardwalk, but there's no public access to the area.

Continuing on the Grand Loop Road
8.2/8.8 P (2) Fountain Paint Pot. Closest parking area entrance for those heading north.

9.0/8.0 White Creek crossing; **Firehole Lake Drive** begins. This side road runs one way south to north.

Firehole Lake Drive*

NOTE: The mileage from the beginning of this side road is given in parentheses. Grand Loop Road mileage continues on page 63 where Firehole Lake Drive rejoins it. All thermal features are accessible along this drive.

(0.0) The dead pines standing in this marshy area have white "socks," a result of absorbing silica from the hot spring runoff water surrounding their roots. Mature lodgepoles here were killed by thermal runoff dammed up by new road construction in the 1960s. Trees killed in this way may stand for decades.

(0.65) **Broken Egg Spring** resembles an upturned egg with the shell broken off.

(0.8) **Firehole Spring** is actually a perpetual spouter rather than a spring. In 1888, George L. Henderson, a tour guide and the namer of many Yellowstone features, wrote: "Every few seconds there arise great globes that seem to revolve like chariot wheels as they rise toward the surface. Then they come faster and faster until they seem to glide into each other and rise into one magnificent dome of liquid splendor. . . . " The runoff channels are lined with some of the park's most beautiful, many-colored bacteria (see picture, page 66).

When you look northward, the beautiful mountain you see in the distance is 10,336-foot (3,150 m) **Mount Holmes**. William H. Holmes (1846-1933) was an artist and geologist who climbed this mountain as a member of the 1878 Hayden Geological Survey, a government-sponsored expedition. In his later years, Holmes was most noted for his work in American archaeology.

(0.9) **Surprise Pool** is a deep black—not blue—pool (for the reason, see "Black Water and Travertine," page 63). An 1895 observer wrote, "If a handful of gravel is thrown into it, it will bubble and sparkle, exactly like bromo seltzer." The modern visitor would substitute "Alka-Seltzer." You could stir the water with a stick for the same result. Please remember that throwing anything into a thermal feature not only destroys its beauty but is illegal. The phenomenon happens because any disturbance causes a bubbling reaction in superheated water, that is, water whose temperature is hotter than the boiling point.

The small creek flowing from the east under the road near Surprise Pool is named White Creek for the white sinter deposits lining it. Geologists have found that no cold water flows into the creek, since any rainwater in the area must percolate through hot ground before it reaches the stream. The White Creek thermal area is now closed to visitation due to excessive use of this sensitive area.

DNA Fingerprinting Started Here!

A team of biologists led by Dr. Thomas Brock found an extremely important *thermophilic*, or heat-loving, bacterium in a hot spring near here in 1965. The bacterium is *Thermus aquaticus*. An enzyme called *Taq polymerase* derived from this bacterium has contributed to medical diagnosis and to DNA fingerprinting. This enzyme is useful specifically because of its unusually high heat stability.

Now many researchers are bioprospecting throughout Yellowstone's *hydrothermal areas* for other thermophiles that may prove useful or even help to solve the mystery of the origin of life on earth.

(1.0) P **Great Fountain Geyser**★★ ranks today as one of the four highest-spouting active geysers in Yellowstone and in the world. While eruptions of the others—Steamboat Geyser at Norris Geyser Basin and Giant and Beehive Geysers at Upper Geyser Basin—are unpredictable, Great Fountain is fortunately quite predictable. Eruptions usually range between 100 and 150 feet (30–45 m) high, but may go higher in an occasional superburst. The average interval between eruptions is now about 12 hours. The next predicted eruption time is usually listed at Old Faithful Visitor Education Center as well as at the geyser.

Although there may sometimes be a shortage of park rangers to write the predicted range of times on the signboard, a knowledgeable geyser gazer is often on hand to predict the next eruption, using a formula based on the duration of the previous eruption. She or he can refine the prediction after noting the length of time water overflows from the central vent. The eruption usually starts more than an hour after overflow begins. Your patience will be amply rewarded by a spectacular eruption! The beginnings of some bursts are accompanied by a so-called "blue bubble"

Great Fountain Geyser erupts straight into the air.

at the base of the water column. Don't be in a hurry to leave—wonderful bursts may erupt from a seemingly empty crater during the next hour.

Even the crater of Great Fountain is impressive, with a vent 16 feet (4.8 m) across, surrounded by concentric rings of geyserite that extend to about 150 feet (45 m) in diameter. Its symmetry so impressed expedition leader Ferdinand V. Hayden in 1871 that he called this geyser Architectural Fountain.

This is perhaps the park's largest *fountain-type geyser*. Such geysers have a very broad pool rather than a cone or narrow vent, and they usually erupt in a series of bursts, sometimes beginning with a blue dome-shaped surge.

About Yellowstone's Geysers

The number of hot springs in the park has been estimated to be around 10,000. Geysers known to have erupted or erupting now number more than 1,200. No one knows the exact numbers. However, the Y.N.P. Spatial Analysis Center is now assembling a baseline inventory of geothermal features. Since 2006 the Thermal Biology Institute of Montana State University at Bozeman has been using this inventory to provide an online data set and to coordinate the efforts of thermal researchers. Browse the geothermal features database at www.rcn.montana.edu/resources/.

Some people are not enthralled by geyser basins. You might agree with Owen Wister, author of *The Virginian*, who visited in 1887: "I do not like them or their neighborhood. The air has drafts of stenches through it sometimes like sulphur, sometimes like a stale marsh. The ground is drilled with hissing puddles and sounds hollow as you walk, and all healthy plants and grass keep at a prudent distance. . . . "

Others of us are more like survey leader Hayden, who, according to Harry J. Norton's 1873 guidebook, "cannot compose himself in presence of a geyser in eruption; but, losing recollection of the material world for the time, rubs his hands, shouts, and dances around the object of his admiration in a paroxysm of gleeful excitement."

To learn more about Yellowstone's geysers, the best guide is *The Geysers of Yellowstone* (2008), by geologist and former ranger T. Scott Bryan. Another major source for the author has been the bimonthly newsletter of the Geyser Observation and Study Association (see the Travel Tips for contact information).

(1.25) **White Dome Geyser** has a 20-foot-high cone atop a 12-foot-high mound (6 m atop 3.6 m), both built up from the deposit of sinter or geyserite. To build such a mound, a hot spring or splashing geyser must have deposited sinter here steadily for centuries before the present feature built the cone. White

Dome is a *cone-type geyser*; erupting its steady column of water from a narrow vent in the cone. Much of the actual cone is not white, but is stained pink from a manganese compound. White Dome's unpredictable eruptions (in recent years about every 15 to 45 minutes) go as high as 30 feet (9 m).

(1.3) The jumble of interlaced channels of hot water coming from the right is aptly named **Tangled Creek**.

(1.65) **Pink Cone** is very close to the road. Its eruptions, about once daily, last up to two hours, as high as 30 feet (9 m). It was rarely seen erupting until 1937.

In this area are a few other small geysers, including **Pink Geyser**, located back from the road near the trees, erupting 15–20 feet (5–6 m) every two to seven hours. Old Bath Lake is farther along the road on the right. Researchers believe prehistoric peoples used and perhaps altered it. Tree sections dam up the spring, creating surprisingly regular sides. Thermal areas to the right and left of the road are closed to all visitation.

(2.1) **P** Parking area for Firehole Lake and its associated hot springs (sometimes called Black Warrior Springs).

Take the boardwalk to the left of the road—and the left branch of the boardwalk—to experience being close to the **Hot Cascades** of water from **Steady Geyser** and see the black and red-brown algal streamers under the bridge. Steady Geyser is a perpetual spouter that may be the world's largest, sometimes erupting to 15 feet (4.6 m). In this area the small oval or scalloped formations (*geyser eggs*) are made of travertine rather than geyserite.

At your left is **Hot Lake**, which is primarily a collecting basin rather than a lake but may have hot springs within it. The outlet (western end) of Hot Lake is cool enough for Canada geese to swim on it. They sometimes nest on grassy hummocks next to the lake. The lake created by Steady Geyser's runoff is **Black Warrior Lake**, named for its unusual dark olive green or almost black lining.

Pink Cone's deposits are tinted by manganese compounds.

Continue past Steady Geyser and cross the road to take the other boardwalk along **Firehole Lake** and its several spouting springs. Firehole Lake, like Firehole Spring (at 0.8 mile on this side road), got its name from the blue flamelike appearance of the large steam bubbles you can often see rising from within it.

Three small geysers on the edge of Firehole Lake may be erupting when you're here. Nearest the road are the many vents of **Young Hopeful Geyser**, erupting almost perpetually from two craters, which formed when it underwent a steam explosion in the 1970s. Close to Young Hopeful is **Gray Bulger Geyser**. Its numerous small vents constantly spray water or emit steam, making an entertaining racket. Farthest from the road is **Artesia Geyser**, whose eruptions are usually under 5 feet (1.5 m) high.

(3.3) Junction with Grand Loop Road. Opposite is the parking area for the Fountain Paint Pot area. Turn left for Old Faithful, right for Madison Junction.

Black Water and Travertine

Why are Firehole Lake and some of the nearby springs black? There are large amounts of manganese oxide being deposited, more than anywhere else in the park. In fact, George Henderson, tour guide in the 1880s and '90s, liked to call this part of the Firehole River Valley "Ebony Basin."

Around Firehole Lake, the mineral *travertine*, which is *calcium carbonate* in the form deposited by hot springs, is deposited along with geyserite. This is unusual, because in all but four of the park's thermal areas, the geysers and hot springs deposit only geyserite. At Mammoth Hot Springs, the terraces are made entirely of travertine. The only other easily accessible area where both minerals are deposited is the Terrace Spring area near Madison Junction. Look for the egglike travertine formations that exist in both Black Warrior and Firehole Lakes.

Continuing on the Grand Loop Road
9.5/7.5 (17) Just south of a quiet meadow (unofficially called Whiskey Flats) is Whiskey Flats picnic area. Yellowstone Park sign maker Virgil Hall gave up making "Whiskey Flats" signs, when 18 of them were stolen in less than two years' time!

9.9/7.1 **(2)** Midway Geyser Basin.

Midway Geyser Basin Loop Walk**

NOTE: This route is wheelchair accessible but has a steep ramp.

The first feature you encounter on the walkway is **Excelsior Geyser**. The tremendous crater and prodigious overflow give you some idea what a stupendous geyser this must have been when active. The crater (sometimes called The Caldron in the park's early days) measures over 250 by 300 feet (75 by 90 m). The constant steaming overflow has been measured at about 4,000 gallons (15,000 L) per minute. For comparison, Old Faithful Geyser takes nearly two months to throw out as much water as Excelsior's crater discharges in one day. The mustard yellow, orange, and brown runoff over the side of Excelsior's crater into the Firehole is a perennial favorite of photographers.

Excelsior Geyser (F. J. Haynes photo, 1888)

Some early visitors called this geyser Hell's Half Acre, but Park Superintendent Norris applied that name to the whole geyser basin in 1881 and changed the geyser's name to Excelsior, meaning "ever higher" in Latin. When Excelsior erupted, enormous volumes of rock were thrown everywhere, and after an eruption, the Firehole River would have three times its normal volume. But these 300-foot (90 m) eruptions themselves may have destroyed the geyser. Whatever the reason, there's been only rare, minor activity during the last century.

Notice the layers and layers of laminated sinter on the crater's walls. Nearby Grand Prismatic Spring may have been overflowing and depositing sinter downslope for many centuries before Excelsior blew out its crater.

If you're walking beside the crater on a cool day, engulfed in steam next to the walls' great drop-off, you may have a feeling of being at the edge of the earth. No photograph can capture that sensation.

If you take the boardwalk to the right when it forks, you'll first encounter **Turquoise Pool**, which greatly resembles the semiprecious stone. The color is caused by light reflecting from minute particles suspended in its water. Grand Prismatic Spring drains into Turquoise, and Excelsior may have an underground connection with it as well. Sometimes the water drains nearly out of sight, but it slowly returns in subsequent months.

Next along the path is **Opal Pool**, which got its name from the opalescence both of its water and its surrounding sinter. Opal is actually a geyser with rare but sometimes high eruptions. Opal sometimes drains its 43-foot-deep (13 m) pool completely, as it did during 2005–7.

Midway Geyser Basin's stellar attraction is **Grand Prismatic Spring [GEO.20]**. The largest hot spring in the park, it measures about 250 by 350 feet (75 by 100 m). Prismatic means "brilliantly colored." The central water in the spring is a brilliant blue, with blue-green near the edges. Radiating out from this are rays of yellow, orange, and brown—the runoff channels. Since early days, visitors have remarked about the beautiful reflection of the pool's colors in the steam.

It's difficult to get a good photo of a spring as huge as Grand Prismatic. Some of the best are taken from the air, but if you are determined to reach a good viewpoint, there's a choice of two hills you might climb. East of the main road there's Midway Bluff, and to the southwest of Grand Prismatic is a burned-over hill skirted by the Fairy Falls Trail (described at mile 11.3/5.7).

What Makes the Colors?

Wandering through Yellowstone's thermal areas, you'll see an amazing range of colors. The centers of the hot springs may be deep blue or blue-green or palest turquoise blue. The edges of the pools and their runoff channels will range from yellow through orange and red to brown, with light and dark greens here and there. What causes these different colors?

Let's start with the blue of the water. Sunlight penetrating the pool is scattered by the minute particles and molecules in the water. However, blue light is scattered more efficiently than red or yellow, so the light coming toward you appears blue. This same phenomenon occurs in the atmosphere to give us blue skies. Thus, in all but very shallow hot springs, we see blue centers. The blue is intensified in many pools where a lot of silica is suspended in the

Grand Prismatic Spring

water. Pools like Emerald Pool in Black Sand Basin (page 72) appear green, combining their yellow or orange microorganisms with the blue water.

Scientists have found many different tiny living organisms in the hot springs, all generally called thermophilic microorganisms, meaning that they reproduce and prosper in hot places. Different species of bacteria, *algae* (*Eukarya*), and *Archaea* thrive at different temperatures and at different degrees of acidity or alkalinity. *Hyperthermophiles*, that is, organisms that thrive in environments above 176°F (80°C), are found in the hottest water, while algae grow best where the runoff water has cooled to about 113–122°F (45–50°C). Their various colors are due to pigments—such as the yellow-green of chlorophyll—in those organisms that use light as their source of energy, that is, the photosynthetic ones. The bright green Cyanidiales order of alga living in a prominent runoff channel in Porcelain Basin at Norris is an example (picture, page 241). Carotenoid pigments may contribute red, orange, or yellow. Another common pigment is melanin, which contributes a dark maroon or brown color to a relatively low-temperature alga (at about 95°F, or 35°C) called *Zygogonium*.

Non-photosynthetic bacteria live in the hottest water, while algae and photosynthetic bacteria occupy the cooler water farther from the hot spring source. Archaea use iron and precipitate it out. There are so many different families and genera of these tiny beings that scientists have only begun to find them and study their characteristics.

Microorganisms thrive in the runoff of Firehole Spring (described on page 59).

As you travel in Yellowstone, you may notice colors around the hot springs other than the ones mentioned here. Not all the colors are organic; some are due to minerals. For example, iron-containing minerals are responsible for various shades of yellow and red around the acidic springs of Norris Geyser Basin. The pinks that stain some geyser cones are due to manganese-containing minerals. A great deal of manganese oxide in water will turn it black. Compounds of sulfur, arsenic, and mercury create some of the reds and yellows. In summary, the colors are due both to the pigments in the microbes and to biochemical processes carried out by metabolism within them, such as the oxidation of iron. Microorganisms are too small to be seen individually with the naked eye, but the colored mats formed by countless masses of them appear everywhere in the park, sometimes as filamentous streamers, other times as masses of color adhering to the geyserite and travertine around the hot springs.

—With contributions by Timothy McDermott

Continuing on the Grand Loop Road

10.6/6.4 Across the Firehole River from the road is **Flood Geyser**; other geysers of lesser interest line both riverbanks. Flood was recently erupting up to 10 feet (3 m) every 30 to 40 minutes, but it has been known to have major eruptions up to 25 feet (7.6 m). The big meander in the river is called Muleshoe Bend by fishermen, who have caught many big trout here.

11.2/5.8 Rabbit Creek crossing. Near the headwaters and elsewhere along this creek is a thermal area with paint pots and hot springs. Unfortunately, this is a dangerous area due both to downed trees and the risk of breaking through the fragile thermal crust into the very hot water below. Visit only in the company of a park ranger or other person knowledgeable about this thermal area.

Before 1970, bears were everywhere along the roads. A garbage dump near here was frequented by grizzly bears. Nearby Grizzly Pool is a spot where the bears sometimes bathed.

11.3/5.7 To the northwest a short road takes you to a large parking area for **Fairy Falls Trailhead**. The entire 5-mile stretch of the former Fountain Freight Road, beginning at the 1903-vintage steel bridge, is open to mountain bikes. To approach by car from the other end, turn off the Grand Loop Road at the "Fountain Flat Drive" sign at mile 5.6/11.4 instead.

There are several small geysers and hot springs near the river (and even in the parking lot). To the north is a spring with a 75-foot-wide (23 m) crater, named **Tire Pool** when two auto tires were removed from it. South of the parking lot and closer to the river is **Egeria Spring**, a name that comes from a water nymph in Roman mythology.

To reach graceful 197-foot (60 m) **Fairy Falls** on Fairy Creek, it's a 2.2-mile (3.5 km) hike along the former road and then west on a level trail. The walk to Fairy Falls is one of the relatively few park experiences that were somewhat spoiled by the 1988 fires, but the falls itself is now easier to see and quite spectacular. **Imperial** and **Spray Geysers** and some fascinating mud pots are about 1.5 miles (2.5 km) farther along the same trail, at the foot of the Twin Buttes.

On the Grand Loop Road opposite this side road and partially concealed up the small hill is **Till Geyser**, named for the loose sand and gravel left by glaciers. It erupts as high as 20 feet (6 m) from several vents about every 10 to 11 hours.

11.9/5.1 **Mallard Creek Trailhead** on the east. This unmaintained trail reaches Mallard Lake in about 4 miles

(6.5 km) and connects with the Mallard Lake Trail to descend to Old Faithful in about another 3.5 miles (5.5 km). Mallard Lake is known to geoscientists for the Mallard Lake *dome* **[GEO.25]**, an area where the *magma* under the Yellowstone Caldera comes unusually close to the surface.

Geyserite formations like biscuits once surrounded Sapphire Pool (W. H. Jackson historic photo).

12.5/4.5 For a short time in the spring you can see a waterfall cascading over the edge of the Madison Plateau if you look southwest while traveling south along this part of the road. Waterfalls enthusiast Mike Stevens, coauthor of *The Guide to Yellowstone Waterfalls and Their Discovery* (2000), calls it Unfaithful Falls for its temporary nature and proximity to Old Faithful.

13.8/3.2 Ⓟ 🥾 **Biscuit Basin** is named for the biscuit-shaped geyserite knobs that were formerly more prevalent in this area. In addition to the three-quarter-mile (1.2 km) boardwalk around the basin, there are other trails starting from here. A recommended trail goes to 70-foot (21 m) Mystic Falls starting near Avoca Spring (see next page).

The **Artemisia Trail** starts opposite the Biscuit Basin turnoff (look for the sign "Artemisia" with a trail symbol). Also recommended, this trail takes you southward past several interesting geysers and hot springs. It joins the paved walkway at Morning Glory Pool in less than a mile (1.5 km). Features along this trail are described from its other end on pages 95–96.

Biscuit Basin Loop Walk

NOTE: ♿ This hot spring area is accessible to wheelchairs, but has no curb cut. See the map on page 83.

The first area after the footbridge has been surprisingly active since 2006. **Black Opal Pool** erupted explosively in May 2009, causing geologists who happened to be present to debate whether it had an especially forceful eruption or a hydrothermal explosion. Late in the 2012 season Black Opal and the next two pools, **Black Diamond** and **Wall**, had merged into one large pool, at least temporarily.

In the distance near the river is a

relatively new perpetual spouter informally called Salt and Pepper for its early tendency to throw out dark rocks in addition to water.

The once crystal-clear **Sapphire Pool** was delightful to watch. Visitors stood transfixed, watching a string of bubbles from far below, followed by an overall sizzling, and then a surging boil that engulfed the whole spring. Then, due to the 1959 Hebgen Lake earthquake, Sapphire began erupting 125 feet (38 m). These violent eruptions increased the size of Sapphire's crater, destroyed its unique "biscuits," and changed its shape from circular to oval. By 1964, the eruptions were much smaller, and a few years later it ceased any significant activity.

Take the boardwalk loop to the right beyond Sapphire to see several other features, including the deep cavernous vent of **Black Pearl Geyser**. Black Pearl was thickly studded with quarter-inch black knobs when it was named in the first part of the twentieth century. At the boardwalk curve is **Mustard Spring**, really two small geysers connected underground.

Avoca Spring is the grotto-like cone located near Mystic Falls Trailhead. Avoca was a boiling spring until 1959, when it developed into an erratic geyser.

Silver Globe Geyser, next to Avoca and connected to it, can mesmerize you when it has silvery white bubbles rising from deep within its clear pool. Here's proof of the erudition of early Yellowstone namers, especially of tour guide George Henderson: he called the geyserite arch in and over Silver Globe Geyser the Zygomatic Arch, because it reminded him of a human cheekbone.

A number of very hot features (including Avoca Spring and others to its south) are grouped into the **Silver Globe Complex**. Geyser expert T. Scott Bryan has suggested that a marked increase in activity here beginning in 1983 was linked to an Idaho earthquake of that year centered 150 miles (240 km) away at Borah Peak (Idaho's highest point).

Starting across from Avoca Spring, the **Mystic Falls Trail** is about 3.5 miles (5.6 km) round trip, with steep sections near the falls. A left turn at the first junction would lead you through backcountry to Summit Lake in 7 miles (11 km) on Yellowstone's western section of the new Continental Divide National Scenic Trail.

To reach Mystic Falls on the Little Firehole River, go left at the next trail junction instead. (The right-hand trail takes you in 0.7 mile (1 km) to an overlook of Biscuit and Upper Geyser Basins.) Trail junctions are not well marked except at the falls itself. If you stay left, you'll follow the Little Firehole River to the 70-foot (21 m) drop of Mystic Falls. This delightful hike may reward you with a profusion of unusual wildflowers.

Back on the boardwalk

Shell Spring (actually a small geyser) has an irregular crater that may remind you of a clamshell. The crater has a mustard-colored lining from sulfurous deposits splashed on during its very frequent small eruptions.

Chances are good that **Jewel Geyser** (at the boardwalk junction) will erupt for you. Jewel generally erupts every seven to nine minutes, sometimes to 20 feet (6 m) high. In the 1930s, rangers found that Jewel would draw down a handkerchief

Jewel Geyser's name comes from the shiny sinter beads around its vent.

placed in one vent and expel it from another during an eruption, but this practice was stopped when injuries occurred. (See "Black Sand Basin Walk," below, for the original Handkerchief Pool.)

Two more very active geysers are located near the Biscuit Basin parking area. Out on an island in the Firehole River to the south is **Island Geyser**, which erupts most of the time. Near the road is **Rusty Geyser**, with an *iron-oxide-*stained crater.

Continuing on the Grand Loop Road
13.9/3.1 Firehole River Bridge.

14.0/3.0 There's limited parking along the road for access to trails. A bicycle and hiking trail southeast leads to Old Faithful and passes near Daisy Geyser. A trail to the west joins the Mystic Falls Trail described earlier.

14.4/2.6 Through the trees you may notice a red-orange stained area partway up the hill to the west. This is **Hillside Springs**, a nearly inaccessible thermal feature. Old-time stagecoach drivers called it Tomato Soup Springs.

15.4/1.6 Black Sand Basin side road southwest (right) to a large parking area. You can see all the features in this geyser basin by walking less than a mile (1.6 km). The basin is now best known for Emerald Pool at its south end. The lovely **Iron Spring Creek** meanders through on its way north to join the Firehole River. There's not a lot of iron in the creek, but there *is* a large amount of reddish brown algae, due to the creek's thermal warming.

The black sand here is composed of grains of hyaloclastite, a type of rhyolitic volcanic glass that formed when lava flowed into water or ice (such as into a lake), cooled extremely quickly, and shattered into tiny fragments.

Black Sand Basin Walk★

NOTE: This hot spring area is accessible to wheelchairs, but has no curb cut. See the map on page 83.

If you take the sidewalk a short distance back along the entrance road, you'll see a couple of spouters, appropriately named **The Grumbler** (splashing angrily below the sidewalk) and **Spouter Geyser**. Spouter's runoff has fed the double ob-

Handkerchief Pool once drew down and regurgitated tourists' handkerchiefs.

long of **Opalescent Pool**, long a popular subject for color photographers. When Spouter is not very active, Opalescent Pool becomes smaller and less colorful.

The geyserite mound southeast of the parking area indicates that there has been a geyser here for a very long time. It's been seen (and heard!) to erupt enough times to earn the name **Whistle Geyser**. Its rare eruptions are characterized by a powerful steam phase, described in a 1931 newspaper article as sounding like "about four locomotives at a distance, with a shrill, ringing tone to it."

As you start along the main boardwalk, **Jagged Spring** and its smaller neighbor **Ragged Spring** are the first features you meet. Actually geysers, they play in unison almost constantly, and Jagged may erupt as high as 15 feet (5 m).

Cliff Geyser across the creek is likely to be erupting, and its major eruptions may go to 40 feet (12 m) from a full pool, then drain the pool suddenly and completely.

Large and sometimes gloriously colored **Green Spring** to the left (south) of the walkway can occasionally act as a geyser.

Turning right when the boardwalk forks, you'll see several bubbling and spouting holes. The most vigorous of these in recent years has been the formerly famous **Handkerchief Pool**. One hundred years ago tourists would place a handkerchief in the water near the edge, watch it be drawn out of sight by convection currents in the water, and then reappear, sometimes in another vent.

During the 1920s, someone jammed logs into Handkerchief Pool, effectively killing it. Some years later sufficient trash was removed from the pool to partially restore its activity, but it's now filled with sinter. Thick beds of cyanobacteria usually surround it. Occasionally in recent years, it's come back to life as a small geyser.

Rainbow Pool and **Sunset Lake** are brightly colored big pools at the boardwalk's end. Both of these have acted as geysers but have not erupted in the past several years. Sunset in particular sometimes boils up a few feet at its center, creating large steam clouds. When conditions are right and Sunset Lake is at its hottest, you'll see impressive concentric waves and reflections of color in the steam. As with all these hot springs, the colors around the periphery come from mats formed of Archaea, bacteria, and algae.

A separate stretch of boardwalk to the south takes you to **Emerald Pool**. This is one of the most famous pools in Yellowstone and is a truly unusual deep emerald green at its center with orange around the edges. The bacteria can grow inside this pool due to its relatively cool temperature (around 150°F/66°C). But watch out! It's *not* cool enough to touch!

Emerald Pool's green is a combination of blue water and yellow bacteria.

A trail you might want to take from here joins the main walkways around Upper Geyser Basin in just under a mile (1.5 km). Park in the Black Sand Basin parking lot and cross the Grand Loop Road (carefully!) opposite the parking lot entrance. The first thermal feature on this former main road segment is Black Sand Pool in about 0.3 mile (0.5 km). Features on this trail are described from its Daisy Geyser end on pages 102–3.

Continuing on the Grand Loop Road

15.8/1.2 Old Faithful interchange. Built in 1969, this urban-type interchange has been called a "disorienting concrete merry-go-round, the park's most intrusive feature" by Eric J. Sandeen of the University of Wyoming.

Take the ramp to the right for Old Faithful Village and Upper Geyser Basin. Continue straight for West Thumb Junction.

16.3/0.7 **(2)** After taking the off-ramp to the Old Faithful area, you then take the first left turn for a service station, general store, and the Old Faithful Inn.

NOTE: Parking in front of the inn is for guests only. Continue past this turn and follow the signs to much more parking.

16.9/0.1 **P** The second available left (after Do Not Enter signs) goes to the visitor center, upper general store, and the Snow Lodge. Turn left again at the stop sign and find parking along the secondary road at the left or in the large West Parking Area (see map, page 74).

17.0/0.0 Taking the last curve to the left brings you to Old Faithful Lodge and cabins and the East Parking Area. Park in either lot for access to Old Faithful Geyser.

Old Faithful Village

(2) (2) (7) (2) (27) After you turn toward Old Faithful Village, the second turn to the left takes you to a fully equipped service station, where car repairs and towing are available; a general store with small restaurant; and the **Snow Lodge** with its restaurants and associated cabins (open in winter as well as summer). The last curve on the access road leads to the **Old Faithful Lodge** (including a cafeteria and cabins) and the East Parking Area, the place to park recreational vehicles. Picnic tables (10) are located at this parking area's southern edge, the Snow Lodge (14), and the general store near the Inn (3).

The 2010 **Old Faithful Visitor Education Center** includes a large bookstore, ranger-interpreters who answer questions and make geyser predictions, and a museum with a large working geyser model and dioramas. Movies and ranger lectures take place in the large auditorium. Note that other wheelchair-accessible restrooms are available in the inn, lodge, and Snow Lodge.

Across the West Parking Area from the visitor center is a post office, as well as a clinic, ranger station, and backcountry office. Between the visitor center and the Lodge is a walk-in center for the Yellowstone Park Foundation.

The name Old Faithful is used in the park to refer to both the village and the geyser. If you've arranged lodging at Old Faithful, you'll find that there are two faces to this village. From about nine in the morning to six in the evening there are cars and people everywhere. But later in the evening, at night, and in the early morning you may find, if not exactly solitude, at least a delightful opportunity to enjoy this long-famous area in relative quiet.

Old Faithful Visitor Education Center, opened in 2010

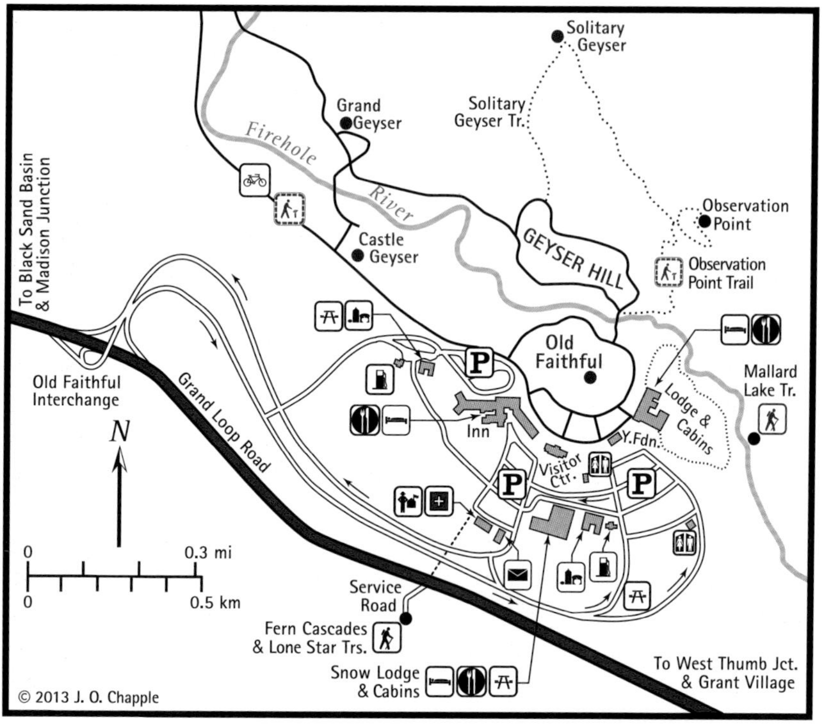

Old Faithful Village

Lodgings

NOTE: There is no overnight camping in the Old Faithful area.

There are four types of lodgings at Old Faithful, all needing to be reserved well in advance (see "Hotels and cabins" in the Travel Tips for details):

- **Old Faithful Inn**, the most interesting (with both inexpensive and expensive rooms)
- The **Snow Lodge**, completed in the summer of 1999, with the most modern accommodations
- The **Snow Lodge cabins**, comfortable and modern
- The **cabins** behind the **Old Faithful Lodge**, some of which lack private bathrooms

Confusingly, but in keeping with early park concessionaires' idea of a lodge, **Old Faithful Lodge** itself has no sleeping rooms at all. Instead, it was built in the 1920s as a spacious recreation hall with a great view of the geyser. Modern needs have dictated that the space be divided for use as a cafeteria, gift shop, desks for cabin rental and activities, a large lobby, and several small snack shops. Showers are available at the lodge even for people not staying in the cabins.

You can find seven cafeterias and restaurants at Old Faithful. In addition to those in the inn and lodge, the Snow Lodge has one grill and one family-style restaurant, and both general stores have small food-service areas.

Old Faithful Inn★★

Reservations to stay in Old Faithful Inn must usually be made several months in advance, but occasionally a room becomes available close to the time you need it. Whether or not you stay in the inn, you'll enjoy seeing it, both inside and out. This National Historic Landmark is a wonderful example of early twentieth century western American architecture.

The inn was built in 1903–4, at a time when visitors were increasingly complaining about the lack of a good place to stay at Upper Geyser Basin. Before that time, most stagecoach tours of the park could allow only half a day here. Coaches stopped at the popular Fountain Hotel and at Lake or Canyon the following night.

Thirty-year-old architect Robert C. Reamer situated the building so that arriving visitors could easily witness an Old Faithful Geyser eruption. For geyser watching he also provided a second-story veranda, extended out over the new porte cochere in 1927. Reamer chose native rhyolite for foundations, lodgepole pine for decorative details, and wrought iron for the lobby clock and door hardware, all worked on the site.

Early morning shadows catch Old Faithful Inn at a quiet time.

A few years after the inn opened, guidebook writer Reau Campbell put it this way:

> Who shall describe this most charming, most unique, queer, quaint, fascinating place? . . . The stairways have the steps of logs split in half with the flat side up; the banisters and newel posts are of knotted, gnarled and twisted branches of the native trees. The galleries are supported by columns and braces cut from trees bent under the weight of snows and grown to fantastic shapes . . . the foundation stones, innocent of the stone-cutters' chisels, were rolled in from the woods with the lichen still on their rugged sides. . . . Here is where you will wish to stay all summer. . . .

Lights were electric from the outset, powered by a steam generator, and there was hot water and central heating, true luxuries for a wilderness hotel at the time. Several rooms shared baths; even today, there are only a dozen private baths in the Old House, as the central portion of the inn is called.

The original log building had 140 rooms. Wings, also designed by Reamer, were completed in 1914 (the east wing) and 1927 (the west wing), bringing the present-day total to about 325 rooms open to guests.

Old Faithful Inn's magnificent lobby by morning light.

If you have time to take one of the twice-daily tours of the inn, led by a knowledgeable inn employee, you'll learn much more about it. At least step inside to see Reamer's majestic lobby, with its 80-foot (24 m) roof ridge exposed above two floors of balconies and its tremendous stone fireplace and wrought iron clock (now electrified). Most of the original inn furniture has had to be replaced, and the fireplace and clock were being repaired in 2012.

The dining room requires reservations but is otherwise informal. Guests of the early days were required to dress for dinner and to be precisely on time. They were entertained by chamber music easily audible from the first balcony's open window. In fact, the author's mother played piano in the Ladies' Ensemble for tea in the afternoons and dancing in the evenings in 1939. A pianist and sometimes other musicians play from about 6:00 to 10:00 in the evening; for twenty years beginning in 1992 it was usually classical pianist George Sanborn. Where else in the world can you enjoy a pleasant dinner or a refreshing drink and look out the window to see a free-roaming bison calmly rubbing his head on a nearby tree? It has happened at Old Faithful Inn!

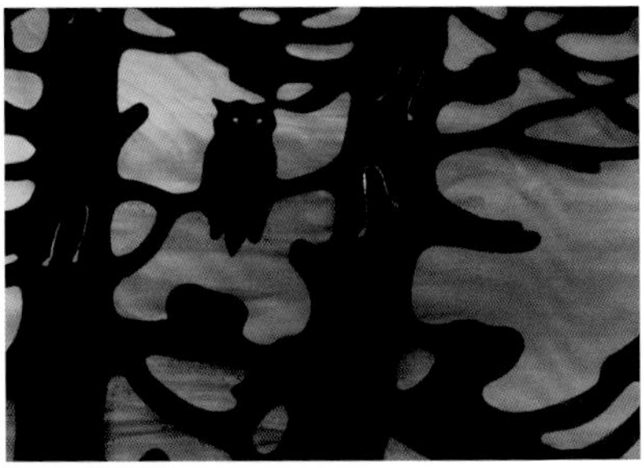

Partner writing desks from 1911 and detail of glass lamp shade.

Twice in its history the inn has been damaged or threatened by the forces of nature. In August of 1959, as a result of the Hebgen Lake earthquake, rocks from the top of the dining room chimney fell through the roof; the chimney was rebuilt in 1987. Then in 1988, the North Fork fire came so close to the inn that people all over the country were holding their breaths that it might be saved. Fierce winds blew embers across the area from the western to eastern hills, and some cabins and employee lodgings were burned. Fortunately, heroic efforts by firefighters, the presence of the huge parking lots, and a last-minute wind shift saved this delightful landmark. We must also thank the outdoor sprinkler system wisely installed the year before.

Major restoration completed in 2008 brought Old Faithful Inn up to modern safety standards and restored it closer to its 1904 appearance.

Hikes from Old Faithful Village

In addition to the walking tours of the Upper Geyser Basin (described in the next section), two other short walks begin from Old Faithful Village.

Take the **Mallard Lake Trail** for a short and easy walk to the **Pipeline Creek Group** of pools and mud pots. The hot springs have had this name at least since the 1920s, when a pipeline ran nearby. The lake is almost 3.5 miles (5.6 km) away and a 700-foot (210 m) climb.

You'll find the trailhead behind the Old Faithful Lodge cabins. Cross the footbridge over the Firehole River. In about 0.5 mile (0.8 km), there's a short side trail at the left toward four or more

*Pink monkeyflowers (*Mimulus lewisii*) along the Mallard Lake Trail.*

mud-filled springs, one a growler that churns like a washing machine. Watch your step and keep small children firmly under control. After about another mile (1.6 km), you cross Pipeline Creek, where pink monkeyflowers (*Mimulus lewisii*) grow.

Fern Cascades Trail. You may encounter some downed lodgepoles on this moderately steep 2.5-mile (4 km) loop, which takes you to some rather small white-water rapids on Iron Spring Creek. Access to the trail is through the employee housing area across the Grand Loop Road from the clinic and ranger station parking lot. The trail intersects with a part of the Howard Eaton Trail that passes Lone Star Geyser (see page 106 for a shorter trail to Lone Star).

Old Faithful Geyser

Old Faithful Geyser**

Old Faithful [GEO.19], the most famous geyser in the world, was named when members of the Washburn Expedition noticed its regularity. This group of men explored the area in 1870 and helped to encourage Congress to set it aside as a park.

Not only is Old Faithful Geyser the top priority for most visitors to see here, it's extremely accessible. Parking is close by, and generous boardwalks and benches border two sides of the geyser's mound. If you happen to be in the inn when the geyser erupts, you can watch it from the porch roof just off the first balcony. In fact, Old Faithful, true to its name, will probably erupt for you even if your time here is very limited.

Haynes Guides from the 1940s on offered some advice about photographing Old Faithful, suggesting that the photographer not stand too close to it and wait to catch the best part of the eruption. "Most people photograph this first display," wrote Mr. Haynes, "and are changing film about the time the geyser attains its maximum height."

For the next eruption time, call (307) 344-2751. See page 359 for Yellowstone webcams to watch from home.

How Faithful Is Old Faithful?

Old Faithful has *never* in recorded time erupted "every hour on the hour" as you may have heard. Here are some figures given for average expected intervals between eruptions: 60 to 65 minutes (1870), 65.5 minutes (1964), 78 minutes (1990). The mean interval has recently varied from a high of 93 to a low of 88 minutes. The range of possible intervals has always been from about 30 to 105 minutes.

Seismic activity *can* affect Old Faithful. Following the strong earthquake at Borah Peak, Idaho, in 1983, the average interval between eruptions became greater, at least for a while. Geoscientists suspect that the geyser may someday seal itself off: a probe sent down its conduit a few years ago revealed a very narrow throat about 22 feet (6.5 m) down, and there's another constriction about 70 feet (21 m) down. Silica may continue building up there, but how fast is anybody's guess. On the other hand, the geyser's water may actually be eroding away the narrow section. No one knows for sure.

In recent years, there's been a rumor that the geyser is losing its power or becoming less regular or much less frequent. The truth is that the average interval between eruptions has lengthened by a few minutes, but the average height has remained about the same for more than 140 years.

Some statistics:

- Old Faithful Geyser's height: 106–184 feet (32–56 m), averaging 145 feet (44 m)
- Eruption length: 1.5–5 minutes
- Elevation at Old Faithful: 7,367 feet (2,245 m)
- Boiling point of water at this elevation: 198°F (93°C)

Predicting Old Faithful's Eruptions

Ask a geyser gazer the rule for predicting Old Faithful's eruptions on a summer day and you would hear: If there is a big crowd around the benches, the eruption will occur within about 15 or 20 minutes. A more precise prediction method involves timing the duration of an eruption from the first heavy surge of geyser water through the last splashes of water above the cone. The longer an eruption lasts, the longer the interval to the next eruption. For example, a two-minute eruption results in about a 55-minute interval; three minutes, a 72-minute interval; four-and-a-half minutes, a 93-minute interval.

Upper Geyser Basin

Upper Geyser Basin stretches in a right triangle from Old Faithful Geyser north and west, mostly along the Firehole River. The hot springs and geysers draw upon the local groundwater for their source of water but also upon deep underground reservoirs. This hydrothermal area contains more than 20 percent of all the geysers in the world, as well as thousands of non-erupting hot springs. T. Scott Bryan, in his book, *The Geysers of Yellowstone*, writes: "To properly experience the Upper Geyser Basin, one should spend at least two or three days to wait for the large and famous geysers to erupt, as well as to enjoy the smaller features. There are minor details to be observed in the basin, too—the colors, wildflowers, forest life, thermophilic communities, and so on—many of which are found nowhere else in the world. To spend less time is to cheat oneself."

What exactly is a geyser?

A geyser is a hot spring that throws forth jets of water and steam intermittently. As you wander through the area, try to guess which seemingly placid hot pools or deep holes may be active geysers, even if they don't erupt while you're watching. Here are some telltale signs of active geysers:

- A deep or wide white crater that does not look cracked and dry
- Areas downhill from the crater that are devoid of life due to hot water
- Puddles of water around a crater when it hasn't been raining
- Dead but standing trees nearby, indicating a relatively new geyser
- Concentric rims or formations of the pale brittle rock called geyserite

The Old Faithful interchange bypasses most of the thermal features. Before it was built, the Grand Loop Road ran past many of them, including Morning Glory Pool and Grotto and Castle Geysers. The only current access to these fascinating but sensitive features is by foot or bicycle. Many bicyclists here are members of the Geyser Observation and Study Association (see page 361).

Vandalism to the geysers and pools has decreased noticeably since the rerouting of traffic, but the road relocation has made it difficult for older or disabled visitors or for those with very little time to view such less-accessible marvels as Grand Geyser and Black Sand Pool. It's some consolation that a wheelchair may be borrowed from the visitor center.

Even the hardy should not be surprised if hills that don't look steep set you to puffing and your heart to beating fast—it's the altitude! A few conveniently located benches are especially welcome on the hilly parts of Geyser Hill.

Precautions for Your Geyser Walks

- Bring **drinking water**, **sunscreen**, and a **hat** for protection from the extra UV radiation at the park's high altitudes.
- The only **restroom** is a chemical toilet near Morning Glory Pool.
- **Stay on the walkways** and **watch children vigilantly**; the water is hot and the crust near the hot springs and geysers is thin and brittle.
- **Do not touch the water**. You can be scalded at 120°F (49°C); the pools and geysers range in temperature from 142° to 205°F (61–96°C).
- **Always wipe off geyser spray** from eyeglasses and camera lenses, since the silicon dioxide can leave permanent spots.

Planning your geyser walk

Here are some ways to visit the geysers:

1. Join one of the ranger-interpreter led tours (1.5 or 2 hours long) listed in the *Yellowstone Today* newspaper you receive as you enter the park.
2. If you have only an hour or two and prefer to be on your own, walk around the Geyser Hill loop. This walk's first half is described below as Geyser Route One, and its return is described from page 97 **(C)** to page 99.
3. If you have half a day or so, check the visitor center for predicted geyser eruption times, then follow one of the geyser routes described here to try to catch one or more eruptions and see other features on the way. Castle, Grand, Riverside, and Daisy Geysers put on rewarding shows. Unfortunately,

Morning sun on geyser runoff and Firehole River, from behind Old Faithful Geyser

Grand Geyser may require a long wait, because its eruptions can only be predicted to within about a four-hour span. Take books and games to entertain yourself while you wait!

4. A tour for true geyser lovers can be taken by those who have one or several days to spend. Wait for one or more of the predicted geyser eruptions, linger over your favorite parts of the basin, or extend your walk to Observation Point, Solitary Geyser, Black Sand Pool, or the extension of the trail beyond Morning Glory Pool.
5. To stay away from crowds, tour the basin at 7 or 8 AM or during the last daylight hours in the evening. These can be wonderful times for picture taking.

TWO WALKING TOURS THROUGH UPPER GEYSER BASIN

Described here are two routes you might take through Upper Geyser Basin. Any combination of walkways is possible, and there's much to see. You might follow one of these Geyser Routes exactly, or plan your own route with the aid of the map on the next page or the large map in the pamphlet that's available at the visitor center and from boxes between the Inn and Old Faithful Geyser and between the Lodge and the geyser. Bicycles are allowed only on Route Two.

Geyser Route One: Geyser Hill and beyond

NOTE: This trail is mostly boardwalk and is not fully wheelchair-accessible.

Geyser Route One is about 3.5 miles (5.6 km) round trip and takes you to two of the two-star features listed in the "Best Sights" list in the Introduction. (Castle and Daisy Geysers are on Geyser Route Two, which begins on page 99.) Extending your walk beyond Morning Glory Pool to Biscuit Basin adds another 1.5 miles (2.4 km) or so. For just the shorter Geyser Hill loop, totaling about 1.3 miles (2 km), start near Old Faithful Geyser as below, but return from near North Goggles Geyser (the area labeled (**C**) on the map and described on pages 97–99).

Starting from the visitor center, circle partway around Old Faithful Geyser, keeping the geyser on your left. There may be bison or elk around the area; allow them plenty of space. Marmots once lived under the old redwood boardwalks here. When the higher recycled plastic boardwalks were put in during 1997–98, coyotes, foxes, and the increased heat probably chased them away.

As you walk toward the Firehole River, notice that Old Faithful and two or three other small features are on a huge mound some 200 feet (60 m) across and 12 to 15 feet (3.6–4.6 m) high. One or more hot springs must have been overflowing and depositing geyserite here for centuries to build such a mound. Yet one study hints that Old Faithful was probably born as a geyser not more than seven hundred years ago.

The trail to Geyser Hill starts down the hill to the right across the Firehole River footbridge.

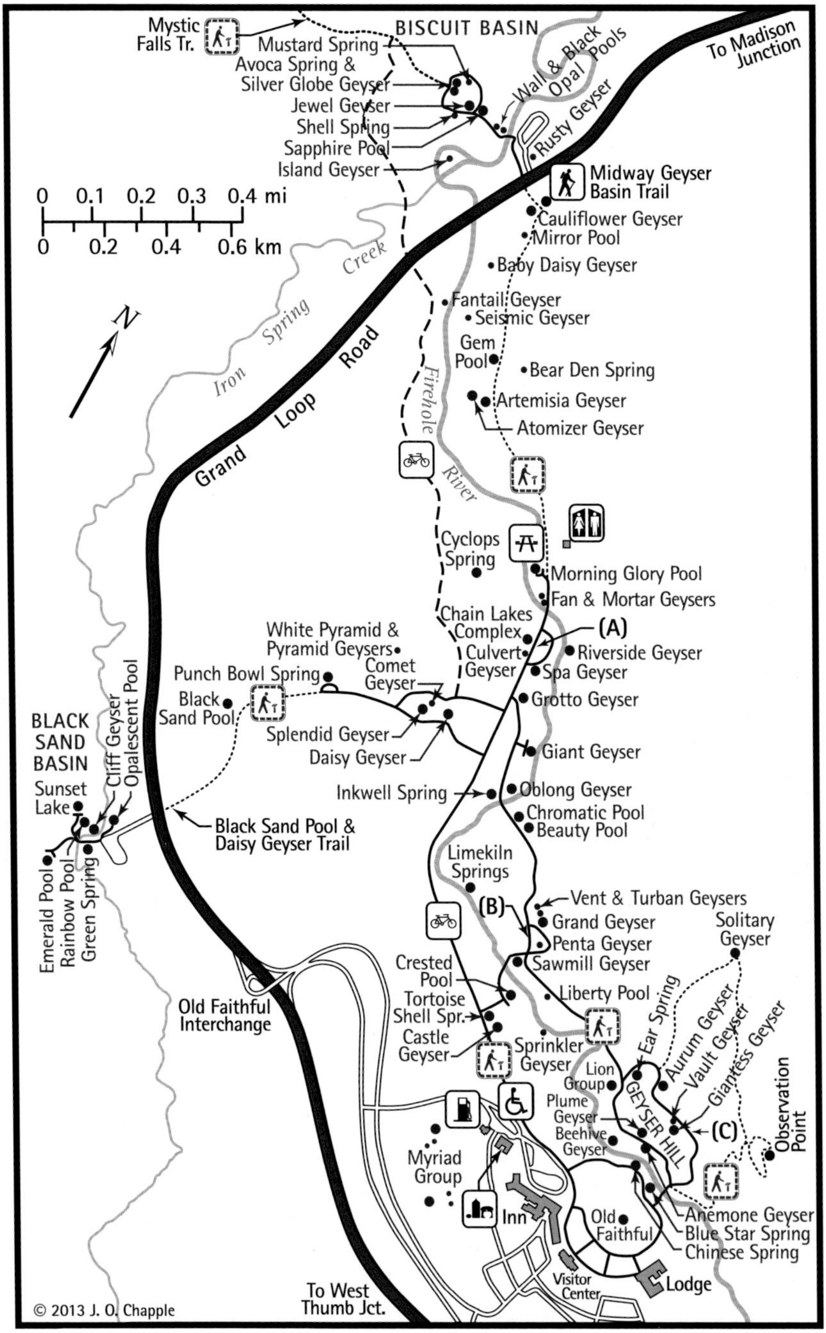

Upper Geyser Basin

Blue Star and Chinese Spring Side Trail

If you take the left fork before going down to cross the river and walk around Geyser Hill, you can take a short side trip to three hot springs. This might be a good way to spend half an hour or so while waiting for Old Faithful to erupt, keeping the geyser in view as you walk.

Blue Star Spring's thin crust sets off the unusually deep blue of its water.

The name of **Blue Star Spring** comes from its geyserite border, shaped like an irregular four-pointed star. After a bison fell in during spring of 1997, the hot spring began a hitherto unseen boiling and doming-up activity. Organisms in the runoff from this spring create a fan of color you can see from across the Firehole.

Down the hill are two bubbling springs, first unsigned **East Chinaman Spring** and then the famous **Chinese Spring**, where an Asian laundryman (actually Japanese) used to draw his supply of water and one day accidentally caused an eruption.

Beyond Chinese Spring the walkway goes to benches that are ideally located for watching Beehive Geyser erupt across the river. Continuing past the benches returns you to Old Faithful Inn and Geyser. Retrace your steps from Chinese Spring to follow the main path.

Back on the main walkway

Stop on the footbridge across the **Firehole River**. Nowhere is the river more beautiful than in this area on the way to Geyser Hill. Wildflowers abound at least until midsummer, the river itself is crystal clear, and the brightly stained banks add to the magical effect.

Observation Point/ Solitary Geyser Side Loop

Just over the bridge and partway up the hill begins the trail to **Observation Point**, a climb of about 150 feet (45 m) in less than half a mile (0.8 km). Observation Point gives you an excellent view overlooking much of Upper Geyser Basin, and it's a fine place to watch Old Faithful. You can continue to Solitary Geyser on this trail, which rejoins the Geyser Hill walkway, or you can retrace your steps down from Observation Point.

Like Chinese Spring near Old Faithful Geyser, **Solitary Geyser** was misused in earlier days, but in this case,

The author learned to swim at the Old Faithful Swimming Pool, housed in this building.

the misuse was officially sanctioned. Its water was piped down to the Old Faithful Geyser Baths, across the Firehole River from Beehive Geyser, beginning in 1915. Its replacement, the Old Faithful Swimming Pool, was used until 1949. Solitary Geyser now commonly erupts less than 6 feet (2 m) high every few minutes, and its water is definitely too hot for bathing! Solitary's pool is surrounded by interesting geyserite egg formations.

Back on the main walkway

If you don't go to Observation Point, climb the paved trail along the river and take the left fork (closer to the river) to walk around Geyser Hill and follow the route described here. (The walkway to the right is described in the other direction on pages 97–99 and labeled (**C**) on the Upper Geyser Basin map.)

Sulphide Spring, the first feature on your right after the walkways split, lives up to its name by emitting a strong hydrogen sulphide odor. Its waters and those of nearby Infant Geyser are acidic rather than alkaline, unlike most Geyser Hill springs.

After a perpetual spouter informally called Improbable Geyser is **Anemone Geyser**, named by geologist Walter Weed in the 1880s, whether for the sea anemone or for the flower, no one is quite sure. The larger of the two vents, the one closer to the boardwalk, may erupt as often as every seven to ten minutes, unless an extended eruption of the smaller one increases the length of the intervals. It's entertaining to watch the larger crater fill with water, begin splashing, erupt for a few seconds as high as 8 feet (2.5 m)—then drain away with a sucking sound.

Plume Geyser, a short distance from Anemone and on the opposite side of the boardwalk, was created by a small steam explosion in 1922, then made itself a new vent in another explosion 50 years later. Plume plays up to 25 feet (7.5 m) in a plume or feathery jet that spews water at an angle about every hour. Plume is prone to some erratic behavior, including "sleeping" at night (erupting only in the daytime) and experiencing extended dormant periods.

The eruptions of **Beehive Geyser**★ are a glorious sight but not really predictable. Nonetheless, the activity of an indicator geyser a few feet away sometimes gives ranger-interpreters a chance to alert visitors to an impending erup-

Beehive Geyser jets 150 to 200 feet (45–60 m).

tion. Although not totally reliable, the indicator has been noted in writings about the park since 1875 or earlier. It usually starts erupting 10 to 25 minutes before Beehive, allowing people around the visitor center to get to Geyser Hill or at least to the viewing benches north of Old Faithful and next to the river in time for the eruption. Beehive erupts once or twice a day for about five minutes.

Historian Hiram Chittenden wrote of Beehive in the late nineteenth century: "The symmetry of its cone is only surpassed by the regularity of its water column. From an artistic point of view it is the most perfect geyser in the Park." Beehive's needle of water is breathtaking even from a distance; the roar of the steam is an extra thrill when you're standing close.

As you leave Beehive, there are several minor geysers to your right (northeast) above the boardwalk. All are difficult to see and not currently active, though they may bubble or steam.

Depression Geyser's blue-green pool west of the boardwalk looks quiet until it erupts 6 to 10 feet (2–3 m); this happens every few hours. Beyond Depression, one or more of a group of small geysers called The Dwarfs may be spouting as you pass.

Arrowhead and **Heart Springs** are quiet pools whose shapes illustrate their names, except that Arrowhead may have got its name from an artifact found within it.

The Lion Geyser Group has four cones. The largest and closest to the boardwalk is **Lion Geyser**. It roars like a lion when it gushes steam from its vent before all but the first of its cyclic eruptions, and its formation looks to some like a reclining lion when seen from the south. Farther back from the boardwalk, right to left as you stand near Lion, are **Big Cub**, **Lioness**, and **Little Cub Geysers**.

Lion has five- or six-minute eruptions up to 70 feet (21 m) and always plays in a series of eruptions spaced one to one-and-a-half hours apart. In the past ten years its mean between cycles has increased from about 9 to 15 hours. Lioness and Big Cub have been inactive in recent years but sometimes boil vigorously. Little Cub erupted frequently to 10 feet (3 m) but has been erratic since 2004. The washed look of Little Cub's formation tells you it is a frequent geyser, never dormant, in fact, in the history of the park.

In 1889 a British visitor toured the Upper Geyser Basin, noted the "pretty and fanciful" names assigned to all the geysers, and wrote about the group you see here: "The first mound that I encountered belonged to a goblin splashing in his tub. I heard him kick, pull a shower-bath on his shoulders, gasp, crack his joints, and rub himself down with a towel; then he let the water out of the bath, as a thoughtful man should, and it all sank down out of sight till another goblin arrived. Yet they called this place the Lioness and the Cubs." The visitor was the 24-year-old Rudyard Kipling.

Goggles Spring and **North Goggles Geyser** are just beyond the Lion Group. Around North Goggle's cone, note the interesting formation of geyser eggs, built up during its sometimes impressive but very irregularly occurring eruptions. To turn back toward Old Faithful, take the right-hand fork at the walkway intersection (see pages 97–99 for the features you will see).

Heading away from Geyser Hill, the main path now takes you through the trees along the Firehole River. You pass nondescript thermal pools, one called Frog Pond, because it actually has frogs in springtime, and Liberty Pool. The last spring was named after its first eruption on July 4, 1887. Across the river, **Sprinkler Geyser** may be spouting, as it does at least half the time.

Tardy Geyser is the first one you encounter in a group called the Sawmill Geyser Complex. The underground plumbing of Tardy and several other geysers is connected in an exchange of function with Sawmill Geyser. Look closely when the water in Tardy's crater is low, and you can see uniform coin- or biscuit-shaped geyserite knobs around the edge, as you can also in Sawmill's crater. Tardy's eruptions are 10 to 15 feet (3–4.5 m) high.

Sawmill Geyser is the tallest—up to about 50 feet (15 m)—and the longest erupting of the group. You'll find it erupting about 30 percent of the time, with intervals between eruptions typically ranging from one to three hours. Its water spins about in a circle in the crater during eruptions, sounding like the moving wooden parts in an old water-powered sawmill. Behind Sawmill (to the west) is **Uncertain Geyser**, a small hole in Sawmill's formation. Sometimes called Sawmill's Satellite Vent, Uncertain erupts when others in the group are quiet, as high as 15 feet (45 m).

Side Trail toward the River

If you turn left at Sawmill to cross the river and visit Castle Geyser, you'll pass **Churn Geyser**—not very active now but known to erupt to 10 feet (3 m). **Scalloped** and **South Scalloped Springs** are on your right. The water deep down in Scalloped Spring reverberates in its cavern with a satisfying gurgle. The low water level indicates that the spring was probably illegally induced to erupt at some time in the past.

The cone high above the river to the right (downstream) is called **Deleted Teakettle Geyser**. Its strange moniker comes from someone having added "deleted" to the records, resulting in that word becoming part of its name. The formation to the left (upriver) is **Chimney Cone** (though sometimes signed as Chimney Geyser).

Across and downriver you may make out some steaming and spouting springs called the **Terra Cotta Springs**. Needy tourists seem to have found one of them, **Washtub Spring**, useful as a laundry tub. An 1883 guidebook advised: "Sometimes the clothes are returned with one or two pieces missing, but generally they are all safely restored in due time."

This geyser route now returns to the main path without crossing the river. Across the Firehole and up the short hill are unique Castle Geyser and its neighbors (described in Geyser Route Two).

~

Back on the main walkway

To see a few more features in the interdependent Sawmill Complex, take the small loop to the east rather than the straight walkway. These include geysers called **Penta** (named for its five vents), which rarely erupts when Sawmill is active, but may go to 25 feet (7.5 m); **Spasmodic**, with its many vents; and **Old Tardy**. Last encountered before you rejoin the main walk is delicately colored **Belgian Spring**, where a tragedy occurred in 1929: a newspaper editor from Belgium died after falling into this pool.

Turn right to rejoin the straight

part of the boardwalk. We'll pick up the missed section of the main walkway on the way back, labeled (**B**) on the Upper Geyser Basin map and described on page 97.

You're approaching what many geyser lovers consider the most exciting geyser of all to watch, **Grand Geyser**. Before reaching Grand you'll come to some small geysers connected to it underground, including **Rift Geyser**, which seems like just an innocuous group of cracks, but, when active, can influence Grand's eruptions; **Triplet Geysers**, of which only **West Triplet** erupts with any frequency now; and **Percolator Geyser**, which *does* sound like coffee percolating. Percolator Geyser has upon occasion been known to play for two hours or so before Grand's eruption. West Triplet is located closest to the boardwalk, and Percolator is in the middle of a direct line from West Triplet to Grand.

How Does a Geyser Work?

After you've seen some geysers, you'll probably want to know how a geyser works. The basic requirements are a water source, a heat source, and some rather complicated plumbing.

The Sources and the Plumbing

Snowmelt and rainfall provide the water by soaking into the ground locally and from the surrounding mountain ranges. The water flows deep into the geyser basin as groundwater, reaching hundreds of yards (meters) below ground level, as shown in the diagram.

The still-hot volcanic rocks found below Yellowstone's geyser basins provide the source for heating the water. The rocks continuously receive heat because there is magma a few miles below the surface.

The plumbing that all geysers have consists of a vent connected to a narrow crack that goes down into the hot rocks, widening into chambers and narrowing into channels as it goes and intersecting a multitude of tiny cracks and pores that feed water into the geyser.

What Happens to the Water

Let's follow the cycle at the point just after an eruption has ended.

1. The vent and crack have been largely emptied of water. A small part of the water that shot up into the air falls back into the geyser vent and drains down the crack. Of course, this water is much cooler than when it shot out.
2. More water now starts to fill the crack by seeping in from the sides. This water is already very hot from having passed through hot rocks. Much hotter water enters the crack deeper down and pushes the overlying water up.

Time-out here to mention three properties of hot water that clarify why geysers act as they do.

- The boiling temperature of water is higher at higher pressures. The weight of a column of water raises the pressure at the bottom, which raises the boiling temperature. This lets the hot rocks raise the water temperature, making it superheated water.

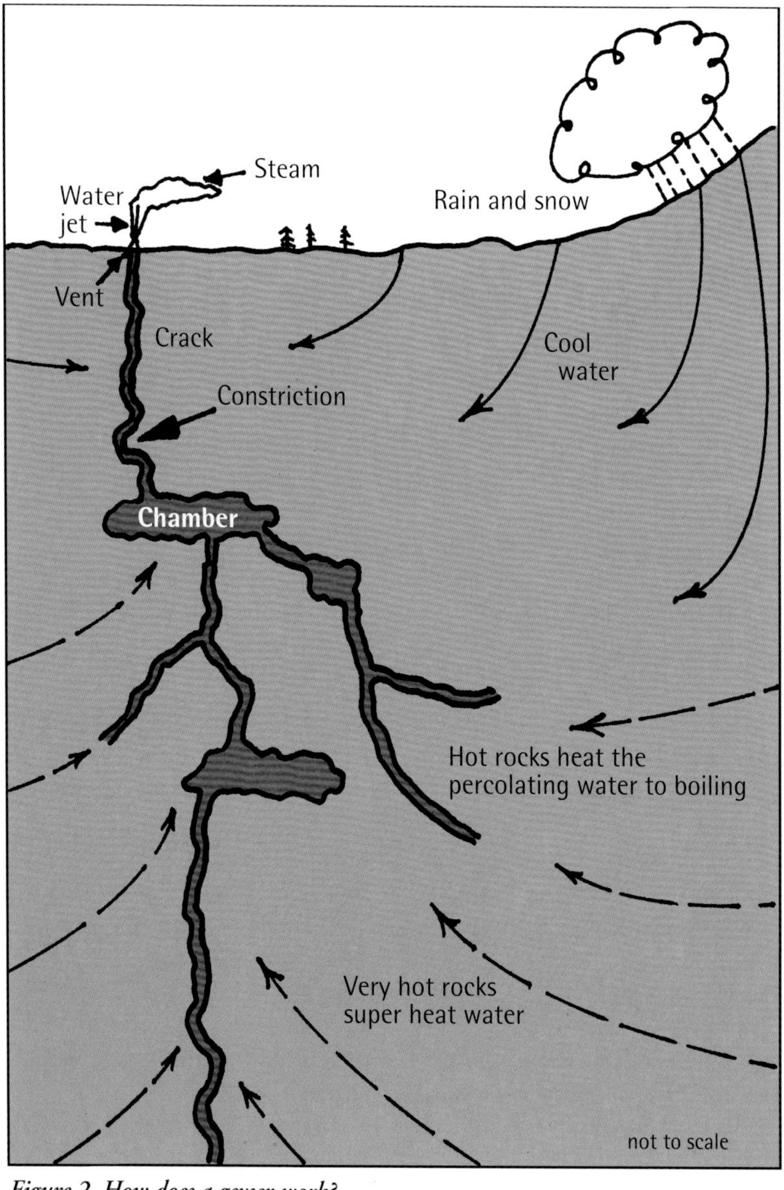

Figure 2. How does a geyser work?

- The same weight of water occupies far more space as steam than it does as liquid water—on the order of a thousand times more space.
- Superheated water flashes into steam if the pressure on it is lowered to ordinary atmospheric pressure.

Now back inside the geyser:

3. As more water enters the crack (or *fissure*), the water level rises toward the surface. The added weight of water increases the pressure near the bottom. The hot water heats the somewhat cooler water already in the fissure. The water level rises past the very narrow parts of the vent.
4. As the superheated water continues to rise in the fissure, it starts to boil gently, forming small steam bubbles that rise and heat the overlying water. Because the deeper boiling water is under higher pressure, it boils at higher temperature, and its steam heats the upper water to its boiling point. More bubbles form, raising the column of water and bubbles in the fissure until it reaches the surface at the vent. Up to this point, the water pressure at depth has been increasing.
5. When water starts to spill out of the vent, the column of water in the fissure is at its greatest height. More steam bubbles from below displace liquid water, some of which spills out at the top. With more steam bubbles in the column now, the weight of the water becomes less, more boiling occurs, even below the constricted parts, and water comes out faster.
6. Next, the steam from below rushes through the constriction like jet engine exhaust. The water is being pushed rapidly toward the surface and spurts out. As more superheated water rises to the upper part of the water column, far more bubbles form, so the column has far more steam in it and thus less weight. This greatly reduces the pressure inside, letting the steam blow the water column out of the vent. The geyser is erupting—an exponentially accelerating catastrophe!
7. When all the steam has managed to escape from below the constriction, there's nothing more to push on the water, and not much water there, so the eruption stops. Then the cycle begins again.

There's more about geysers in the Geological History chapter.

Watching powerful **Grand Geyser**★★ from close by is an unparalleled experience for its raw natural energy. Maybe the obligation to wait a long time in the hot sun (or in below-zero temperatures in the winter!) adds to the thrill when it does erupt, but it's truly a stellar attraction.

Grand erupts from a rather large vent a safe distance from the boardwalk and benches. Early in the park's history, Grand erupted only at widely spaced

Grand Geyser's eruptions are always worth waiting for.

intervals, but the interval gradually decreased between 1930 and the 1980s. In recent years, the range of time between eruptions is mostly from about seven to about ten hours. Your wait for Grand may be long, but it's very likely to be rewarding, since Grand has become the world's tallest predictable geyser.

Turban Geyser (the more impressive geyserite mound to the north of Grand) is not the main attraction, yet will usually oblige you with five minutes of play about every 17 to 22 minutes. The blobs of geyserite in its crater do resemble turban headdresses, but please don't go off the boardwalk to get a closer look! Turban erupts about 5 feet (1.5 m) above its rim, except that for an hour or two after Grand has erupted, it may go to 20 feet (6 m).

The relationship between Turban's eruptions and the overflow and ebbing away of water in Grand's pool can indicate how soon Grand will next erupt. When Turban erupts without lowering Grand's pool, waves will begin to disturb the water surface more and more vigorously, and Grand's eruption will usually begin.

When Grand finally begins, a wonderful roaring from underground will accompany a tremendous burst of water up to 150 or 200 feet (45–60 m). But that's not all—Grand may put forth as many as four of these bursts—or even more. Some people claim the first part of the second burst is always the most fun.

Observer James C. Fennel wrote a description of Grand's first burst in 1892 that's valid years later. "[W]ith earthshaking and tremendous rumbling that sounds like smothered thunder, the fountain without receiving warning of attack is shot aloft into the air two hundred feet in an immense column of steam and water. . . . From the main column numberless jets are discharged at all heights and angles draping the Colossus in an agitated fringework of ever-changing patterns."

Vent Geyser next to Turban might be called Companion Geyser: its eruptions always accompany Grand and sometimes Turban. It erupts as high as 70 feet (21 m) at a slight angle and may continue after Grand's eruption for an hour or more.

In approximately the next quarter mile (0.4 km), there are only five named springs before the bridge over the Firehole. You pass springs connected to Grand called **Economic Geyser** (named for its habit of reclaiming almost all its erupted water), **East Eco-**

Beauty Pool shows a full range of color in its water and bacterial mats (1996).

nomic Geyser, and **Wave Spring**, and come to **Beauty Pool** and neighboring **Chromatic Pool**.

Beauty and Chromatic Pools illustrate extremely well the exchange of function between connected thermal features. Beauty Pool was for a time in recent years decidedly the more beautiful of the two; in 1995 Chromatic Pool became hotter and therefore more colorful for about two months. The situation then reversed itself again and continues to do so. However, since 2000, neither pool has been at its best.

Across the Firehole bridge is **Inkwell Spring**, which has diminished its flow recently. Bubbling water leaves inky manganese oxide stains on its cone.

The trail passes **Oblong Geyser** at quite a distance, due to the fact that Oblong can erupt as high as 25 feet (7.5 m) in a large boiling dome, pouring a huge volume of water into the Firehole River. You can infer its long history from the wide buildup of geyserite to Oblong's west. Oblong has been active recently, with intervals ranging from three to seven hours and upward. It frequently erupts in the morning, especially when the wind is calm. It's known for the thumping noises it makes and the prodigious amounts of water it throws out.

On a short spur to the right beyond Oblong you can visit **Giant Geyser** and its neighbors. This group is interdependent and connected to Grotto Geyser to the north as well. Some of the smaller features here are (left to right): **Bijou Geyser** (French for "jewel"), which plays almost constantly from its bacteria-covered cone, **Catfish Geyser**, and **Mastiff Geyser**. Mastiff's name may refer to its growling sound or to its watchdog function next to Giant. It has had periods of amazing energy. Usually Mastiff and Catfish have erupted simultaneously with Giant.

Beginning in the middle of 1996, tremendous eruptions of Giant Geyser occurred frequently. Since 1955 there had been eruptions *years* apart, but for a time in the late 1990s and again from

Giant Geyser displays its incredible power.

2005 into 2008 they occurred a few *days* apart. Eruptions always occur during hot activity in Giant and its neighbors, but nearby Grotto Geyser's eruptions can take the energy Giant needs.

With eruptions sometimes reaching 250 feet (76 m), Giant has built a massive 12-foot-high cone (3.6 m) with an enormous central cavity. An estimated 1 million gallons of water (nearly 4 million L) pours out during an eruption. Giant Geyser ranks with the rarely erupting Excelsior and Steamboat Geyser as Yellowstone's three most powerful.

A short distance north of Giant, this route joins the paved walkway. Next, the bizarrely shaped **Grotto Geyser** is the central attraction. Grotto's unique cone has probably been built up over fallen trees that became encrusted with geyserite. The interval between Grotto's eruptions averages six or seven hours but may be more than a day. It may erupt for an hour or perform a 36-hour marathon, height about 15 feet (4.5m). It's better to take Grotto's picture when it's not erupting, so that water and steam don't obscure the view of its remarkable formation.

Grotto Geyser has the park's most grotesque cone.

Three geysers near Grotto erupt briefly just before or during Grotto's long eruptions. They are **Rocket Geyser**, which erupts from its cone in unison with Grotto, sometimes up to 50 feet (15 m); **Grotto Fountain Geyser**, which can throw a thin stream of water up to 65 feet (20 m) and precedes most of Grotto's eruptions; and smaller **South Grotto Fountain Geyser,** which also may erupt just before Grotto. The last two are far back from the walkway.

Spa Geyser was named for the mineral spring in Belgium that gave its name to all such springs used for medicinal bathing. Don't try bathing in this spa—the water is over 190°F (88°C)! Spa's infrequent but explosive eruptions, sometimes as high as 60 feet (18 m), are linked to Grotto's activity.

Riverside Geyser Spur

Turn east toward the river at Spa Geyser to see the most gracefully situated and aesthetically satisfying geyser eruption in the park. **Riverside Geyser★★** has been for a century the park's most regular geyser. A 1909 guidebook stated that it erupted every eight hours for about 15 minutes. Now erupting about every six hours, it is predictable to within half an hour. The visitor center posts predicted times for all predictable geysers.

During its eruption, Riverside ejects water from several vents in its chair-like formation on the far side of the Firehole. Water overflowing the edges of the formation indicates that it will erupt within an hour or so, while water beginning to spout from the highest

Riverside Geyser's spray creates a rainbow in the sunlight.

hole at the left means the eruption will occur in about half an hour. The first few minutes of the eruption are the most spectacular, with water arching over the river up to 75 feet (23 m) from the cone. The eruption continues for about 20 minutes. Some eruptions spread a veritable curtain of droplets out over the river.

Back on the main walkway

On the far side of the bridge are two geysers so closely related that they are always mentioned together and are effectively one geyser. **Fan Geyser's** eruptions come from 10 or 11 vents, some with water spouting 125 feet (38 m) and over the trail. One vent even jets water *downward* toward the Firehole. **Mortar Geyser**, whose name may come from the cannon-like sound of its eruptions, has fewer vents and lower jets of water—up to 80 feet (24 m). Everyone fortunate enough to witness a major eruption of these geysers is invariably thrilled. So far this century, Fan and Mortar have erupted every few days during most summers, but with several months-long dormant periods. Geyser gazers wait for hours

Mortar (on left) *and Fan Geysers put on an exciting show* (2001).

and are able to chronicle in great detail the "preplay," or varying minor activity, from the many vents. Certain combinations of vent activity are known to trigger eruptions most of the time.

Spiteful Geyser is closer to the walkway than Fan and Mortar. Dormant in the early 1990s, it more recently emitted a constant spray toward the boardwalk. Witness its angry-seeming spitting and you'll understand the name. Opposite Spiteful is an unnamed feature that is unofficially called the **Norris Pools**. From 1998 to 2001, these pools underwent a major change and the southern one became a geyser that erupted when Fan and Mortar did.

A restroom is off the trail to the right.

Morning Glory Pool, on a short spur to the left, was famous for its brilliant blue color and tube shape, which made it resemble the common morning glory blossom. But late in the season when its temperature drops, it may be green in the center with yellow, orange, and brown microorganisims around its edges. Morning Glory's great fame may account for the tremendous vandalism it has suffered. In one cleaning-out in 1950, rangers found 112 different kinds of foreign objects, including logs, nearly $100 in coins, and "delicate items of underclothing." Vandalism was one reason why the Grand Loop Road was relocated a considerable distance away from this pool in the 1970s.

Morning Glory Pool

Extension to Biscuit Basin

NOTES: This extension can also be approached from the other end by parking at Biscuit Basin (see page 68). To head back to Old Faithful, skip to page 96 for the features; see page 83 for the map. Bicycles (allowed on Geyser Route Two) must be parked in the rack here.

The unpaved trail from Morning Glory Pool to Biscuit Basin (the former Grand Loop Road) takes you about 0.8 mile (1.3 km) over a hill to several splendid springs and geysers. Since few people explore beyond Morning Glory, it's a great place to escape the crowds and see some Yellowstone treasures. The following description identifies the unmarked thermal features on this trail for you. Be sure to stay on the trail!

Three or four small geysers line the riverbanks just beyond Morning Glory Pool, most notably **East Sentinel Geyser**, whose cone makes an island near the east side of the Firehole River when the water is high.

About 0.4 mile (0.6 km) from the Morning Glory area are two geysers below the wall that supported the old road.

Artemisia Geyser takes its name from the scientific name for sagebrush (*Artemisia tridentata*), which shares its gray-green color with some of the geyserite deposits under the water at the turquoise blue pool's edge. Its eruptions surge as much as 30 feet (9 m) with very little warning, at intervals ranging from 9 to 34 hours. Uphill from Artemisia are two milky bubblers, one with a beautiful mossy overhang and rust-stained edge.

Atomizer Geyser (also called Restless Geyser) consists of the two small cones between Artemisia and the slope down to the river. It's named for the device that breaks a liquid down into a fine spray. The geyser's atomizer-like spraying action and chugging sound come from the cone farthest from the river, but only during major eruptions. Such eruptions, which may go to 50 feet (15 m) high and last ten minutes, occur about twice a day.

More small geysers line both sides of the river near here, but they are difficult to see through the trees. One of these was so directly a creation of the 1959 Hebgen Lake earthquake that it's called **Seismic Geyser**. It erupted as high as 75 feet (23 m) during the following 15 years. In 1999 and 2000, a new and unnamed vent close to Seismic erupted frequently as high as 20 feet (6 m) and sometimes much higher. Geyser gazers call it **Aftershock Geyser**.

Across the river from Seismic and from the trail, another very short-lived geyser, called **Fantail Geyser** for its angled eruptions, performed impressively for one spring and summer (1986), then almost not at all since.

Beyond Atomizer, you'll find oblong **Gem Pool**, which overflows constantly. East of Gem Pool and across the trail is **Bear Den Spring**, where, in spite of bubbling water at the bottom, a crawl space under the rock ledge served at least once (in 1958) as a bear's winter home.

After descending the hill, look toward the west (left), where **Baby Daisy Geyser** may be steaming. A smaller version of Daisy (page 101), Baby Daisy began erupting 30 or 40 feet high (9–12 m) about every 45 minutes early in 2003 and continued through 2004. Farther along and close to the trail, you reach pale sapphire blue **Mirror Pool**, with yellow to brown bacteria around the edges.

Finally, you pass **Cauliflower Geyser** south of the small footbridge before you reach the highway. The "cauliflowers" are the same type of formation as the biscuits of Biscuit Basin (across the highway), but bigger. They are nodules of geyserite.

At the footbridge near Cauliflower Geyser, a trail leading north parallels the Grand Loop Road to join the Mallard Creek and Fairy Falls trails about 2 miles (3.2 km) from Biscuit Basin.

Geyser Route One features you may have missed

As you return from Morning Glory Pool, you'll have the chance to see a few hot springs and geysers you missed if you took the recommended side trails on the way out. Three stretches of the main trail are described below in sections labeled (**A**), (**B**), and (**C**). These letters correspond to labels on the Upper Geyser Basin map, page 83.

(**A**) After recrossing the bridge over the Firehole near Fan and Mortar geysers, continue straight ahead (unless Riverside Geyser is about to erupt, in which case, don't miss it!). Here you'll pass the **Chain Lakes Complex**, which consists of several hot springs and geysers related both to each other and to the Grotto Complex. The **Bottomless Pit** was described by the geologist Albert C. Peale of the 1878 Hayden Survey as "a beautiful blue cavern-like spring of great depth." **Link Geyser** can (very infrequently) erupt to 100 feet (30 m) high.

Culvert Geyser has an interesting story. Road engineers building the original Grand Loop Road (now the walkway) buried one spring nearby and built a culvert around this one. This gave Culvert Geyser the energy to enlarge its crater and begin spouting to 2 feet (0.6 m), which it continued to do for some years. It is now a clear or colored pool with prominent overhanging edge.

(**B**) Between Grand Geyser and Sawmill Geyser, the straight walkway has only three small springs. **Bulger Spring** (on the right as you walk toward Old Faithful Village) is actually a small geyser. The seemingly unremarkable springs on the left are interesting because they are not connected underground, according to geyser expert T. Scott Bryan, although their apertures are only one foot (0.3 m) apart. **Crystal Spring**, named for its very clear water, is connected to the Grand Geyser Complex, but **Crystal Spring's Geyser** (a round hole right by Crystal Spring's runoff channel) is a member of the **Sawmill Geyser Complex**.

(**C**) Back on Geyser Hill. When the boardwalk splits near North Goggles Geyser, turn left to take the upper part of the loop and see the features you missed at the start of Geyser Route One.

Ear Spring is obviously named for its shape and used to be called the "Devil's Ear." *Haynes Guide* in the 1920s reported that "it not only resembles an ear in shape, but the lobe is pierced and the earring is a tiny geyser. It is here that messages are transmitted, so the story goes, to regions below." Sometimes Ear Spring's water becomes superheated (hotter than boiling), and bubbling occurs around its rim.

The western end of the trail to Solitary Geyser and Observation Point joins the main boardwalk between Ear Spring and nearby Beach Spring. In rainy summers, the meadow north of here is filled with wildflowers.

Beach Spring in the boardwalk's corner may get its name from the beach-like terrace its water intermittently flows over, the sandy color of the sinter in its central bowl, or perhaps the sound it makes during boiling periods: like surf at a beach. If you watch for a few minutes, you may be hypnotized by seeing the water rise, bubble, and fall repeatedly a short way down in the bowl.

*Aurum's bubbling and erupting causes geyser eggs (*foreground*) to form.*

Aurum Geyser, Latin for "gold," gets its color from iron oxide inside its tiny geyserite mound. Aurum erupts for about one minute at intervals varying from about 3 to 12 hours, with the more frequent intervals in winter and spring. Sometimes it sprays the boardwalk with spurts up to 25 feet (8 m) high. Notice the large and uniform geyser eggs in Aurum's overflow pool.

Giantess Geyser, September 5, 2001

Doublet Pool was called The Quaker by nineteenth century tour guide, George Henderson. Standing near it, you can sometimes hear and feel vibrations, probably caused by the collapse of steam bubbles within the pool. Its overhanging geyserite ledge is unusually wide and thin (and dangerous!); other ledges partway down indicate previous lower water levels.

Sponge Geyser is barely a geyser at all, but it may have been one in the past or at least has been building its cone for a very long time. It resembles a sponge both in its highly perforated surface and its light beige color. When active, its water boils up to the rim, then sinks out of sight.

Pump Geyser and two small vents nearby called **The Pump** can be counted on to splash more or less vigorously almost without a break. Their constant runoff creates ideal conditions for large beds of orange and brown microbes.

Giantess Geyser rests in a deep pool high atop Geyser Hill. The boardwalk is placed a safe distance away, because when the geyser is active, it can erupt as high as 200 feet (60 m) with very little warning. Giantess is surely the queen of the hill, with influence over many other springs and geysers; her eruptions are known to affect Vault, Teakettle, Infant, Sponge, Doublet, Beach, Ear, Plume, and Beehive. Early writers who saw Giantess erupt described "globular masses of vapor" that were "domed at the top like a crystal cupola." Steam phases, which can alternate with water phases, make a deafening roar that may be heard a mile away. Eruptions can last many hours—one induced by the 1959 earthquake lasted over four days. However, their rarity (an average of three per year since 1984) means that you'll have to be very lucky to see one, as was Nathaniel Langford, who named it in 1870.

Closer to the boardwalk are deep-welled Teakettle Spring with its punch-bowl-shaped crater, and Vault Geyser. **Teakettle Spring** is an excellent example of how springs change with time. Until 1947, its crater was full to the rim. Now the water level sits deep out of sight, but the bubbling from inside still sounds rather like a teakettle.

Some of **Vault Geyser's** eruptions occur after Giantess starts and may go to 15 feet (4.5 m), but it can erupt independently of Giantess. An unusual attribute of Vault is that it erupts from far below ground level rather than first filling its crater, as most geysers do.

Active once or twice a month, **Dome Geyser** sits high up the hill to the east. Twin craters in the shape of butterfly wings nearby (but out of sight of the trail) belong to **Butterfly Spring**, which surprised observers by bursting out in major 30–40-foot (9–12 m) muddy eruptions—but only during May 2003.

Infant Geyser sometimes has tiny eruptions when Giantess Geyser is active. If its cloudy, acidic water is low in the oval cavity, you can see an unusual deep-red lining.

Geyser Route Two: Castle and Daisy Geysers and an extension to Black Sand Pool

NOTE: This is an approved bicycle route to the Grand Loop Road near Biscuit Basin about 2.5 miles (4 km) to the north. To reach Biscuit Basin, turn left on the northern trail to the Daisy Group, then turn immediately right (see the map, page 83).

The 2.4-miles (4 km) round trip to view Castle and Daisy Geysers on Geyser Route Two is paved and can be traversed by wheelchair or bicycle. You may shorten the distance a little by parking in the lot for the general store near Old Faithful Inn. The side trail past Daisy Geyser to Punch Bowl Spring and Black Sand Pool (not fully paved and not open to bicycling) can add another mile (1.6 km) to this excursion.

From the visitor center, follow the former main road past the east wing of Old Faithful Inn, keeping Old Faithful Geyser on your right. After passing the inn's parking area and the side trail to Chinese Spring, you'll see a large meadow on your right, where bison and elk can find grass even in winter due to warming from hot springs.

West of the store and service station, you may see steam surprisingly close to the buildings. The steam comes from the Myriad Group, where hundreds of hot springs have been counted, including at least one historically interesting feature. **Round Geyser** erupted as high as 150 feet (46 m) in a few widely spaced years, with long dormancies in between. It rivaled the height of Old Faithful itself. There's no public access to the area.

Castle Geyser* is the first thermal feature you come to—about a half mile (0.8 km) from the visitor center. This

Castle Geyser is Yellowstone's largest regularly erupting cone-type geyser.

cone-type geyser erupts from the center of a large geyserite edifice that looks very much like a crenelated medieval castle. Castle's cone is about 12 feet (4 m) high and 6 feet (2 m) in diameter. Major eruptions usually occur about 13 to 16 hours apart but with longer intervals after minor eruptions.

Castle typically erupts explosively for 15 to 20 minutes in its water phase, spouting to as high as 100 feet (30 m). Then 30 to 45 minutes of steam phase follow, accompanied by a thrilling roar. Castle is changeable and has displayed other types of eruption patterns in the past. It's also hundreds if not thousands of years old. A hot spring predating the geyser probably built up its mound of geyserite, and the cone's lower shelf dates from about AD 1100.

Castle's Neighbors Toward the River

Tortoise Shell Spring boils violently in its geyserite cone. It's one of the hottest springs in the park—207°F (97°C) or hotter—and seems to have no connection with neighboring Castle Geyser. According to some close observers, you can visualize not just the shell but the head, tail, and legs of a tortoise in the spring's shape. Campers in the early days used this superheated spring to boil their food.

Crested Pool★ is 42 feet (13 m) deep and sometimes boils as high as 10 feet (3 m). According to one of the first guidebook writers, Harry J. Norton (1873): "For delicacy of coloring and beauty of ornamentation it surpasses any we visited. It is more quiet than others, yet its surface is gently rippled by constant vibrations."

Sad to relate, in 1970 a nine-year-old boy was scalded to death in a few seconds in the superheated water of this pool. The guardrail here and additional warnings of danger throughout the geyser basins were erected in response to the tragedy. Old names for Crested Pool, such as Fire Basin and Devil's Well, may have been apt after all.

Back on the main walkway

Across the pavement from Castle is a fenced hot spring called **Shield Pool** for its shape.

Leaving Castle and continuing on the paved trail, you'll pass a meadow where a few springs quietly give off steam. This area had a short-lived geyser in 1986, when **South Orange Geyser** erupted quite regularly.

Look through the trees to the right, just before the walkway comes close to the Firehole River, to see a brilliantly colored mound the shape of a kiln, alive with microorganisms in the runoff from **Limekiln Springs**. This is a favorite subject for color photographers.

Before you reach the path to Daisy Geyser, the Round Spring Group of springs and occasional spouters to the west makes the idea of cutting across

Crested Pool has an almost perfectly symmetrical ten-sided rim.

this open space very unwise (as well as forbidden!).

If you started from the visitor center, you will have traveled a little more than a mile (1.8 km) by the time you reach the first (southern) path to Daisy and the sign: "Daisy Geyser may erupt within *x* minutes of *y*." The time is posted both here and at the visitor center after the first eruption or two of the day. The path to the west here and the bicycle path a short distance north both pass the Daisy Group of geysers. They rejoin west of those geysers to become one path toward Black Sand Basin.

To your east you can see the distinctive cone of Giant Geyser. It's described on page 92.

In the group at the top of the small hill, Daisy Geyser is the only regularly and predictably active geyser, but about ten features here are closely related. Two of the geysers have interesting names. Park geologist George Marler named **Radiator Geyser** for sounding like a boiling car radiator. Its eruptions are mostly subterranean when Daisy is active, but above ground when Splendid is active. **Daisy's Thief Geyser**, when it first appeared in 1942, used to erupt occasionally *instead of* Daisy, lowering the water in Daisy and preventing its normal eruption. Later, it seemed to serve as a precursor to Daisy. The Thief has now been dormant for many years and is hard to see. Sometimes, nearby **Bonita Pool** would overflow and Daisy would become dormant.

Daisy Geyser★ erupts as high as 75 feet (21 m). Its eruption interval was about two-and-a-half hours in 2012. The eruption lasts three or four minutes, always followed by a steam phase with a roar like that of an old steam engine.

Geologist Marler proved by experiment that Daisy's eruptions would be much longer if so much cooled water did not flow back into the crater. Daisy's intervals react to windy conditions, becoming longer when the wind is strong. Note the wind direction while waiting for Daisy to erupt, or you may be the recipient of a "geyser kiss" from Daisy's water.

It's not known whether Daisy's name came from a popular old expression: "Hey, it's a daisy!" (slang for first-rate) or from the nickname of an early assistant superintendent.

Splendid Geyser may have the most on-again-off-again history of eruption activity of any of Yellowstone's geysers, starting with its first mention in 1834 by explorer Warren A. Ferris. It has been

Daisy Geyser erupts dependably and at a graceful angle.

known to erupt over 200 feet (61 m) high in its active periods, and eruptions sometimes seem to be caused by falling barometric pressure.

Splendid and its neighbor Daisy sometimes erupt simultaneously. This unpredictable occurrence is breathtaking—they may both jet to more than 100 feet (30 m).

The relatively recent (mid 1990s) simultaneous eruptions of Daisy and Splendid provide a fine example of the reason we should never pronounce a geyser dead. An article about Yellowstone Park in a 1940 *National Geographic Magazine* stated: "Daisy sprang into existence in 1892 with the demise of Splendid Geyser, fifty feet away." But Splendid wasn't dead, just dormant for about half a century!

There may be a deep east-west fissure connecting Splendid Geyser and Giant Geyser, which is about 1,200 feet (360 m) to the east. In 1951 and the mid 1990s, these two magnificent geysers ceased dormancy and entered very active periods within a few months of each other.

Comet Geyser's cone is to the west of Daisy and closer to the northern walkway. Deposition of minerals from water droplets splashing almost constantly has built the cone.

Extension to Black Sand Pool

If you continue west where the two walkways around Daisy become one, you'll see the **White Pyramid** (or White Throne), the cone of an extinct geyser, across the meadow to the north. At its base is small but active **Pyramid Geyser**.

A little farther west is the almost perfectly circular **Punch Bowl Spring★**. The center of this beautiful spring boils a foot or so above its rim, which is nearly 2 feet (0.6 m) in height. It overflows constantly, creating a colorful runoff channel.

Geyserite precipitating from Punch Bowl Spring has created a finely sculpted bowl.

It's a short distance to **Black Sand Pool★**, the last major feature on this route. Black Sand acts infrequently as a geyser and has a large and colorful runoff stream to its west. The area at the base of the runoff was named **Specimen Lake** (when it had more water) for the "specimens" of still-standing silicified trees killed by Black Sand's runoff. In and around Black Sand Pool you'll see good examples of the black volcanic sand that gives the pool and the geyser basin to its southwest their names.

The small but deep, dangerous crater just across the path and south of Black Sand Pool is called **Demon's Cave**. Avoid going near its overhanging ledge.

You can continue from here to Black Sand Basin (described on pages 70–72) or turn back to the Daisy Group.

If you return via the northern path past Daisy, you'll meet the bicycle path toward Biscuit Basin. Biscuit Basin is 1.3 miles (2.1 km) from here (described on pages 68–70). This path (a former service road) goes through meadow and burned forest and passes near a large hot spring, **Cyclops Spring**.

The ridge at the south end of the bicycle path is **Wylie Hill**, the site of a tent camp from the 1890s until 1916. William W. Wylie set up several such inexpensive camps around the park for stagecoach passengers. His managers at this camp piped water from Punch Bowl Spring to the tents, in this case without apparent deleterious effect to the spring. They made a notch in the geyserite rim (obvious even today), through which most of the spring's runoff still drains.

A short distance beyond the bicycle path, Geyser Route Two ends at the main walkway. To return to the Old Faithful Village area, turn right. To see more of the geyser basin, turn left. Grotto Geyser is just up the short hill, and Riverside Geyser is not far beyond. The walk from Grotto to Morning Glory Pool is described on pages 93–95.

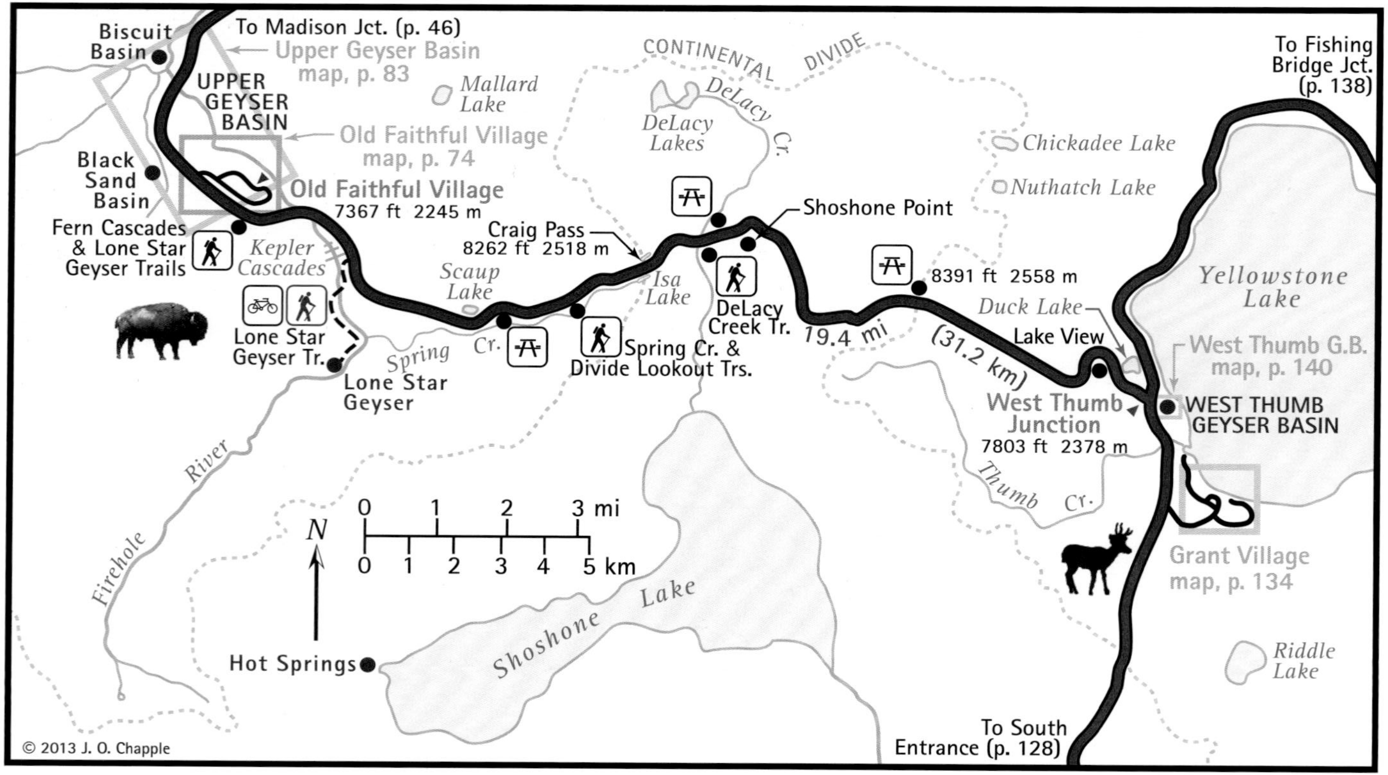
Biscuit Basin
To Madison Jct. (p. 46)
Upper Geyser Basin map, p. 83
UPPER GEYSER BASIN
Mallard Lake
Old Faithful Village map, p. 74
Black Sand Basin
Old Faithful Village
7367 ft 2245 m
Fern Cascades & Lone Star Geyser Trails
Kepler Cascades
Lone Star Geyser Tr.
Lone Star Geyser
Spring Cr.
Scaup Lake
Craig Pass
8262 ft 2518 m
Isa Lake
Spring Cr. & Divide Lookout Trs.
CONTINENTAL DIVIDE
DeLacy Lakes
DeLacy Cr.
DeLacy Creek Tr.
Shoshone Point
19.4 mi
(31.2 km)
8391 ft 2558 m
Chickadee Lake
Nuthatch Lake
Duck Lake
Lake View
West Thumb Junction
7803 ft 2378 m
Thumb Cr.
Yellowstone Lake
West Thumb G.B. map, p. 140
WEST THUMB GEYSER BASIN
To Fishing Bridge Jct. (p. 138)
Grant Village map, p. 134
Riddle Lake
To South Entrance (p. 128)
Firehole River
N
0 1 2 3 mi
0 1 2 3 4 5 km
Hot Springs
Shoshone Lake
© 2013 J. O. Chapple

Old Faithful Village to West Thumb Junction

From Old Faithful Village to West Thumb Junction

From Old Faithful to West Thumb is a distance of about 19 miles (31 km), as measured from the visitor center. Worth stopping for on the way are Kepler Cascades, Lone Star Geyser Trail, and Isa Lake at the western crossing of the *Continental Divide*, as well as the views from Shoshone (pronounced "show-SHOW-nee") Point and from above West Thumb Junction.

Road Log

0.0/19.4 Old Faithful Village and Visitor Center. Follow signs to exit the area or to find facilities in the village (described on page 73, map on page 74).

1.6/17.8 Old Faithful Interchange with the Grand Loop Road. West Thumb Junction is to the east, Madison Junction to the north.

2.3/17.1 Employee housing area on the south. Slow down for the pedestrian crossing!

Not far from here and just south of the present Old Faithful Clinic was the site of the Bears' Feeding Ground in the early twentieth century.

2.6/16.8 Small unpaved parking area for trails to Fern Cascades (west) and Lone Star Geyser (south). The **Lone Star Geyser Trail** is a section of the old Howard Eaton trail. For a shorter walk to Lone Star Geyser, park at mile 4.2/15.2. (See page 78 for the Fern Cascades Trail.)

Fire damage from the 1988 North Fork fire can still be seen.

3.2/16.2 Firehole River bridge. From here the Madison Plateau extends southwest as far as the Bechler River in the park's corner and as far north as the Madison River. This plateau is a huge, relatively young, lava flow—that is, about 100,000 to 200,000 years old.

4.1/15.3 **P** **Kepler Cascades** of the Firehole River. Kepler was the

Kepler Cascades tumbles down a gorge near Old Faithful Village.

given name of the 12-year-old son of Wyoming Territory's Governor John Hoyt. The boy was with his father in a group searching for suitable routes from Wyoming into the park in 1881, and he was such a good sport, that Supt. Norris named these pretty cascades for him.

The Firehole River has cut a deep gorge in the Madison Plateau lava here. Where the erosion is continuing, a series of cascades or small waterfalls drops a total of more than 100 feet (30 m). Downstream from the viewing platform, the canyon narrows radically. These steep walls below the cascades (called Devil's Gate or Devil's Gorge) claimed the life of a Yellowstone Park employee who was climbing here in 1976.

Hell and the Devil in Yellowstone

The first observers of Yellowstone Park's features were often reminded of the Prince of Darkness and his abode. As historian Aubrey L. Haines writes in *Yellowstone Place Names: Mirrors of History* (1996): "For a time, the devil had a proprietary interest in thirty-nine Park features, with the word 'hell' appearing in eight others and 'Satan' in one. But in the last half century, he has been largely dispossessed, so that his influence is now minimal. A mere three place names remain: Devils Thumb and Devils Kitchen at Mammoth Hot Springs, in addition to the Devils Den… " (located near Tower Fall).

Park Historian Lee Whittlesey, in his book *Yellowstone Place Names*, adds Devil's Stairway (on the former Mary Mountain road), Devil's Well near Icebox Canyon, and Devil's Inkstand on Mount Washburn. His book also describes Devil's Gate, visible below Kepler Cascades.

4.2/15.2 🥾 🚲 🐎 **Lone Star Geyser Trailhead.** A short road to the west leads to the parking area. This round trip of about 5 miles (8 km) is a level trail also suitable for biking, since it is a former automobile road. The route soon passes the source of the Old Faithful Village water supply.

In about 1.8 miles (2.9 km), the Spring Creek Trail intersects this one. You can follow it up to the Grand Loop Road, but coming *down* the Spring Creek Trail might be more to your liking (description at mile 8.2/11.2).

The Lone Star Trail passes some small hot springs and a beautiful meadow

Lone Star Geyser

before reaching the geyser. **Lone Star Geyser** erupts to as high as 45 feet (14 m) from a pink-stained steep cone as wide as it is tall—about 10 feet (3 m) in each dimension. Its major eruptions are 20 to 30 minutes long.

Lone Star's eruptions occur almost exactly three hours apart, and the interval has averaged 2.5 to 3 hours with no interruption ever since the park was founded. Rangers no longer post eruption predictions at the Old Faithful Visitor Center, but you can help other visitors by recording the time of any eruption you witness in the logbook near the geyser.

The backcountry trail continues past Lone Star's thermal area to Shoshone Lake and Geyser Basin (another 6.2 mi/10 km). Before the lake, a (southern) branch leads to the vast and undeveloped Bechler Region in the park's southwest. A much closer trail to Shoshone Lake's north shore is at mile 10.5/8.9, the DeLacy Creek Trailhead.

6.5/12.9 Scaup Lake to the north. A scaup is a type of duck related to the canvasback and sometimes seen in the park.

Not far from here, along Spring Creek (which the road used to follow), the most profitable—to the robber!—of Yellowstone's five stagecoach robberies took place. The victims of this 1908 crime called it "the greatest stage coach hold up and highway robbery in the twentieth century." One man was able to stop 17 coaches and take more than $2000 in money and jewelry from the passengers. He was never caught.

Scaup Lake was the center of a more recent scandal, according to Alston Chase's book, *Playing God in Yellowstone.* This was one of the places in the park where geologists were allowed to use dynamite as part of a 1980 borehole project, possibly causing the extinction of a rare species of salamander.

6.8/12.6 P Small pond, Congress Lake (named because it "just sits there and does nothing") to the south, and large parking area a little farther east for easy trail access down Spring Creek Trail.

As the road climbs you may see patches of snow along the road, even in July.

7.2/12.2 **(10)** Spring Creek picnic area on the right (south). Near the restroom is a trailhead for the Spring Creek Trail that shortens the hike down the creek to the Lone Star Geyser Trail by over a mile.

8.2/11.2 Spring Creek and Divide Lookout marked trailheads.

The **Spring Creek Trail** follows the creek and the Firehole River for a total of about 6 miles (9.5 km) from this trailhead to the Lone Star Trailhead parking area (at mile 4.2/15.2). The trail uses the route of an 1890s stagecoach road through Spring Creek canyon, described in early literature as "one of the prettiest short trips on the Loop," and as having "irregular walls" and "rock needles pointing skyward."

Spring Creek was named for the several small cold springs that flow out from beneath the rhyolite along its course. The downside of having so many springs is that parts of the trail are marshy, while the upside is that wildflowers thrive here. On the east side of a 20-foot-high (6 m) rock located partway down the trail is a turtle shape engraved by natural forces. The rock has always been called Turtle Rock and was the site of the successful stagecoach robbery described above. The trail could be highly recommended were it not so difficult to get through the narrow part of the canyon at Turtle Rock and to traverse the marshy areas near the trail's bottom.

The steep **Divide Lookout Trail** goes to the site of a former fire tower about 2.5 miles (4 km) south of the road and nearly 8,800 feet (2,680 m) above sea level.

Along the road between here and Isa Lake, as well as east of the lake, you can spot beautiful patches of altered rhyolite in some of the road cuts and hillsides. There are many colors: cream, yellow, orange, salmon pink, red, dark brown. At some time in the past, hot water and gases altered the minerals in these rocks, creating the colors.

Water lilies cover Isa Lake in midsummer.

9.3/10.1 **P** **Isa Lake** has parking space at both ends, 0.2 mile apart. The lake was named in 1893 for a Cincinnati tourist, Isabel Jelke, but was sometimes called Two Ocean Lake because of its location. It's directly on the Continental Divide at 8,262 feet (2518 m).

The flow directions from the two ends of this lake are the opposite of what you'd expect. The seeming paradox will become clear to you with a look at the map and explanation in "Understanding the Continental Divide."

Understanding the Continental Divide

Driving between Old Faithful and West Thumb, you twice pass signs identifying the Continental Divide. This makes it difficult to understand the concept of a *drainage divide* or to visualize where the water is going. Maps show the Continental Divide as a thin line crossing irregularly from the park's western boundary to leave the park near the southeast corner. What does this line represent?

A drainage divide is a geographer's term for the topographic boundary between adjacent drainage basins or watersheds. Runoff from precipitation that falls on one side of the divide will find its way into one stream system; on the other side, surface runoff discharges into another stream system.

The Continental Divide, (also known as the Great Divide) is the main watershed boundary of the North American continent. As shown in Figure 3, the divide separates areas that drain to the Pacific Ocean (green) and the Atlantic Ocean (lighter green). The area around Old Faithful Village drains

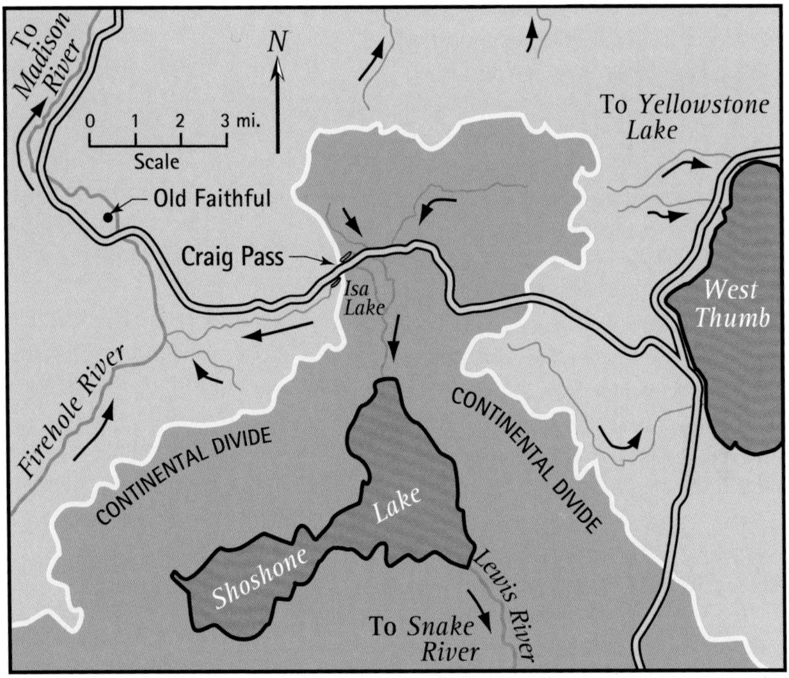

Figure 3. Map showing stream flow directions (black arrows) *and the Continental Divide.*

to the Atlantic Ocean via the Firehole River, a tributary of the Madison River. About 9 miles east of Old Faithful, the Grand Loop Road crosses the Continental Divide at Craig Pass, entering the watershed of the Lewis River, which flows to the Pacific Ocean via the Snake River and eventually the Columbia River. A raindrop falling on one side of Craig Pass may be destined for Astoria, Oregon, while a drop falling a few feet away on the other side of the pass could meet the Gulf of Mexico near New Orleans.

Isa Lake is situated right across this line at Craig Pass. This is a rare type of place where the top of the divide is actually flat enough to permit a small depression where the small pond, Isa Lake, has formed. Looking at the lake, you would think that the water from its southwestern outlet would flow to the Pacific and that from the northeastern outlet to the Atlantic, but just the opposite is true.

In this area the Continental Divide doubles back on itself and the road crosses it again, as you can see from the sketch. Using the old name, continental watershed, might make it easier to visualize.

—With contributions by Linton A. Brown

This high point on the road is called **Craig Pass**, named for the first tourist to cross the pass on the "new" road in 1891. From near Craig Pass, logs to build Old Faithful Inn were cut in the winter of 1903–4 and dragged down on sledges.

The grade descending northeastward from Isa Lake was so steep in the early days of the first stagecoach road that drivers dubbed it Corkscrew Hill. According to Lee Whittlesey's book *Yellowstone Place Names*, drivers enjoyed terrifying the "dudes" by rushing down this narrow and tortuous hill. Since that time, realignment has reduced the grade so much that you hardly notice the hill.

10.5/8.9 **DeLacy Creek Trailhead** opposite the parking area. This trail leads through forest and meadow south 3.5 miles (5.6 km) to the shore of Shoshone Lake, connecting with trails around that lake and along Lewis Lake channel to Lewis Lake and the South Entrance Road. During most of the summer, it may be hard to keep your boots dry. Parallel deep tracks show heavy use by hikers and fishermen.

Walter W. DeLacy, for whom the creek was named, was an army captain and civil engineer who passed through this part of future park territory in 1863 with a party of prospectors. Shoshone Lake was called DeLacy's Lake for a time, in honor of his discovery that it is part of the Snake River's drainage, not Madison River's, as previously believed.

10.8/8.6 **(11)** DeLacy Creek picnic area on a short side road.

11.1/8.3 **Shoshone Point** turnout for a view of distant Shoshone Lake. The Teton Range about 50 miles (80 km) away may also be seen on a clear day.

In 1914, here on the Grand Loop Road, a stagecoach robber stole more than $1000 in cash and jewelry from 165 passengers. This time (unlike after other similar incidents) the robber was caught and served time in prison. He was Edward Trafton, a notorious horse thief and robber.

Shoshone Lake can be reached only by hiking, riding horseback (trailhead at 4.2/15.2), or paddling a canoe up the Lewis River from its neighbor, Lewis Lake—or on skis in winter. Shoshone is the second largest lake in Yellowstone and sports a major geyser basin near its western shore.

Before it was called Shoshone, this large lake bore the name Madison Lake and then the names of several men who named it for themselves. Finally, Prof. Frank Bradley, chief geologist of the 1872 Hayden Expedition to Yellowstone, decided it should be named for the Native American Indians who frequented it. The Shoshoni tribe—their name probably meaning "grass house people"—lived in the area between the mountains of Wyoming and the present state of Oregon and as far south as Nevada.

The Grand Loop Road crosses the east summit (at 8,521 ft / 2,597 m) before reaching the next crossing of the Continental Divide.

15.3/4.1 Continental Divide (8,391 ft / 2,558 m). This is the east side of the Continental Divide's loop. Though it's more than 100 feet (30 m) higher than Craig Pass, this point lacks a name. Now you've left the Columbia River tributary area (see Figure 3 in "Understanding the Continental Divide").

About 1 mile (1.6 km) to the southwest of this point, old maps showed an unnamed lake, later a "Two Ocean Pond." Although old-timers claimed to have seen this lake (and to have fished it) as early as 1915 and as late as 1938, recent maps made from aerial photos do not show it. Was it a transient meltwater pond or a shallow lake that became a meadow? It remains a mystery.

15.6/3.8 (14) Divide picnic area (also called East Divide) on the left (north).

18.7/0.7 P Near a major curve there is parking on both sides of the road for a panoramic view of Yellowstone Lake. This spot was called **Lake View** as early as the 1890s. Between then and now the lodgepoles grew tall but then burned, allowing us to see lake and mountains in a 180° arc once again.

Lake View Panorama

If the day is clear you can see, left to right (north to south):

West Thumb Bay's northern edge in middle ground.

Absaroka Range in the distance—these are 50-million-year-old volcanic mountains. Absaroka was the name that the Crow called themselves, meaning "children of the large-beaked bird" and pronounced ab-SAHR-o-ka. Due east of the viewpoint are four closely grouped, pyramid-shaped peaks: Doane, Langford, and Stevenson are inside the park (and all more than 10,000 ft / 3,050 m high), and Plentycoups, the highest at 10,937 feet (3,334 m), on the eastern border.

Duck Lake in middle ground, **West Thumb Bay**'s eastern edge in the background, with more Absarokas behind it.

View of Yellowstone Lake and Absaroka Range from above Duck Lake

Flat Mountain just beyond the bay (elevation 9,168 ft / 2,794 m), noted for its red cliffs.

Mt. Sheridan at the far right and relatively close to the viewer (elevation 10,305 ft / 3,141 m).

Referring to this lake view, explorers David E. Folsom and Charles W. Cook wrote prophetically in 1869:

> We ascended the summit of a neighboring hill and took a final look at Yellowstone Lake. Nestled among the forest-crowned hills which bounded our vision lay this inland sea, its crystal waves dancing and sparkling in the sunlight as if laughing with joy for their wild freedom. It is a scene of transcendent beauty which has been viewed by few white men, and we felt glad to have looked upon it before its primeval solitude should be broken by the crowds of pleasure seekers which at no distant day will throng to its shores.

For a similar view completely off the highway, take the recommended Yellowstone Lake Overlook Trail from West Thumb Junction (described on page 139).

19.0/0.4 P 🥾 Short, steep, unmaintained trail to **Duck Lake [GEO.16]**. This little lake has an unusual geologic history. About 6,000 to 8,000 years ago a glacial ice dam gave way and allowed water to drain out quickly. Removal of the load of water drastically lowered the pressure above a group of hot springs, allowing the superheated water to flash to steam. Duck Lake is an explosion crater filled with water.

See page 139 for a good trail to Duck Lake from West Thumb Geyser Basin.

19.4/0.0 West Thumb Junction. For West Thumb Geyser Basin turn left (north), then an immediate right (east). For Fishing Bridge Junction and other points on the Grand Loop Road, also turn left (north). Grant Village and the South Entrance are to the south, Old Faithful Village to the west.

West Thumb Geyser Basin and facilities at West Thumb are described on pages 140–43 and Grant Village on pages 133–35.

II. THE BECHLER REGION

Proceeding counterclockwise from the West Entrance, the next roads that go into the park are two very short ones branching off Green Timber Road (see map) that don't connect with any other Yellowstone roads. This corner of the park is often called the Bechler Region, but its official name is Cascade Corner. It is well supplied with water and contains a great many waterfalls. It's a great place for backpackers and horsepackers (and recently llama packers) who want to escape the crowds, but a long trip for most day visitors.

Access to the Bechler Ranger Station and Cave Falls is on good paved and gravel roads from southeastern Idaho or via a very poor and primitive dirt road called Grassy Lake Road (or Ashton-Flagg Ranch Road), which runs outside the park to Flagg Ranch (see page 126). We'll only describe the better route here. If you want to take the Grassy Lake Road, inquire locally about its current condition before starting on it. From Idaho Falls to Ashton is 53 miles (85 km); from Ashton (population 1,100) to the Bechler Ranger Station is 23 miles (37 km); from West Yellowstone to Bechler is about 80 miles (130 km).

FROM WEST YELLOWSTONE OR ASHTON TO THE BECHLER REGION

Not far west of West Yellowstone, Montana, on U.S. Highway 20 is Targhee Pass, used by the Bannock tribe on their annual trek to hunt buffalo. South of the pass is a wide fertile valley, a checkerboard of private and national forest lands. State parks near Henrys Lake and Island Park Reservoir offer camping and hiking possibilities and fishing for trout and whitefish. Harriman State Park on Island Park Reservoir is an important wintering spot for trumpeter swans and home to a variety of other wildlife. The park also has a visitor center and over 20 miles (32 km) of trails.

For years this edge of clear-cut forest outside the park's west boundary was the second most visible man-made feature, besides the Great Wall of China, as seen from outer space. However, the Forest Service has done considerable replanting in Caribou-Targhee National Forest.

Traveling along U.S. 20 between West Yellowstone and Ashton, Idaho, you might take one or both of the following side excursions in the national forest.

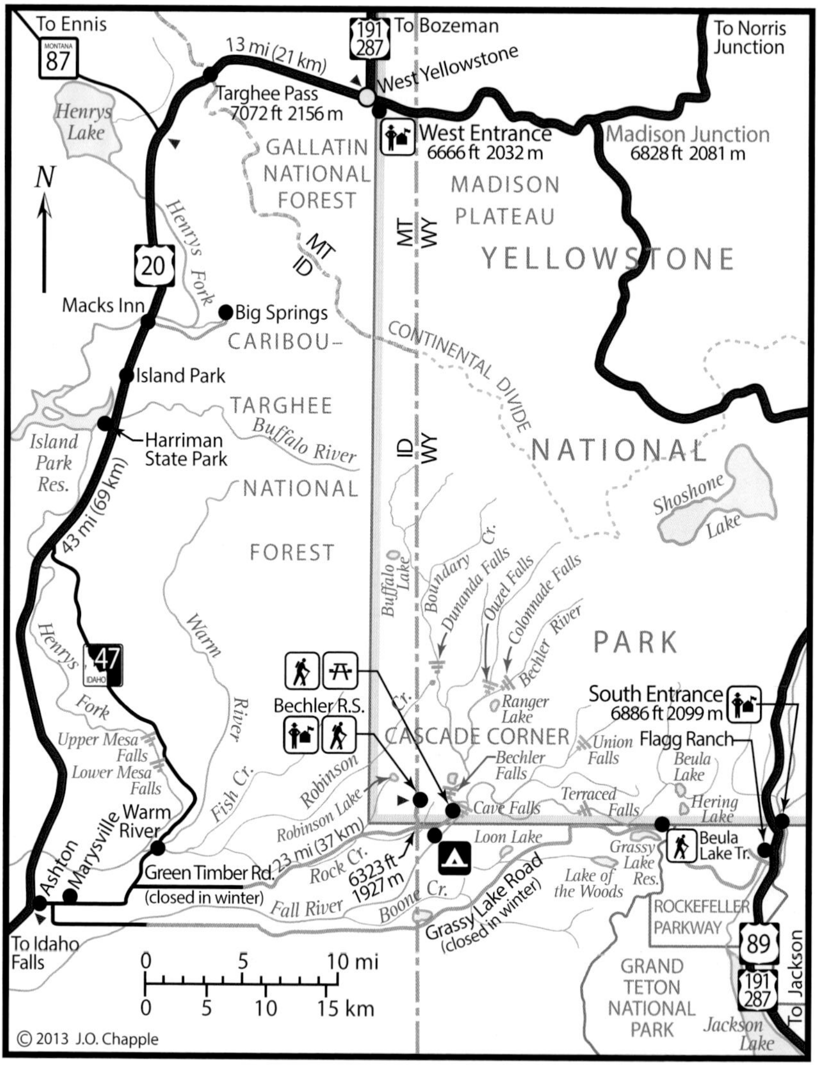

The Bechler Region and Environs

Side excursion to Big Springs

A side road leading east from U.S. 20 at the tiny town of Macks Inn takes you east 3 or 4 miles (5–6 km) to **Big Springs**, the major source of Henrys Fork of the Snake River and a truly beautiful spot. Small rafts or boats without motors may use part of the river, and there's a trail along it.

Side excursion to Mesa Falls

Big Springs harbors islands of flowers.

For a delightful short trip very close to the western edge of Yellowstone, visit Upper and Lower Mesa Falls on Idaho Highway 47. These two beautiful waterfalls on Henrys Fork cascade over the edge of lava that formed the eastern edge section of the Henrys Fork Caldera. The Henrys Fork Caldera is just to the southwest of the Yellowstone Caldera and is smaller and twice as old **[GEO.8]**. (For more about these calderas, see the Geological History chapter.)

To reach Upper and Lower Mesa falls from the north, take Idaho 47, which intersects U.S. 20 about 36 miles south of West Yellowstone. Coming from southeastern Idaho, go east from Ashton about 5 miles (8 km) and then north on Idaho 47.

The 114-foot (35 m) **Upper Mesa Falls** is about 12 miles (19 km) from the U.S. 20 turnoff. Following the short trail leading to the falls, you stand above its exhilarating roar. The Big Falls Inn, privately built by power company officials in 1916, was rarely used as an inn but is now an interpretive center, with full access for wheelchairs. Major improvements to the inn building, the trails and boardwalks, and the interpretive signs have necessitated an entrance fee of $3 per car.

A short distance south of Upper Mesa Falls is the turnoff for the less spectacular 65-foot (20 m) **Lower Mesa Falls**, with its attractive 1930s stonework.

Upper Mesa Falls waters a lush green garden of moss.

There are three Forest Service campgrounds along Idaho 47. Near Warm River, the road drops steeply over the Henrys Fork Caldera rim. The contrast between forested mountain terrain and gently rolling farmland is sudden and striking. Potatoes, barley, and alfalfa are grown in these fertile plains. To the east you'll catch views of the Tetons.

Continuing to the Bechler Region

About 6 miles (9.5 km) east of Ashton on Idaho 47, you can take Green Timber Road eastward to reach Cascade Corner in about another 17 miles (27 km). Before long, the pavement changes to a good quality gravel surface, just as you enter Caribou-Targhee National Forest. You cross into Wyoming just before reaching the roads leading to Bechler Ranger Station and Cave Falls.

The Bechler Region, or Cascade Corner, and Its Water

Named for Gustavus Bechler, a topographer who entered the area with the 1872 Hayden Expedition, the Bechler Region is best characterized in one word: water. Streams and marshes are everywhere. The park ranger at Bechler remarked on one June 30: "Bechler Meadows is a lake!" The whole corner abounds in waterfalls. Within a 10-mile (16 km) radius of Bechler Ranger Station are Cave, Bechler, and spectacularly beautiful Union Falls (250 ft / 76 m high), as well as Rainbow, Iris, Colonnade, Ouzel, Dunanda, Silver Scarf, and Terraced Falls. Farther along the trails are numerous others.

The drawbacks to all this water are several: hikers must wait until the latter part of the summer to enjoy the area—and even then must be prepared to ford streams that may be as deep as mid thigh—and mosquitoes and other pesky insects like it here, too. Fortunately, they die off in late summer.

In the 1920s, this copious supply of water inspired repeated proposals to dam the Bechler or Fall Rivers and deliver the water to Idaho farmers, allowing the use of Yellowstone Park water for irrigation or even removing the Bechler Region from park territory. Yellowstone's supporters successfully defeated congressional bills, and no dams were built in the park.

Around the same time, a member of the National Parks Association, writing about his exploration of the area, stated a bit cheekily: "Persons living near a national park who feel themselves harmed by their situation must bear their burden cheerfully" (quoted in *The Yellowstone Story* by Aubrey L. Haines). Idaho potato farmers get water instead from Grassy Lake Reservoir (built in the late 1930s) and from Jackson Lake.

~

IN YELLOWSTONE'S BECHLER REGION

Just after entering Wyoming, turn left to cross into Yellowstone Park and reach the ranger station in about a mile. In the historic 1911 building, a ranger is available in summer from 8 AM to 4:30 PM to answer questions and issue fishing and overnight camping permits.

Since Cascade Corner is a totally undeveloped area, horseback, llama, and backpacking trips, hiking, and fishing are the only activities here. At the ranger station, you can pick up a free guide to day trips that start from the station or from Cave Falls. Many long trails lead into the backcountry, starting from here or from the Grassy Lake Road. Backcountry trail books and good maps are essential for these trails.

To reach Cave Falls, continue to Green Timber Road beyond the ranger station turnoff for a little over a mile and find the Forest Service campground just outside the park boundary. There are no NPS campgrounds in this part of Yellowstone.

Cave Falls takes its name from a large cave to the left of the picture.

In 0.3 mile the **South Boundary Trail** is signed to the east and the **Bechler River Trail** to the west (leading to the ranger station). Taking the South Boundary Trail from here involves fording the wide and deep Fall River.

P Parking is available on the right at 0.9 mile. From here you can walk a short distance to **Cave Falls** of the Fall River. In 2008 the namesake cave collapsed and filled with rocks; it can no longer be entered. Falling over a lava flow, Cave Falls is remarkably broad, 250 feet wide and 20 feet high (76 m by 6 m).

(4) **(2)** Two-tenths of a mile beyond the Cave Falls parking area are picnic tables and the **Bechler River Trailhead**. The trail follows the river north to **Bechler Falls** in about a mile. Continue on to join several backcountry trails.

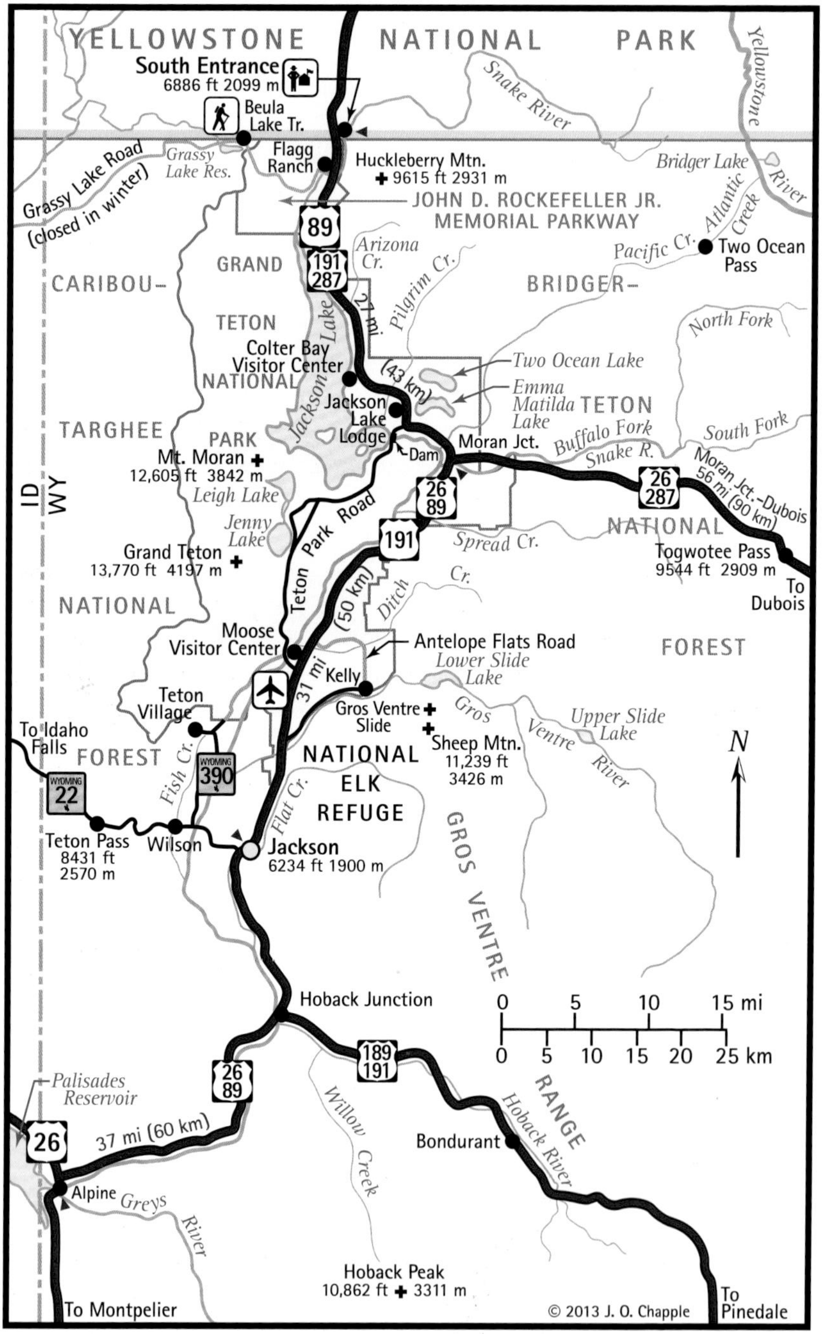

Approaches to the South Entrance

III. SOUTHERN SECTION

Approaches to the South Entrance

You'll be entering Yellowstone through the South Entrance if you include a visit to Grand Teton National Park in your travel plans. It's also the closest entrance for those interested in water sports or in backcountry hiking in the relatively undeveloped southern one-third of the park. The spectacular Tetons loom above the valleys from east or west and afford splendid photographing opportunities. Note that one fee (currently $25 per car) covers entry to both parks for one week.

As much as nine thousand years ago, Native American Indians left evidence that they were here. Then in the last two centuries, many colorful characters have passed through Jackson Hole. Beaver trappers came as early as the 1820s, and gold prospectors followed in the 1860s, but the latter never found pay dirt in commercial quantities. Some people found this a good place to escape the law, but many came as homesteaders and established ranches. By the beginning of the twentieth century, dude ranches were catering to wealthy Easterners. Today tourism and cattle are both important to the economy.

Jackson, Wyoming, has an airport and rental car agencies. Accommodations are plentiful, as are outdoor activities of every kind. The distance from Jackson to the South Entrance is 58 miles (93 km).

There's another way to approach Yellowstone's South Entrance, one that comes from the southeast rather than passing through Jackson. It follows U.S. Highways 26 and 287 from the town of Dubois near the northern end of the Wind River Range, across beautiful Togwotee Pass, and northwest to reach Yellowstone. Togwotee Pass road reconstruction was completed in 2012.

Jackson, Wyoming, and Environs — **Jackson Hole Airport**

Population: 9,600 — *8 mi. (13 km) N*

Since World War II, Jackson has become a full-blown summer and winter tourist center, replete with motels, restaurants, shops, and sports outfitters. Perhaps symbolic of its cachet, President Bill Clinton and family chose the area twice in the mid 1990s for their August vacation, and former Vice President Dick Cheney has a home nearby. Not surprisingly, you will pay more here for most accommodations and restaurant food than in any other gateway city around Yellowstone. There are numerous upscale ranches, houses, and condominiums in and around Jackson.

Fur trappers named the large valley east of the Teton Range Jackson's Hole for a fellow trapper. A hole to them meant this type of valley surrounded by mountains. In 1895, a wagon road was completed from West Thumb in Yellowstone Park through the South Entrance to the new Wyoming settlements to the southeast.

This is an area with many things to do; in fact, you need a day or more just to visit the most outstanding stops in Grand Teton National Park, with perhaps a boat trip or a short hike.

A Sampling of Summer Activities in Jackson Hole

- In and near Jackson: rodeos and "shootouts," chairlift at Snow King, National Wildlife Art Museum, National Fish Hatchery
- In Teton Village: aerial tram to Rendezvous Mountain, Grand Teton Music Festival classical concerts in July and August
- In and around Grand Teton National Park: ranger-led hikes and campfire lectures, float trips and white-water rafting trips, horseback riding and pack trips, fishing, climbing, and biking
- Near G.T.N.P. headquarters at Moose: the excellent Murie visitor center, former home of conservationists Olaus, Adolphe, Mardy, and Louise Murie and now devoted to the conservation of wildlife and wild places; the exhibits and trails of the Laurance S. Rockefeller Preserve

The **Snake River** has its source in the southern backcountry of Yellowstone, then traverses Jackson Hole. Its name does not come from the snakelike path it takes through the area, but rather from the French Canadian trapper name for the Shoshoni tribe: Snakes (Serpents in French). According to some researchers, the trappers misunderstood the sign Shoshoni people used to identify themselves: a sinuous hand motion with index finger extended, indicating that they were grass weavers. Instead, the trappers thought the sign meant the track of a snake.

Grand Teton National Park came into being in 1929 after much disagreement between advocates for adding the Teton country to Yellowstone and local ranchers interested in keeping the land private. At that time, Congress decided not to extend Yellowstone Park in this direction, but simply placed the land in the public domain. Grand Teton reached its present size only in 1950, with the addition of the part of Jackson Hole that includes the outer road (U.S. Highways 26/89/191).

For complete information about this park, write to The Superintendent, Grand Teton National Park, P.O. Drawer 170, Moose, WY 83012; call (307) 739-3300; or visit www.nps.gov/grte.

FROM JACKSON TO MORAN JUNCTION

As you leave town going north on U.S. Highway 89/191 from the center of Jackson, you'll pass the National Wildlife Art Museum, the National Elk Refuge, and the National Fish Hatchery. At Gros Ventre Junction, a paved road to the northeast leads to a campground and the town of Kelly.

A few miles farther north is the **Jackson Hole Airport**. Private aircraft and commercial 737s use this airport, located completely within Grand Teton National Park.

At **Moose Junction**, about 13 miles (21 km) north of Jackson, you'll have to choose your route to Jackson Lake Junction. Either turn onto Teton Park Road, which takes you closer to the lakes and mountains, or stay on U.S. Highways 26/89/191, which is a bit longer, yet faster and with equally spectacular views. On each road, there are lots of turnouts and several interpretive displays.

Northwest of Moose Junction is a Grand Teton National Park entrance station. Visitor centers are at Moose, South Jenny Lake, and Colter Bay. We'll describe only the eastern highway route.

The wide Snake River flows past the Tetons.

The Tetons and How They Got So High

The name Tetons (Les Trois Tetons—The Three Teats in the somewhat indecent French of the early trappers) comes from the three great summits you can see from the Idaho side, although there are many more than three peaks in the range. These mountains are truly awe inspiring: 12 peaks exceed 12,000 feet (3,650 m), and the Grand Teton is 13,770 feet (4,197 m) high.

The striking difference in elevation from that of Jackson Hole is what makes these mountains so special. There aren't a lot of places where you can gaze up at a sky full of mountain peaks whose tops are 5,000 to 7,500 feet (1,500–2,300 m) above you while you stand at their base—with no foothills in between! As author Owen Wister wrote over one hundred years ago: "The way in which they come up without any heralding of foothills seems as though they rose from the sea."

How did these mountains get so high? The eminent author John McPhee, although not a geologist, describes the process in his book, *Rising from the Plains*: "The crust extends, the earth stretches, the land pulls apart—and one result is a north-south-trending normal fault, fifty miles long. On the two sides of this fault, blocks of country swing [as though] on distant hinges like a facing pair of trapdoors—one rising, one sagging. The rising side is the rock of the nascent Tetons, carrying upward on its back the stratified deposits."

Geoscientists have proven that the Tetons certainly *did* rise, though not from the sea, as it seemed to Wister. This range of mountains was formed as part of the east-west pulling apart of the North American plate—an activity that is still going on from Arizona to Idaho and Wyoming. In the Teton area, when the pulling apart overcame the strength of the rocks, they broke to form a *fault* where the two sides move past each other. This fault runs roughly north to south and slants down steeply to the east. The more the rocks are pulled apart, the more space needs to be filled in. The block that is sinking helps to fill the gap that would otherwise develop.

The steepness of the mountain front that looms over Jackson Hole testifies to the strength and resistance to erosion of the 2.7-billion-year-old rocks recently exposed by the fault. The fault is still active, the land continues to sink, and the mountains continue to rise, but streams have brought sediments in to fill the valley floor. This process has been going on for about 7.5 million years so far, according to *Creation of the Teton Landscape* by David D. Love, John C. Reed, and Kenneth L. Pierce (Grand Teton Natural History Association, 2003).

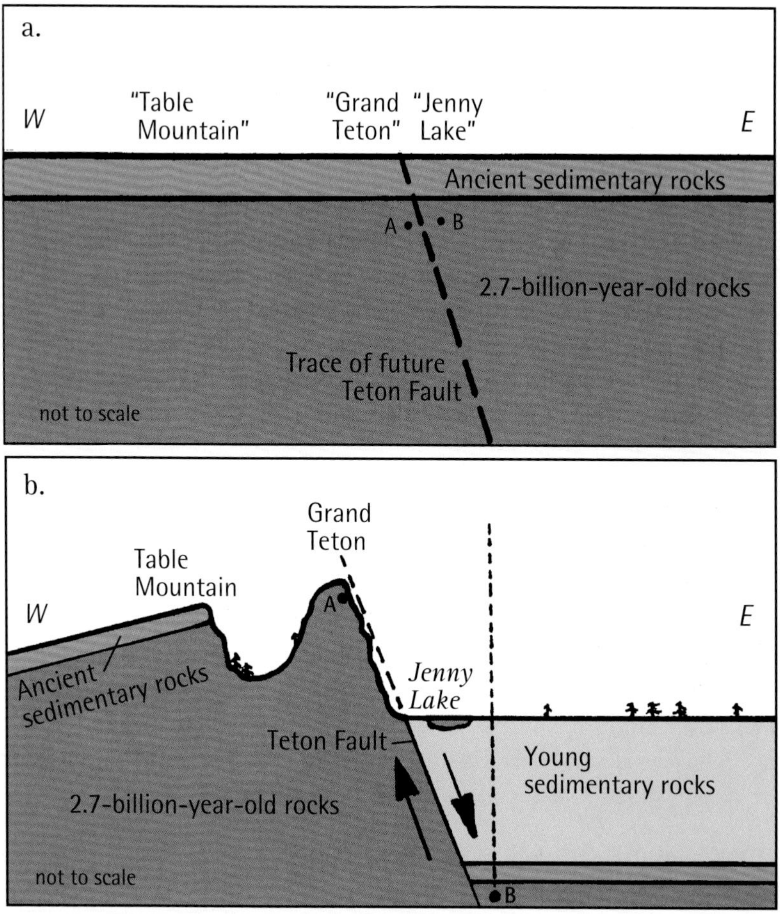

Figure 4. Cross sections showing the formation of the Teton Range.
View looking north, **4a**, shows the situation just before faulting started, where the features named in quotation marks are not yet formed. **4b** shows the situation today. The fault is indicated by a solid line, which continues as a dashed line in order to show where the fault was before the rocks were eroded. Point B started out opposite point A, but the eastern side moved down while the western side rose, separating the two points by about 19,000 feet (5,800 m). Primarily we notice how the Grand Teton towers over Jenny Lake, but the tension pulling the plates apart is east-west. The fault motion relieves the tension by moving point B eastward from adjacent to point A to a point indicated by the vertical dotted line. The ancient sedimentary rocks, which are about 525 million years old, were deposited before the faulting, whereas the young sedimentary rocks have been forming since the faulting, especially on the lake bottoms.

U.S. Highways 26/89/191

Continuing straight north beyond Moose Junction, the highway intersects with Antelope Flats Road, which leads to several campgrounds, the town of Kelly, and the Gros Ventre slide. Gros ventre—pronounced GROW VAUNT locally—means "big belly" in French. The low mountain range here and a subgroup of the Blackfeet tribe share this name.

The **Gros Ventre Slide** left an enormous scar that's still visible—though it happened nearly a century ago—on the hillside east of the main highway. It's interesting to compare this landslide with the Quake Lake slide near the West Entrance to Yellowstone (see page 36), which buried a campground and killed 28 people in the 1959 Hebgen Lake earthquake. The Gros Ventre landslide occurred when the unusually wet spring of 1925 caused sandstone layers overlying slippery shale to give way suddenly, shaken by a relatively minor earthquake. The landslide itself killed no one, but two years later the natural dam it had created suddenly gave way, flooding the town of Kelly downriver and killing six of its citizens.

To visit the slide and the Forest Service exhibits at its base, turn right at Gros Ventre Junction, pass the little town of Kelly, then continue more than a mile to a road on the right that passes guest ranches in the next 5 miles (8 km) and arrives at several interpretive signs. The best view of the slide is down a short trail near the signs. Drive less than a mile farther for a view of lovely Lower Slide Lake, which dammed a nineteenth-century wagon route into Jackson Hole.

Eighteen miles (29 km) from Moose Junction you reach Moran Junction. (See "From Moran Junction to the South Entrance.")

FROM DUBOIS TO MORAN JUNCTION

Instead of traveling via Jackson from the south, you may choose to reach the South Entrance via the southeast, from Dubois.

DUBOIS, WYOMING

Population: 970

DUBOIS MUNICIPAL AIRPORT
3.5 mi. (5.5 km) NW

A small western town with one main street, Dubois (called DOO-boys by residents) is about 83 miles (134 km) from the South Entrance on an excellent road over high Togwotee (TOE-guh-dee) Pass. Dubois has inexpensive motels, several restaurants, and the National Bighorn Sheep Interpretive Center, where tours can be arranged to visit the sheep's fall and winter range.

U.S. Highways 26 and 287

Outside the town, once a center for the production of railway ties, are now cattle and guest ranches. Spectacular striped hills, composed of alternating red clay stone and white tephra layers, line the road west of town.

Shoshone and Bridger-Teton National Forests offer two high-altitude picnic areas and two campgrounds as you cross **Togwotee Pass**, at 9,544 feet (2,909 m) a higher mountain pass than any inside Yellowstone. Togwotee was a medicine man and chief of the Sheepeater tribe. He led early explorers across this pass and guided Gen. Philip H. Sheridan on his expedition in 1882.

After you cross the pass, rolling hills and meadows greet the eye, with high mountains on all sides. You descend to the Buffalo Fork of the Snake River and cross the east boundary of Grand Teton National Park. Reaching Moran Junction, continue toward Yellowstone or turn left for the Tetons or Jackson.

FROM MORAN JUNCTION TO THE SOUTH ENTRANCE

One of two Teton Park entrance stations is located at **Moran Junction**, just north of where U.S. 26/287 joins U.S. 89/191. Going north for about 3.5 miles (5.5 km) takes you to Jackson Lake Junction, where the Teton Park Road joins the U.S. highway.

Mt. Moran rises majestically over Willow Flats and Jackson Lake.

South of the junction is **Jackson Lake Dam**, first completed in 1911 and rebuilt in 1989. The dam has raised the water level of Jackson Lake as much as 39 feet (12 m). In August and September of dry years, drawdown for irrigation creates mud flats in the northern section of Jackson Lake.

A short distance north of Jackson Lake Junction is the turnoff for **Jackson Lake Lodge**, famous for its luxurious accommodations and its views of the mountains. It was built by John D. Rockefeller, Jr. and opened in 1955.

The next turnoff to the west is for **Colter Bay Village**. It has complete visitor facilities, including a campground, a marina, and the Indian Arts Museum, where guest artists demonstrate traditional crafts. About a mile beyond the Colter Bay turnoff is one for **Leeks Marina** and the University of Wyoming/NPS environmental research center.

In the last 10 miles (16 km) of highway within Grand Teton National Park, there are four picnic areas and the **Lizard Creek campground**. You'll find another picnic area along the Rockefeller Parkway just to the north.

Stretching about 7 miles (11 km) between Grand Teton and Yellowstone Parks is the **John D. Rockefeller, Jr., Memorial Parkway**. Congress created the parkway in 1972 in recognition of Rockefeller's work in establishing or expanding several national parks. Though called a parkway, it's more than just a road; it encompasses many acres of land between the two big parks.

About 2 miles (3 km) from the Yellowstone boundary is **Flagg Ranch Resort** (with facilities opened in 1996), where you'll find cabins and motel-style rooms, campsites with full RV hookups, a restaurant, general store, laundry, and service station. In winter, Flagg Ranch is the southern point of departure for snowmobiles and snowcoaches to travel over the unplowed roads to Old Faithful. The entrance road to Flagg Ranch is also the eastern end of the Grassy Lake Road, along which there are eight free campsites. This area suffered a forest fire in the summer of 2000.

About 10 miles (16 km) west of Flagg Ranch, at Grassy Lake Reservoir's eastern tip, is **Beula Lake Trailhead** (see map, page 114). This trail, at first climbing rather steeply, goes less than 3 miles (5 km) into Yellowstone to a lake prized for its cutthroat trout (catch and release only). Farther west along the Grassy Lake Road are other trailheads for backcountry trails into Yellowstone. Backcountry trail books and topographic maps are essential for hiking these trails.

To the east of the Rockefeller Parkway between Flagg Ranch and Yellowstone's South Entrance rises **Huckleberry Mountain**, topped with 2-million-year-old Huckleberry Ridge tuff.

From the South Entrance to West Thumb Junction

Along this entrance road, you'll find two fine waterfalls and views into Lewis River Canyon. Just east of West Thumb Junction is West Thumb Geyser Basin.

Engineer Hiram Chittenden reported the South Entrance Road in 1900 as being "in a wretched condition and a disgrace to the Government." Improved very gradually, it was not heavily used until after the establishment of Grand Teton National Park. It's now the second most popular entrance.

It's about 21 miles (35 km) from the South Entrance to West Thumb Junction and the Grand Loop Road.

Road Log

0.0/21.5 Yellowstone Park boundary.

0.1/21.4 South Entrance station. Stop here to pay the entrance fee (see the Travel Tips for fee information). For backcountry, boating, or fishing permits, visit the ranger station.

The **Snake River Ranger Station**, built in the 1990s, is at the right (east) just beyond the entrance station.

To take the South Boundary Trail to the east, you must ford the river either near the ranger station or south of the park boundary. Prospector Walter DeLacy wrote in 1863 of hot springs with high cones near the junction of the Snake and Lewis Rivers, but access is difficult, so most of us will not see them. There used to be a hand-propelled cable ferry that park personnel used in crossing the Snake River, until it was washed away in 1995.

The **South Boundary Trailhead** to the west is much more accessible. You can find it by walking through the government housing area and going in a straight line from the north edge of the horse corral, where you see a trail sign to Grassy Lake and "Bechler Ranger Station 24 mi." In less than 1 mile (1.5 km), you glimpse Tanager Lake, but the trail bypasses it. The lake was named after the official park bird, the western tanager. The most interesting feature of this trail is the perfectly straight vista created by the downing of lodgepole pines, which are still lying about. The pines were cut down in 1911 to mark the south boundary and have decomposed very little. Even today, hunters need to know exactly where the boundary is. Moose are sometimes seen around the lake, and mosquitoes and biting flies may be plentiful, even in late summer.

0.2/21.3 **(10)** **(3)** Snake River picnic area, between the road and the Lewis River.

A pleasant 1-mile (1.6 km) trail from the north end of the picnic

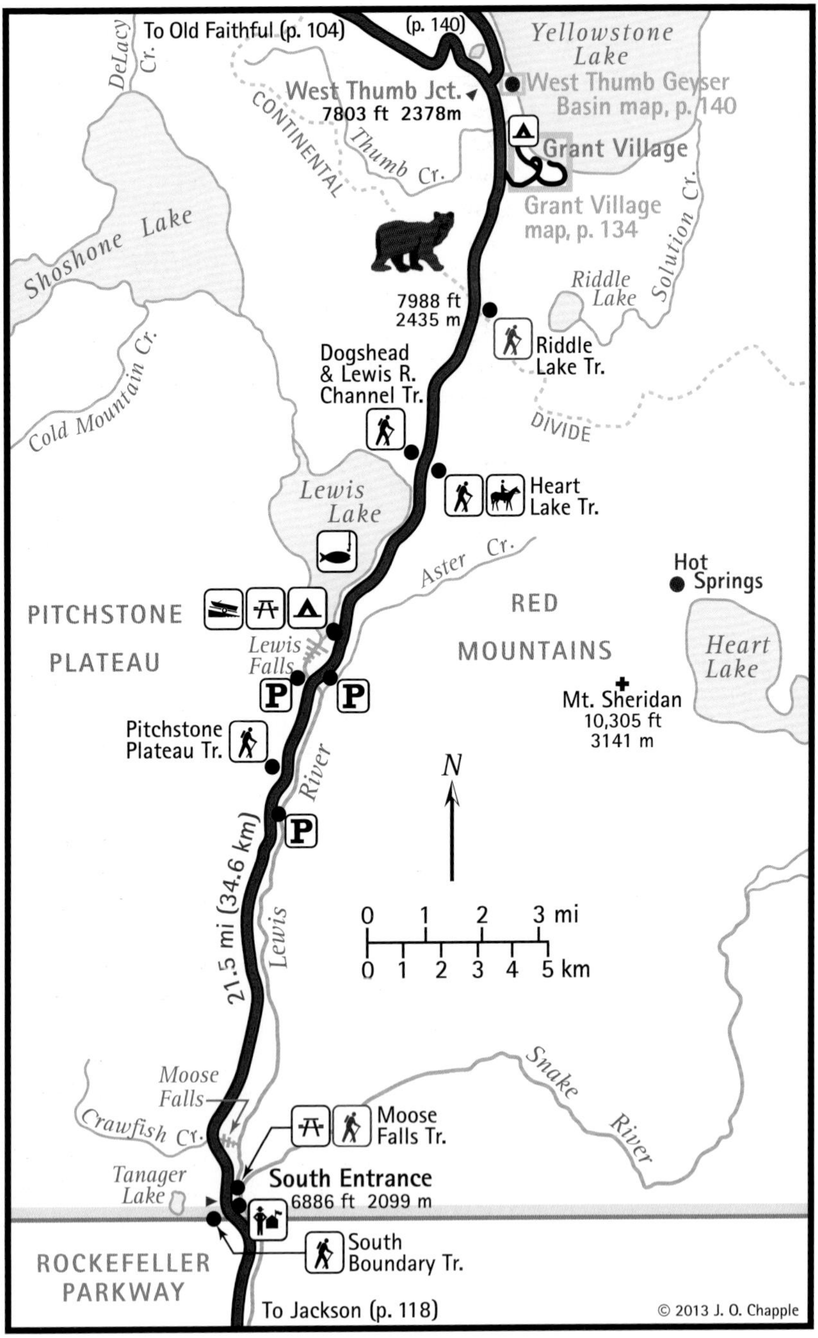
To Old Faithful (p. 104)
(p. 140)
DeLacy Cr.
Yellowstone Lake
West Thumb Jct.
7803 ft 2378m
West Thumb Geyser Basin map, p. 140
CONTINENTAL
Thumb Cr.
Grant Village
Grant Village map, p. 134
Shoshone Lake
Solution Cr.
Riddle Lake
7988 ft 2435 m
Riddle Lake Tr.
Dogshead & Lewis R. Channel Tr.
Cold Mountain Cr.
DIVIDE
Heart Lake Tr.
Lewis Lake
Aster Cr.
Hot Springs
PITCHSTONE PLATEAU
RED MOUNTAINS
Lewis Falls
Heart Lake
Mt. Sheridan 10,305 ft 3141 m
Pitchstone Plateau Tr.
River
N
21.5 mi (34.6 km)
Lewis
0 1 2 3 mi
0 1 2 3 4 5 km
Snake River
Moose Falls
Crawfish Cr.
Moose Falls Tr.
Tanager Lake
South Entrance
6886 ft 2099 m
South Boundary Tr.
ROCKEFELLER PARKWAY
To Jackson (p. 118)
© 2013 J. O. Chapple

South Entrance to West Thumb Junction

area takes you to Moose Falls. The first 0.4 mile (0.6 km), a popular area with fishermen, follows the Lewis River after its confluence with the Snake.

1.5/20.0 **P** Bridge and parking for **Moose Falls** on Crawfish Creek. A short trail takes you down to the brink of a delightful, small waterfall in a mossy sylvan setting and then on down to the bottom. Near the falls and overlook, you can find shiny jet-black pebbles and swirls of obsidian in the rock. Crawfish Creek is named for the small freshwater crustaceans, same as crayfish or crawdads, that thrive in its thermally warmed water.

The long, gradual ascent of the road beginning here takes you up the southern flank of the Yellowstone Caldera.

4.2/17.3 South end of Lewis Canyon. Fire damage that begins just north of here is from the 1988 Snake River complex of fires. You can still see where the fire crossed the canyon and burned down into it.

6.7/14.8 **P** An interpretive sign about the 1988 fires.

6.8/14.7 **P** Best overlook of several possible ones (only usable when going north) at the north end of **Lewis Canyon [GEO.10]**. Don't stop on the dangerously soft gravel shoulders along here—use the areas with widened pavement.

The rocks you see across the canyon near the tops of the cliffs are Lava Creek tuff, part of the vast eruption that

Moose Falls rushes over hard lava toward the Lewis River.

formed the Yellowstone Caldera 639,000 years ago. The Lewis River has cut down through these easily eroded rocks and is now exposing older lavas at the bottom of the canyon. Younger rhyolite lavas are west of the road. (For more about the caldera, see "The Yellowstone Caldera" in the Geological History chapter.)

8.0/13.5 Approximate point where the Lewis River begins to cut its canyon.

8.3/13.2 **Pitchstone Plateau Trailhead**. This trail climbs steadily from the road to the plateau and then descends gradually some 1,500 feet (475 m) in its 18-mile (29 km) course across the plateau to Grassy Lake Reservoir just south of the park.

The Eight Plateaus

Over the years of Yellowstone Park's history, explorers and geologists have discovered and named eight plateaus within the much larger Yellowstone plateau (see map for approximate locations). Four were created by volcanic flows; the other four are simply plateaus, raised land that is relatively flat.

1. **Pitchstone Plateau** is a geologically new expanse of rhyolite lava that flowed out of the caldera only 70,000 years ago in the most recent of the 30 or so relatively small eruptions of lava and tephra since the last great caldera explosion. Since rain and snowmelt percolate rapidly through this ground, few streams are created, and trees grow only along the ridges. Today's hiker can find the pressure ridges caused by the wrinkling of lava that cooled at the surface. *Pitchstone* is another name for obsidian, though it is not especially common on this plateau.

2. **Two Ocean Plateau** is a nonvolcanic, high, rolling area about 10,000 feet (3,050 m) high in the remote Thorofare corner. Its name comes from an area just south of the park boundary, from which creeks flow toward the two oceans. Not far from Two Ocean Pass—about 6 miles south of the Yellowstone border in the Teton Wilderness area (see upper right corner of the map on page 118)—are the sources of both the Snake and the Yellowstone Rivers. Mountain man Jim Bridger knew the plateau well and may have been its discoverer in the early nineteenth century.

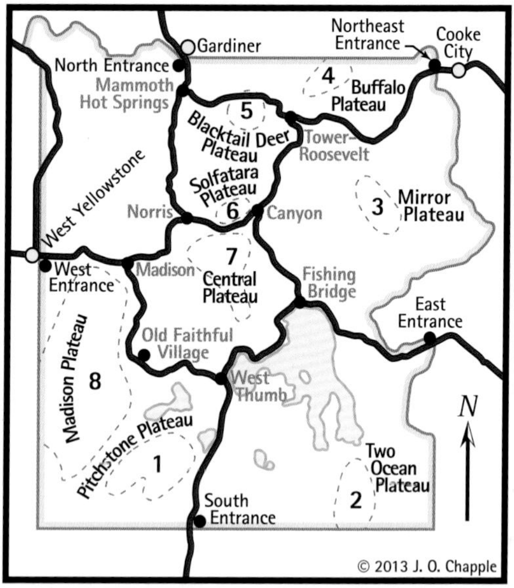

Approximate Locations of Yellowstone Plateaus

3. **Mirror Plateau**, another nonvolcanic area, has an average elevation of about 9,000 feet (2,750 m). It takes its name from little Mirror Lake, which is located on the drainage divide between the Lamar and Yellowstone Rivers.

4. **Buffalo Plateau** was named by a group of prospectors in 1870, when

it was a grazing ground for thousands of buffalo. Most of the rock here is 2.7 billion years old, more than half the age of the earth itself.

5. **Blacktail Deer Plateau** is an expanse of grass- and tree-covered glacial deposits about 7,000 feet (2,130 m) high.

6. **Solfatara Plateau** is a small and fairly recent volcanic flow dating back 110,000 years. The first known *solfatara*, near Naples, Italy, is a volcanic crater that exhales hydrogen sulfide, sulfur dioxide, and steam. In Yellowstone, the Solfatara Plateau is an area with many fumaroles.

7. **Central Plateau** is centered in the lower loop of the Grand Loop Road. The Nez Perce lava flow on this plateau is 160,000 years old.

8. **Madison Plateau** is the result of several lava flows of different ages. The West Entrance Road and the Grand Loop Road near Old Faithful both pass along its edges.

10.2/11.3 **P** **Lewis Falls** parking along the road at both ends of the Lewis River bridge. At the falls the flow of the Lewis River turns sharply from south to east. A rocky climb to the top of the falls on the upstream side of the bridge provides a pleasant short hike.

The river is gradually cutting down through the Pitchstone Plateau lavas that filled the Yellowstone Caldera to overflowing in this area. The presence of black shiny obsidian shows that the lava cooled too fast to form crystals. Lewis Falls is approximately at the caldera's southern boundary.

Lewis Falls drops about 30 feet (9 m).

East of the bridge, the river turns south again. The wide, calm river in its peaceful meadow gives no hint of the deep canyon it's scouring a few miles downstream. Soggy meadows like this one are good places to find moose, who love to browse standing in water.

11.4/10.1 **(10)** **(2)**

A short side road to the west leads to **Lewis Lake Campground**, picnic area, and boat launch site. The campground has 85 sites available on a first-come, first-served basis. There are no showers here. Ironically, this campground may be closed early in the summer due to excess water.

Lewis Lake formed where the rocks of the caldera rim resisted erosion by the Lewis River, creating a natural dam. The lake is about 3 miles (4 km) long and nearly as wide, with a maximum depth of 108 feet (33 m). Anglers catch unusually large nonnative lake trout and brown trout here.

The lake was named for Captain Meriwether Lewis of the famous 1803–6 Lewis and Clark Expedition. Although the men did not enter the park's territory, the expedition added a great deal to the knowledge of the vast American west and bestirred the public's curiosity about it.

All types of boats up to 40 feet in length are permitted on Lewis Lake. A popular option is to launch a canoe here and follow the western shore of the lake to the channel that connects to Shoshone Lake about 3 miles (5 km) to the north. Both boating and overnight permits are required.

14.3/7.2 **Heart Lake Trailhead**, from a large parking area on a short side road to the east. The trail is heavily used by both hikers and horseback parties. Before reaching Heart Lake in about 7 miles (11 km), you'll notice the many hot springs and small geysers along Witch Creek. The trail's first 4 or 5 miles are relatively flat. Then it passes along the side of Factory Hill at the northern edge of the Red Mountains before descending about 500 feet (150 m) to reach the lake, which abounds in large trout. From this trail you can also climb to the summit of Mount Sheridan—a 2,700-foot (820 m) climb in about 3 miles (5 km).

Heart Lake Geyser Basin saw the tragic death of Yellowstone's Research Geologist Roderick A. Hutchinson and a colleague in an avalanche in March 1997. Hutchinson contributed much to the understanding of the park's thermal areas in his 27 years as a staff member.

Historians believe that Heart Lake was named for 1840s hunter Hart Hunney and that the spelling was changed from Hart to Heart in the 1870s because of the lake's shape. However, you can see on any map of Yellowstone that Lewis Lake is the one that's more conventionally heart-shaped! Heart Lake has both cutthroat and lake trout; in fact, it yielded the largest fish ever caught in the park—a 42-pound (19 kg) lake trout.

14.5/7.0 Dogshead and Lewis River Channel Trailheads to the west. These are two routes to the same place, Shoshone Lake, the second largest lake in Yellowstone.

Dogshead Creek flows south into Lewis Lake. The Dog's-Heads in Greece are a range of hills where a famous Roman victory was won, but whether this was the source of the name in Yellowstone, or whether the name originally referred to a coyote or wolf, no one knows for sure. The **Dogshead Trail** is the shorter but less interesting of the two trails, reaching Shoshone Lake in about 4.5 miles (7 km).

The **Lewis River Channel Trail** reaches the channel in 3 miles (4.8 km) and Shoshone Lake in about 7 miles (11 km), skirting Lewis Lake on the way. The channel is a favorite with fishermen in the fall, when brown trout are spawning.

If you're traveling south, you'll see the **Red Mountains** looming almost ahead of you in this area, with Mount Sheridan their highest point. Mount Sheridan sports one of the three fire lookouts remaining in the park.

17.4/4.1 **Riddle Lake Trailhead** to the east. An easy hike of about 4.5 miles (7 km) round trip traverses burned forest and meadows full of wildflowers. The lake is covered with lily pads and backed by Mount Sheridan. Before mid July this trail may be soggy, and it's usually closed for bear management until that time.

The name Riddle Lake is an old one. Early hunters who thought this lake was located directly on the Continental Divide and drained to both oceans may have called it "Riddle" Lake. The name Biddle Lake sometimes shows up on old maps in this location or where Jackson Lake is, presumably honoring Nicholas Biddle, the Philadelphia publisher of William Clark's map. Riddle Lake actually drains into Yellowstone Lake and thence to the Atlantic Ocean. A U.S. Geological Survey party in 1885 decided no riddle should be without a solution, so they named the lake's outlet "Solution Creek."

Bear Management Areas

In recent summers, the Riddle Lake area has been closed until mid July for bear management. This means that the park's Bear Management Office limits bear/human interactions in an effort to keep bears from becoming habituated to people and especially to allow grizzly bears large areas of wilderness without human contact. Humans are thus less likely to be injured, and bears do not have to be relocated or killed. The program, inaugurated in 1983, appears to be paying off in the relatively few cases of bears injuring people and in the apparent increase in the bear population. (There's more about bears in the Living Things chapter.)

17.5/4.0 Crossing the Continental Divide. The land here is so nearly flat that you wouldn't notice a divide if it weren't for the sign.

19.8/1.7 Grant Village side road to the east.

This road passes the law enforcement ranger station and in less than 1 mile (1.6 km) reaches the village, the newest facility in the park.

Named for Ulysses S. Grant, the president who signed the act establishing the park in 1872, Grant Village was built between the late 1960s and the 1990s. The Snake River complex of forest fires threatened the settlement in 1988 and burned some campground buildings.

FACILITIES AT GRANT VILLAGE

As you enter the Grant Village area, you'll find a service station and mini-store on the left.

The large general store with lunch counter and the registration building for arranging accommodations in the motel rooms are slightly farther along on the right.

Small boats of all kinds may be launched on Yellowstone Lake from the boat launch site at the end of the first road on the right after the service station. The Grant area is the best part of the lake for sailboats, but the former marina here was damaged by winter storms and subsequently closed. Required permits and regulations for boating are available at the visitor center. (See page 153 and the Travel Tips for more about lake recreation.)

(2) Grant also has a post office, a family restaurant (where reservations are required), the Lake House (for breakfast and dinner only), a cocktail lounge, a gift shop, the **Grant Visitor Center**, and an amphitheater for ranger lectures. An excellent exhibit about the 1988 Yellowstone fires and the park's history of fire is on display at the visitor center.

On the way to the **Grant Village Campground** are a self-service laundry and showers. Several campsites and restrooms in loops A and B are wheelchair-accessible.

Grant Village is situated along West Thumb Bay.

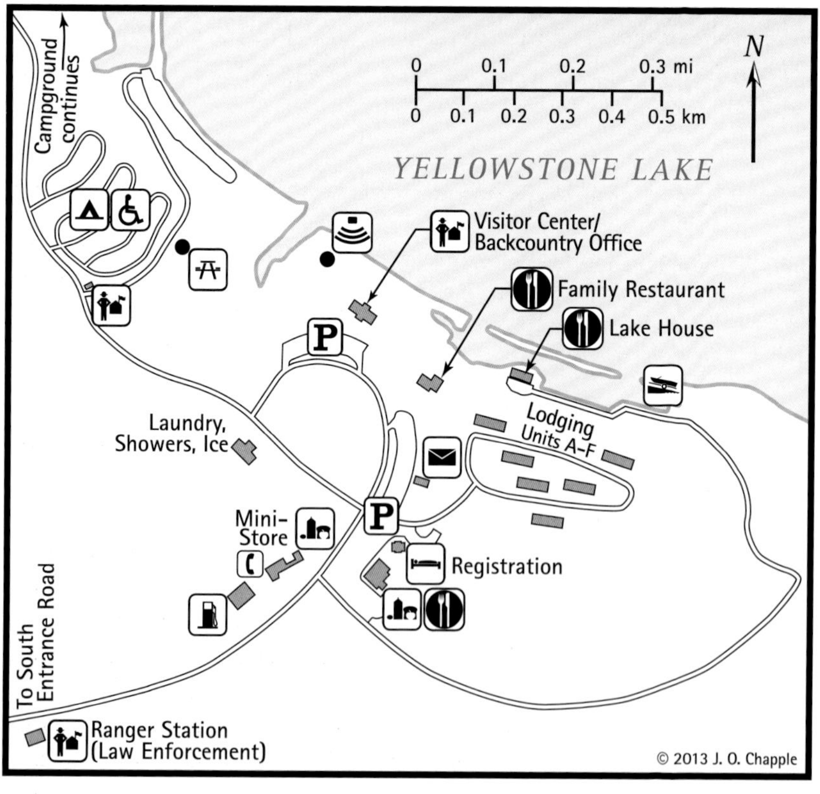

Grant Village

(15) **(2)** Near the entrance to the campground is a small ranger station and a picnic area with some fire grates.

Wheelchair-accessible restrooms are available at the general store, family restaurant, visitor center, laundry building, and picnic area.

Politics and Grant Village

The construction of Grant Village had a long and complicated history, starting from preliminary surveys of the area in 1947. At that time the National Park Service decided it was desirable to relocate West Thumb's facilities farther away from the thermal features of the geyser basin. Construction at Grant began somewhat later and was halted as many as seven times for various reasons, according to Alston Chase's controversial 1986 book, *Playing God in Yellowstone*.

A major difficulty with this site is its proximity to several important trout spawning streams, where grizzly bears like to fish in late spring and early summer. The expensive large marina at the east end of the village was closed for many years due to undercutting of the shoreline by the lake's waves.

In spite of these problems, Grant Village has become a convenient and heavily used area for campers, boaters, and other tourists. It has more than 400 campsites and 300 motel rooms.

Continuing on the Grand Loop Road

20.8/0.7 Thumb Creek bridge. This is one of the prime trout spawning creeks in the area.

21.5/0.0 West Thumb Junction. West Thumb Geyser Basin is described in the next section; Fishing Bridge Junction is to the northeast; Old Faithful Village and Madison Junction are to the west (straight ahead).

The Fires of 1988

In the summer of 1988, fires raged through Yellowstone Park, generating the most media attention and the greatest wildfire fighting effort in American history up to that time. About 36 percent of the park's acreage was affected, either by canopy burns—in which the treetops burned, trunks were partially consumed, and ground cover turned to ash—or by less severe partial burns. About 41percent of Yellowstone's 1988 fires were of the canopy burn type.

More than 40 different fires burned in the Greater Yellowstone Ecosystem that summer, ignited both by lightning and by humans. The most destructive one, the North Fork Fire, began accidentally, started by a woodcutter near tiny North Fork Creek in Caribou-Targhee National Forest. Along the most severely affected roadsides, from the West and South Entrances, you still see

The fire closely threatened Old Faithful Village.

standing snags, but almost everywhere new lodgepole pines (see picture, page 228) have grown from their *serotinous cones.*

Study of fire frequency in Yellowstone has revealed that fires with the intensity of these have occurred only once in every three hundred years. The causes were a very unusual combination of drought, dry storm fronts bringing lightning and high winds, and long-term buildup of fuel.

After the 1988 fires were out—with the snows of early September—a careful census was made of the wildlife whose lives had been lost. Surprisingly, very few large animals perished. Less than 1 percent of the elk in Yellowstone that summer died—about 250 of 32,000. The one species that has become rarer is the moose, which suffered due to the decline of old-growth forest.

Positive results from the 1988 fires continue to be discovered. Wildflowers flourished, especially in the first few subsequent years, since the fire killed almost none of the plant parts underground. The fires opened up distant vistas visitors could not see before. Fire specialists know that smaller wildfires will continue to proliferate in our climate-changed future, and prescribed fires are periodically ignited to reduce fuel buildup.

Most animals continued their lives unaffected. As John D. Varley and Paul Schullery concluded in evaluating the effect of the fires on Yellowstone's fish: "Wildland . . . has all the time in the world to regenerate and maintain itself. It scars and heals itself on a scale of centuries, and with no regard for the much briefer scale of a human lifespan."

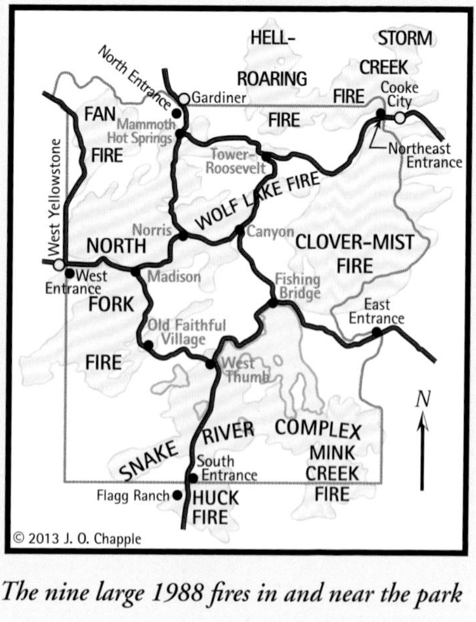

The nine large 1988 fires in and near the park

From West Thumb Junction to Fishing Bridge Junction

The Grand Loop Road going north from West Thumb follows the lakeshore closely most of the way to Fishing Bridge Junction, almost 21 miles (33 km) away. You'll drive along America's highest large freshwater lake and glimpse its surrounding mountains. The Absaroka Range is beyond the lake to the east, and the Red Mountains are to the south. There are many places to pull over by the lakeside to stroll, wade, take pictures, or fish.

Road Log

NOTE: There are several short side roads along this stretch of the Grand Loop Road. The mileage for such roads is given at approximately the midpoint between the two ways to enter the loop.

0.0/20.6 From West Thumb Junction the road north goes toward Bridge Bay Marina, Lake Village, and Fishing Bridge Junction. To the west is Old Faithful Village; to the south is the South Entrance and Grand Teton National Park.

0.2/20.4 Entrance to parking for West Thumb Geyser Basin, an information and bookstore building, and a picnic area.

West Thumb

West Thumb Geyser Basin—just east of the junction—is the most beautifully situated thermal area in the park and is well worth visiting.

West Thumb history and facilities

NOTE: Consult the map of West Thumb Geyser Basin on page 140 for West Thumb facilities.

P ? (The information and bookstore building, where the Yellowstone Association sells books and pamphlets, is housed in the former ranger station dating from 1925, now used as a warming hut in winter.

(5) (4) Reached from this parking lot are the West Thumb picnic area, two hiking trails, and the West Thumb Geyser Basin boardwalks. There is no running water.

The rather strange name of this spot, West Thumb, refers to the shape of this bay in Yellowstone Lake. Early explorers thought the lake resembled a hand with fingers protruding southward. Early surveyors even thought for a while that

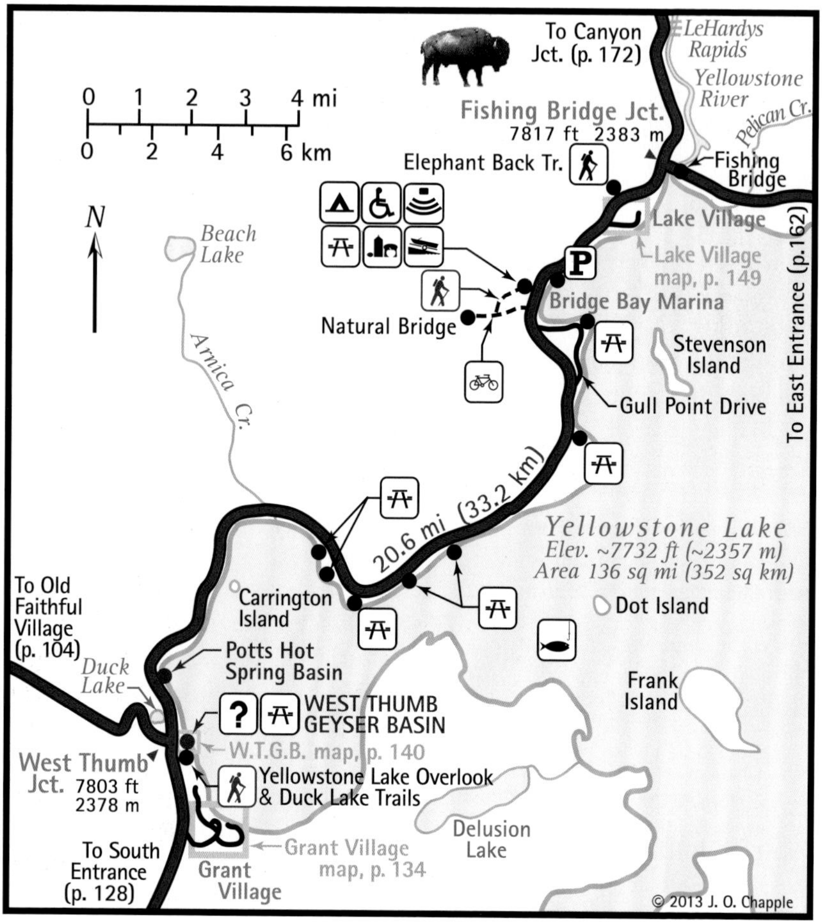

West Thumb Junction to Fishing Bridge Junction

there was a fifth finger. When it turned out that the small body of water was not connected to the larger lake, it was named Delusion Lake.

You could take a steamboat from West Thumb to a dock at Lake Hotel from the 1890s until soon after automobiles were allowed into the park in 1915. At that time the steamboat line was abandoned as unprofitable.

Until 1989, there were various facilities for visitors at West Thumb, but these were moved to Grant Village to separate them from the fragile hot spring area. It has been rumored that the gas station's underground storage tank was located where the ground temperature is one degree below the flash point of gasoline!

West Thumb Bay is actually a smaller, more recent caldera formed within the

Evening at West Thumb Geyser Basin with alpenglow on the distant Absarokas

main Yellowstone Caldera about 200,000 years ago and then flooded. Water for its hot springs and geysers comes up through fractures at the edge of this crater.

The lake's water level is now above its level of 50 years ago, contributing to the periodic drowning of some of West Thumb's lakeside thermal features. Geoscientists have discovered that the lake basin has risen and fallen numerous times in the 15,000 years since the Yellowstone glaciers started to melt. The movement of the lake is attributed to uplift in the central part of the Yellowstone Caldera, the axis of which passes by LeHardy's Rapids. When there is uplift Yellowstone Lake's outlet and northern part rise, and a tilting of the lake's water level occurs. For more about Yellowstone's slow ground movements, see page 318.

Two short hikes from West Thumb

Yellowstone Lake Overlook Trail is a loop of a little over 2 miles (3.2 km). Start by walking southwest from the West Thumb parking lot. After crossing the South Entrance Road (where there's limited roadside parking), turn right for the shortest way to the top of "Savage Hill," so called by concessionaire employees, who call themselves Savages. Pass a riot of wildflowers in the burned forest, and notice a couple of modest combinations of mud pots, fumaroles, and hot pools on your way up the moderately strenuous 400-foot (120 m) climb. On a clear day, you'll be rewarded with a fantastic view of much of the lake and its surrounding mountains.

You can take the **Duck Lake Trail** northwest from the same West Thumb parking area. Duck Lake Trailhead is shown by a painted pedestrian crosswalk that crosses the Grand Loop Road north of West Thumb Junction. This hike is about one-half mile (0.8 km) through burned forest to a view of Duck Lake and another one-third mile (0.5 km) to its shore. Since Duck Lake is in an explosion crater, the last part of the trail goes steeply up and down over the crater's edge.

West Thumb Geyser Basin Loop Walk★

The boardwalk around West Thumb Geyser Basin is about one-half mile (0.8 km) long. It takes you to the main portion of this basin, which has few geysers but is outstanding for its scenic setting and beautiful hot springs. Since there is less sulfur in the chemical mix brought up from below, the rotten egg smell so common to other basins is less strong here.

In some seasons and some years, the colors in and around the hot springs are spectacular. Thermal features are changeable, however, so if the colors you see are rather ordinary at the time you're here, come back another time! Bison, deer, and waterfowl are often seen in the area. A pamphlet describing the basin is available.

NOTE: The boardwalk through the basin is nearly level and accessible to wheelchairs, but on the hill farthest from the parking lot, assistance may be required.

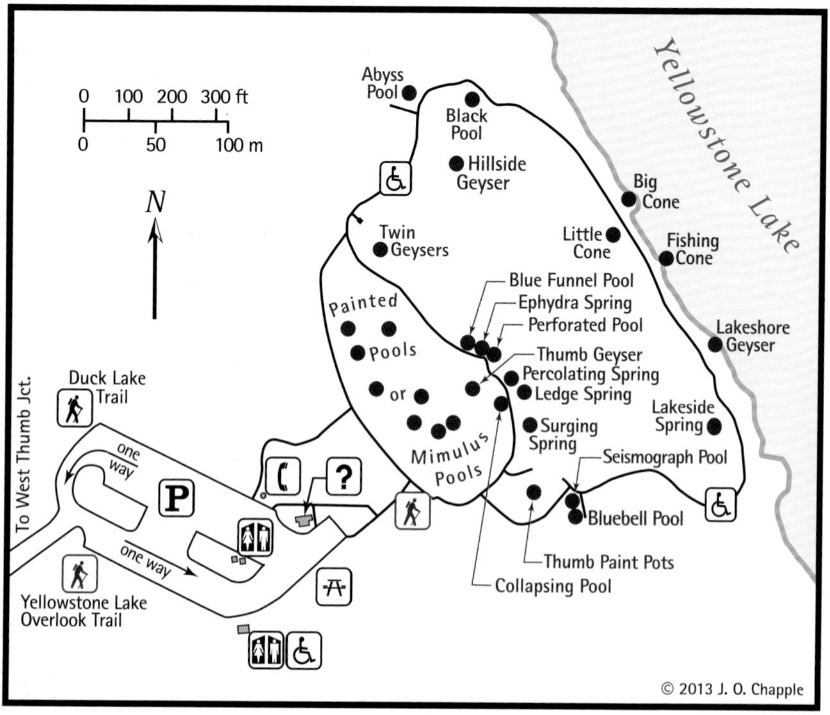

West Thumb Geyser Basin

Walking toward the lake from the parking lot, stay to the right to find the **Thumb Paint Pots [GEO.23]**, named Mud Puffs when the pastel colors were remarkable in the nineteenth century. Now they are duller and vary from muddy to dry depending on recent rainfall. The mud is formed by sulfuric acid in the water acting on the rock as it passes through.

Seismograph and **Bluebell Pools**, on a spur to the right, differ from each other in temperature and sometimes in coloring. Seismograph's name dates to about 1960, when it was noticed that small earthquakes caused turbidity and a rise in the pool's temperature. There may be extremely thick, colorful mats of bacteria and algae in both pools' runoff (see "What Makes the Colors?" on page 65).

At the lakeshore are **Lakeside Spring** and **Venting Pool**, unremarkable features when they're cool. However, when Lakeside Spring's water is hot, its microorganisms are beautifully colored. Look down from the boardwalk to see a remnant of the concrete that supported a boat dock here a century ago. A sign explains the West Thumb caldera.

When the lake's water level is high, the next features are entirely or almost submerged. **Lakeshore Geyser** has a sizeable cone, indicating considerable activity and a lower water level in the past—geoscientists tell us sinter cones like these usually aren't built under water.

A pool to the left of the boardwalk shows what happens when thoughtless visitors throw things into hot springs, filling the vents and causing the water to cool. Ugly brown microorganism mats cover the bottom or float to the top.

Fishing Cone is the most famous feature at West Thumb. It was where "unfortunate trout find catching and cooking painfully near together," as

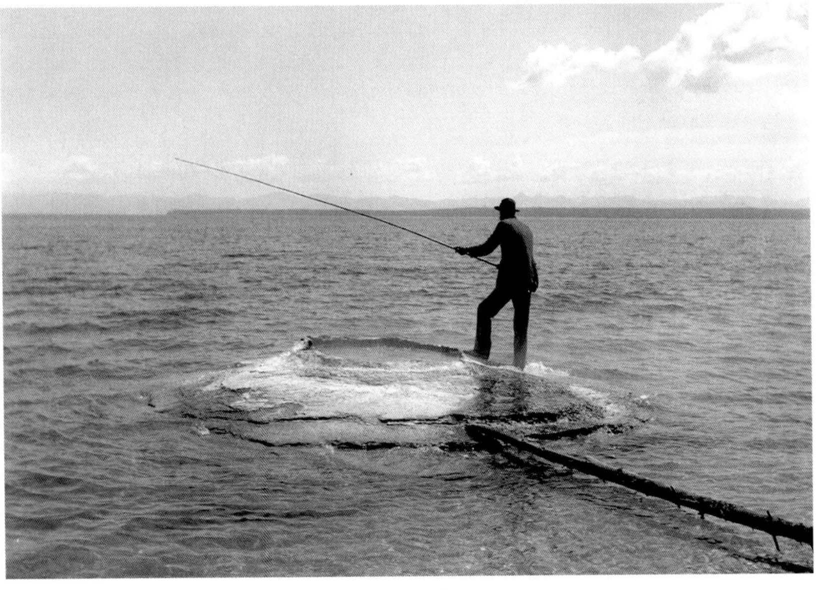

Fishing Cone in the late 1800s, by W. H. Jackson.

historian Chittenden wrote in 1895. In other words, early day tourists could catch a fish here and cook it without removing it from the hook. Regulations now prohibit fishing at or near West Thumb, since at least five people have perished over the years after falling into these hot springs.

Two more cones (**Big Cone** and **Little Cone**) complete features at the lakeshore before the path leaves the lake. Inactive Little Cone is above the boardwalk, well away from the water.

You'll next encounter Black Pool at the left and Abyss Pool a bit farther on at the right. Perhaps 50 yards (or meters) from the boardwalk next to Black Pool is **King Geyser**, whose eruptions are extremely rare but discharge an impressive amount of water when they occur.

In 1991, **Black Pool** became much hotter than before and erupted for a brief period. This activity killed the bacterial mats, whose oranges and browns had combined with the usual blue of the water to give the pool an almost black color. Now Black Pool is often a lovely blue or green and is gradually cooling.

West Thumb is anything but a static place! Proof of this is given by the recent history of **Abyss Pool**. A very explosive geyser in the early years of the twentieth century, Abyss then became dormant for something like 80 years. Then in 1991 and 1992, it erupted numerous times up to 100 feet (30 m), causing some of the nearby pools to drain. Since then, Abyss has quieted, but no one can guess how long it may remain that way. At 53 feet (16 m) deep, it's one of the park's deepest pools. It's sometimes difficult to see the bottom through the lightly bubbling blue-green water.

As you ascend the boardwalk's hilly stretch, you can see that trees to your left have been killed by mineral-laden water. In this area, **Hillside Geyser** was erupting to 70 feet (20 m) or more between 1995 and 2005.

Black Pool turned blue in 1991.

To the west of the boardwalk intersection beyond the Twin Geysers overlook, an unnamed steam vent often makes a furious racket. Just above here, road builders many years ago diverted the steam of a fumarole away from the construction site by cramming a pipe into it. The pipe ends here.

The higher section of boardwalk (the former Grand Loop Road) returns you to the parking lot, past large hot pools called the **Painted Pools** or **Mimulus Pools**, after the Latin name for monkeyflowers. The pools show a range of colors. Some are clear, others opaque; some quiet, others bubbling. To see several other geysers and hot springs, follow the lower boardwalk to the left. This part of the geyser basin is especially prone to energy surges, that is, brief periods when hot springs become geysers and known geysers increase their frequency and size.

It's hard to believe that the now relatively calm springs called **Twin Geysers** could ever have been the largest geysers at West Thumb and a spectacular attraction, but in some decades of the twentiethth century, this was the case. Rising temperature and boiling activity in 1998 preceded renewed eruptions that August and occasional eruptions since. The temperature in one of the pools has sometimes measured 203°F (95°C)—above the boiling point of water at this elevation.

Some of West Thumb's Painted Pools

The next notable feature is **Blue Funnel Pool**, an almost perfectly circular pool whose shape somewhat resembles Morning Glory Pool.

Ephydra Spring was named in the 1960s for the brine fly (*Ephydra bruesi*) that is common in alkaline thermal areas and feeds on microbes growing in the hot water.

Several springs lie in an almost straight line; apparently they have developed along a slightly curving fracture under the earth. These springs include Blue Funnel, Ephydra, **Perforated Pool**, an unnamed pool with a black lining, **Percolating Spring**, **Ledge Spring**, and **Surging Spring**. Some have erupted as geysers, including Ledge Spring during the summer of 1999 and into this century. On the opposite side of the walkway is **Thumb Geyser**—which has been known to erupt up to 25 feet (7.5 m)—and also **Collapsing Pool**.

Continuing on the Grand Loop Road

Turn right (north) out of the West Thumb parking area to continue along the lake toward Fishing Bridge Junction. The first steam you will see comes from the Lake Shore Group of thermal features, where there is no public access. **Lone Pine Geyser** in this group has been the most interesting in recent years. It was known to erupt up to 50 feet (15 m) high, recently performing once a day to once in 36 hours. Lone Pine Geyser's namesake pine tree on a nearby rock fell into the lake in 1997.

1.8/18.8 Potts Hot Spring Basin is indicated only by a small widening along the road. Please heed the Danger—Thermal Area and Do Not Enter signs. This is the northernmost group of geysers and hot springs of the West Thumb area. The sinter buildup at least 18 feet (5.5 m) high indicates that it's a very old thermal area.

The Grand Loop Road used to run right through Potts Basin, named for trapper Daniel Potts, who wrote about his 1826 traverse of this area.

Looking across Bluff Point to Mount Sheridan.

2.4 to 4.2/18.2 to 16.4 (P) Lakeside turnouts near historic **Bluff Point.**

3.9/16.7 Carrington Island is the tiny, rocky bird roost just off shore, submerged at times of high water except for one tree. It's named after the zoologist of the 1871 Hayden Expedition, E. Campbell Carrington, who sketched the shoreline of Yellowstone Lake from the first boat ever known to sail upon it, the *Anna*. Half the nonnative lake trout are believed to spawn near here.

5.7/14.9 (P) Small parking area on the lake side of the road. One of the two rutted, unmaintained trails across the road is a remnant of the main stagecoach road from West Thumb to Bridge Bay, used from 1902 to 1926. In this area, the builders of the Old Faithful Inn found some of the strikingly deformed logs used in the inn's interior, according to historian Aubrey Haines. The other unmaintained trail goes up Arnica Creek to remote Beach Lake.

Arnica Creek is named after a yellow flower with heart-shaped leaves (picture, page 336), often found in lodgepole forests. Geologist Arnold Hague, who spent many summers in the park in the nineteenth century, advised rubbing arnica flower on sore muscles.

Not visible here due to the thick stand of trees is the western end of a wave-built sandbar in the lake. A road along the shore used the sandbar as its roadbed for a few years, but it proved too difficult to maintain—rangers later called it "Hard Road to Travel." Water from the lake flows through the sand below the sandbar to form the lagoon.

The intense fire damage you see for over a mile in this area was caused by the 2009 Arnica fire.

6.5/14.1 (5) Picnic area located in a partial burn.

7.4/13.2 (P) Wide turnout where you can stop to walk along the east end of the natural sandbar.

7.9/12.7 (3) (2) Unmarked road to south, leading to Park Point picnic area. From the picnic area, there's a beautiful view of the lake and the **Red**

The sandbar once used as a roadbed still graces Yellowstone Lake a century later.

Mountains to the south. Their highest peak is **Mount Sheridan**, (10,305 ft / 3,141 m), named for General Sheridan, Civil War Union general, commander during the wars with Indian tribes, and a staunch supporter of the park who paid several visits to the area.

8.7/11.9 **P** **Pumice Point**, with access to the lake. This point marks the northern boundary of West Thumb Bay. *Pumice* is a porous form of volcanic glass that can be powdered and used as an abrasive.

The closest mountain across the lake to the south is **Flat Mountain** (9,168 ft / 2,794 m). It marks the southeastern edge of the Yellowstone Caldera.

9.7/10.9 **(2)** Unmarked lake access road at **Spruce Point**.

10.8/9.8 **(4)** Exhibit picnic area with an interpretive sign about the forests. Blue-green Engelmann spruce and subalpine fir trees can be found along with lodgepole pines in the moister environment near the lake. For hints about identifying these trees, see the Living Things chapter.

Visible out to the east in the lake are **Dot** and **Frank Islands**. Boat operator E. C. Waters kept bison and elk penned on Dot Island in the early 1900s. It was a sort of zoo for the tourists who traveled between West Thumb and Lake Hotel on his boat, the *Zillah*. The hull of this boat is probably the one seen by divers in 1994 about 200 yards (180 m) out from Lake Hotel.

Yellowstone Lake

No writer has better described Yellowstone Lake than did renowned naturalist John Muir in an *Atlantic Monthly* article of 1898:

> It is about twenty miles long and fifteen wide, and lies at a height of nearly 8,000 feet above the level of the sea, amid dense black forests and snowy mountains. Around its winding, wavering shores, closely forested and picturesquely varied with promontories and bays, the distance is more than 100 miles....
>
> It is full of trout, and a vast multitude of birds—swans, pelicans, geese, ducks, cranes, herons, curlews, plovers, snipe—feed in it and upon its shores; and many forest animals come out of the woods, and wade a little way in shallow, sandy places to drink and look about them, and cool themselves in the free flowing breezes.
>
> In calm weather it is a magnificent mirror for the woods and mountains and

sky, now pattered with hail and rain, now roughened with sudden storms that send waves to fringe the shores and wash its border of gravel and sand.

Yellowstone Lake is North America's largest high altitude lake (7,732 ft / 2,357 m) at about 14 by 20 miles (23 by 32 km) in width and length and with more than 141 miles (227 km) of shoreline. The lake has an average depth of 139 feet (42 m); its deepest spot is 430 feet (131 m) just east of Stevenson Island.

Tributaries

Approximately 125 tributary streams feed into Yellowstone Lake, mostly from the south and east. One of the streams is the Yellowstone River's source, which enters the southeast arm of the lake from the mountains in Bridger-Teton National Forest. Thus, the lake's outlet at Fishing Bridge is not really the headwaters of the Yellowstone River.

Islands

The seven named islands in Yellowstone Lake are, from largest to smallest: Frank, Stevenson, Dot, Peale, Molly (actually two islands named Sandy and Rocky), Carrington, and Pelican Roost. Frank, Peale, and Molly were named by or for members of the 1871 and 1878 Hayden Expeditions.

Winter and the Lake

In winter, ice nearly 3 feet (1 m) deep covers much of the lake, except where shallow water covers hot springs. The lake freezes over by early January, and the ice doesn't break up until late May or early June. Rangers on ski patrol used to take a shortcut to the Thorofare in the southeast by crossing the ice from Lake Ranger Station to Park Point on the east shore.

Science and the Lake Bottom

In recent years, scientists have explored some of the lake's bottom using a submersible robot called a Remotely Operated Vehicle (ROV). They've learned that Mary Bay at the lake's north end, where temperatures up to 212°F (100°C) have been measured, is a major hydrothermal explosion crater complex that erupted about 13,000 years ago. They've also found deep pits that may be old explosion craters.

At least two other hot areas in the lake are being studied. West Thumb Bay is one of these areas, with huge hot gas eruptions that stir up food for enterprising trout. Another is east of Stevenson Island, where many active hydrothermal springs are found.

Spires as tall as 26 feet (8 m) grow in clusters on the lake bottom at one lake hot spot, Bridge Bay. These pinnacles are made of the siliceous shells of diatoms, microscopic algae that live and die near the lake bottom. Exactly how these hydrothermal features form is as yet unknown.

Lava flows that are still very hot underlie much of the lake. Thus all the possible thermal features that we see in the rest of the park are here, only modified by having a lake sitting on them. The result is that many explosion craters dot the lake perimeter, and we know from recent research that there are more on the lake floor. There are also domelike features, some one-third of a mile (0.5 km) in diameter, bulging up perhaps due to steam.

An ongoing study called the Molecular All-Taxa Biodiversity Inventory is discovering species previously not known to live in the lake, ranging from the smallest bacteria to crustaceans and insects.

14.1/6.5 (14) (2) Sand Point picnic area. The tables have no view of the beach, but there's a shore access trail with a good view of long, narrow **Stevenson Island** and the Absaroka Mountains across the lake. The island was named for James Stevenson, the skillful manager of all three Hayden surveys of Yellowstone in the 1870s. Stevenson and a companion explored the island and reported it to be a dense jungle with abundant animal tracks.

On the far side of Stevenson Island lies the wreckage of a 125-foot (38 m) wooden steamboat, the *E. C. Waters*, named for her owner. Launched in 1905, she was never licensed to carry passengers and lay aground until 1930, when her boilers were removed and used to heat the Lake Hotel. The boat's capstan has recently been added to the park's artifact collection at Gardiner.

15.4/5.2 (21) (2) Gull Point Drive (south end). This is a two-way loop road about 2 miles (3 km) long, closed in times of high lake water. Gull Point marks the south edge of Bridge Bay and extends into the lake for some distance when the water level is relatively low. California gulls come to Yellowstone in mid spring to nest on the Molly Islands in the Southeast Arm of the lake.

16.9/3.7 Gull Point Drive (north end) on the lake side.

Natural Bridge Trailhead on the west side of the Grand Loop Road. This is the best place to begin a bike ride to the Natural Bridge, a round trip of about 2 miles (3.2 km), but there's very little space for parking here.

To hike to the Natural Bridge, it's best to turn in toward Bridge Bay Marina 0.3 mile (0.5 km) north, park in the large lot next to the marina, and follow the trail that starts from the west side of the campground and then joins the old road. Natural Bridge from there is about a 3-mile (4.5 km) round trip. Be aware that bears feed on the spawning trout in Bridge Creek early in the season, so inquire about trail closures at a visitor center before hiking here.

Natural Bridge was cut by Bridge Creek through a cliff of rhyolite lava. Its graceful arch is about 50 feet high and 30 feet across (15 m by 9 m). The Grand Loop Road passed this way from 1901 to 1926. It climbed and descended

Natural Bridge stereograph view, about 1880

a 16-percent grade before reaching this point. (This is the north end of the former road from Arnica Creek mentioned at mile 5.7/14.9.)

17.0/3.6 Bridge across the entrance to Bridge Bay. The bay did *not* get its name from this bridge, as you might think, but, like Bridge Creek, was named by Superintendent Norris after the Natural Bridge.

17.2/3.4 (23) Bridge Bay Marina entrance road. Bridge Bay is one of the newer park villages, completed in the early 1960s. **Bridge Bay Campground** is the largest in the park, with over 425 reservable campsites, three of them wheelchair-accessible. A picnic area with an ice machine is close to the bay.

An amphitheater for nighttime ranger-interpreter talks and slide shows is in the campground. If you attend a ranger talk, be sure to return the same way you came in—it's a vast campground with no exit signs for the unwary!

Bridge Bay Marina, although located on a natural bay, was deepened in the 1970s to better accommodate large boats. It is one of only two places to launch motorized vessels on Yellowstone Lake. At the marina you can find rowboat and outboard rentals, as well as rental slips for private boats.

(5) There's a tackle shop, a mini-store, and a ranger station, too. The rangers have mounted interesting displays about fishing and the lake.

Lake cruises run by the park concessionaire go out for one-hour trips several times a day, in vessels holding 47 passengers each.

The nearest food service and general store are at Lake Village, about 2 miles (3 km) north. For more groceries, gasoline, and self-service laundry, continue to Fishing Bridge, another 2 miles beyond the Lake Village turnoff. (See pages 168–69 for these facilities.)

17.3/3.3 **P** Unmarked side road for fishing access or strolling along the lake. No picnic tables.

19.0/1.6 Entrance to Lake Village.

FACILITIES AT LAKE VILLAGE

Lake Village has the oldest and most beautifully situated hotel in the park and serves visitors with its many other practical facilities, including a clinic (with an emergency heliport), a general store, post office, lodge, and cabins.

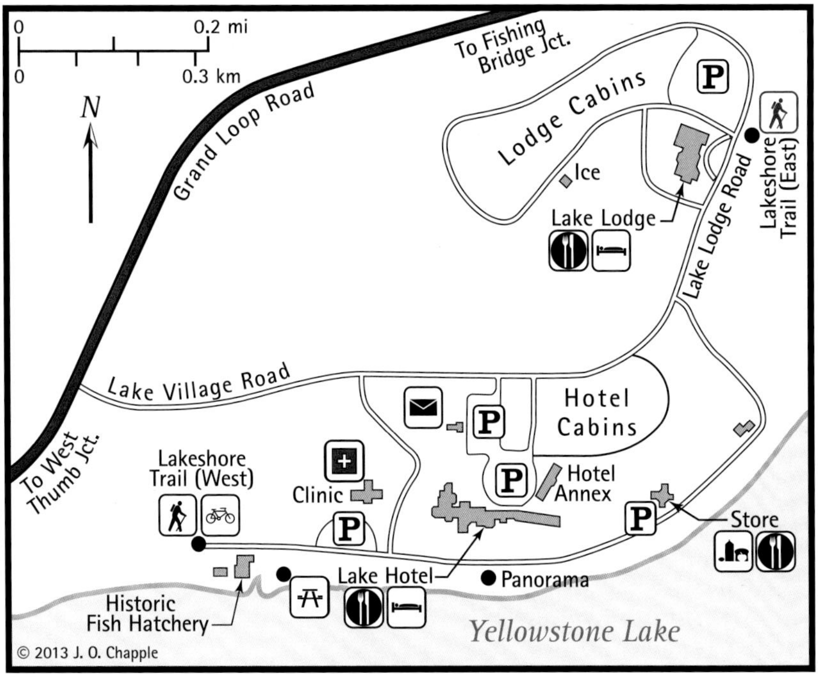

Lake Village

(2) After the turn onto the Lake Village side road, the first right turn leads toward the shore. If you turn right again off this side road, you'll find the clinic. West of the clinic there are a couple of lakefront picnic tables. In front of Lake Hotel, where a boat dock used to be, is a beautiful mountain panorama over the lake. Here you can see a large part of the southeastern quadrant of Yellowstone Park, from Pyramid Peak south to Mount Sheridan.

The large building at the far end of this side road is the now-closed Lake Fish Hatchery, for many years the largest game fish hatchery in the United States. From 1913 until the 1950s, fish were raised to fingerling size from harvested eggs, then planted in lakes and streams throughout the park and sent to many localities outside the park.

Wheelchair-accessible restrooms are available at Lake Hotel and Lake Lodge and outside the general store.

There are two segments of trail along the lakeshore stretching from about 1 mile (1.6 km) west of the hatchery building past Lake Hotel and Lake Lodge northeast to Fishing Bridge Junction. This was a stretch of the Grand Loop Road until the Lake bypass was constructed in the early 1970s. Biking is allowed on the segment of the old roadbed west of the clinic.

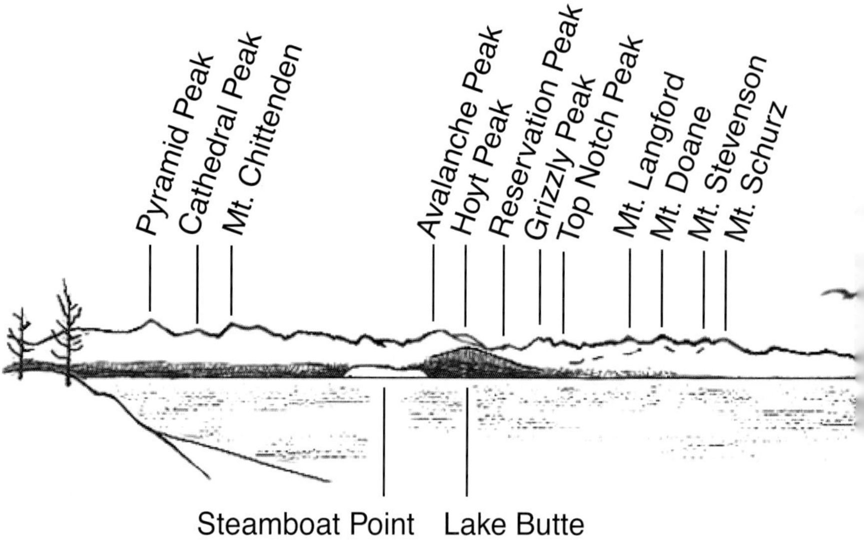

Lake Hotel Panorama*

Left to right (east to southwest):

Pyramid Peak (10,508 ft / 3,203 m) and jagged **Cathedral Peak** (10,765 ft / 3,281 m).

Mt. Chittenden (10,177 ft / 3,102 m) and its neighboring peak to the south form a saddle on the eastern boundary of the park.

Mountains outside the park boundary.

Steamboat Point on the lakeshore.

Flat-topped **Avalanche Peak** (10,568 ft / 3,221 m) and **Hoyt Peak** (10,506 ft / 3,202m) slightly behind and to its right. In front of Avalanche and Hoyt is **Lake Butte**, covered with trees.

Reservation Peak (10,629 ft / 3,240 m), with its diagonal border capping of dark rock, is much farther back and to the south of the East Entrance Road.

Grizzly Peak (9948 ft / 3,032 m) and **Top Notch Peak** (10,238 ft / 3,121 m) are next (the notch is not visible from here).

The next three pyramid-shaped peaks are named for early explorers of the park:

Mt. Langford (10,750 ft / 3,277 m) farthest back and **Mts. Doane** (10,656 ft / 3,248 m) and **Stevenson** (10,352 ft / 3,155 m). Nathaniel P. Langford and Lt. Gustavus C. Doane were leaders of the 1870 expedition through the park. James Stevenson was geologist Ferdinand V. Hayden's manager and chief assistant on all his western ventures.

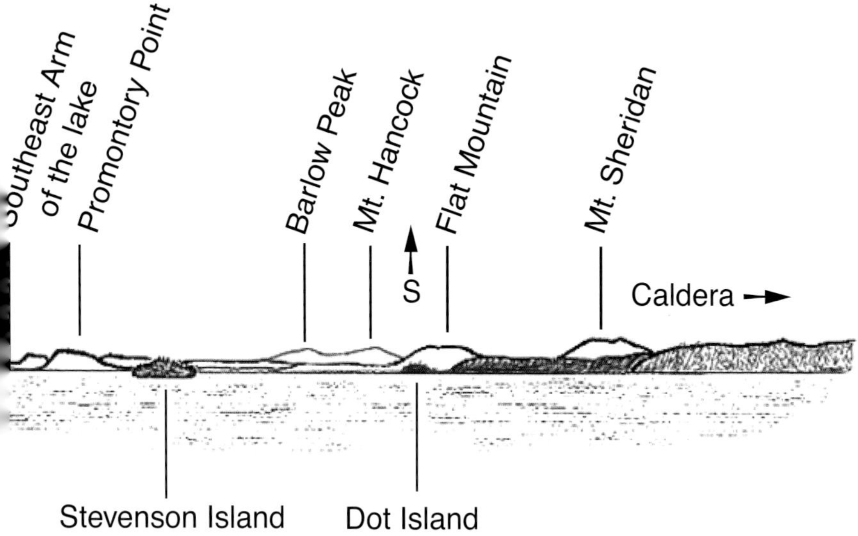

Just to the right of Mt. Stevenson is **Mt. Schurz** (11,163 ft / 3,402 m), named for Carl Schurz, secretary of the interior (1877–81) and strong supporter of the park.

The highest peaks in the park show their tops to the right of Mt. Schurz, and the relatively level area in front of them (to the southeast) reaches to the Thorofare Corner 30 miles away.

You can see where the **Southeast Arm** of the Lake occupies a gap in the high ground.

Promontory Point between the two arms, and the north end of **Stevenson Island** obscuring the **South Arm**.

Almost due south is the long top of **Flat Mountain** (9,168 ft / 2,794 m), with **Dot Island** in front of it. At the left flank of Flat Mountain is the much higher **Mt. Hancock** (10,214 ft / 3,113 m) near the park's south boundary, and to the left of it another high mountain, **Barlow Peak** (9,622 ft / 2,933 m). Gen. W. S. Hancock, a Union general wounded at Gettysburg, was Commander of the army's Department of Dakota in 1871, when the peak was named for him. In 1871, Capt. John Barlow led an expedition in tandem with Hayden's expedition and explored in this area.

Mt. Sheridan (10,305 ft / 3,141 m), farthest to the right, honors a champion of Yellowstone, Gen. Philip H. Sheridan.

Lake Hotel★

Lake Hotel (called Lake Yellowstone Hotel by the concessionaire in recent years) suggests 1920s casual elegance. The Lake String Quartet has played in the sunroom during cocktail and dinner hours since 1999. The dining room (reservations required) has an outstanding ambience and good food. The hotel is the most carefully planned and comfortable in the park. Lake Hotel also has a deli and gift shop.

U.S. presidents Warren G. Harding and Calvin Coolidge stayed here on their trips through the park. From the *Haynes Guide* for 1912: "Hotel at the Outlet.—This spacious and elegantly appointed hotel tends greatly toward making Yellowstone Lake the resort par excellence of the Park. Here everything is so arranged that guests can spend the entire season, if they so desire, making short, easy trips of sight-seeing or exploration to all points of the great reserve." Few people have the time or inclination to spend "the entire season" these days, but the hotel has not changed much.

The central portion of the hotel was completed in 1891, and additions were finished in 1902, 1903, 1923, and 1928. If you look closely, you can see that the east wing does not quite line up with the hotel's central portion. It was believed that a large rock underground had changed architect Robert Reamer's plans, but no such rock has been found, leaving an unsolved mystery.

Reamer added some of the colonial touches at the time of the additions, including the imposing Ionic columns, dormer windows, and small third-floor balconies. He also extended the lounge toward Yellowstone Lake; guests now enjoy views in three directions from the lounge windows. The porte cochere over the hotel driveway was added in 1920. After extensive renovations took place in the early 1980s, there are now nearly 300 rooms, including those in the annex and simple cabins at the rear.

To see the **Lake Hotel Panorama** of almost the entire southeastern quadrant of the park (described on the previous two pages), go down to the site of a former boat dock directly in front of the hotel.

Lake Hotel, Yellowstone's most elegant accommodations.

East of Lake Hotel along the shore you'll find a general store with lunch counter and the now closed 1922 Lake Ranger Station, with its octagonal community room and central four-sided stone fireplace.

Beyond the store and ranger station is **Lake Lodge** and its many cabins, with 186 spaces (for two to four visitors). The lodge, built and added to between 1919 and 1929, contains the cabin registration office, cafeteria, gift shop, and self-service laundry.

The **Lakeshore Trail** eastern section begins in the meadow below Lake Lodge and continues about 1 mile (1.6 km) northeast to Fishing Bridge. Although somewhat marshy, this is a beautiful way to enjoy views of the lake and mountains.

Yellowstone Lake Recreation

Swimming in Yellowstone Lake is strongly discouraged, even forbidden at West Thumb. This is due to the extremely cold water—after all, the lake's elevation is nearly 8,000 feet (3,400 m). On a recent hot July day the surface water temperature behind Fishing Bridge Visitor Center was 55°F (13°C), but this was rare, and lakes like this one have colder layers beneath the surface. Signs at Bridge Bay are explicit: "Warning—water extremely cold. Survival time limited to twenty minutes."

Boating is allowed from several launch sites, but motorboats are restricted to Grant Village and Bridge Bay Marina. Permits and flotation devices are required; see the Travel Tips for more information. Be careful when boating! The lake is famous for sudden squalls, especially in the afternoon, when waves can be as high as 6 feet. At least 40 drowning deaths have occurred on the lake in the park's history; most have involved small boats.

Fishing opens on June 15th in Yellowstone Lake, but permits and regulations must be acquired first from a ranger station, visitor center, or general store. See the Living Things and Travel Tips chapters for more about fish and fishing in the park.

Continuing on the Grand Loop Road

19.6/1.0 Elephant Back Trailhead. A 4-mile (6.4 km) trail with a loop at the top climbs **Elephant Back Mountain** about 800 feet (250 m) to a spectacular view of Yellowstone Lake, but be aware that early in the season you need to inquire about grizzly bear activity in the area. The mountain's name, one of the park's oldest, stems from the shape of its steep sides and rounded summit. Elephant Back Mountain is part of a very large 153,000-year-old lava flow.

Across the road from the trailhead, a short trail leads to Lake Lodge.

20.6/0.0 Fishing Bridge Junction (sometimes called Lake Junction). Fishing Bridge and the East Entrance are to the east; Mud Volcano, Hayden Valley, and Canyon Junction to the north; Lake Village, Bridge Bay Marina, and West Thumb to the southwest. For facilities at Fishing Bridge, see page 168.

IV. EASTERN SECTION

From Cody to the East Entrance

Starting your trip at Cody, Wyoming, you may enjoy visiting one or more of the town's five western museums or attending a rodeo. Accommodations are available in Cody and at numerous guest ranches along the road leading to Yellowstone's East Entrance, 53 miles (85 km) from the town.

Heading directly west, at Buffalo Bill Dam you'll find a visitor center with interesting exhibits. Campgrounds and numerous places for water sports are available in the state park around the reservoir. For several miles before you reach Yellowstone, wonderfully bizarre rock formations line the road.

A longer but very scenic road over the mountains from Cody to Yellowstone is the Chief Joseph Highway. To take the longer route, go north from the center of town and turn northwest (left) on Wyoming Highway 120 in less than one-half mile (0.8 km). After about 17 miles (27 km), turn left (or west) on Wyoming 296 to cross Dead Indian Pass and descend to Cooke City, Montana,

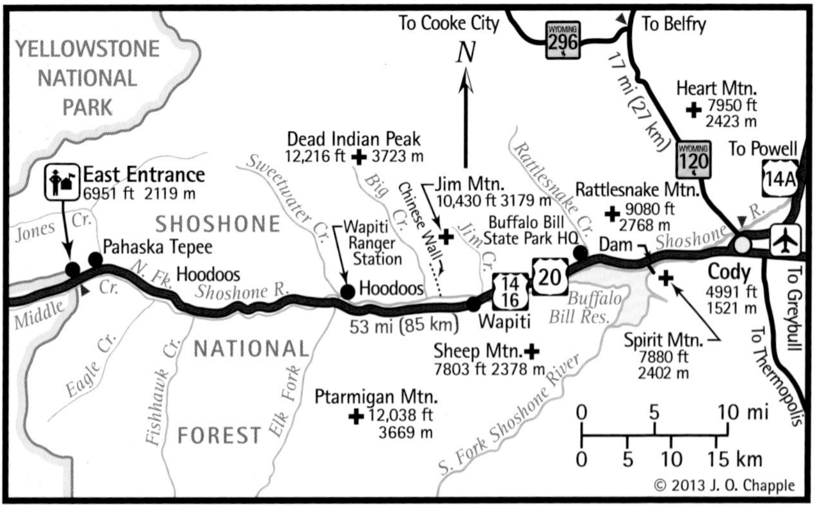

Approach to the East Entrance

and the Northeast Entrance. It's a total of 81 miles (130 km) by this route from Cody to the park. (See page 195 in "Approaches to the Northeast Entrance" for a description of the Chief Joseph Highway.)

CODY, WYOMING | **YELLOWSTONE REGIONAL AIRPORT**

Population: 9,520 | *2.3 mi. (3.7 km) SE*

Among the Wyoming gateway communities, the growing town of Cody is rivaled only by Jackson for its complete range of tourist attractions and facilities. Cody has the advantage of having considerably lower-priced accommodations than does Jackson.

William Frederick Cody, who, with George Beck, founded the town in 1896, was world famous as Buffalo Bill, a name he won as a young man by killing more than 4,000 buffaloes in a few months' time. His prowess as a hunter and Indian scout was exceeded only by his fame as a showman. From 1883 well into the twentieth century, he toured the United States and Europe extensively with his Wild West spectacle. He made a fortune but lost almost all of it in well-meant, but mostly unsuccessful, speculative ventures.

The town of Cody was the terminus of the Burlington Route, a railroad that operated from 1901 to 1956. Cody still has some historic buildings, including the 1902 Irma Hotel, named for Buffalo Bill's daughter.

The Buffalo Bill Historical Center houses five fine museums. For one admission price, you can visit the **Whitney Gallery of Western Art**, the **Buffalo Bill Museum**, the **Plains Indians Museum**, the **Cody Firearms Museum**, and the **Draper Museum of Natural History**, whose interactive exhibits center around the Greater Yellowstone Ecosystem. Worth a stop is the **Old Trail Town** just west of town on the road to Yellowstone. It's a collection of historic western buildings, including one used by Butch Cassidy and the Wild Bunch.

Other attractions include a nightly rodeo during summer months and, on a June weekend, the **Plains Indian Museum Powwow**, a social gathering that includes competitive dancing. There are two annual events in July: the **Cody Stampede** and the **Yellowstone Jazz Festival**. The Stampede is two days of "whooping it up," with parades, rodeos, barbecues, and Western entertainment.

U.S. Highways 14/16/20

This road (called the Buffalo Bill Scenic Byway by the Forest Service) goes west from Cody to Yellowstone. Just beyond the rodeo grounds, if you park near the last building on the right (north) side of the road, you can walk to the rim of the canyon of the Shoshone River (properly called the North Fork of the Shoshone) to see what's left of a geothermally heated pool at DeMaris Springs. A sulfur mine was located a bit farther along the road before World War I.

"Colter's Hell" and John Colter

The area along the Shoshone River here was called Colter's Hell by nineteenth-century trappers. Native American Indians and trappers used the Shoshone River Canyon and Sylvan Pass as an east-west passage through the high Absaroka Range. Probably the first white person to use this pass and the first to see Yellowstone's marvels was mountain man John Colter. Colter reported information about his 1806–8 traverse of the area to Capt. William Clark of the Lewis and Clark Expedition, who recorded it on a map. John Colter may have seen at least some of the hot spring basins and must have told people about them, but they did not believe him.

A large tar spring that gave off sulfurous odors near the junction of the North and South Forks of the Shoshone River came to be called Colter's Hell, and the river was called the Stinkingwater River throughout the nineteenth century. In 1835, "Colter's Hell" showed up in Washington Irving's version of an early explorer's journal, *The Adventures of Captain Bonneville.* Somehow the name had become transposed to the whole of the Yellowstone thermal area as a derisive term, with the implication that Colter had not seen the wonders he had described.

The dual confusion over Colter's veracity and exactly where Colter's Hell was located persisted until about 50 years ago, when historian Merrill J. Mattes determined that the name referred to hot springs in the Shoshone River Canyon and not to Yellowstone Park.

The Wyoming Legislature changed the name Stinkingwater River to Shoshone River in 1901, when Cody was first being settled and the road into Yellowstone was being improved.

You enter the Shoshone Canyon and cross the river almost simultaneously, with Rattlesnake Mountain on the north and Spirit Mountain (also called Cedar Mountain) on the south. This whole area was important to the people of the Crow tribe. Young Crow vision questers, seeking to become tribal leaders and medicine men, visited the land that is now under Buffalo Bill Reservoir.

Automobile use of the Shoshone Canyon road began in 1915. Here's what it looked like to the author's grandfather, Montana mountaineer Fred Inabnit, as he drove up the old road in 1918:

> The Shoshone canyon is so narrow and winding that you can hardly see from the bench [rim of the canyon] where the valley cut through. You follow the river closely here as there is no other way possible, at times several hundred feet above it and then dipping down almost into the water. The roads are rocky, some places on and through solid rock and up and down steep hills. . . . The

> canyon is a beautiful sight, both its sides reaching up to near timber line, either perpendicular or steep. We could see the dam something over a mile away and before reaching it the road climbs way up above the river only to take another dip so as to make a good long steep climb to reach the level of the dam again.

The road was reconstructed after World War II, so that traveling through it has become much less of an adventure. In fact, on the modern road you'll hardly notice the more than 3,500-foot (1,080 m) climb from Cody to Sylvan Pass inside the park, a distance of 60 miles (96 km).

Seven miles (11 km) from Cody and immediately beyond the long third tunnel is 353-foot-high (108 m) **Buffalo Bill Dam**, the tallest dam in the world when completed in 1910. Looking down from the dam is rather like peering from the top of a 35-story building, with the added thrill of roaring water below creating a tremendous spray.

Shoshone Canyon road in 1917, by Jack Haynes.

You may want to pick up a pamphlet about the facilities available in **Buffalo Bill State Park** either at the visitor center or at the park's headquarters about 3 miles (5 km) up the road to the west.

The road passes along the northern edge of Buffalo Bill Reservoir, crosses the Shoshone River, and then passes the little town of Wapiti, named after the *wapiti* (elk). Soon after the sign about the local geology, you'll enter an area covered by what geologists call the Absaroka Volcanics. Around 50 million years ago, about a dozen major volcanic centers spread lava and tephra over a huge area from beyond the northwest corner to well southeast of Yellowstone Park (see the map of the Absaroka Volcanics, page 159).

Look at relatively low **Jim Mountain** to the north, where you can see the edges of the old volcanic lava flow layers. In the distance beyond Jim Mountain, you may catch a glimpse of high **Dead Indian Peak**, another of many mountains made of lava.

West of Wapiti, you'll be entering America's first national forest, the **Shoshone National Forest**, created in 1891 and called at that time the Yellowstone Timber Land Reserve. It was set aside to be a cushion of protection east and south of Yellowstone.

As you drive west, you'll begin to see the fantastic rock formations or hoodoos this road is famous for. About a mile (1.6 km) into the national forest, on the left (south), is the first of many named hoodoos, **Laughing Pig Rock**.

On the north side and almost perpendicular to the road is the **Chinese Wall**, actually a *dike*, a thin vertical sheet of hardened magma. In 4 to 5 miles (6–8 km), you'll see **Hanging Rock**, hanging almost over the road. Less than 1 mile (1.5 km) from this is **Goose Rock** at right center on the cliff top. In the same turnout area is the **Holy City**. Many equally fantastic shapes may inspire you to name them yourself.

One of the most easily recognized hoodoos is Goose Rock.

What's a Hoodoo?

To geologists, a *hoodoo* is a standing column or odd shape left when sedimentary rock has eroded unevenly. Here the process of making hoodoos began when the lava flows and tephra in the extensive Absaroka Range volcanic mountains were eroded. Rain sometimes turned the slopes to mud, mud slides came surging down the mountains, filled the valleys, and hardened into conglomerate rock, a sedimentary rock that consists of fragments from previously formed rock. The fragments range in size from tiny up to greater than fist size.

Over the millennia, other lava flows covered some of these sediments. After relatively minor earth stresses fractured the rocks, rain and the freezing and thawing of water in the vertical cracks eroded the rock to form cliffs or columns. The tops of the columns occur where a layer of rock more resistant to erosion sheltered the underlying soft layers. Some of these columns developed into the bizarre shapes called hoodoos.

Observers have used their imaginations in naming about 60 hoodoos. At one of them, Chimney Rock, about 16 miles (26 km) west of Wapiti, the road goes close enough to reveal how the flat-lying layers of pebbly rock alternate with finer-grained sandy layers.

Extent of Absaroka Volcanics

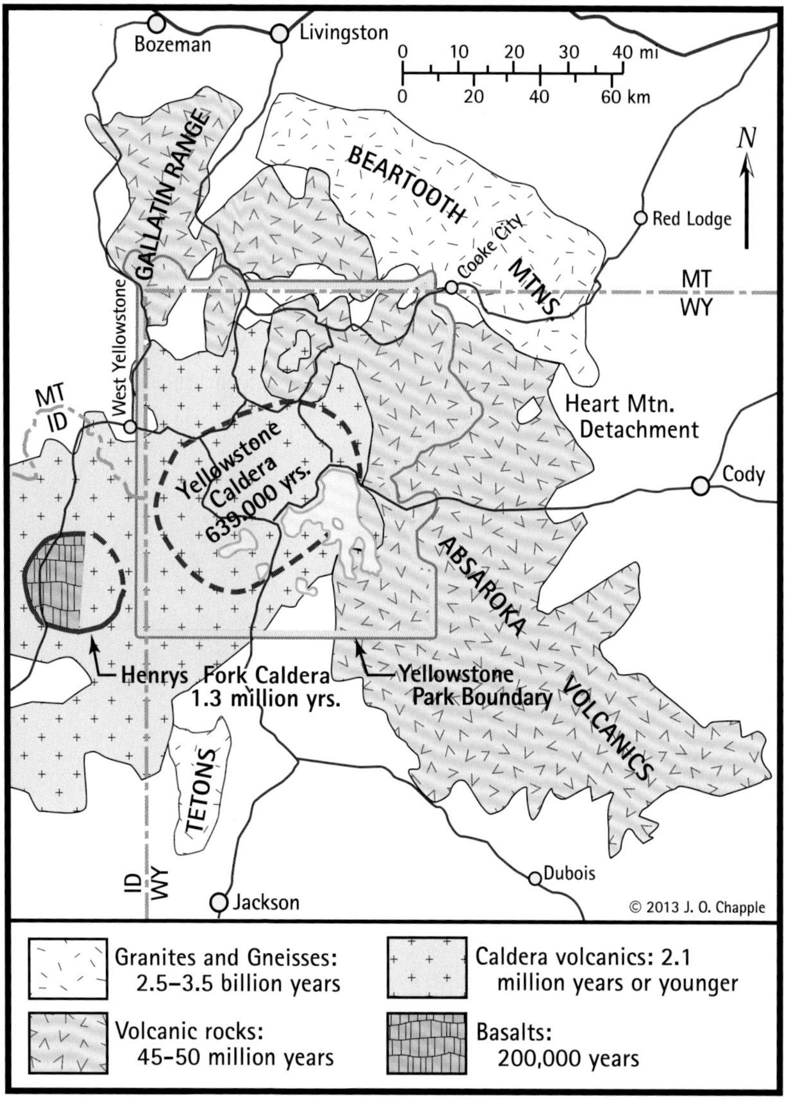

Adapted with permission from Mountain Press Publishing Company's *Roadside Geology of Montana*, 2nd edition, 1991, by David R. Lageson and Darwin R. Spearing.

About 20 miles (32 km) northwest of these roadside formations is another extensive area of hoodoos called Hoodoo Basin. It's in a remote spot near Yellowstone's eastern border. An easily accessible place to see hoodoos inside the park is at Devil's Den just north of Tower Fall.

In about 2 miles (3 km), you'll find the **Wapiti Ranger Station**, which dates from 1903–4 and is the oldest built with U.S. government funds. Midday tours of the old ranger station are sometimes offered. There's also an information center close to the road. The nearby wayside exhibit commemorates one hundred years of the U.S. Forest Service, 1891 to 1991.

The rangers will give you information about the nine Forest Service campgrounds along this road, backcountry trails in the area, and recent bear sightings.

For a few miles after the ranger station, the valley widens, making room for many guest ranches. There are no more hoodoos for a stretch. This area was severely burned in the 2008 Gunbarrel fire. Near Rex Hale Campground is a site called Mummy Cave (not open to the public), where archaeologists have discovered evidence of sporadic human habitation for about 9,000 years. In the same area are a few petrified trees, turned to stone by the same geologic events as in Yellowstone Park.

The last two easy-to-find hoodoos near the road are **Elephant Head** and **Chimney Rock**.

Chimney Rock has eroded away from its neighboring cliff.

About 2 miles (3 km) east of Yellowstone's boundary, the road crosses the North Fork of the Shoshone, which it's been following since Cody. From here into the park, we ascend **Middle Creek**, centered between other North Fork tributaries called Jones Creek and Eagle Creek.

You pass Sleeping Giant Campground and ski area (for cross-country and downhill skiing) and historic **Pahaska Tepee**, Buffalo Bill's hunting lodge, one hundred years old in 2004 and now open for free tours. The road from Cody is kept open this far all winter. The lodge's associated cabins and restaurant are the last facilities before entering Yellowstone.

From the East Entrance to Fishing Bridge Junction

The East Entrance Road is most noted for passing among high mountains and over Sylvan Pass, as well as for spectacular views of Yellowstone Lake and of nearby mountain ranges. Sparkling Eleanor and Sylvan Lakes catch your eye at the top of the pass, and farther along are viewpoints from which you can often see all the way to the Grand Tetons. Before reaching Fishing Bridge, the road closely follows the lakeshore. It's 26 miles (42 km) from the East Entrance to Fishing Bridge Junction.

Special Caution: Much of the area accessible from the East Entrance Road, especially around the Pelican Creek drainage, is prime grizzly bear territory in the first half of the summer, when the bears are feeding on spawning trout. It is prudent to check with rangers before hiking and never to hike alone.

Road Log

0.0/26.0 Yellowstone Park boundary.

0.1/25.9 (2) East Entrance station. Stop here to pay the entrance fee (see the Travel Tips for fee information). A side road leads north to service buildings and the ranger station. Restrooms are just inside the entrance.

Yellowstone Park's Eastern Edge

A glance at any current map of Yellowstone Park, such as the map on pages 2–3, shows that its boundaries are mostly straight, except for the eastern edge. In fact, if you look closely at that ragged edge, you can imagine the outline of a cute snub-nosed bear cub. Its ear sticks up at the Northeast Entrance, its brow and nose squiggle through the northern Absaroka Range—and you might even make a case for a right paw east of Yellowstone Lake!

The original Yellowstone National Park was a perfect rectangle, its borders specified by the 1872 act of Congress that set aside the land. The eastern border ran along the 110th meridian "passing ten miles to the eastward of the most eastern point of Yellowstone lake." Then why is this side of the park so irregular today?

In 1929, the original eastern border was revised, turning over to the Forest

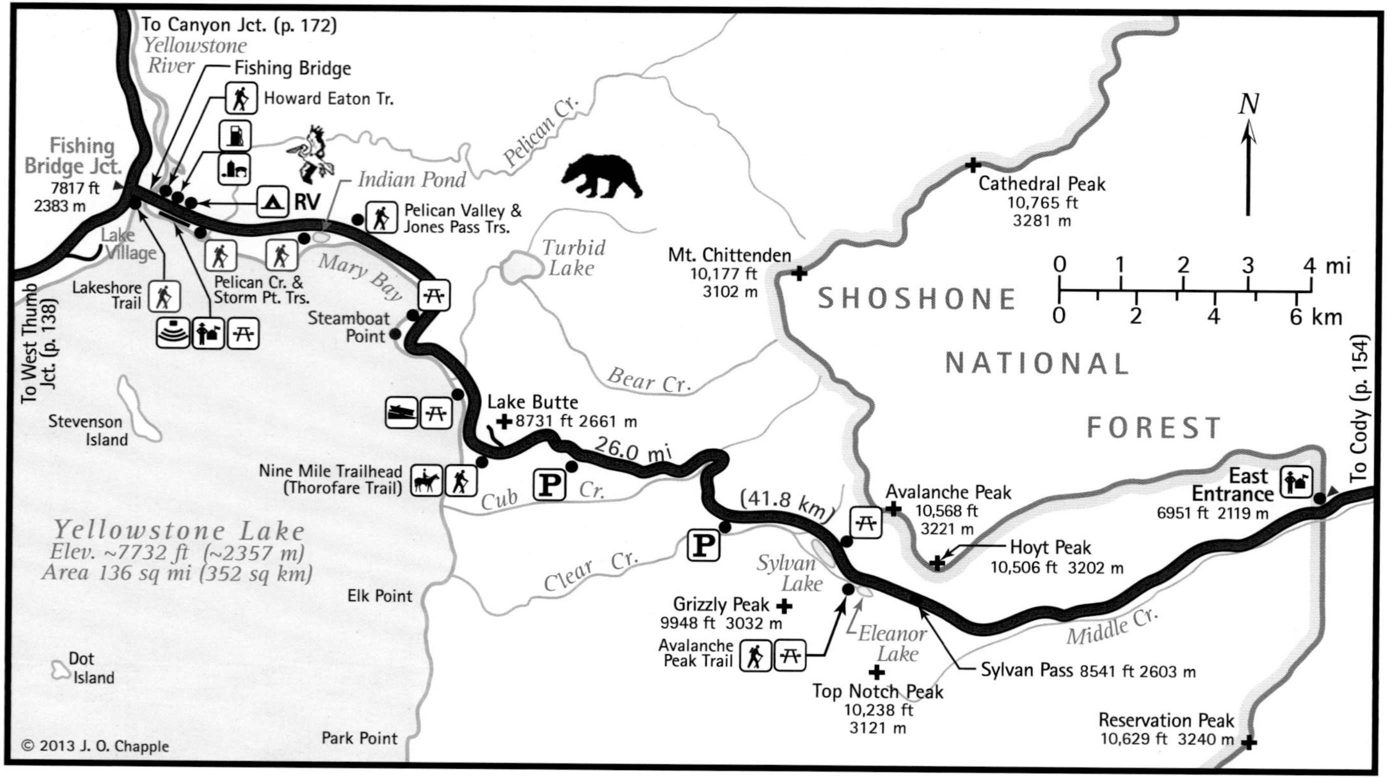
To Canyon Jct. (p. 172)
Yellowstone River
Fishing Bridge
Howard Eaton Tr.
RV
Fishing Bridge Jct.
7817 ft
2383 m
Indian Pond
Pelican Cr.
Pelican Valley & Jones Pass Trs.
Lake Village
Lakeshore Trail
Pelican Cr. & Storm Pt. Trs.
Mary Bay
Steamboat Point
Turbid Lake
Bear Cr.
Mt. Chittenden
10,177 ft
3102 m
Cathedral Peak
10,765 ft
3281 m
N
0 1 2 3 4 mi
0 2 4 6 km
SHOSHONE
NATIONAL
FOREST
To West Thumb Jct. (p. 138)
Stevenson Island
Lake Butte
8731 ft 2661 m
26.0 mi
(41.8 km)
Nine Mile Trailhead
(Thorofare Trail)
Cub Cr.
Clear Cr.
Yellowstone Lake
Elev. ~7732 ft (~2357 m)
Area 136 sq mi (352 sq km)
Elk Point
Dot Island
Park Point
© 2013 J. O. Chapple
Avalanche Peak
10,568 ft
3221 m
Hoyt Peak
10,506 ft 3202 m
Sylvan Lake
Grizzly Peak
9948 ft 3032 m
Avalanche Peak Trail
Eleanor Lake
Top Notch Peak
10,238 ft
3121 m
Sylvan Pass 8541 ft 2603 m
Middle Cr.
East Entrance
6951 ft 2119 m
To Cody (p. 154)
Reservation Peak
10,629 ft 3240 m

East Entrance to Fishing Bridge Junction

Service any land east of the Absaroka summits and, at the same time, annexing some of the headwaters of streams already in the park. Thus, Crow and Jones Creeks, which flow east out of the mountains north of Sylvan Pass to the North Fork of the Shoshone River, are entirely outside the park. Almost all the tributaries of the Lamar River (farther north) are within the park. Most of the eastern border now follows drainage divides, meandering along ridge crests and over mountain peaks.

3.0/23.0 (P) For the next mile or so, there are several parking areas and a road toward Middle Creek. Some of the turnouts provide good views of the mountains.

The original East Entrance Road followed Middle Creek more closely than it does now. Pleasant features of the present road in early to mid summer are the riot of color from roadside wildflowers and the numerous small waterfalls that rush down from the hillsides above. But don't drink the water—it may not be safe.

As the road gradually climbs toward Sylvan Pass, you'll see trees on both sides that are dying from a mountain pine beetle infestation. Damage from fires in 2001 and 2003 is also visible to the south.

Corkscrew Bridge afforded a manageable grade up Sylvan Pass on the original East Entrance Road.

6.5/19.5 Stop at the **Corkscrew Bridge Viewpoint** to see a trace of the very unusual Corkscrew Bridge (also called Spiral Bridge). You can now see only a gently curving smooth path, but a century ago it was an engineering marvel. At the bottom of the Sylvan Pass grade was a large and excellent cold spring, Mammoth Crystal Spring, the source of Middle Creek. The spring is now very hard to locate.

6.9/19.1 Sylvan Pass (8,541 ft / 2,603 m). In 1901, Army Engineer Captain Chittenden, who designed this road, wrote that Sylvan Pass **[GEO.6]** is "unique among mountain passes in that it is almost entirely loosened from the cliffs on either side by the action of frost. This broken rock varies in size from fine pebbles to pieces a cubic yard in volume." You may wonder why it was named Sylvan, meaning forested, when it's so rocky. The pass is named after the larger of the two tree-ringed lakes near it.

North of the road is **Hoyt Peak** (10,506 ft / 3,202 m), named for John W. Hoyt, first governor of the Territory of Wyoming and later University of Wyoming president. Hoyt Peak is part of the volcanic Absaroka Range.

7.6/18.4 (2) **Eleanor Lake**, probably named in 1901 by road engineer Chittenden for his infant daughter.

In Praise of High Mountain Passes

A Yellowstone experience that's always a delight in good weather is the opportunity to sample a high pass in the Rocky Mountains. At three places in the park, the main road climbs above 8,000 feet (2,440 m). Besides Sylvan Pass, the other high passes are Craig Pass between Old Faithful Village and West Thumb Junction (8,262 ft / 2,518 m), and Dunraven Pass, the highest (8,873 ft / 2,704 m), between Tower Fall and Canyon Junction.

What's Different about Mountain Passes?

You can tell you're in a special environment even without getting out of your car. In June and early July, there are still mounds of snow along the road. Waterfalls spill onto the road and fall down to the river.

You'll see a profusion of wildflowers in July and August. They have only a few weeks to show their splendors and produce their seeds.

Trees that grow this high on the mountainsides belong to species that have adapted to the climate, predominantly subalpine fir and whitebark pine. In very high windy places, they may show crooked growth called *krummholz*, German for "crooked wood," with branches only on the side away from the wind.

Sometimes there are gorgeous vistas at or near the mountain passes. In the case of Sylvan Pass, the best views are a few miles to the west of the pass itself.

Some park animals spend the summer months this high or higher. Bears gorge themselves at the end of summer on berries and whitebark pine nuts. Especially around Dunraven Pass, you may see bighorn sheep if you look up to the crags above the road.

How Do You Feel?

At altitudes of over 8,000 feet (2,400 m), almost everyone feels some effects from the thinner air. You may feel dizzy, faint, or seem to have trouble getting your breath. The atmospheric pressure is 27 percent less than at sea level, thus the air around you is less dense, and you're only getting about three-quarters as much oxygen per breath. However, if you stay at high altitude for a few days, your body will usually accommodate at least partially to the reduced oxygen supply. Another high-altitude effect is increased UV radiation, even on cloudy days.

Look above the east end of the lake for a delightful small waterfall, named **Crecelius Cascade** for Chittenden's subordinate, who was responsible for building this stretch of road.

You can park in the picnic area at the west side of the lake for **Avalanche Peak Trail**. This trail takes you in a very steep 2 miles (3.2 km) to the top of Avalanche Peak. Rangers sometimes lead hikes up this trail; inquire at Fishing Bridge Visitor Center.

Snow avalanches are common in this area of steep mountainsides. In the spring, park rangers fire a cannon to try to create small snowslides and prevent the snow buildup that causes greater avalanches.

An unmaintained fisherman's trail, not shown on current maps, starts south of Eleanor Lake and follows Clear Creek down to the Thorofare Trail.

From Eleanor Lake to the edge of Mary Bay, evidence remains of the Grizzly East complex of fires, which burned more than 25,000 acres of forest in late summer of 2003.

8.7/17.3 (8) Sylvan Lake picnic area, with tables near the lake and across the road. Fishing in Sylvan Lake is catch and release only.

The mountain visible beyond the southeast end of Sylvan Lake is the aptly named **Top Notch Peak**. Above the trees to the south and closer to the lake is **Grizzly Peak**. Look on Grizzly Peak's northwest side for an obvious *cirque*, a natural amphitheater carved by a glacier.

Sylvan Lake may retain its ice into early summer (2008).

9.1/16.9 **P** Northwest end of Sylvan Lake.

11.0/15.0 **P** Teton Point turnout for the first good view of part of Yellowstone Lake, Mount Sheridan across the lake, and (on clear days) the Tetons.

12.3/13.7 The road makes a horseshoe curve to cross Cub Creek.

14.2/11.8 Unnamed ponds can be seen briefly along the road. The gas bubbles and turbid water in the ponds and colorful hillsides beyond them indicate a hydrothermally active area.

14.8/11.2 **P** The excellent panorama here, historically called the Teton Overlook, is described on page 166.

Yellowstone Lake and Mountains Panorama

Far left to right:

Three sharp peaks of the **Absarokas** poke above the trees: Grizzly, Doane, and Stevenson.

To the south are the **Tetons**, 60 miles away.

Flat Mountain at the southern edge of Yellowstone Lake.

To the right and behind Flat Mountain, **Mt. Sheridan**, with its fire lookout.

Frank Island, Yellowstone Lake's largest island, heavily burned in a 2003 fire, and **Dot Island**, with **West Thumb Bay** to its right. Behind and between the islands is high, flat **Thorofare** country.

To the far right is **Stevenson Island**, the long, narrow one that can become two islands when water is very high in the lake.

16.3/9.7 **Lake Butte** side road to the north, about 0.8 mile (1 km) to a pretty view. The butte is the most westerly peak of Absaroka volcanics in this part of the park.

The panoramic view from the top of this road takes in more of Yellowstone Lake and distant mountains than you can see from any other road in the park. The view stretches (right to left) from the white **Sulphur Hills** above rounded **Mary Bay** and the hydrothermally altered rocks of **Steamboat Point** to the northwest, through the distant Gallatin Range in the northwestern corner of the park, across the Yellowstone Caldera to the west, to the mountains near the southern arms of the lake and to the faintly visible Tetons.

17.0/9.0 Nine Mile Trailhead for the **Thorofare Trail** on a short side road to the south. This is a long pack trail that parallels the lakeshore to the park's Thorofare corner.

The southeast area of the park is called the Thorofare. The name dates from the fur-trading days of the 1820s and 1830s, when the only known southern route into the Yellowstone Plateau was by way of Two Ocean Pass and down the Yellowstone River. Today the Thorofare patrol cabin has the distinction of being the place farthest from a maintained road in the contiguous United States.

Between here and Butte Springs, we cross into the Yellowstone Caldera; here the caldera rim runs approximately northeast-southwest.

18.2/7.8 **(1)** **Sedge Bay**, a canoe launching spot. Look out in the lake along this stretch of road to see **Pelican Roost**, a tiny rocky point that may be all but submerged in early summer.

18.3/7.7 Butte Springs, a small thermal area north of the road. Fire damage from 2003 extends more than 10 miles from here east.

19.6/6.4 **P** Two turnouts in this area afford excellent views of the lake at **Steamboat Point**. The lower turnout displays a sign about Mary Bay's hot lake bed. Geologist Albert C. Peale wrote in 1878 that at this spot there was located "a powerful steam vent from which a vast column of steam escapes with a continuous roar that exactly resembles the escape from a huge steamboat," but you can no longer hear that sound. The red stain on Steamboat's formation is *cinnabar*, mercuric sulfide, which is poisonous.

Steamboat Point has two hydrothermal features, Steamboat Spring and Locomotive Vent.

20.0/6.0 (5) Turnout at **Holmes Point**, named for W. H. Holmes after the initials W. H. H. were found on a rock here. Holmes was the artist and geologist with the 1872 and 1878 Hayden Surveys.

From this point the road follows **Mary Bay** of Yellowstone Lake for a while. Mary Bay was named for Mary Force, the girlfriend of Henry Elliot, artist with the 1871 Hayden Survey. Mary's name remains on the bay, though when Elliot returned home, he married someone else.

The rounded forms and steep sides of Mary Bay attest to the fact that it is an explosion crater. The Mary Bay crater dates back about 13,800 years. The bay has lots of underwater hot springs and the hottest spot in the lake, measured at 212°F (100°C).

21.6/4.4 Beach Springs north of the road is a small thermal area that often gives off a strong sulfur odor. Here the road is actually on a sandbar. The Beach Springs area was turned into a lagoon by the buildup of sand and gravel washed in by wave action during storms, forming an offshore bar.

22.7/3.3 Short road to the northeast leads to parking for the backcountry **Pelican Valley Trails**. Until early July, this area is closed by the park administration for bear management (see page 133 for more information). Make sure you consult a ranger at Fishing Bridge Visitor Center about current grizzly bear activity in this neighborhood before using any of these trails.

22.9/3.1 P Parking for Indian Pond and for Storm Point Nature Trail to the south. **Indian Pond** (called Squaw Lake for some years) was named in 1880 by Superintendent Norris, who had found Native American Indian wickiups, corrals, and lodgepoles in the area. A few years later, geologist Arnold Hague wrote that this was a favorite place for the Indians to manufacture implements, being near to stone quarries and to good hunting and fishing grounds. Notice the very steep sides of Indian Pond **[GEO.17]**, which, like Mary Bay, was created by a steam explosion, this one only 3,000 years ago.

During summer, daily ranger-led hikes cover the **Storm Point Nature Trail's** round-trip route, a walk of a little more than 2 miles (3.2 km). You might see yellow-bellied marmots or some of the local waterbirds. The circular depressions in the sandy soil are likely to be bison

Storm Point, named for the storms out of the southwest that it intercepts.

wallows where the animals roll, seeking warmth in winter and protection from biting insects in summer.

The beach between Mary Bay and the outlet of the Yellowstone River is called Diamond Beach because of its sparkling sand. The lake is usually too cold for swimming, but wading can be pleasant. Just north of Storm Point is **Concretion Cove**, where early day visitors found strangely shaped rocks and thoughtlessly carried them all away long ago.

24.2/1.8 [P] Short trail to a view of the lake and Pelican Creek's delta.

24.3/1.7 The mouth of **Pelican Creek** is a great place to see many types of ducks, Canada geese, California gulls, and pelicans.

24.4/1.6 Pelican Creek crossing and a 1,500-foot-long (460 m) causeway for the road. Pelican Creek drains the Mirror Plateau to the north.

If you could look down on Pelican Creek from above, you'd see several oxbow lakes, crescent-shaped ponds left behind when loops in a meandering stream are cut off.

Near here in 1839, fur trapper Osborne Russell and a companion were attacked and wounded by Piegan (Blackfeet) Indians, and five other trappers were killed. The creek was named for a later incident in which a prospector shot a large bird for dinner; it was not a goose as he'd thought, but an unsavory pelican—hence the name.

24.6/1.4 **Pelican Creek Nature Trail**. This short loop (less than 1 mile/1.5 km) to Yellowstone Lake consists of a boardwalk across a marsh and a path through the woods.

FACILITIES AT FISHING BRIDGE VILLAGE

NOTE: See the map on page 162.

25.2/0.8 **Fishing Bridge RV Campground** road. This campground is the only place in the park where recreational vehicle owners can find a sewer hookup at each site. No tents or tent trailers are allowed. The more than 325 sites must be reserved in advance. A small concession building and a self-service laundry and showers are nearby.

25.3 to 25.6/0.7 to 0.4 A short frontage road to the north parallels the main road for Fishing Bridge facilities.

From east to west along the frontage road are an ice machine, public telephones, general store with soda fountain, and gas station. Housing for employees is also located here.

To hike on a segment of the **Howard Eaton Trail**, park along the service road a short distance behind the service station. This segment of the trail follows the east side of the Yellowstone River all the way from here to the South Rim of the Yellowstone River's canyon. It's a 6.5-mile (10.5 km) round-trip hike to view LeHardy's Rapids downstream. As with all trails in this area, check first with the rangers about recent bear activity.

A Case of Bears Winning Out over People

When park policy ended the feeding of bears by removing all park garbage dumps in 1970, encounters between humans and grizzly bears increased. Something had to be done, especially at Fishing Bridge, a popular spot for camping.

The bears come every year to fish in Yellowstone Lake's outlet and in its many tributaries. Now bears have been given first priority at this site. Visitors may not stay overnight, except in RVs. The campground across the main road was closed in 1990, and many cabins near the river were razed.

25.5/0.5 (11) (2) Road to **Fishing Bridge Visitor Center** and amphitheater. The picnic tables are to the west along the road, while restrooms are a short distance up a trail on the opposite side of the parking area. A pleasant sandy beach is just outside the back door of the visitor center.

Do you know what a phalarope looks like? You can find out in the visitor center, a National Historic Landmark that opened in 1931. You'll find lake bird and grizzly bear dioramas, a large map of Yellowstone Lake and environs, exhibits about lake habitats, and a small bookshop. (A phalarope is a small shorebird, as you can see in the museum display.)

25.7/0.3 P Alternate parking on the north for Howard Eaton Trail (described above) or for Fishing Bridge.

25.8/0.2 Fishing Bridge. Closed to fishing since 1973, Fishing Bridge should now be called Fish-Watching Bridge.

Fishing Bridge Visitor Center and Museum

Fishing from Fishing Bridge in 1925 (Frantz & Sharpe photo)

While the crowds of anglers catching their hooks in each other's hair are gone, many people do enjoy watching the cutthroat trout and long-nosed suckers, especially during spawning season. Both trout resident in the lake and those from the outlet are believed to spawn in this part of the Yellowstone River. The park's no-fishing policy at the bridge helps the trout and allows the traffic to pass without tie-ups.

The first Fishing Bridge, built in 1903 when the East Entrance Road was completed, crossed the outlet diagonally and was a little closer to the lake. It was steeply arched to allow the passage of rowboats. The present bridge dates from 1937 and has no arch but includes much-needed walkways.

25.9/0.1 (P) (hiking) Parking for Fishing Bridge and for the **Lakeshore Trail**. Head up the steps south of the road for this pleasant, easy trail. It goes for about 2 miles (3 km) round trip along the lake to the Lake Lodge area. Parts of this trail may be marshy.

26.0/0.0 Fishing Bridge Junction (sometimes called Lake Junction). To the southwest along the lake is West Thumb Junction, to the north are Canyon Junction and Canyon Village, and to the east is the East Entrance to the park.

From Fishing Bridge Junction to Canyon Junction

Leaving Fishing Bridge Junction and heading north, the Grand Loop Road closely follows the Yellowstone River all the way to the Grand Canyon of the Yellowstone. Highlights include the unusual thermal features of the Mud Volcano area, long views of the river as it descends gradually through the Hayden Valley, many convenient stops for fishing access and picnicking, and the summer home of bison, moose, pelicans, sandhill cranes, and Canada geese. Wolves of the Mollie's and Canyon Packs are sometimes seen from Hayden Valley turnouts, as is the occasional grizzly bear. The distance from Fishing Bridge to Canyon is about 15 miles (24 km).

Road Log

0.0/15.4 Fishing Bridge Junction (sometimes called Lake Junction). Canyon Village is to the north; Lake Village, Bridge Bay Marina, and West Thumb to the south; Fishing Bridge facilities and the East Entrance to the east.

About two miles north of the junction, burned areas on the road's west side remain from the 2008 LeHardy fire.

2.3/13.1 **Fishing Bridge Meadows**. A good spot for watching pelicans, gulls, ducks, and geese.

2.8/12.6 P Here and just to the north are two **LeHardy's Rapids** parking areas. A boardwalk and footpaths lead to the river, where in June and early July you can spot trout leaping up the rapids, returning to the lake after spawning in the river.

The walkway from the north parking lot is wheelchair-accessible and well marked.

Paul LeHardy met trouble at these rapids. He was a topographer accompanying a military reconnaissance of the park in 1873. At the rapids his makeshift raft was sucked to the bottom, forcing him and his partner to salvage what they could and tramp downriver to join their expedition near the falls of the Yellowstone.

The rapids are located along the center of the caldera and are part of the evidence that the tilting up of the lake basin at this end is due to movement of magma deep in the earth.

4.0/11.4 **(5)** LeHardy's picnic area.

4.7/10.7 **(6)** Cascade picnic area.

4.9/10.5 Interpretive signs about cutthroat trout and other wildlife. According to fish expert Todd Koel,

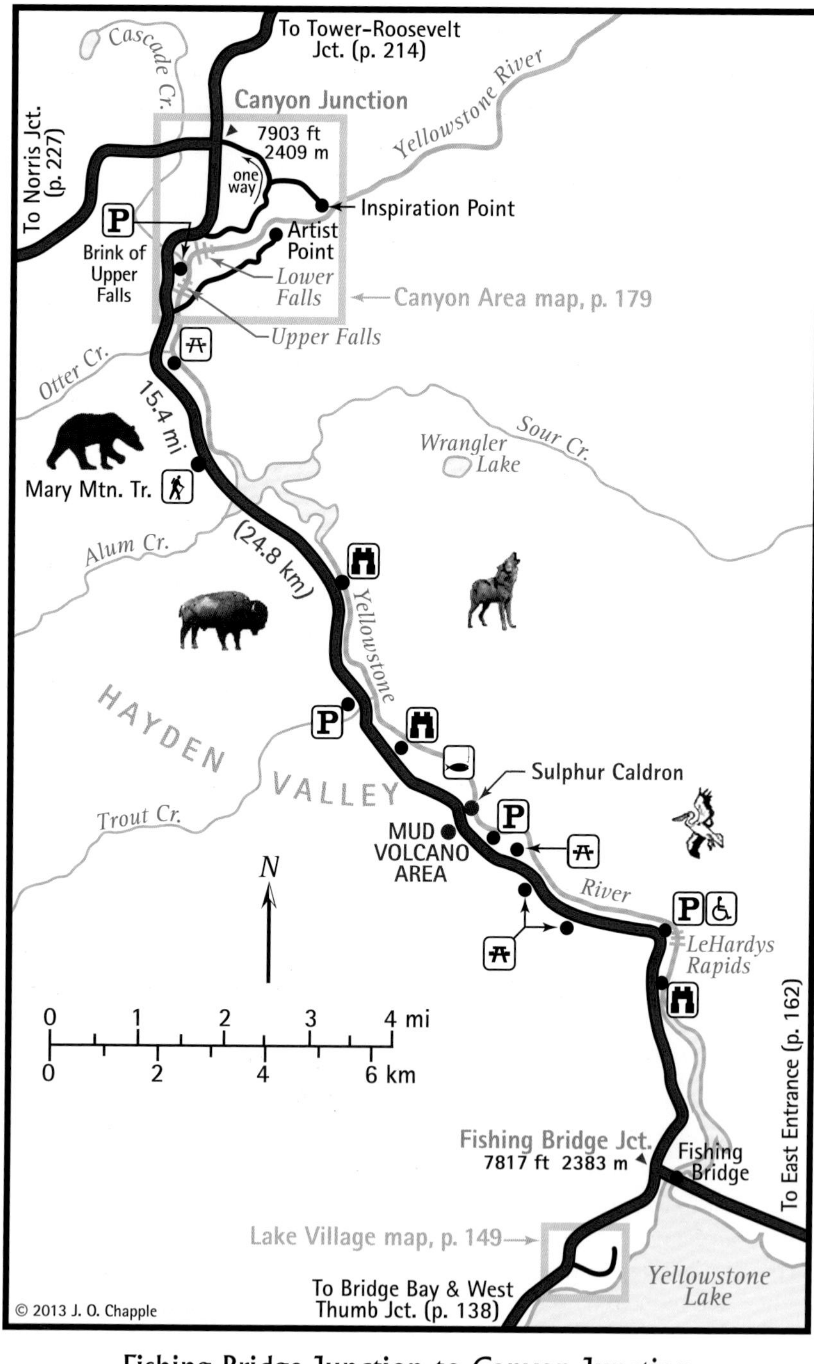

To Tower-Roosevelt Jct. (p. 214)
Cascade Cr.
Canyon Junction
Yellowstone River
To Norris Jct. (p. 227)
7903 ft 2409 m
one way
Inspiration Point
Artist Point
Brink of Upper Falls
Lower Falls
Canyon Area map, p. 179
Upper Falls
Otter Cr.
15.4 mi
(24.8 km)
Sour Cr.
Wrangler Lake
Mary Mtn. Tr.
Alum Cr.
Yellowstone
HAYDEN VALLEY
Sulphur Caldron
Trout Cr.
MUD VOLCANO AREA
N
River
LeHardys Rapids
0 1 2 3 4 mi
0 2 4 6 km
To East Entrance (p. 162)
Fishing Bridge Jct.
7817 ft 2383 m
Fishing Bridge
Lake Village map, p. 149
To Bridge Bay & West Thumb Jct. (p. 138)
Yellowstone Lake
© 2013 J. O. Chapple

Fishing Bridge Junction to Canyon Junction

The Name of This Ford

The name used for many years for this spot, Buffalo Ford, stems from a winter about 50 years ago when two rangers discovered several bison frozen in the ice here. However, Nez Perce Ford has been the official name since 1981. Here the Nez Perce crossed the river as they were fleeing the U.S. Army in 1877, attempting to reach Canada. Their route began in Idaho and ended in northern Montana, where they were finally forced to surrender.

many cutthroat spawn in the Yellowstone and its tributaries, then move back to the lake.

5.0/10.4 (17) Nez Perce Ford picnic area side road. No fishing is allowed in the west channel of the river here. Above and below this stretch of the river are areas extremely popular with fishermen, even though it's for catch and release only. According to data collected by the U.S. Fish and Wildlife Service, the same trout may be caught and released nine times in one season.

5.4/10.0 **P** Parking for river access and informal trails to two springs. The closer bubbling spring is surrounded by grasses, but the one in sparse trees and nearer the river, **Cold Water Geyser**, has a considerable rock crater and a crevice filled with water and bubbles of carbon dioxide. It erupted more or less regularly for about 50 years of the twentieth century and occasionally since then. In 1912 at least one tourist party used it as a natural bathtub. The carbon dioxide that powered this geyser is probably derived from the *limestones* below the caldera's volcanic rocks. There's a similar geyser near Green River, Utah.

5.8/9.6 **P** (4) Turnoff for Mud Volcano.

MUD VOLCANO AREA

If you have only a short time to spend, be sure to see Dragon's Mouth Spring and Mud Volcano at the north end of the walkway. For a longer visit, you might want to pick up a pamphlet from the box near the parking lot and follow the walk described below.

Unlike the water-driven basins of geysers and hot pools you find on the western Grand Loop Road, Mud Volcano is a vapor-driven system. Here steam rather than water rises from deep underground, and rain and snowmelt provide most of the water to the features. Before railings and boardwalks, early tourists considered the place "most repulsive and terrifying."

Near the center of the parking area's edge is **Mud Caldron**, a large, bubbling, gray lake that seems to have worn away or blown out the cliff behind it. In 1999, a hole created by hydrothermal action suddenly appeared in the parking lot. Features here are roiling, not boiling. There are no geysers.

Rangers sometimes lead hikes to visit fascinating off-trail features in this area; inquire at Fishing Bridge Visitor Center.

Mud Volcano Loop Walk

This trail loops around all the features in less than one mile (1.5 km). The climb is a little more gradual going clockwise (starting to your left).

NOTE: Only the north length of boardwalk, which includes Dragon's Mouth Spring, is wheelchair-accessible, since there are steps above Mud Volcano.

The first feature encountered, **Mud Geyser**, viewed from above, was a spectacular geyser when the park was first explored. It erupted to 40 or 50 feet (12–15 m) from its large pool and then drained dramatically. It's now usually a bubbling muddy lake with rare eruptions.

You can see evidence here that the soil is now too hot for any trees to grow. In 1978–79 a surge of local earthquake activity caused changes, including an increase in soil temperature that killed lodgepole pines, which were then blown down all around. The increased heat also created the **Cooking Hillside**, where the trail goes uphill. **Sizzling Basin** and **Churning Caldron** (up the hill) were affected, too. Sizzling Basin used to sizzle more than it does now, while Churning Caldron is now too hot for bacteria to form.

The newest large feature, south of the main walkway, is a seething mud pot, **Black Dragon's Caldron**, which formed in the winter of 1947–48. It must have begun with a terrific explosion, because trees were blown out by their roots, but no one happened to be here to see it. The pool has since grown much larger: it's about 200 feet (60 m) long. Hydrogen sulfide bubbles to the surface. The black color (or sometimes a deep gray when there's lots of water) is due to iron *sulfides*.

Huge and very acid **Sour Lake** beyond Black Dragon's Caldron is less hot than some of its neighbors, allowing bacteria and algae to thrive and color the water green. As you can see from the steam rising beyond Sour Lake, there are more thermal features where the boardwalk doesn't go. Please don't leave the boardwalk unless you're with a ranger.

The walkway crosses quiet meadow and forest, where you may see wildlife before reaching **Grizzly Fumarole**. This feature changes seasonally from a large, spattering mud pot to some quiet, steaming holes, depending on its water supply.

Mud Volcano★ is reached by boardwalk today, but in 1870, when the Washburn exploration party named it, there was only a steep hillside. Those

Black Dragon's Caldron (1986)

Acid Hot Springs

The Mud Volcano area and Norris Geyser Basin are the two easily accessible thermal basins that have great concentrations of acid hot springs. Sulphur Caldron, across the road and just north of here, has water that is more acidic than lemon juice (with a pH of 1.3). So much acid and sulfur in the water prevent the growth of multicolored bacteria and algae seen elsewhere.

Can you believe that anything can live in such an environment? Surprisingly, at least one microbe *(Sulfolobus acidocaldarius)* thrives here and actually feeds upon sulfur compounds such as hydrogen sulfide. It oxidizes the sulfur, turning it into sulfuric acid. Formerly classified as a bacterium, *Sulfolobus* is now known to belong to Archaea, a different domain of very old organisms. It is quite content in Yellowstone, growing well even at the amazingly high temperature of 194°F (90°C). These acidic pools and soils also harbor a more complex organism, a type of alga *(Cyanidium caldarium)* that grows only in acid conditions and lives at temperatures up to 133°F (57°C).

In the backcountry less than a mile from here, microbiologists have found a very hot pool with a diversity of life forms hitherto unimagined. In Yellowstone, scientists continue to learn about some of the oldest forms of life on earth.

who climbed the hill saw a cone from which mud splashed into the trees as much as 100 feet up and 200 feet away (30 and 60 m), making a tremendous racket. Only two years later, Superintendent Langford returned to find that "the loud detonations which resembled the discharges of a gun-boat mortar were no longer heard, and the upper part of the crater and cone had in a great measure disappeared, leaving a shapeless and unsightly hole much larger than the former crater. . . ." Today, Mud Volcano's dark gray water continues to bubble and churn inside a deep hole at the base of the hillside.

Dragon's Mouth Spring

Dragon's Mouth Spring★ is still fun to visit, although its activity has diminished in recent years. The belching waters from deep within its cavern make an amazing thumping sound. You may be mesmerized by the sound and the repetition of the surging action.

Continuing on the Grand Loop Road

5.9/9.5 (P) Sulphur Caldron parking area. A hot spot burst through the pavement here in about 1980, requiring a protective fence.

Sulphur Caldron is below the level of the road. You'll see more than one large pool and smaller bubbling or steaming ones. Sulphur Caldron is sometimes nearly dry; to its left is green **Turbulent Pool**. Sulfur and microorganisms that live on sulfur contribute to the yellow-green color. Acidic gases rotted the supporting wall; a new one was built in 1985.

6.2/9.2 South edge of **Hayden Valley**. The vista opens out here to take in a wide swampy valley. This is an excellent place to see wildlife, especially bison, large birds, and maybe wolves. You'll find several convenient turnouts in the next few miles.

The valley's namesake, Dr. Ferdinand Vandiveer Hayden, directed three scientific surveys of the Yellowstone region. Educated as a medical doctor, he had a strong interest in geology and the west, leading him to persuade Congress to fund exploratory parties into this area in 1871, 1872, and 1878. The reports from his first survey helped to convince Congress to establish Yellowstone National Park in 1872.

6.3/9.1 (P) Interpretive sign about Hayden Valley.

Yellowstone Lake Was Bigger Back Then

At the south end of Hayden Valley you can see terraces across the river that mark the shoreline of the much deeper lake that was here about 10,000 years ago, at the time when the last ice age was ending. At one point, Yellowstone Lake was 270 feet higher than at present and covered the entire valley. A glacier dammed the river downstream and filled the valley with water.

The lake sediments and the *till* (clay, sand, and gravel) left by the glaciers combined to form a densely packed type of soil that water can't soak through readily. The poor drainage prevents trees from becoming established. Notice where the trees are growing now—this tree line was always higher than the water level of the lake. Now that the ice has melted, the Yellowstone River and its tributaries meander lazily across the wet valley.

6.9/8.5 **Wildlife Overlook**. Hayden Valley is an excellent sanctuary for wildlife. Animals and birds you might see include bison (almost always), elk, deer, coyotes, wolves, grizzly bears; Canada geese, ravens, ospreys, pelicans, gulls, sandhill cranes, marsh hawks, eagles, peregrine falcons, and great blue herons; mallard, merganser, and Barrow's goldeneye ducks.

7.4/8.0 Elk Antler Creek crossing.

7.6/7.8 P Turnout to the west overlooks **Trout Creek**. If you stop and look down from the cliff, you'll see a maze of waterways that are all one stream.

Meanders and the Northern Pacific Railway

Trout Creek is an excellent example of *meanders*, or the windings a stream forms when it flows across nearly level ground. As the water flows through this remnant of the former lake bottom, it gradually cuts through the glacial till and lake sediments. If the river encounters a small obstruction, it goes around it. As a curve develops, the water flows faster on the outside of the curve, cutting still further, while on the inside of the curve, where the water flows slower, a sandbar of deposited sediment builds up.

Over a century ago people noticed that Trout Creek's meanders at the time resembled the Chinese yin and yang symbol, which represents the passive and active forces of the universe. In 1893, the Northern Pacific Railway, which brought tourists from the eastern U.S., chose the thousand-year-old yin-yang symbol for the logo of their Yellowstone Park Branch Line, proudly pointing out that the same symbol was found in Yellowstone. However, natural events have altered the stream.

The word meander comes from the Meander or Menderes River in western Turkey (ancient Phrygia), proverbial for its windings.

Near Trout Creek, the stagecoach road led across the Central Plateau west to Lower Geyser Basin. This road, completed in 1880, was used until the road from the Upper Geyser Basin to West Thumb over Craig Pass replaced it as the main route in 1892. Today there's only a faint trace of the 1880 road's eastern end.

7.8/7.6 Trout Creek crossing.

9.6/5.8 Turnout on the east above a large meander in the Yellowstone River. Called **Grizzly Overlook**, this is a good place to spot wildlife. It's also the best place to see the surface expression of the Sour Creek Dome **[GEO.26]**, where the magma under the caldera comes quite close to the surface. The dome's center forms part of the eastern horizon.

10.0/5.4 View of Avalanche Peak about 13 miles away when traveling south.

Meanders on Trout Creek.

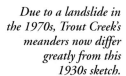

Due to a landslide in the 1970s, Trout Creek's meanders now differ greatly from this 1930s sketch.

There's Molten Rock below Sour Creek Dome

As you drive along the north end of Hayden Valley, you're about as close as the road goes to the Sour Creek Dome (see map, page 302), one of the two areas in the park that overlie molten rock—as close as 3 to 4 miles (5–6 km) below the surface.

Even a very modest rise of the Sour Creek Dome affects the shorelines of Yellowstone Lake. Raising Hayden Valley raises the lake outlet (the Yellowstone River), which in turn raises the lake level. This is a different phenomenon from the rise in lake level due to sudden spring thaws that cause the Yellowstone River to flood.

10.6/4.8 [P] Alum Creek bridge. Alum Creek drains some hot springs reached by the Mary Mountain Trail. Though the water may not actually contain *alum*, which was sometimes used to contract blood vessels, plenty of legends have risen from the belief that it does. Coach drivers were fond of telling tales about how its waters could shrink practically anything—such as the one about the guy who, upon riding his horse across the creek, found that the horse's hooves had shrunk to pinpoints. Another legend had it that water from this creek, when sprinkled on park roads, caused the distances to shrink.

Alum and other creeks join the Yellowstone River in Hayden Valley, creating an area like a small lake.

Eight miles up Alum Creek, the government's first attempt to save the buffalo was made in 1895–96, a time when public sentiment was strong for trying to keep the magnificent animal from extinction. The animals were penned up for feeding in winter. Some segments of fence still stand, but no buffalo were actually saved in this effort.

Looking south from Alum Creek, you can see the steam from Sulphur Mountain, also called Crater Hills, a hot spring and mud pot area. Early tourists who took the Central Plateau route reached this hydrothermal region by a side road. However, the area is no longer open to visitors unless accompanied by a ranger.

11.3/4.1 **Mary Mountain Trailhead** and interpretive sign on the east side. This is the north end of Hayden Valley and a place where waterbirds large and small love to congregate.

Mary Mountain Trail across the road leads southwest across Hayden Valley and the Central Plateau to rejoin the Grand Loop Road near Lower Geyser Basin

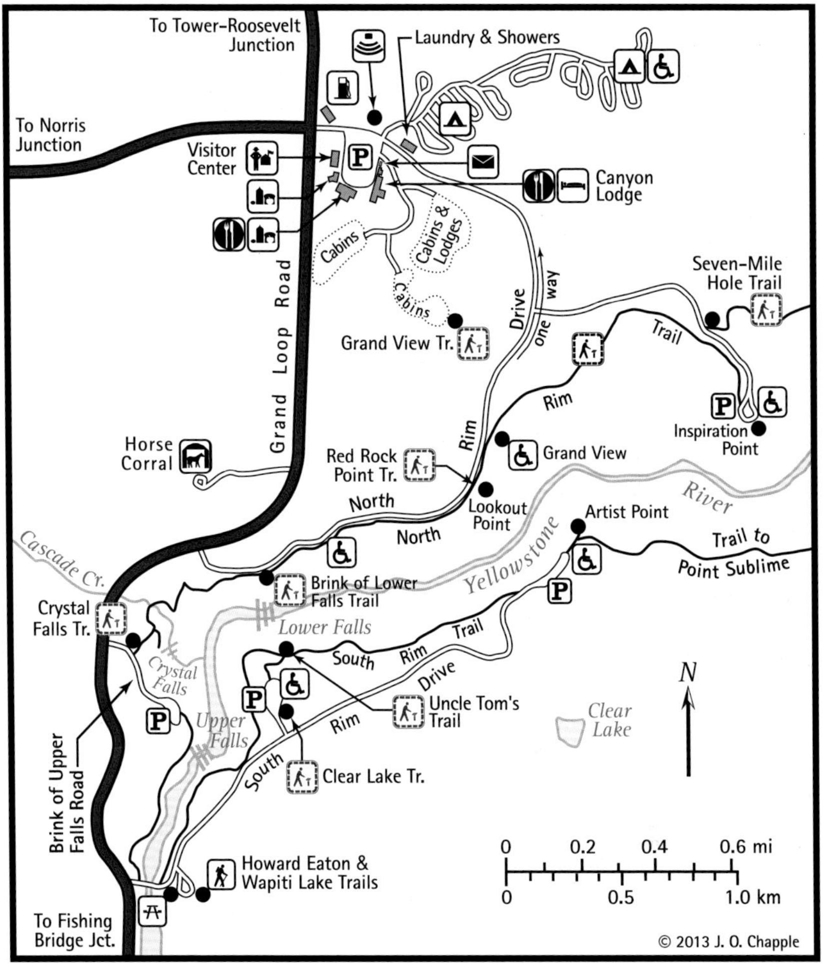

Canyon Area: Village and Falls

about 20 miles (32 km) from here. Prime grizzly habitat, the entire area is closed to overnight camping.

12.4/3.0 (picnic symbol) **(6)** Otter Creek picnic area at the riverside.

12.6/2.8 Otter Creek crossing. Until the 1940s, Otter Creek was the site of a bear feeding ground, where tourists watched a nightly "show" of the bears eating hotel garbage. A photographer was killed by a grizzly in the same area in 1986.

13.1/2.3 Side road to Artist Point along the Grand Canyon of the Yellowstone. This 1.6-mile (2.6 km) road, **South Rim Drive**, takes you to two viewpoints for the canyon and opportunities for hiking. There are also five viewpoints on the north rim (see page 184).

This side road first crosses the Yellowstone River on **Chittenden Bridge**, named after Hiram Chittenden, the captain in the Corps of Engineers who planned and directed the construction of many of Yellowstone's roads between 1891 and 1906. He followed a parallel career as a historian, writing *The Yellowstone National Park: Historical and Descriptive* and three other histories of the American West.

Incidentally, this canyon was often called Grand Canyon, until Grand Canyon National Park was set aside in Arizona in 1919. Now people simply call the area Canyon or sometimes Grand Canyon of the Yellowstone.

Here's what naturalist John Muir wrote in 1898 about Hayden Valley, the Yellowstone River, and its falls:

> For the first twenty miles its course is in a level, sunny valley lightly fringed with trees, through which it flows in silvery reaches stirred into spangles here and there by ducks and leaping trout, making no sound save a low whispering among the pebbles and the dipping willows and the sedges of its banks. Then suddenly, as if preparing for hard work, it rushes eagerly, impetuously forward rejoicing in its strength, breaks into foam-bloom, and goes thundering down into the Grand Cañon in two magnificent falls, one hundred and three hundred feet high.

SOUTH RIM DRIVE

P (4) **Howard Eaton** and **Wapiti Lake** trailheads are just over the bridge. There's access both for picnicking and for hiking the backcountry trails.

(0.5) **P** **(4)** Uncle Tom's Trail parking area on your left. Here you may choose to leave your car to see the Upper Falls, take Uncle Tom's Trail partway down the canyon, or hike either the South Rim Trail or the Clear Lake Trail. You may want to pick up a Yellowstone Association pamphlet about the whole Canyon area from the dispenser near the parking area.

Uncle Tom's Overlook at the canyon rim is a wheelchair-accessible viewing area for the **Upper Falls** of the Yellowstone and **Crystal Falls** of Cascade Creek (across the canyon).

An early park tour guide and enterprising character, "Uncle Tom" Richardson, built the first crude trail into the canyon in 1898. After ferrying visitors across the Yellowstone above the Upper Falls, he would show them how to descend into the canyon with the help of wooden ladders and ropes.

Canyon Lodge and cabins stood at the west end of today's parking area from 1925 to 1957. The Lodge's loyal employees returned year after year and produced musical shows to entertain the guests.

Above Upper Falls the water "breaks into foam-bloom" (John Muir).

The Canyon and Falls of the Yellowstone

Don't be confused by the names of the two famous falls of the Yellowstone River **[GEO.18]**. Upper Falls is upstream from Lower Falls, but Lower Falls is nearly three times taller than Upper Falls.

- Upper Falls: 109 feet (33 m)
- Lower Falls: 308 feet (94 m)
- Canyon depth: 800–1,200 feet (240–360 m)
- Canyon width: 1,500–4,000 feet (450–1,200 m) in the area of the overlooks
- Canyon length: about 20 miles (32 km) from the Upper Falls to Tower Junction.

You can't see or photograph both waterfalls from any point, since the Yellowstone makes a big bend between Upper and Lower Falls. The canyon area has been hydrothermally active since not long after the formation of the caldera, and this activity has altered the lava that flowed hundreds of thousands of years ago to fill in the area. The rock was thus easily eroded by the Yellowstone River after the retreat of the glaciers. The falls have formed on the more resistant layers in the lava flows and where hydrothermal alteration was less. To read about carving the canyon, see page 313.

Trails from Uncle Tom's Overlook

Special Caution: At least ten people met their deaths falling into the canyon in the twentieth century and one in 2012. Please exercise caution, stay away from the edge, and keep small children firmly under control.

Uncle Tom's Trail has 328 steps in a descent of less than one-half mile (0.8 km), so it's not for the faint of heart, but it's pleasant when you reach the bottom and find yourself delightfully close to the Lower Falls. The steps are made of metallic mesh, which may seem a little scary as you descend—but there's a railing. Allow plenty of time both for rest and enjoyment. It's no longer possible to descend to the very bottom of the canyon in this area.

Uncle Tom's Overlook has a fine view of Upper Falls and Canyon Bridge.

A much longer but easier and less crowded trail is **Clear Lake Trail**, which begins at the Uncle Tom's Trail parking area. Cross South Rim Drive, go uphill to the Wapiti Lake Trail intersection, and turn left (east). Clear Lake is less than a mile (1.5 km) away; an area with steaming holes and small mud pots lies another few hundred yards (meters) beyond.

You might return the same way you came. Backcountry hikers can continue past Lily Pad Lake and along the canyon rim to Artist Point. The one-way hike would be less than 3 miles (4.8 km) long if you have a drop-off and pick-up arrangement at Uncle Tom's and Artist Point parking lots. You can also hike from Uncle Tom's parking area in either direction along the South Rim Trail.

(1.6) ♿ The side road ends at **Artist Point★★**, a must-see for the full effect of the colorful canyon and Lower Falls. Although every book about Yellowstone describes or pictures this wonderful vista, there's no substitute for standing here yourself. Absorb the unbelievable coloring of the rocks, the depth of the canyon, the grace of the falls with their faint roar nearly a mile away, and the thrill of the rushing river below you. Even the attractive stonework dating from 1938 adds to the beauty of the place.

Artist Point was probably named by park photographer F. J. Haynes for the painter Thomas Moran—or even for himself!

If you think you see steam in the canyon from several viewpoints, you're not mistaken. There are several hot springs, perpetual spouters, and geysers below you.

Part of the **South Rim Trail** east from Artist Point reveals some of the most

Lower Falls on the Yellowstone River is by far the most often photographed of Yellowstone's many waterfalls.

awe-inspiring sunset colors you will see anywhere, with the sky and canyon rivaling each other on a beautiful evening. The NPS warns hikers of uneven footing and steep drop-offs here; it is also narrow and sometimes slippery. This trail cannot be recommended to casual walkers.

Hikers prepared for backcountry conditions can continue on to a view of the many pinnacles historically called Castle Ruins and also to Point Sublime. The trail turns south before Point Sublime to a junction and goes straight on to Clear Lake Trail (see previous page) or left at the junction to Lilypad and Ribbon Lakes.

Continuing on the Grand Loop Road

To reach Canyon Junction and Canyon Village when leaving the South Rim Drive, go north after the bridge (that is, turn right onto the Grand Loop Road). For Fishing Bridge Junction, go south (left).

13.7/1.7 P (2) **Brink of Upper Falls Road** to the east. Park at the end of the short side road for a very short walk right to the top of Upper Falls, an exhilarating place to be.

From the parking area, you can also reach **Crystal Falls** on Cascade Creek. Walk back along the side road, crossing over a small creek, to the North Rim Trail. Then walk an easy 200 yards (or meters) to Crystal Falls, which drops 129 feet (39 m) in three stages. When the trail forks, take the right fork for the best views of the falls. The unmaintained trail to the left crosses the bridge above the falls and continues on the North Rim Trail.

The cool green glen at the top of Crystal Falls was Superintendent Norris's favorite spot in the park. In 1875 he gave the name **Grotto Pool** to the "broad, deep pool of placid water, nearly hidden

Canyon Colors

The colors in the Grand Canyon of the Yellowstone derive both from minerals and from living organisms. There are infinite shadings of yellow and orange, and also reds and pinks, off-whites, browns, greens, and black. Most of these colors result from the weathering of the rocks and from the dissolved minerals that precipitated and deposited out of the hot water that rose from below.

Rainwater and the oxygen in the air break down the rhyolite that is the predominant rock of the canyon. At the same time, hot water and steam react with minerals in these rocks. These processes convert some of the elements, such as iron and manganese, to new minerals. The result gives us colors such as rust or brick red (iron oxide), black, or bright yellow.

Some of the black shadings are probably magnetite, a jet-black iron oxide, while some of the black is lichen growing on the rocks.

In moist places, such as near the hot springs at the base of the canyon, algae and moss grow and lend a lush green color to the rock surfaces. There may also be colorful microorganisms present around the few hot springs, but the living ones make a modest contribution to the riot of color in the canyon. Dead microorganisms leave no residual color.

You may think the Yellowstone River got its name from the yellow of this canyon, while historians have written that the Native American Indian name came from the color of the sandstone cliffs lining this river for hundreds of miles downriver from Billings. However, members of the Crow tribe believe that early French travelers to the area mistranslated the Crow word for elk, calling the river *La Roche Jaune* ("the yellow rock") to translate the Crow name for Elk River. The Crow word for elk sounds very similar to their word for yellow stone.

Few visitors to Canyon see Crystal Falls at close range.

under the narrow shelf of rocks between the two leaps of the cataract."

14.1/1.3 Entrance to North Rim Drive (one way south to north).

The magnificent Canyon Hotel was located just up the hill from the intersection here until it burned to the ground in 1960 (see picture, page 187).

NORTH RIM DRIVE

In 2008 the North Rim Drive was completely reconstructed and became one-way from south to north. Approximately 2 miles (3 km) long, this road provides four beautiful and varied views into the canyon and opportunities to hike partway down. Restrooms are available along the way. The trail along the rim is paved and accessible with assistance near the Lookout Point and Grand View parking areas.

As you visit this unique treasure, you'll realize that the canyon is not a static place. The steep walls will further disintegrate and the canyon will become wider and deeper over the years due to earthquakes, storms, the freezing and thawing of winter ice, the continual action of the river, and the friable (that is, easily crumbled) nature of the thermally altered rock.

Special Caution: At least ten people met their deaths falling into the canyon in the twentieth century and one in 2012. Please exercise caution, stay away from the edge, and keep small children firmly under control.

Instead of driving you might park at one end of the **North Rim Trail**, which runs along the rim between Chittenden Bridge and Inspiration Point.

(0.0) Enter the North Rim Drive from the Grand Loop Road at mile 14.1/1.3.

(0.2) **P** (4) The first parking area is for **Brink of (Lower) Falls Trail**, a strenuous but rewarding drop of some 600 feet (180 m) in about one-half mile (0.8 km). At the bottom of the trail, you stand at the very point where water tumbles over the top of thundering **Lower Falls**.

(0.8) **P** At **Lookout Point** you take switchbacks and steps to **Red Rock Point**, a paved but very steep trail of about 1 mile (1.5 km) round trip. This is the best place to see, hear, and feel the water of the Yellowstone pounding through its narrow canyon or to take the best photos from the North Rim of Lower Falls and its mossy walls. With binoculars, you may spy osprey nests on the pillarlike formations of canyon rock.

A little over one hundred years ago an enterprising Montanan applied to build an elevator to the bottom of the canyon at the falls. Author Owen Wister got wind of the scheme and mentioned it disparagingly to an acquaintance, who asked, "But why should your refined taste . . . interfere with the enjoyment of the plain people?" To which Wister answered, "Have the plain people told you or anybody that the one thing they lie sleepless craving for is an elevator to go up and down by those falls the way they do in hotels?" "They would like it if it was there," replied the acquaintance. Wister agreed, but asked, "Is that a reason to vulgarize a supreme place of wild natural beauty for all time?" The acting military superintendent, Captain F. A. Boutelle, recommended against it and the elevator was never built.

Experience the thrilling power of falling water at the Brink of Lower Falls.

Just east of here was a spot called Moran Point, where artist Thomas Moran sketched in the 1870s. (Despite its name, Artist Point across the canyon was not Moran's sketching spot.) Moran subsequently painted his huge masterpiece of the Grand Canyon, which hung for many years in the nation's capitol and now belongs to the U.S. Department of the Interior. The point had become inaccessible by the mid 1900s.

(0.9) P ♿ The colors are decidedly photogenic at **Grand View★**, the next-to-last stop along the road. There is no view of either falls at this point.

(1.3) Inspiration Point side road (two way). On the way to Inspiration Point, you'll see the *granite-gneiss* **Glacial Boulder [GEO.13]**, as large as a small house and surrounded by trees. Because there's no bedrock like this anywhere near, geoscientists have concluded that boulders like this one must have been carried from the Beartooth Mountains about 40 miles (64 km) north long ago by a glacier.

The strenuous **Seven-Mile Hole Trail** leads to the bottom of the canyon from Glacial Boulder. The "hole" refers to a good fishing spot in the Yellowstone River. The trail is not quite 7 miles (11 km) long, but it's very steep.

Less ambitious hikers might park near the boulder and use the Seven-Mile Hole Trail only to hike along the canyon rim. It's a pleasant 2.5 miles (4 km)

Grand View is a great place to see the canyon colors.

round trip and includes a view of slim **Silver Cord Cascade** on Surface Creek. It drops about 1,200 feet (366 m) into the canyon from the other side and is probably the park's highest waterfall.

(P) (♿) **Inspiration Point★★** was originally called Promontory Point because it protrudes into the canyon, affording fine views in both directions, including some wheelchair-accessible views. Fifty steps lead down to a panoramic view. You see only a slice of Lower Falls from here because of a bend in the river, but the colors of the rocks are marvelous. An earthquake in 1975 caused a large part of this promontory's rock to fall into the canyon.

Innumerable writers, artists, and photographers have tried to reproduce what they see in this canyon. One can never tire of gazing at it. Here's a late-nineteenth century attempt to describe the colors:

> The whole gorge flames. It is as though rainbows had fallen out of the sky and hung themselves there like glorious banners. The underlying color is the clearest yellow; this flushes onward into orange. Down at the base the deepest mosses unroll their draperies of the most vivid green; browns, sweet and soft, do their blending; white rocks stand spectral; turrets of rock shoot up as crimson as though they were drenched through with blood. It is a wilderness of color.
>
> —Dr. Wayland Hoyt, as quoted in the *Haynes Guides*.

After returning to the North Rim Drive and turning right, you'll find the Canyon Campground and Canyon Village before reaching Canyon Junction in less than a mile (0.8 km).

~

Continuing on the Grand Loop Road

14.5/0.9 A side road leads west to the **Canyon Horse Corral**, from where guides will take you on one- or two-hour horseback rides along area trails during the summer months. Cascade Meadows here is a good place to see bison, elk, and birds of prey.

15.4/0.0 Canyon Junction. Canyon Village to the east; Dunraven Pass, Tower Fall, and Tower Junction to the north; Norris Junction and Norris Geyser Basin to the west; Fishing Bridge Junction to the south.

FACILITIES AT CANYON VILLAGE

NOTE: See the Canyon Area map on page 179.

At the northeast corner of Canyon Junction is a full-service gas station, including towing and maintenance.

Most of Canyon's facilities are arranged in a semicircle south of the gas station. First is the **Canyon Visitor Center**, whose two floors include a

Canyon Hotel

The famous Canyon Hotel, incorporating an earlier hotel, opened to guests in 1911. Arguably the all-time gem of Yellowstone Park hotels, this was the largest and most elaborate one ever built in Yellowstone.

Designed and supervised by architect Reamer, who had completed the Old Faithful Inn seven years before, Canyon Hotel was a massive and elegantly appointed hotel whose foundations were said to measure a mile around. It was five stories high and had 430 rooms, a huge lobby, and a spiral staircase reputedly copied from the Paris Opera House. The author of this guide remembers passing by as a child with her parents and being told we couldn't go there, because it was a hotel for rich people.

Canyon Hotel was built in the wintertime. Supplies were hauled the 40 miles from the Gardiner railhead on sleds pulled by six horses. Over 100 carpenters worked seven days a week to make it ready for the 1911 tourist season.

Elegant Canyon Hotel opened for business in 1911 (Elliot W. Hunter photo).

large bookstore and displays about Yellowstone geology and the Native American Indian presence in the park—all well worth a visit.

(2) Next around the loop are a sporting goods store and a general store with lunch counter.

(3) (2) Continuing around the loop are the **Canyon Lodge** facilities. There are three places to eat: cafeteria, snack bar, and dining room, then a cocktail lounge and gift shop. Next come the registration building for the many motel-like cabins (opened in 1957) and two small 1990s lodges (Cascade and Dunraven), and finally the post office. Wheelchair-accessible restrooms are available at the cafeteria and the cocktail lounge.

The only picnic spots near Canyon Village are at the east end of Chittenden Bridge (map, page 179), 1.3 and 2.4 miles north of Canyon Junction (map, page 214), and 3.0 miles south of the junction (map, page 172).

A pleasant, paved trail about one-half mile (0.8 km) long leads through the woods from the "P" loop of cabins (next to P23–26) to the **Grand View** area, which can also be reached by the one-way North Rim Drive.

North of the other facilities is the **Canyon Campground**, with more than 250 sites (3 of them accessible), and a building containing self-service laundry and showers. The amphitheater for ranger talks is between the campground and the service station.

V. NORTHEASTERN SECTION

Approaches to the Northeast Entrance

If you decide to enter Yellowstone by the Northeast Entrance, you are given the choice of two unforgettable mountain roads that lead to Cooke City and the Northeast Entrance. Most popular is the Beartooth Scenic Byway, which crosses the Beartooth Plateau and reaches almost 11,000 feet (3,350 m) at its summit. The highway is a remarkable piece of engineering that affords spectacular views of mountains, lakes, and valleys. The summer display of wildflowers is unsurpassed, and the chance to throw snowballs in July will appeal to the kids.

A less well-known but also beautiful way to reach the Northeast Entrance is by the Chief Joseph Scenic Byway, where the 8,000-foot (2,440 m) summit reveals other mountains and valleys in profusion.

To take the Beartooth Highway, turn south from Interstate 90 at Laurel, Montana, onto U.S. Highway 212. You'll reach Red Lodge in 43 miles (69 km)—or a total of about 60 miles (97 km) from Billings. At Red Lodge you continue on U.S. 212, which becomes the Beartooth Highway. The distance from Billings to the Northeast Entrance over this route totals about 130 miles (210 km).

The Chief Joseph Highway (Wyoming Highway 296), is easily accessible either from Billings or from Cody. By the Billings-Belfry-Wyoming 120-Chief Joseph Highway route, you reach the park in about 150 miles (240 km). It's less than 80 miles (130 km) from Cody by this route.

Red Lodge, Montana — **Red Lodge Airport**

Population: 2,125 — *1.2 mi. (2 km) NW*

The small ranching, tourist, and summer home community of Red Lodge was built in 1884 on the site of a summer camp used by the Crow tribe, who painted their tepees with red clay.

From about 1892 to 1952, miners dug coal near Red Lodge and from several mines to the south for the Northern Pacific Railway's locomotives. Immigrants came from Austria, Croatia, Serbia, Italy, and Finland; in the 1920s, Red Lodge had some 5,000 people. After the completion of the Beartooth Highway, Red Lodge began catering to increasing numbers of visitors. Now the town has

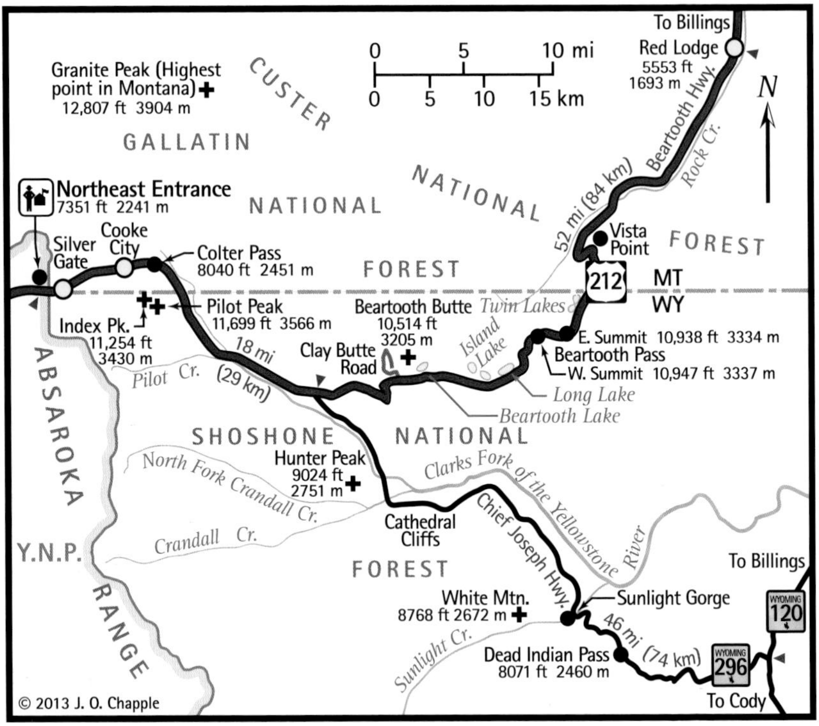

Approaches to the Northeast Entrance

festivals, fishing, and hiking in summer, and skiing from December to April. There's a historical museum and several buildings listed on the National Register of Historic Places.

THE BEARTOOTH SCENIC BYWAY

NOTE: Road construction may delay traffic on segments of this highway for the next several years.

The Beartooth Highway, open only between Memorial Day weekend and early October, covers the 70 miles (113 km) between Red Lodge and Yellowstone's Northeast Entrance. In *American Places* (1993), novelist and Western environmentalist Wallace Stegner wrote: "Yesterday, coming over the Beartooth Scenic Highway . . . we looked across from the 11,000-foot comb of Beartooth Pass and saw not a town, not a ranch, not a cabin, not a road or pole line, not a smoke, only miles beyond miles of forested mountains, shark-tooth peaks, the turquoise sets of lakes, bare stone, snow, wildness, serenity, the blue of distance."

You'll traverse parts of three national forests and the Beartooth Plateau between Red Lodge and Cooke City: Custer National Forest near Red Lodge,

Gallatin National Forest near Cooke City, and Shoshone National Forest in Wyoming.

This unique road first follows Rock Creek out of Red Lodge and in 8 miles (13 km) enters Custer National Forest, where there are four campgrounds on Rock Creek Road. A serious wildfire burned part of this area in August 2000.

Where Rock Creek comes down from the mountains, its valley shows the *U-shape* typical of a valley carved out by glaciers, with the stream at the bottom of the U.

Rock Creek Valley, nestling below the Beartooths, was created by now-melted glaciers.

U.S. 212 leaves the valley and climbs by way of four major switchbacks or horseshoe curves, partly following a Crow path dating from the nineteenth century. It was considered an engineering miracle when opened in 1936. Notice how the quick change in altitude makes your ears pop due to the rapid reduction in atmospheric pressure. (See page 164 for more about high altitude effects.) Across the valley, you can see a road built to bring chromite (chromium ore) down from a mine high in the mountains during World War II.

About 20 miles (32 km) from Red Lodge, you reach the **Rock Creek Vista Point** and restrooms. You can take the short accessible walkway to a fine view of upper Rock Creek Canyon and the mountains and plateaus to the west.

Between here and the summit of the highway, and after four more switchbacks, another deposit was tapped for chromite in the 1940s. Near the east summit, you'll see where winter sports enthusiasts mount their snowmobiles or take the (experts only!) ski lift. Several trails lead from both sides of the summit to the sparkling lakes of the Absaroka-Beartooth Wilderness high country.

In this rarified atmosphere, the animals you're most likely to see are the yellow-bellied marmot (related to the woodchuck) and the tiny pika, a tailless, round-eared animal. (See the Living Things chapter for more about the animals and plants of the mountain passes.)

In July and early August, the wildflowers are marvelous; stop at

Moss campion

Sugarbowl

Phlox

Rosecrown

turnouts to get a closer look. It's hard to believe the flowers can grow in such a hostile environment, with about a 45-day growing season, but they somehow survive, clinging to the small amount of soil above the bedrock. Where there's a bit more soil, permafrost lurks just below their roots. This is arctic tundra. Nevertheless, you can find miniature and brilliantly colored flowers, including forget-me-nots, bluebells, moss campions, and occasionally the bitterroot, state flower of Montana.

There's snow near Beartooth Pass all year. The road is not fully plowed until late May or early June; at that time, you may be traveling through white canyons higher than your car (see picture, page 326). A little later in the summer, the snow may be pink, indicating the presence of a microscopic plant that grows on its surface and makes its meltwater unsafe to drink.

Upon crossing the Montana/Wyoming state line, you enter Shoshone National Forest, which has surprisingly few trees. Timberline at this latitude is about 10,000 feet (3,000 m). On windy slopes below timberline, you'll find only the stunted trees called krummholz.

It's always windy and many degrees cooler up here than in nearby valleys. At the **West Summit** the short side road to the ridge crest affords wonderful views of the Absaroka Range, especially to the southwest.

Twin Lakes

Descending through more switchbacks, you'll see many alpine lakes, including **Frozen**, **Long**, and **Little Bear Lakes** near the road. These lakes are free of ice for only a few weeks of the year.

You'll pass trailheads for several backcountry hikes on the south side of Beartooth Highway's summit. The trailhead for the Beartooth High Lake Trail is at **Island Lake**, which also has a campground and a boat ramp. Be prepared for cold nights if you camp here—the elevation is about 9,500 feet (2,900 m).

Island Lake and dozens of others in this part of the plateau are connected by small streams and fall into patterns of straight lines. Geologists call such small, usually circular lakes in a glacial valley paternosters, because they resemble a rosary or string of beads.

Crystal-clear **Beartooth Lake** has a campground, picnic area, and boat ramp, and lies at the foot of a monumental beige and red cliff, Beartooth Butte. Not far below the summit of this butte, fossil fish have been discovered.

Why Are There Fish Fossils on Top of the Mountain?

The Beartooth Plateau is part of the large block of mountains making up the Beartooth uplift. The uplifted area is about 75 miles long and 40 miles (120 by 65 km) across (see map, page 159), rising to its present elevation along nearly vertical faults. It is composed of very ancient granites and gneisses, some of which are at least 3.3 billion years old, and none of which are younger than 2.7 billion years old. When the uplift started about 50 million years ago, these ancient rocks were buried under about 12,000 feet (3,660 m) of younger sedimentary rocks. These younger rocks have largely been eroded away but remain in a few areas, such as Beartooth Butte.

The strata in the cliff face across Beartooth Lake include a lens-shaped reddish brown layer that is about a third of the way down from the top. The bright colored sediments were deposited in the brackish waters of a stream where it entered the ocean. Many fish fossils have been found in these sediments. These were among the earliest fish on earth about 400 million years ago. Today, those fish are about 10,000 feet (3,050 m) above sea level, thanks to the ride they got during the Beartooth Plateau uplift.

Beartooth Butte is reflected in Beartooth Lake.

A little over a mile (0.8 km) west of Beartooth Lake, a gravel road goes north to reach the Clay Butte Forest Service lookout tower in about 2.5 miles (4 km). In July and August, visitors are welcome to enjoy the view and the panorama of mountain photographs on display in the small building at the top. Clay Butte is another remnant of sedimentary rocks similar to Beartooth Butte, but the fish fossil strata have been eroded away.

Descending on the Beartooth Highway, you may notice the prominent white ledge across the wide valley from you. It extends for miles. This is a 100-foot-high (30 m) cliff of Pilgrim Limestone, over 500 million years old—a very tough sedimentary rock resistant to erosion. Other limestones and volcanic rocks lie above this layer.

A short side road takes you to an excellent overlook for **Pilot** and **Index**

Peaks to the southwest. Glaciers carved both peaks out of volcanic rocks. Pilot, the pointed one, is a glacial horn; four glaciers carved its pyramidal shape.

In this area a few snags are left standing from the 1988 Clover-Mist fire that devastated much of the northeastern quadrant of Yellowstone.

Waterfall enthusiasts should look for the lovely **Lake Creek Falls** on a bend of the old road that's supported by well-preserved rockwork. It's about 6 miles (10 km) west of the Clay Butte road. Look for a new bridge and a wide turnout north of the road to find it.

Pilot and Index Peaks have long served as landmarks to explorers and visitors.

About 14 miles (23 km) east of Cooke City is the junction with Wyoming 296, the Chief Joseph Highway. To continue to the Northeast Entrance, see "The continuation of U.S. 212 to Cooke City" on page 198.

CHIEF JOSEPH SCENIC BYWAY

NOTE: This road is described from east to west. See map, page 190.

Instead of taking the Beartooth Highway, you may choose to reach the Northeast Entrance via another beautiful mountain pass, using Wyoming 296, the Chief Joseph Highway. Dead Indian Pass (the former name for this entire route) is nearly 3,000 feet (900 m) lower than Beartooth Pass, so this route receives somewhat less snow and is plowed (though not daily) in winter.

Why Was This Route Named Dead Indian Pass?

The marker at the summit of the Chief Joseph Highway attributes the name Dead Indian Pass to an incident in 1877 involving the Nez Perce tribe and the U.S. Army. Chief Joseph led his people that year from their home in Idaho, across Yellowstone and the Absaroka Range, then down through Clarks Fork Canyon, a route considered impassable by the pursuing army. One Nez Perce was killed in the area, but about seven hundred members of the tribe successfully evaded the troops. The group attempted to flee to Canada but was eventually forced to surrender to the army not far short of the Montana-Canada border. Where their route is known, an occasional marker now points out the Nez Perce National Historic Trail.

The Nez Perce story is commonly accepted as the source of the old name for this pass, but another conflict occurred near here the following year. Col. Nelson A. Miles surprised a camp of Bannock Indians, killing and capturing many of them. Also, one of the Bannocks was killed and buried here by Crow scouts. 1878 was the last year of troubles between Native American Indians and the U.S. government in and around the national park.

The Chief Joseph Highway begins at the intersection of Wyoming 296 with Wyoming 120, signed Sunlight Basin Road. It's about 17 miles (27 km) north of Cody or about 32 miles (51 km) south of Belfry, Montana.

As you drive on Wyoming 120, you can see a distinctive mountain to the east, partly flat-topped, partly craggy, and standing by itself. People of the Crow tribe called this mountain Four Tops Father or sometimes Buffalo Heart Mountain. This is now called **Heart Mountain**, famous both for the shameful internment of Japanese-Americans at a camp at its base during World War II and for the Heart Mountain fault or detachment (see "The Case of the Wandering Mountains" on page 198). An excellent museum called the Heart Mountain Interpretive Learning Center opened here in 2011.

The first 10 miles (16 km) of Wyoming 296 climb from the dry, wide Big Horn Basin to viewpoints dominated on the northeast by a red rock butte and on the south by **Pat O'Hara Mountain**, named for an old-timer who lived near here. To the right (northeast) of the road is a bright-red hogback, a 200-million-year-old sedimentary rock ridge with one steep face and one gentle one.

If you stop on the way up to enjoy the view or the wildflowers, don't be surprised if you think you hear a trumpet or a saxophone! Northwest College of Powell, Wyoming, has a jazz camp located on this side of the pass.

At the summit, there's a generous parking area, two wheelchair-accessible restrooms, and a historic marker. Here you have one of the most wonderful panoramas a Rocky Mountain pass can offer, from the Absaroka Range crossing the horizon on the south to the Beartooth Plateau on the north.

Summit View at Dead Indian Pass

Some of the mountains and valleys from left (south) to right (north) are:

Numerous snow-covered peaks of the **Absaroka Range**, many above 11,000 feet (3,350 m).

The broad flat valley of **Sunlight Basin** way below.

The perfect pyramid of **White Mountain** (picture, page 197).

Windy Mountain, farther away and higher, and **Steamboat Hill** in the foreground.

A little to the right and farther away than Steamboat Hill are the two peaks of **Sugar Loaf Mountain** and a flat-topped hill called **Antelope Mesa**.

The Clarks Fork River and its canyon are too deeply incised to be seen from here but are marked by the steep rise of the **Beartooth Plateau** on the far side.

The switchbacks west of the summit were paved in the late 1990s. There are several Shoshone National Forest campgrounds, along with ranches and summer homes.

After descending from the summit, the road goes around the "prow" of **Steamboat Hill**. Then, about 2 miles (3 km) after passing Dead Indian Creek and Campground, a gravel road (Wyoming 7GQ) leads west to mountain-ringed Sunlight Basin. One-half mile (0.8 km) beyond the gravel road turnoff, park on the right near the highest bridge in Wyoming for a breathtaking look into deep **Sunlight Gorge**.

Sunlight Basin shelters ranches, summer homes, and a Forest Service campground.

Sunlight Creek enters the Clarks Fork of the Yellowstone a couple of miles below here. In 1990, 20.5 mi (33 km) of that river received a Wild and Scenic River designation from Congress, preserving it from any development. You can launch kayaks upstream at Crandall Creek Bridge, but only the most experienced kayakers should consider running the section called The Box, and then only when the water is not too high.

In another 14 miles (23 km) or so, Wyoming 296 meets U.S. 212.

The Case of the Wandering Mountains

A number of peaks you see from the Chief Joseph Highway, including Heart Mountain, Steamboat Hill, and Cathedral Cliffs, are part of an amazing geological enigma, the Heart Mountain detachment. An enormous area of old sedimentary rock, extending from south of Cooke City to near Cody, became detached from the underlying rocks and slid to the southeast. Some of the pieces of this "landslide" remain intact and upright; others appear jumbled. Several dozen such blocks, some in excess of 10 miles (16 km) across, are spread over an area 66 miles (97 km) long. The sliding surface is nearly horizontal and today has an average slope of only 2 degrees. Younger volcanic rocks lie between and on top of the older sedimentary slide blocks and may be part of the slide itself.

Geoscientists agree on where these huge blocks of rock came from, but there is no agreement on the mechanics of how they got there. However, consensus is building that the movement occurred during the unstable time when the volcanic Absaroka Mountains were forming.

The continuation of U.S. 212 to Cooke City

Going west at the junction of Wyoming 296 and U.S. 212 takes you to Cooke City and Yellowstone's Northeast Entrance; east is the Beartooth Highway to Red Lodge. Wyoming 296 leads southeast over Dead Indian Pass to Wyoming 120 and Cody, Wyoming, or Belfry, Montana.

Watch for **Crazy Creek Falls**, about 2.5 miles (4 km) west of the highway junction and nearly opposite the campground with the same name. It's an unusually broad waterfall.

There are five forest service campgrounds and several trailheads between the junction and Cooke City. Those south of the Wyoming/Montana state line are in the Shoshone National Forest and those north of it in the Gallatin National Forest.

You'll find good fishing access for the **Clarks Fork River**. Clarks Fork joins the Yellowstone River near Laurel, Montana. Don't confuse this river with the Clark Fork of the Columbia in western Montana.

Cooke City & Silver Gate, Montana

Combined Population: 75 (doubles in summer)

Cooke City was settled in 1870 by miners soon after gold was found. The area was first called the New World Mining District and the town "Shoo-Fly," but the name was soon changed to honor the banker and railway magnate, Jay Cooke, Jr., who had promised to bring in a railroad. The mining boom peaked in the 1880s, when hundreds of mining claims were recorded in the New World

District and the population exceeded 1,000. Hopes for a railroad faded, and most mining claims were abandoned, but deposits of gold, copper, lead, silver, chromium, and zinc remain in these mountains.

A huge gold mine was proposed near here in the 1990s by a Canadian mining company. After considerable national outcry over the damage Yellowstone could suffer from mine tailings and other impacts, development was averted—at least for a time—by a land exchange and the withdrawal of the area from mining claims.

This store on Cooke City's only paved street, U.S. 212, was built in 1886 to serve miners.

Mineral Mountain (10,531 ft / 3,210 m) is seen northwest of Cooke City, and **Republic Mountain** (10,170 ft / 3,100 m) rises to the south. Inquire locally or see the Forest Service maps for four-wheel-drive roads and hiking trails in the area.

An all-day hike or horseback trip can be made to a famous spot about 12 miles (19 km) above Cooke City to the north: Grasshopper Glacier, where grasshoppers were frozen into the ice about three hundred years ago. This glacier has been known and photographed since the 1890s. There are others in the Beartooth Mountains, but no glaciers at all inside Yellowstone Park today.

Silver Gate, the smaller and newer town 3 miles (5 km) from Cooke City, was founded in the 1930s. The architectural standards for the town site require log construction and rustic architecture.

On the hillsides to the north, you can see how the Storm Creek fire seriously threatened Silver Gate and Cooke City in 1988. The fierce Clover-Mist fire to the south also dropped burning embers in the area. A backfire was set, destroying four buildings when it raged out of control, but in the end, both communities were spared serious damage. A sign along the road (later removed) was altered by a local wit to read "Cooked City."

There are several motels and a few restaurants in Cooke City and Silver Gate. The nearest park accommodations are about 30 miles (48 km) west in the Tower-Roosevelt area.

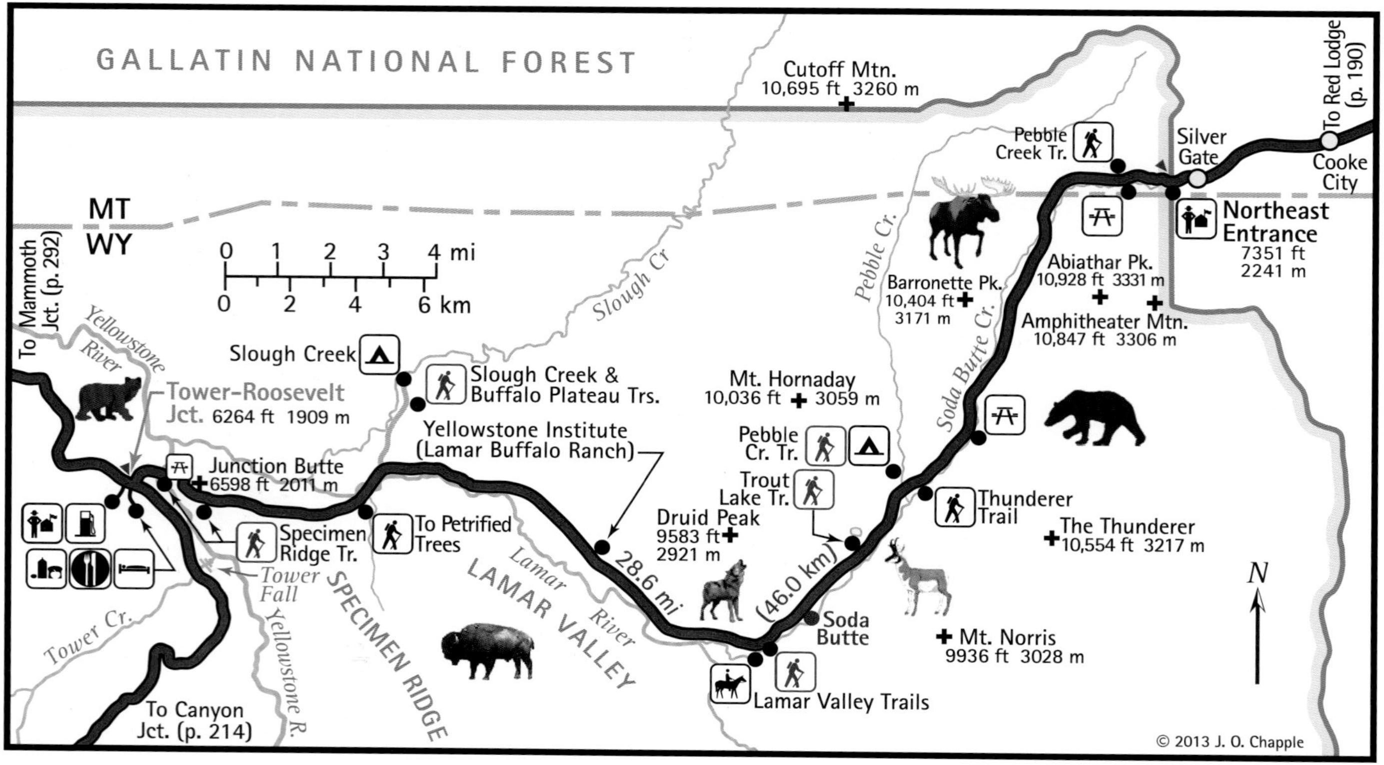
GALLATIN NATIONAL FOREST
Cutoff Mtn.
10,695 ft 3260 m
MT
WY
To Mammoth Jct. (p. 292)
Yellowstone River
0 1 2 3 4 mi
0 2 4 6 km
Slough Cr
Slough Creek
Slough Creek & Buffalo Plateau Trs.
Tower-Roosevelt Jct. 6264 ft 1909 m
Yellowstone Institute (Lamar Buffalo Ranch)
Junction Butte 6598 ft 2011 m
Specimen Ridge Tr.
To Petrified Trees
Tower Fall
Tower Cr.
Yellowstone R.
SPECIMEN RIDGE
Lamar River
LAMAR VALLEY
28.6 mi
(46.0 km)
To Canyon Jct. (p. 214)
Mt. Hornaday
10,036 ft 3059 m
Pebble Cr. Tr.
Trout Lake Tr.
Druid Peak
9583 ft
2921 m
Soda Butte
Lamar Valley Trails
Pebble Cr.
Barronette Pk.
10,404 ft
3171 m
Soda Butte Cr.
Pebble Creek Tr.
Silver Gate
Cooke City
To Red Lodge (p. 190)
Northeast Entrance
7351 ft
2241 m
Abiathar Pk.
10,928 ft 3331 m
Amphitheater Mtn.
10,847 ft 3306 m
Thunderer Trail
The Thunderer
10,554 ft 3217 m
Mt. Norris
9936 ft 3028 m
N
© 2013 J. O. Chapple

Northeast Entrance to Tower-Roosevelt Junction

From the Northeast Entrance to Tower-Roosevelt Junction

This area saw more human activity than any other part of park territory, both before the park was set aside and shortly thereafter. This route along Soda Butte Creek and the Lamar River was an important trail for Native American Indians, trappers, and miners in the nineteenth century.

If miners and railroad interests had had their way in the 1880s and '90s, the Cinnabar and Clarks Fork Railway would have been built through the valley. Congress considered but rejected several bills that would have authorized a right-of-way or eliminated territory from the park's northeast corner in order to bring in a railroad. Interest in the idea waned in the early twentieth century.

The total distance from the Northeast Entrance to Tower-Roosevelt Junction and the Grand Loop Road is about 29 miles (46 km). The road follows Soda Butte Creek, turning toward the northwest after Soda Butte. Here the Lamar River Valley offers the chance to see part of the park's northern bison herd. Early or late in the day, you might catch a glimpse of a wolf, especially with binoculars or a spotting scope.

The road follows the Lamar River past Specimen Ridge, where there are *petrified* trees still standing upright. The Lamar joins the Yellowstone River just before Tower Junction.

Road Log

0.0/28.6 Yellowstone National Park boundary.

0.4/28.2 Northeast Entrance station. Stop here to pay the entrance fee (see the Travel Tips for fee information). The restroom is to the east (left) of the road and outside the entrance station.

The Northeast Entrance Station, dating from 1935, is listed as a National Historic Landmark.

0.5/28.1 Side road to the north for regional ranger headquarters.

1.5/27.1 (7) Warm Creek picnic area and access for fishing in Soda Butte Creek.

Abiathar Peak exhibits layers of lava and volcanic mudflows.

1.6/27.0 [hiker icon] Short road to parking for the **Pebble Creek Trail**. The trail is a 12-mile (19 km) loop that passes between Barronette Peak and Mount Hornaday through forests, meadows, and mountain views. The trail meets the entrance road again at Pebble Creek campground.

2.2/26.4 **P** Turn out to get a good look at red-streaked **Abiathar Peak** (pronounced uh-BYE-uh-ther). Paleontologist Charles Abiathar White helped the early Yellowstone expeditions, and the U.S. Geological Survey honored him with his own mountain. Behind Abiathar is **Amphitheater Mountain** on the park's eastern boundary.

Timberline

What determines how far up a mountainside trees will grow? This depends on the latitude and the characteristics of the particular mountain. Factors such as rainfall, amount of wind and sun, temperature, steepness, and type of soil also affect tree growth. At Yellowstone's latitude (44–45 degrees N), timberline is usually at 9,500 to 10,000 feet (2,900–3,050 m). However, the upper slopes of the mountains you see in this part of the park are so steep that trees cannot grow even at 8,500 or 9,000 feet (2,600–2,750 m).

Botanists use the word *timberline* for the upper limit of fully erect trees and the expression *tree line* to mean the upper limit of all trees, including those that are stunted.

2.3/26.3 Montana/Wyoming state line. When Montana and Wyoming Territories became states, surveyors intended the boundary to follow the 45th parallel, the line of latitude midway between the equator and the North Pole. However, surveying was less accurate in the 1880s, when the tools were a compass for observing directions and a theodolite for measuring angles. Mountainous country was especially difficult to survey. The true 45 degrees N latitude is more than 100 yards (or meters) south of the state line in this vicinity.

3.3/25.3 First crossing of Soda Butte Creek, which the road follows for its first 15 miles (24 km) inside the park. Before the 1930s, the road stayed on the west side of the creek; the old roadbed is now used as a cross-country ski trail.

4.2/24.4 Sign for **Barronette Peak.** The mountain to the west was named for "Yellowstone Jack" Baronett, who came to the area in 1864 to prospect for gold. (See also "Baronett's Bridge and Its Successors," page 212.) The misspelling of his name by members of the 1878

Why Do the Mountains Look Striped?

On all the nearby mountains, you can see stripes or horizontal layers, which are highlighted until midsummer by bands of snow. Abiathar Peak east of the road is layered by chocolate-colored lava flows and volcanic mud flows that were part of the Absaroka volcanic outpourings about 50 million years ago **[GEO.5]**.

Facing Abiathar from west of the highway is Barronette Peak (pictured on page 304), which is also topped by similar chocolate-colored volcanic layers **[GEO.2]**. The lower slopes of Barronette, however, consist of buff to gray layers of ancient sedimentary limestones that are about 350 million years old.

Similar sedimentary rocks underlie Abiathar Peak, but they are difficult to see from the highway. All of these rocks are practically undeformed and are still lying in nice horizontal layers, a phenomenon sometimes called layer-cake geology.

Hayden Expedition later became the officially approved name of this peak. In the 1880s a former miner named Red Sowash built and ran a saloon in this meadow.

Early in the season, you can see dozens of small waterfalls catapulting off Barronette Peak.

7.5/21.1 (9) Soda Butte Creek picnic area, with some shade.

7.8/20.8 North end of **Ice Box Canyon.** This steep canyon is so situated that the sun never penetrates to the bottom; in earlier years, ice remained on the east wall well into summer. There's no good vantage point for seeing to the bottom of the canyon.

The rock exposed on the west side of the road (opposite the canyon) consists of Absaroka volcanic materials brought here roughly 50 million years ago in a mudflow of mixed rock and water called a lahar. Since this flow is near the Lamar Valley, geologists cannot resist calling this one the "Lamar lahar."

8.3/20.3 South end of Ice Box Canyon.

8.8/19.8 **Thunderer Trailhead**. This steep trail crosses a pass about 1,000 feet (300 m) below the summit of The Thunderer, the mountain directly to the east here. The trail provides a route between The Thunderer and Abiathar Peak to reach the backcountry Cache Creek Trail.

Named for its supposed tendency to attract thunderstorms, this mountain saw the death of a lone hiker who fell from the summit in 1985.

9.5/19.1 Pebble Creek Trailhead, with a small parking area. This is a way to join the Pebble Creek Trail without passing through the campground.

9.7/18.9 Crossing of Pebble Creek and side road to **Pebble Creek Campground**, one of the seven Yellowstone campgrounds that do not take reservations. This campground has more than 30 sites with chemical toilets and no showers.

For a pleasant short hike to see an interesting geologic outcrop, park at the upstream end of the campground and walk a few hundred yards (meters) along the start of the **Pebble Creek Trail**. Layers and layers of limestone about 350 million years old are exposed in cliffs in a lovely canyon cut by the creek. This limestone was laid down at the bottom of a vast sea, and looking closely at the rock reveals bits of tiny marine organisms, fossil *crinoids*. The trail continues for about 12 miles (19 km) through spectacular mountain scenery to come out near the Warm Creek picnic area.

To the northwest of the main road is **Pyramid Mountain**; out of view behind it is **Mount Hornaday**. The latter was named for Dr. William T. Hornaday, a noted naturalist and zoo director who helped preserve the bison from extinction a century ago.

The road passes along the edge of the broad, swampy meadow called **Round Prairie**, where Pebble Creek and Amphitheater Creek join Soda Butte Creek.

10.9/17.7 Trout Lake Trailhead. The trail marker appears partway up the trail. A rather steep but rewarding hike of about 1 mile (1.6 km) round trip takes you up a hillside strewn with wildflowers to a sparkling mountain lake with playful otters and verdant meadows.

Trout Lake was called Fish Lake when it was a major source of food for Cooke City residents. Some of the early residents broke the law and killed trout with charges of dynamite.

There's an abundance of trout in this deep lake, but they're not easy to catch. Remains of an old weir or fence for catching fish are still at the lake's outlet, a remnant from the days when fish eggs were collected here.

13.0/15.6 Soda Butte. This landmark is worth a short stop, especially if you're entering the park for the first time. It's the lone thermal feature in this corner of the park. Soda Butte is an extinct hot spring cone made of travertine, the same rock that forms Mammoth Hot Springs' terraces. Pieces of the travertine shine like marble. Although the butte has not done any cone building during recorded history, it or its neighboring hot spring often gives off an odor of hydrogen sulfide. Prospector A. Bart Henderson named Soda Butte in 1870. He mistakenly thought the feature was made of sodium carbonate, or washing soda.

Take the path behind Soda Butte to see a colony of cliff swallows. The seepage of warm water here was called Soda Butte Medicinal Springs by Superintendent Norris.

Soda Butte imitates the shape of Abiathar Peak a few miles away.

In the Vicinity of Soda Butte

Due east of Soda Butte is Mount Norris. Philetus W. Norris was the eccentric but effective second superintendent of the park (1877–82). He was also a prolific writer; his writings include poetry about the west, a road guide to the park, and excellent superintendent's reports that are invaluable to historians. Besides Mount Norris, several other park features carry his name, including Norris Geyser Basin and Norris Pass.

Superintendent Norris

In 1886, when the U.S. Cavalry patrolled the park, a soldier station was built just across the road from Soda Butte. Later used as a ranger station, the wooden structure was moved to the Lamar Buffalo Ranch in the 1930s. In army days, the park had 19 soldier stations, sometimes called snowshoe cabins. They were lonely outposts built to shelter soldiers on patrol in the wintertime. Scattered about the park today are about 40 patrol cabins that shelter rangers, but the rangers don't usually stay in them for weeks at a time as the soldiers often did.

The mountain to the northwest here is Druid Peak. If you're traveling west, this is the last you will see of the striated lava-topped mountains so common in this part of Yellowstone.

From about this point to the Lamar Canyon (mile 20.8/7.8) is the area where you are most likely to see **wolves**—or people with spotting scopes looking for them. The most visible wolf pack from 1996 until 2010 was the big Druid Peak pack, decimated that year by various causes including mange and dispersal. No such easily observable pack has taken its place.

Special Caution: Stay at least 100 yards (109 m) away from wolves.

14.0/14.6 Lamar River Trailhead, and a large parking area for **Specimen Ridge**, **Lamar Valley**, **Cache Creek**, and **Miller Creek Trails**. This is the starting point for long trails up Specimen Ridge or into the remote backcountry. One can hike or ride horseback up the Lamar River and east of the Mirror Plateau into mountainous areas to Yellowstone's eastern boundary and beyond.

All trails cross a sturdy footbridge

over Soda Butte Creek. The apparatus near the bridge measures the flow of water.

Historic remnants hike. History buffs might enjoy a short walk from this trailhead to some historic points from the nineteenth century. Cross the Soda Butte Creek footbridge to look for remnants of the Gardiner to Cooke City miners' road. According to the late Yellowstone historian Aubrey Haines, the two deep tracks that can still be seen paralleling Soda Butte Creek were left by miners dragging an *arrastre* (a heavy apparatus for grinding ore, pronounced a-RASS-treh) along the valley.

Farther along the trail, you might look for the scant remains of a cabin built for gamekeeper Harry Yount in 1880. About 1.6 miles (2.6 km) from the parking area, you can still find chimney stones and traces of a spring box at the base of the hill near the trail junction. Tall, deep green rye grass still gives away the area where Yount pastured his horses. If you reach the point where you would have to ford the Lamar River, you've gone beyond the remnants.

14.4/14.2 Alternate access to the Lamar Valley trails. This one is used especially by horseback riders, who take guided pack trips into the mountains.

14.9/13.7 Located just up the hill from the present road was an especially steep section of the old road, the Jackson Grade. George Jackson squatted (that is, settled without legal claim) near here in the 1880s.

15.3/13.3 Confluence of Soda Butte Creek with the Lamar River. High snowmelt here in June 2011 washed out half the road—quickly repaired.

Chances of seeing bison are excellent in the Lamar Valley, their summer feeding ground.

Near here was the site of an elk corral, used to trap elk and reduce the size of the herd for about 30 years in the mid twentieth century.

The Lamar River and Its Valley

The glacier-carved Lamar Valley entered the historical record as far back as 1836 in *Journal of a Trapper* by Osborne Russell. He praised the "Secluded Valley" for its "wild romantic scenery." Evening light brings forth a particularly beautiful luster.

The Lamar is a long river that originates on the eastern boundary of the park. First called the East Fork of the Yellowstone, in 1885 it was officially named for President Grover Cleveland's secretary of the interior, who bore the melodious classical name Lucius Quintus Cincinnatus Lamar. As interior secretary, Lamar was a good friend to Yellowstone. He later became an associate justice of the Supreme Court.

Death Gulch

Up Cache Creek, above where it enters the Lamar River, is an interesting hot springs area. Located about 5 miles from the road and across the creek from the trail, the area has been called Death Gulch since 1888, when geologist Walter Weed discovered that numerous animals had died there from inhaling poisonous gases. About 15 years later the hot springs in Death Gulch were named Wahb Springs after a fictional grizzly bear that met his end there in *Biography of a Grizzly*, by self-taught naturalist Ernest Thompson Seton.

Creeks with Mineral Names

A veritable mineral collection of names graces the creeks flowing into the Lamar from the Mirror Plateau and Specimen Ridge to the southwest: Flint, Opal, Chalcedony, Amethyst, Jasper, and Crystal Creeks. Two others flow into the Yellowstone River from high on the opposite side of Specimen Ridge: Agate and Quartz Creeks. All these silica-rich minerals have been found in Yellowstone Park, though not necessarily near these creeks.

15.8/12.8 North of the road you may notice a rectangular, fenced-off area of lush plant growth. Biologists call this an *exclosure*, a place where they keep out the larger browsing animals (moose, bison, elk, and deer), in order to compare the protected area with its surroundings. Botanists study the composition and growth rates of the vegetation in several such exclosures in the park.

16.3/12.3 [P] Interpretive sign about Lamar Valley animals. Near the river you'll see three prominent types of trees that thrive in the relatively low altitude here: black and narrowleaf cottonwoods and quaking aspen. See more about these trees on page 347.

18.0/10.6 Sign at south opposite the service road gives Buffalo Ranch history. Lamar Ranger Station and summer headquarters of the Yellowstone Institute. A ranger residence and facilities for the Yellowstone Institute (educational arm of the Yellowstone Association) are located here, but no visitor facilities. (For details about the Yellowstone Association and Institute, see the Travel Tips.)

[bicycle] Bicycles are allowed on the service road at the north end of the cabin area for 1 mile (1.6 km) up Rose Creek, but, since wolves have been reintroduced in the area, anyone wishing to go there should first check with a ranger.

Shadows lengthen in the early evening at Lamar Buffalo Ranch.

Buffaloes, Wolves, and Coyotes

As you pass the ranger station and Yellowstone Institute buildings, you might ponder how three of Yellowstone's larger mammals can coexist here. This was the site of the Lamar Buffalo Ranch from 1907 into the 1950s, a part of the park's efforts to revive the population of the nearly extinct buffalo (often so called, although zoologists prefer to call them bison). Here the animals were kept in corrals and were fed hay cut in the valley. The imported plains herd interbred with native mountain bison, and some of their descendants live in the park today.

Four cowboys rounding up a bison in the Buffalo Ranch corral in 1935, by Jack Haynes.

Wolves lived here at the park's founding but were systematically exterminated as undesirable predators. In the mid 1990s a few Canadian wolves were brought to the park, some of them to an acclimatization pen located on Rose Creek, just a mile or so above the Yellowstone Institute cabins.

In the valley, you're still more likely to see a coyote than a wolf. Wolves will kill coyotes that are competing for food, and when the wolves were reintroduced, they began to make an immediate difference in the park's coyote population. Coyotes may be almost anywhere at almost any time of day, hunting small prey and foraging for carrion. They have little fear of man and may attack people if habituated to them.

There's more about all these animals in the Living Things chapter.

Special Caution: Do not feed any animals in the park. It can be dangerous for you and for them.

19.3/9.3 **P** **Lamar Valley view**. If you're traveling toward the Northeast Entrance along the main road, you have a long, beautiful view here of nearly 20 miles up the valley to Saddle Mountain and other peaks in the Absaroka Range near the eastern boundary of the park.

Several miles beyond Saddle Mountain is a remote area first described by Superintendent Norris after he explored it in 1880; he named it Hoodoo Basin. *Haynes Guide* described "tall, massed eroded rock pinnacles, which reveal to those who let loose their imaginations a large variety of forms of humans and beasts." (See "What's a Hoodoo?" page 158.)

20.8/7.8 East end of **Lamar Canyon**. In 1885, Historian Hiram Chittenden described Lamar Canyon's many boulders as "almost spherical in shape, and, in many instances . . . as smooth as if from the hand of a stone glazier. They are piled up like billiard balls, to such a depth that the stream flows entirely out of sight beneath them."

The large outcrops along the road **[GEO.1]** in this canyon consist of rocks that are among the oldest in the park, about 2.7 billion years old. In fact, there are few areas in the world where older rocks are exposed. These rocks are granites and gneisses, formed deep within the earth at a time when a mountain range was being made above them. Those mountains have long since eroded away.

21.7/6.9 West end of Lamar Canyon.

22.8/5.8 Side road to **Slough Creek Campground** and Buffalo Plateau and Slough Creek Trailheads, with several bird-watching spots from turnouts. At this unimproved campground are 29 nonreservable campsites located about 2 miles (3 km) up the Slough Creek road.

To take one of the two trails, stop at the parking area before the campground.

The **Buffalo Plateau Trail** goes north to join several other trails in the Absaroka-Beartooth Wilderness. A 21-mile (34 km) loop goes from the Slough Creek Campground out of the park and back in, joining the Hellroaring Creek Trail west of Tower Junction.

The **Slough Creek Trail** is popular with fishermen. A hike of about 4 miles (6.5 km) round trip (steep in the beginning) takes you through thriving wildflowers to tranquil First Meadow (as fishermen call it), where a patrol cabin for rangers' use is located.

The Slough (pronounced SLOO) Creek Trail has an unusual reason for being. Just north of the park boundary is the private Silver Tip Ranch, homesteaded in 1913, which is now accessible by air but was previously only reached by this trail or wagon road. At a point called the Slough Creek Transfer, supplies for the ranch are still transferred from trucks to horsedrawn vehicles kept just for traversing a particularly bad section of road through the meadows. Even now, you may see stagecoaches or wagons as you hike this trail.

23.3/5.3 Lamar River bridge and mouth of Crystal Creek, which enters the Lamar River from the south.

23.6/5.0 On an unmaintained trail, you can ascend the ridge to your south, following Crystal Creek to see some petrified trees on **Specimen Ridge**. Because it's a strenuous hike and the trees are not easy to find, get a map and instructions from the Tower Ranger Station before you go. Better yet, go with a ranger or other knowledgeable person.

24.4/4.2 **P** This wide turnout at the south side of the road is the best place to try to see petrified trees near the top of Specimen Ridge. You can see them only with good binoculars and you need to know exactly where to look.

On the opposite side of the road not far from here was Little America, a 1930s camp for men of the Civilian Conservation Corps, who found the weather in this valley early and late in the season to be a lot like Antarctica. The original Little America, on the continent of Ant-

Petrified Trees

South of the road is a remarkable phenomenon: high up on the slopes, trees that used to grow here have been turned to solid stone. This happened during the Eocene epoch, 50 million years ago, long before the caldera events that left us Yellowstone's present-day thermal features. The trees became petrified; that is, the wood was converted to stone by dissolved minerals in water at the time when they were covered with volcanic lava, tephra, and tremendous mudflows. Other areas contain petrified wood—the best known in the United States is Petrified Forest National Park in Arizona. But Yellowstone has more well-preserved upright trees than any other known locality.

Preserved by *petrification* were cool-climate trees (spruce and willow, such as grow here today), temperate trees (like sycamore and walnut), and subtropical trees (like breadfruit and avocado). Researchers have concluded that the climate at the lower altitudes must have been much warmer than it is today and that the trees common to cooler climates were washed down—some still upright—in mudflows from higher altitudes. There must also have been much more rainfall, perhaps 50 to 60 inches (130–150 cm) per year, compared to today's 15 to 18 inches (38–45 cm) per year. This area may have resembled present-day Guatemala.

~

On a lighter note, historian Hiram Chittenden contributes the following, inspired by tales told by trappers:

Sage brush, grass, prairie fowl, antelope, elk, and bears
May there be seen as perfect as in actual life.
Even flowers are blooming in colors of crystal,
And birds soar with wings spread in motionless flight,
While the air floats with music and perfumes siliceous,
And the sun and the moon shine with petrified light!

Another entertaining version of the story has birds sitting on "peetrified" branches, singing peetrified songs.

In present-day Yellowstone, only one of the standing petrified trees is easy to reach—the others require strenuous off-trail climbs. To see this specimen, take the short side road west of Tower Junction, described at mile 16.7/1.4 in the road log "From Mammoth Junction to Tower Junction."

arctica, had been established by Richard Byrd late in 1928. Today this area is called Little America Flats.

Turnouts along the last 5 miles east of Tower-Roosevelt Junction provide access to many ponds, including the Trumpeter Lakes some distance from the road, where trumpeter swans have sometimes nested. Ducks and other aquatic birds, yellow-headed and red-winged blackbirds, as well as otters and muskrats sometimes make these ponds their home. However, the water may dry up by midsummer, and the birds and animals then disperse throughout the area.

26.7/1.9 **Specimen Ridge Trailhead** on the south. This is not a trail where you'll find petrified tree specimens, but rather a trail along the top of Specimen Ridge. You can get to the same trail at mile 27.4/1.2.

P An interpretive sign on the north side of the road explains the evidence left all around by the glaciers.

Traces the Glaciers Left Here

In the 4 miles (6 km) between the Lamar River bridge and Junction Butte, you'll see a particularly rich collection of evidence that this valley was buried in ice not so very long ago **[GEO.14]**. In fact, the ice was about a half mile thick (800 m), with its base at about the level of the highway, so that even Specimen Ridge was covered.

A nursery rock shielded this Douglas fir tree as a seedling.

You'll see numerous small ponds, called *kettle ponds* or kettle holes, mostly on the north side of the road, and a great many large boulders, or *glacial erratics* that differ from the local bedrock. These are all evidence of glaciers **[GEO.15]**. See page 312 in the Geological History chapter for an explanation of these phenomena.

A fascinating attribute of the glacial erratics leads some of them to be called nursery rocks by botanists. These rocks have one Douglas fir tree growing just north or west of them, where the seedling could get a bit of shade, more soil moisture, and shelter from the wind.

As you approach Tower Junction, keep your eyes open for black bears. The Tower area is one of the places where they like to live during the summer.

27.0/1.6 Junction Butte, just north of the road, rises above the spot where the Lamar River joins the Yellowstone.

27.4/1.2 (9) Yellowstone River picnic area and **Specimen Ridge Trailhead** (alternate access) on the south.

If you climb the trail above the picnic area, you'll be treated to some spectacular views into the Yellowstone River canyon and a much more extensive view of Calcite Springs than can be seen at the

Baronett's Bridge and Its Successors

After prospector and hunter Jack Baronett built his wooden toll bridge in 1871, the trip from Gardiner to Cooke City was much easier for miners (although some of them couldn't pay the toll), as well as for park staff and visitors. Ascending along the Yellowstone River's south side, the prospectors formerly had to make the difficult crossing somewhere near the junction. They wanted to follow the Lamar River to reach the rich diggings near Cooke City.

The bridge figured in the Nez Perce tribe's escape from General Howard's pursuing troops in 1877: the Nez Perce burned the bridge, delaying the troops some three hours while Chief Joseph and his people escaped up the Lamar River Valley.

In 1880, Baronett rebuilt his bridge and continued to collect tolls until 1899, when the government finally bought the bridge. It remained here in a dilapidated state until 1905, but a steel one was built just upstream in 1903.

Look south as you cross the present concrete bridge, dedicated in 1963, and you'll see some colorful thermally altered rocks on the banks of the river. Near that spot, a worker lost his life in a tragic accident in 1939. He had been lowered into a deep pit dug to explore a possible site for a new bridge foundation, but he lost consciousness and could not be hoisted out of the pit for 20 minutes. He died of exposure to hydrogen sulfide and carbon dioxide gases.

"Yellowstone Jack" Baronett's bridge over the Yellowstone River.

Calcite Springs Overlook on the other side. (The overlook is described at mile 1.7/16.6 in the road log "From Tower Junction to Canyon Junction.")

In about 2 miles (3 km) the trail leaves the canyon and continues for many miles along Specimen Ridge. A branch of this trail leads back to the highway at mile 26.7/1.9, the Specimen Ridge Trailhead.

27.7/0.9 P Short side road northward to parking area. Below the point of land formed by the junction of the two rivers, about one-half mile (0.8 km) north of this point on the road, stood the first bridge ever built over the Yellowstone River, Baronett's bridge.

27.9/0.7 Yellowstone River bridge, also called Tower Bridge for its proximity to Tower Fall.

28.6/0.0 Tower-Roosevelt Junction. The junction here is both the confluence of the Yellowstone and Lamar Rivers and the intersection of the Northeast Entrance Road with the Grand Loop Road.

(2) Just west of the intersection is a service station and, slightly farther west, the Tower Ranger Station.

Follow the short road straight across the intersection (directly south) for Roosevelt Lodge, its associated cabins, and a small store.

Mammoth Hot Springs Junction is farther to the west; Tower Fall, Dunraven Pass, and Canyon Junction to the south; the Northeast Entrance to the east.

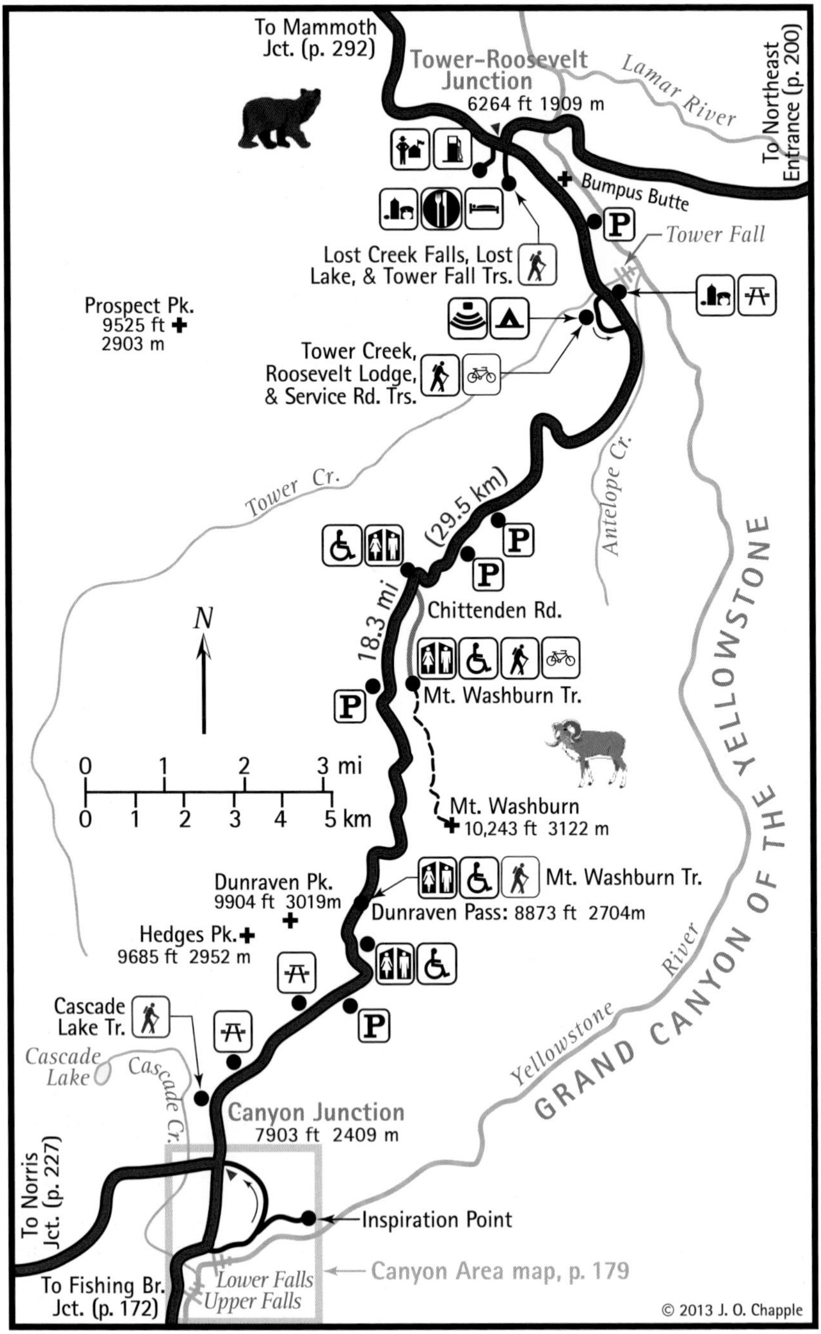
To Mammoth Jct. (p. 292)
Tower-Roosevelt Junction
6264 ft 1909 m
Lamar River
To Northeast Entrance (p. 200)
Bumpus Butte
Tower Fall
Lost Creek Falls, Lost Lake, & Tower Fall Trs.
Prospect Pk.
9525 ft
2903 m
Tower Creek, Roosevelt Lodge, & Service Rd. Trs.
Tower Cr.
Antelope Cr.
(29.5 km)
18.3 mi
Chittenden Rd.
N
Mt. Washburn Tr.
0 1 2 3 mi
0 1 2 3 4 5 km
Mt. Washburn
10,243 ft 3122 m
GRAND CANYON OF THE YELLOWSTONE
Mt. Washburn Tr.
Dunraven Pk.
9904 ft 3019m
Dunraven Pass: 8873 ft 2704m
Hedges Pk.
9685 ft 2952 m
Cascade Lake Tr.
Cascade Lake
Cascade Cr.
Yellowstone River
Canyon Junction
7903 ft 2409 m
To Norris Jct. (p. 227)
Inspiration Point
To Fishing Br. Jct. (p. 172)
Lower Falls
Upper Falls
Canyon Area map, p. 179
© 2013 J. O. Chapple

Tower-Roosevelt Junction to Canyon Junction

From Tower Junction to Canyon Junction

This stretch of the Grand Loop Road takes you first to the popular Tower Fall area, then climbs steeply to cross Dunraven Pass, opened to wagon travelers in 1905. Near the top of this highest pass in Yellowstone, you can stop for excellent mountain panoramas in three different directions. The midsummer wildflowers are outstanding.

The distance from Tower-Roosevelt Junction to Canyon Junction is about 18 miles (29 km).

Road Log

NOTE: Construction on the Chittenden Road to Tower Junction segment may necessitate nighttime or total closure in 2013 and beyond. Check with Yellowstone authorities for up-to-date information.

0.0/18.3 Tower-Roosevelt Junction. The main road toward the south leads to Tower Fall, Dunraven Pass, and Canyon Junction; west is Mammoth Hot Springs Junction; east is the Northeast Entrance. Just west of the intersection is a service station and, slightly farther west, the Tower Ranger Station. On a short side road directly across from the entrance road is Roosevelt Lodge and cabins.

Roosevelt Lodge and cabins

(2) The lodge, named for President Theodore Roosevelt, contains a dining room, wheelchair-accessible restrooms, and registration office for cabins and activities. You may arrange horseback rides, stagecoach trips, and Old West cookouts.

(2) There's a general store nearby with tables on its porch. The store sells firewood for cabin stoves and campsites.

For the unmarked, short **Lost Creek Falls Trail** (about 0.3 mi / 0.5 km long), walk behind Roosevelt Lodge and go left at the signboard—don't cross the creek as you would for Lost Lake. It's a moderately steep climb with loose gravel on the trail near the top, but the 40-foot (12 m) falls and its setting are a delightful reward. In late summer, look for raspberries along the trail. Lost Creek Falls was described in Hiram Chittenden's 1903 guidebook as providing "a scene of quiet beauty rarely found in so wild and rough a country." Compared with the "wild" crowds you may find at Tower Fall, you will find this nearby but little-visited waterfall a welcome contrast!

Lost Lake is less than a mile (1.5 km) west up the **Lost Lake Trail** that starts behind the lodge and across the creek. It's an easier hike from the opposite end, starting near the Petrified Tree (1.4 miles west of Tower Junction). A third trail from Roosevelt goes to Tower Fall, starting behind the lodge or from the corral, reaching the waterfall in about 3.5 miles (6 km).

0.2/18.1 Xanterra horse corral and stagecoaches.

0.9/17.4 Rainy Lake was named because the bubbling springs in the lake make it look like it's raining on the surface.

Bumpus Butte (at top left) above Calcite Springs

The Springs Down by the River

At Calcite Springs Overlook, you may see steam or smell a rotten egg smell coming up from below. The Calcite Springs area is interesting to know about but only accessible to experienced and hardy hikers.

Explorers have known this thermal area since the early 1800s, sometimes calling it Burning Spring. In 1869, explorers watched as "several gallons of a black liquid ran down and hardened upon the rocks . . . it proved to be sulphur, pure enough to burn readily when ignited," quoted in Lee H. Whittlesey's *Yellowstone Place Names.*

Calcite Springs is one of the very few hot springs in the world that emits a petroleum-like material. This material apparently forms by one or both of the following processes. High water temperatures underground may cause rapid reactions in the plant or animal debris in ancient underlying sediments. Alternatively, downward seepage of the surface waters carrying dissolved plant matter and bacteria may be heated at depth, causing the organic materials to react to form oily compounds. However it forms, steam carries this material up to surface vents along the banks of the Yellowstone River.

The hot gases emitted here have the highest known concentration of hydrogen sulfide gas of any of the park's thermal areas—a very lethal 5 percent. Also near Calcite Spring's vents are deposits of gypsum (hydrous calcium sulfate) and pyrite (iron disulfide), and crystals of calcite (calcium carbonate) and barite (barium sulfate), in addition to the nearly pure sulfur.

1.1/17.2 The hill east of the road is **Bumpus Butte**, named for Dr. Hermon Carey Bumpus, the naturalist and educator who set up the park's first museums and roadside exhibits. In addition, Bumpus wrote and illustrated small guides to the natural features in the 1930s.

Not far from here, President Theodore Roosevelt's entourage set up camp during his two-week visit to the park in 1903.

1.7/16.6 **P** **Calcite Springs Overlook.** There's a short loop trail with interpretive signs here and views into the colorful canyon and across it to the Lamar Valley. This part of Yellowstone's canyon is called **The Narrows**, since it's the narrowest part of any of the four canyons of the Yellowstone River.

Along the stretch of road between the overlook and Tower Fall, there is limited parking at turnouts.

Special Caution: Several people have slipped and fallen to their deaths while climbing on the canyon side of the road between this overlook and Tower Creek bridge. Make sure you stand in a safe place to look at the views and take photos.

Basalt columns at Overhanging Cliff dwarf passing cars.

2.1/16.2 Overhanging Cliff [GEO.12], with limited parking along the road. The road excavation has undercut a fine example of columnar *basalt* that is 2.2 million years old. As you might expect, landslides here have been a major problem for road builders.

Lava Columns

Columns in lava are formed when the lava flowed, stopped, cooled enough to become solid, and then continued to cool and shrink. A solidified lava flow can easily shrink in a vertical direction and still remain homogeneous and unfractured; it simply becomes a thinner lava flow. Cooling rock, however, shrinks in all directions, not just vertically. As it shrinks in the horizontal direction, cracks must form. The cracks extend and intersect with others, making columns that are polygons, with space between the columns. The process that makes the columns is very much like the formation of mud cracks. Just as the sun shining on a mud puddle causes the mud to dry, shrink, and crack, basalt shrinks into columns, but it's due to cooling rather than drying.

Not all lava flows exhibit columns; they are most commonly seen in basalt lavas, but also occur in rhyolite lavas. The columns in basalt lavas are more closely spaced and regular in form than those in rhyolite lava. There are examples of both in the park.

Basalt columns in an ancient lava flow are overlain by younger sediments in The Narrows of Yellowstone Canyon.

The area near Tower has some clear examples of basalt lavas that look like stockade fences. You can see them at the roadside at Overhanging Cliff as well as across the canyon, where two lava flows run horizontally for miles. All of these are fine examples of columnar jointing, that is, structures that look like closely packed, vertical logs of lava.

Another example of basalt lava columns is at Sheepeater Cliffs, but the columns at Obsidian Cliff and Mount Jackson formed in rhyolite lava.

—B.J.G/J.S.

2.2/16.1 P **Devil's Den** (with very little parking along the road) is a collection of fantastic rock formations just above Tower Fall and extending up Tower Creek's canyon. When F. V. Hayden named this feature, he was probably thinking of a thicket called the Devil's Den on the battlefield at Gettysburg, a battle fought only eight years before.

Devil's Hoof, with an obvious cleft, stands tall and alone in the Devil's Den jumble. The rock in these formations is not formed by columnar jointing. The Devil's Den rocks were deposited by streams or mudflows as horizontal layers of volcanic debris. Vertical cracks formed in the beds of debris, the rain and the river eroded material from the cracks, and pillars remained. Such formations are called hoodoos. Similar hoodoos in even more bizarre shapes occur on the approach road to the East Entrance.

2.4/15.9 Tower Creek bridge. Tower Creek has been found to be the coldest stream in the park, with a typical summer temperature of 45°F (7°C).

2.5/15.8 (3) One-way road to the west to **Tower Fall Campground** and picnic area large Tower Fall parking lot to the east. This campground has 32 nonreservable sites, pit toilets, and an amphitheater for evening ranger programs.

Three trails begin in or near the Tower Fall campground. **Tower Creek**

Trail, mostly used for fishing access, begins in the campground and goes almost 3 miles (5 km) up Tower Creek. The upper part of the trail's route was severely burned in the 1988 fires.

Bicyclists, as well as hikers and cross-country skiers, may use a former road (called the **Old Chittenden Service Road**) that goes south from the campground to rejoin the Grand Loop Road in 2 miles (3 km).

The **Roosevelt Lodge Trail** goes north from the campground's entrance road, parallels the main road (above Overhanging Cliff), and ends behind Roosevelt Lodge in a one-way distance of a little over 3 miles (5 km).

Tower Fall★

Tower Fall is the beautiful and popular 132-foot (40 m) waterfall on Tower Creek.

P (7) **(2)** The Tower Fall area is extremely crowded all day, since it offers a general store with ice cream counter, as well as trails to and along the Yellowstone River. Come very early or late in the day to enjoy relative solitude.

From the parking lot at the store, the easy, paved walkway (about 0.3 mi/0.5km round trip) takes you out to a platform at the canyon edge, where there's a fine view of Tower Fall and an interpretive sign about its hanging valley.

Although reconstructed in 1985, the trail down to the base of Tower Fall has been impossible to maintain. There is no view of or access to the bottom of the fall.

Tower Fall

Continuing on the Grand Loop Road

2.7/15.6 End of Tower Fall Campground one-way road; entrance is at mile 2.5/15.8.

The Grand Loop Road parallels Antelope Creek for about 1.5 miles (2.4 km). From 1935 until 1942 a "show herd" of about 30 bison was kept near Antelope Creek.

4.8/13.5 **P** A short road to the south leads to a parking area with access to a section of the Howard Eaton trail. The trail is now often closed for bear management (see "Bear Management Area" on page 133).

5.6/12.7 Barred road to the north is the south end of the 2-mile-long (3.2

Tower Fall on Tower Creek

• Tower Fall is the only waterfall in the park officially called "fall" rather than "falls," maybe due to its one clean drop to the creek below. Its name, derived from the many pinnacles or towers above, was given by members of the Washburn Expedition in 1870.

• Just above Tower Creek's mouth, Antelope Creek joins the Yellowstone River. This is the location of the Bannock Ford, where members of the Bannock tribe crossed the Yellowstone on their annual buffalo-hunting trek. It was the only good way to cross the Yellowstone until Baronett built his 1871 bridge about 2.5 miles (4 km) downstream.

• Old drawings and photographs of Tower Fall show a large boulder precariously poised at the edge of the fall. Members of the 1871 Hayden expedition placed bets on when it would fall, but not until June of 1986 did it finally topple over the brink—when no one happened to be watching.

• The boulder that fell in 1986 now lies among the other large rounded hunks of granite-gneiss near the fall's base. Several of these boulders are as much as 10 feet (3 m) in diameter and may weigh up to 30 tons. According to geologists, they are 2.7-billion-year-old glacial erratics carried here from the Beartooth Mountains to the north and east when the area was covered with glaciers a few tens of thousands of years ago.

• Unlike the Yellowstone River, which has cut its canyon through relatively easily eroded rocks, Tower Creek has encountered rocks that are more resistant. Also, the smaller volume of water means much less cutting power. Consequently, the Yellowstone has been able to cut down faster and leave Tower Creek perched on the side of the canyon, thus creating a hanging valley and a beautiful waterfall.

km) Old Chittenden Service Road Trail that starts at Tower Fall Campground.

7.1/11.2 P Interpretive sign about grizzly bears and their habitat. You might spot elk or moose as well as grizzlies in the valley below or in the foothills across Antelope Creek.

7.6/10.7 P Turnout to view Antelope Creek Valley and tiers of distant mountains in a nearly 180-degree sweep. Below here the Antelope Valley fire burned more than 5,000 acres in September 2010.

8.2/10.1 Mae West Curve, though not an official name, is a commonly used one for this hairpin turn in the road. The famous Hollywood actress and writer of plays and films, Mae West (1892–1980), was notorious for her directness as well as for her curves.

Antelope Valley Panorama

From northeast to south (left to right):

Beartooth Mountains in the far distance—outside the park.

Cutoff Mountain (10,695 ft / 3,260 m), part of the Absaroka Range. It has an abrupt cliff at its west end but was named because the summit was "cut off" from the park outside the boundary. Higher and snowier mountains of the Beartooths can be seen beyond it.

Specimen Ridge is the long, irregular, grassy ridge that extends from northwest to southeast in the middle distance. **Amethyst Mountain** (9,614 ft / 2,930 m) is the ridge's highest point and the center of this panorama.

Grand Canyon of the Yellowstone, extending north-south, is visible in the middle distance. Due east of here you can see where Deep Creek's canyon joins the Yellowstone's at an oblique angle.

Mirror Plateau lies beyond the Yellowstone River. A vast area with no maintained trails, it stretches to the headwaters of the Lamar River and to the high **Absaroka Range** in the far distance. Several hot spring groups emit steam in the area, including **Coffee Pot Hot Springs.**

Mt. Washburn (10,245 ft / 3,122 m) is nearby to the south. It is the high peak with the square fire tower.

What's in a name? Beartooths, Beartooth Mountains, Beartooth Plateau, Beartooth Range—all are names applied to a continuous block of mountains and plateaus composed of ancient granite and gneiss north and northeast of the park. The Absaroka Range refers to mountains composed of younger volcanic materials south of the Beartooths and extending along the eastern part of the park. The map on page 159 shows the extent of these mountains.

~

If you look closely at the rocks in this area, you'll see that they contain innumerable angular rock pieces cemented together. This is volcanic breccia, evidence of the explosive volcanism of Mount Washburn **[GEO.4]** some 45 million years ago.

8.4/9.9 Chittenden Road leads 1.3 miles (2 km) up the northern slope of Mount Washburn to a view of the summit and access to the **Mount Washburn Trail**. (A part of this trail is described from the opposite end at mile 13.3/5.0). Gen. Henry D. Washburn (picture, page 320) was the Civil War Union veteran and surveyor-general of Montana who led the 1870 expedition of the park area and was the first of his party to climb this mountain.

Restrooms are found both at the parking area and at the fire tower, where there's a public telephone. This is one of the three fire lookouts still in use.

You can hike or bike to the top of Mount Washburn (about 3 mi / 5 km) from the parking area, but take drinking water and be prepared for sudden drastic changes of weather, including lots of wind and possible summer lightning storms. The view from the fire tower is superb. You may also access the trail from the Dunraven Pass parking area; by following this route, you avoid a narrow ridge that must be traversed just before the summit.

Expect to see bighorn sheep, which are amazingly tame here and may pose for your camera. The older rams have huge horns curved nearly in a circle, while young rams and ewes have short, slightly curved horns.

A pink species of paintbrush thrives north of Dunraven Pass.

Wildflowers abound in the entire area in July and early August. It's possible to find Indian paintbrush, phlox, forget-me-nots, lupine, sticky geranium,

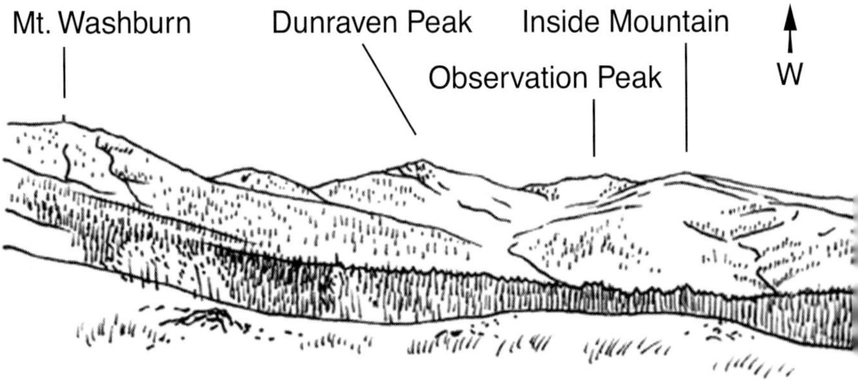

Mount Washburn North Side Panorama

Stretching from left to right (south to north):

Mt. Washburn with its square tower, then

An unnamed round hill.

Dunraven Peak (9,904 ft / 3,019 m) with a rocky top and **Hedges Peak** (9,685 ft / 2,952 m) behind it (visible only from the rocky promontory). Cornelius Hedges was the Washburn expedition member who was long thought to have originated the national park idea.

The next peak is **Observation Peak** (9,397 ft / 2,864 m), and the higher of the pair to its right is **Inside Mountain** (9,681 ft / 2,951 m), inside the semicircle of the Washburn Range.

larkspur, silky phacelia, and many others.

Even as late as mid July, you may see patches of snow. Watch for small waterfalls everywhere. They're pretty to look at, but the water is not safe to drink.

8.6/9.7 🚻♿ **P** Rest area with view to the west.

10.3/8.0 **P** Mount Washburn north side view. Here you see a mountain panorama totally different from the two that are 3 miles north and 4.5 miles south of this point.

13.3/5.0 Dunraven Pass★ (8,873 ft / 2,704 m), the highest point reached by road in the entire park.

🥾 🚻♿ The south end of the **Mount Washburn Trail** is located here.

Penstemon

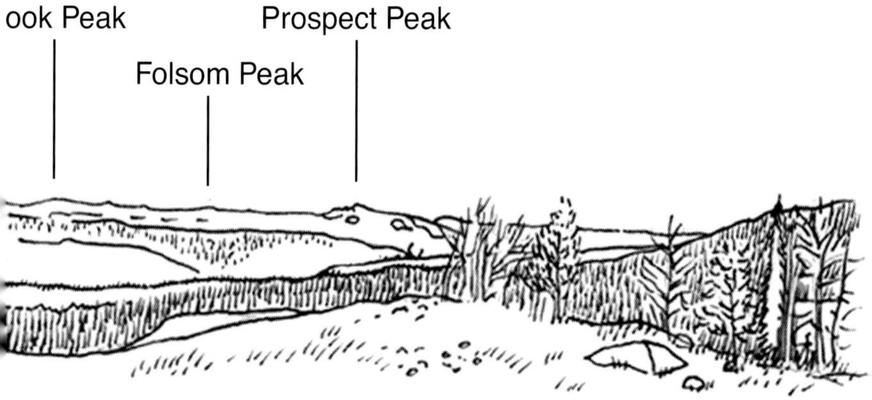

Farther away in the center of the view are **Cook Peak** (9,742 ft / 2,969 m) and **Folsom Peak** (9,338 ft / 2,846 m), named for two of the three men who explored and wrote about this territory in 1869.

On very clear days, you can see **Electric Peak** (10,969 ft / 3,343 m) between Cook and Folsom, over 20 miles away.

Prospect Peak (9,525 ft / 2,903 m), named by geologist Arnold Hague in 1885, is closer by on the right.

Peaks of the **Beartooth Mountains** line the far northern horizon.

No bicycles are allowed on this part of the trail. To hike to the top of Mount Washburn, you might prefer to start by driving up Chittenden Road (see mile 8.4/9.9) to access a shorter but steeper route with an elevation gain of 1,500 feet in 2.25 miles (460 m in 3.6 km).

The first half mile (0.8 km) or so of the Mount Washburn Trail is not terribly steep and is well worth exploring. Along the south-facing hillside here is one of the best wildflower displays in the park!

An interpretive sign at the trailhead explains alpine tundra and describes the rigors of the Mount Washburn trail, where elevation gain is nearly 1,400 feet in about 3 miles (430 m in 5 km).

Dunraven Peak and Dunraven Pass were named for the fourth Earl of Dunraven, the British sportsman who wrote *The Great Divide: Travels in the Upper Yellowstone in the Summer of 1874*. Many Europeans were first introduced to Yellowstone through reading his book. Dunraven waxes eloquent about contemplating the view from Mount Washburn.

Viola

13.8/5.5 Restroom turnout.

14.8/3.5 Interpretive sign about the caldera. At approximately this point, the Grand Loop Road crosses into the Yellowstone Caldera, the major geological feature that helped to shape the Yellowstone landscape (further explained in "At the Edge of the Yellowstone Caldera" on pages 44–45).

The view here is worth another stop.

Washburn Hot Springs Panorama

From east to south (left to right):

Washburn Hot Springs' steam can usually be seen rising from below, as can that from two other hydrothermal areas.

Grand Canyon of the Yellowstone River's far wall is in the middle distance.

To the east are tree-covered **Mirror Plateau** and the distant **Absaroka Range**.

To the south, beyond a nearby clump of live and dead trees, is a glimpse of **Hayden Valley**.

On the clearest days you can make out the peaks of the **Tetons** 75 miles away, and, though Yellowstone Lake is out of sight, you can see part of Mt. Sheridan south of the lake.

Only an unmaintained trail leads from here to **Washburn Hot Springs**, which cluster on both sides of Sulphur Creek before the creek empties into the canyon of the Yellowstone. The springs can be reached from a maintained trail that descends sharply from the top of Mount Washburn down its east flank, or from the Glacial Boulder near Canyon Village.

15.9/2.4 (12) Dunraven Road picnic area on the west.

17.0/1.3 (16) Cascade Lake picnic area, where you may join the Cascade Lake Trail at the picnic area's south end.

17.5/0.8 P Park for the **Cascade Lake Trail**, which goes 4.4 miles (7 km) round trip to the lake. It's a pleasant, nearly level walk through meadows rampant with wildflowers and a mixed green and burned forest. Another trail branches off for a much more difficult hike to Observation Peak.

Cascade Lake is a popular catch-and-release fishing lake for cutthroat trout and grayling. It's surrounded by grass and willows, and beaver have made their lodges here. Bison, moose, and grizzly bears are sometimes seen. This lake is the source of Cascade Creek, which falls over Crystal Falls into the Yellowstone between the Upper and Lower Falls.

18.3/0.0 Canyon Junction. Just to the east are Canyon Village and the end of the one-way loop road along the canyon rim. See pages 184–86 for sights along North Rim Drive. Canyon's sights and facilities are described beginning on page 187; map page 179. South from Canyon Junction is Fishing Bridge Junction; west is Norris Junction; north are Dunraven Pass, Tower Fall, and Tower-Roosevelt Junction.

NOTE: Construction on the Chittenden Road to Tower Junction segment may necessitate nighttime or total closure in 2013 and beyond. Check with Yellowstone authorities for up-to-date information.

From Canyon Junction to Norris Junction

The Canyon to Norris road (historically called the Norris Cutoff) was first built in 1885–86. Although it was often in bad repair during its history, the road was substantially improved in the 1960s and provides a convenient 12-mile-long (19 km) connection between the eastern and western sides of the Grand Loop Road, providing the center part of the figure eight. There's not a lot to see on the drive, but you'll find some pleasant trails to lakes and waterfalls, as well as fly-fishing opportunities in the Gibbon River.

Road Log

0.0/11.6 Canyon Junction. To the west is Norris Junction; north are Dunraven Pass, Tower Fall, and Tower Junction. East are Canyon Village and the north rim of the Yellowstone River canyon, and south is Fishing Bridge Junction.

0.5/11.1 **Cascade Creek Trailhead**. It's about 2.5 miles (4 km) from this trailhead to the lake. This route is used by horseback groups as well as hikers. You may prefer the slightly shorter and more pleasant Cascade Lake Trail (see mile 17.5/0.8 in the road log "From Tower Junction to Canyon Junction").

3.1/8.5 A tiny lily pond to the north may be covered with yellow blooms in midsummer. The burned forest is a result of the 1988 Wolf Lake fire.

3.5/8.1 Short road to generous parking for Grebe Lake Trailhead. A popular fishing spot and one of the few bodies of water in the park that may still have Montana grayling, **Grebe Lake** is about 3 miles (5 km) from the road. It was named for the western grebe (*Aechmorphus occidentalis*), a medium-large waterbird. The trail follows a former road most of the way and joins the Howard Eaton Trail east of the lake.

Grebe Lake figured prominently in the story of the second stagecoach hold-up to occur in the park. In August of 1897, two masked men held up a caravan consisting of an army ambulance and 15 stagecoaches south of the lake. They got away with $630 in cash, but evidence found at Grebe Lake soon helped to convict the men, who served two-and-a-half years' imprisonment for the crime.

The whole relatively level area north of the road is called the Solfatara Plateau, where sulfur deposits, acid soil, and hot sulfurous steam abound.

4.9/6.7 **Cygnet Lakes Trailhead** to the south. The lakes and their surrounding meadows are reached in about 4 miles (6.5 km); an unmaintained trail continues across the flat Central Plateau.

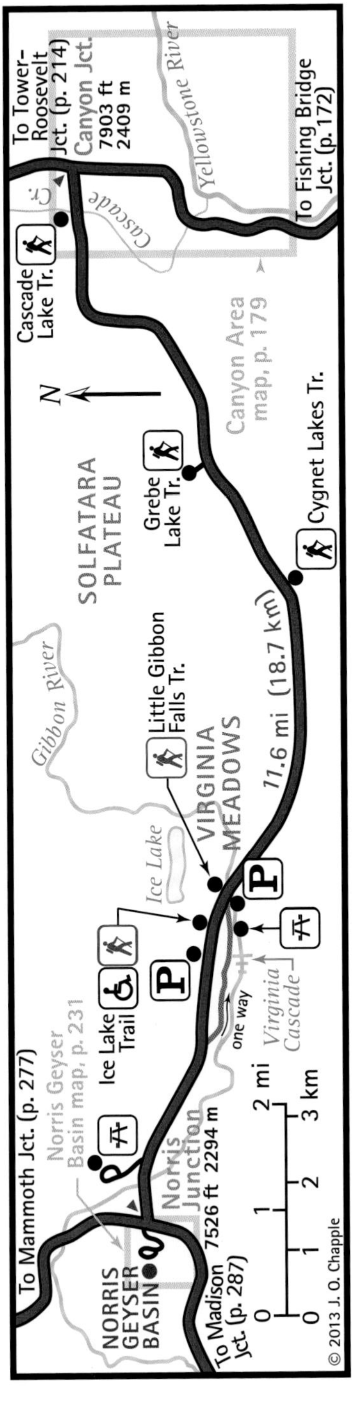

Canyon Junction to Norris Junction

On the trailhead sign-in box, there's a warning: Bear Frequenting Area!

As you top the hill going west, Mt. Holmes and neighboring mountains, over 13 miles (21 km) away, come into view.

The road turns northwest and descends Blanding Hill, named for the foreman of the first road crew here in 1885. Until the road was realigned in 1957, this was a notoriously steep place and was the first part of the road to become impassible in early winter. It's steep because this is the very edge of the 110,000-year-old Solfatara Plateau rhyolite lava flow.

7.9/3.7 Just west of the Gibbon River crossing is a parking area for Virginia Meadows fishing access and for the Little Gibbon Falls and Wolf Lake Trailheads.

Cross the road and walk a few yards toward the river to find **Little Gibbon Falls Trail**, which is not marked at the roadside. A hike of about 1 mile (1.6 km) through Virginia Meadows and up a small hill brings you to gentle, 25-foot (7.6 m) **Little Gibbon Falls**.

Much of the remaining 2.5 miles (about 4 km) to **Wolf Lake** is not well maintained. North of here is one of the park's large mountainous areas with no roads or trails, which includes the Washburn Range and its foothills.

The name Gibbon in the park comes neither from the ape nor from the famous English historian, but rather from Gen. John Gibbon. The general led a group of soldiers through Yellowstone in 1872. They ran out of provisions entirely and were subsisting on roots, squirrels, and blue jays when they encountered the Hayden Survey, who provided them with flour and sugar.

8.0/3.6 End of the one-way loop road (do not enter here) that passes the Virginia Cascade and picnic area.

8.2/3.4 **Ice Lake Trailhead**. This wheelchair-accessible trail—relatively wide and level—is the shortest way to reach tree-bordered Ice Lake (0.3 mi/0.5 km from the road). The name comes from the days when ice was cut from the lake for use at the now long-gone Norris Hotel. This lake has one backcountry campsite accessible to the disabled.

In the twentieth century, Ice Lake was repeatedly but unsuccessfully stocked with grayling. North of Ice Lake, this trail joins the long Howard Eaton Trail to the Norris campground area on the west.

To the east, the trail passes Wolf, Grebe, and Cascade Lakes on its way to the Canyon area. Fishing is excellent in these three lakes, but there may be grizzlies about.

8.5/3.1 **P** Parking on both sides of the road for the boardwalk to the **Fire and Blowdown exhibit**, with no warning sign for those traveling east. A tornado-force wind tore through here in 1984, followed four years later by the big fire. In this locality there is slower regeneration of growth than in most other badly burned areas, perhaps because the soil was scorched by the burning of dry trees that were already lying down.

9.9/1.7 **(6)** **Virginia Cascade Road** affords several good views of the Gibbon River's 60-foot (18 m) plunge over volcanic rock. The 2-mile (3.2 km)

This forest, severely burned in 1988, showed patches of grass and young lodgepole pines in 1996.

Twenty years after the fire, lodgepoles were thriving. Both pictures were taken at the Fire and Blowdown exhibit.

side road is narrow, steep, and curving—and difficult for the park to maintain. Engineer Hiram Chittenden called it "a positive menace to the lives of travelers."

Virginia Cascade and the nearby Virginia Meadows, through which the Gibbon River flows, were named for the wife of Charles Gibson, head of the Yellowstone Park Association, a late-nineteenth-century hotel concessionaire.

A picnic area is at the far east end of the one-way loop road.

11.0/0.6 **(16)** Norris Meadows picnic area. The Gibbon River meanders past on its way to drain Norris Geyser Basin to the west.

11.6/0.0 Norris Junction. The lodgepole snags standing to the southwest of the junction are left from a prescribed burn in 2007.

Norris Geyser Basin is straight ahead (west), Obsidian Cliff and Mammoth Hot Springs are to the north, Madison Junction to the south (then southwest), and Canyon Junction to the east.

Norris Geyser Basin*

Give yourself a few hours at Norris Geyser Basin for a walk through a thermal area very different from all the others in the park. A ranger-interpreter is often roving in Norris Geyser Basin during daylight hours, and it's always worthwhile for a visitor to go along with him or her to learn what's currently interesting in the basin. The features at Norris change so rapidly that only someone on the spot almost daily can keep up.

(6) The short Norris Geyser Basin side road goes directly west from Norris Junction. At road's end, you'll find restrooms and cold drink machines—very welcome on a hot summer day. There are no restaurants, hotels, or grocery stores near this area.

Down a short walkway from the parking lots are a small bookstore and the **Norris Museum**, built in 1930 and now a National Historic Landmark. Inside the museum, you'll find displays about Yellowstone's and other regions' hydrothermal areas. A pamphlet about Norris's trails and features is available from a dispensing box near the museum. Read the precautions for a safe and pleasant geyser basin walk in the Travel Tips and in the Upper Geyser Basin section.

What's at Norris Geyser Basin?

About 50 of the most easily seen and interesting hot springs, geysers, and mud pots are mentioned in this guidebook. Some may be insignificant features but have such irresistible names they beg to be listed. There are actually over 180 features here, according to geyser enthusiast Rocco Paperiello's *Report on the Norris Geyser Basin for 1984*. No guidebook can keep up to date with the constantly changing features of this basin.

Two sometimes-steaming springs greet you before you even start on the basin walkways. To the east of the museum is rarely erupting Harding Geyser, named when it first erupted in 1923 for President Warren G. Harding, who visited the park that year only a month before he died.

Behind the bookstore is the site of Steamvalve Spring. Have you wondered while visiting the park how engineers have managed to avoid placing roads and buildings in the path of hydrothermal activity? Steamvalve Spring is an example of a place they misjudged. Here a seemingly dead mud hole—now covered with downed lodgepoles—has been filled with asphalt twice, only to come bursting through with renewed activity, erupting frequently with extraordinary rumbling noises. No more asphalt has been applied!

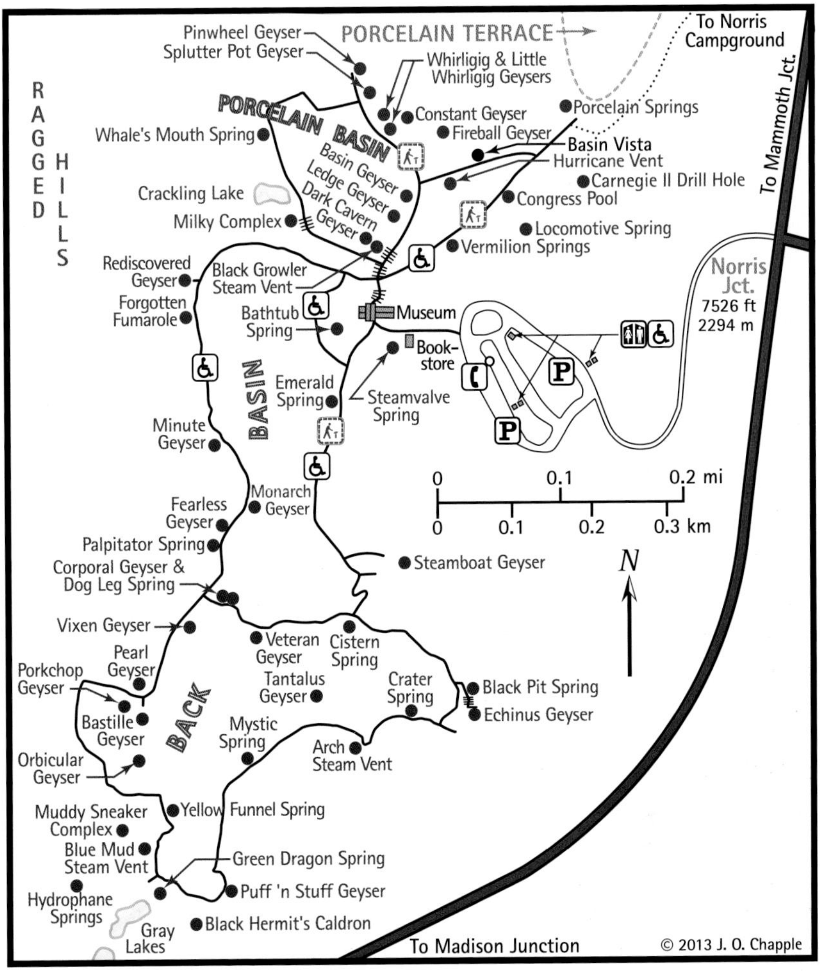

Norris Geyser Basin

Loop trails divide the area open to visitors into two parts, Back Basin and Porcelain Basin. Relatively remote areas called the One Hundred Spring Plain and the Gap are hot, active, wet, and dangerous; therefore, they are not furnished with boardwalks.

Back Basin is where you'll find the sometimes predictable Echinus Geyser and Yellowstone's tallest (but notoriously erratic) geyser, Steamboat. The entire Back Basin loop is about 1.5 miles (2.4 km) around. The loop past Steamboat Geyser and Cistern Spring is wheelchair-accessible.

Porcelain Basin is a vast, delicately tinted plain with many small geysers, hot springs, lakes, and fumaroles. The western loop around this area and the walkway to Porcelain Terrace on the east side are each about 0.5 miles (0.8 km) long. Part of the eastern walkway is wheelchair-accessible.

Norris Geyser Basin in the History of Yellowstone

None of the famous early expeditions visited this geyser basin. It was not until 1872 that a man named Eugene S. Topping and his companion happened to notice steam rising far to the south from the top of Observation Peak (their name for present-day Bunsen Peak near Mammoth). Topping and party were the first known visitors to the area, but Superintendent Norris, for whom the basin is named, was the first to explore and describe it fully a few years later.

Now there's no hotel at Norris, but a succession of facilities followed each other in this area in the early years, ranging from tent camps and lunch stations to a rather fine hotel opened in 1887 and destroyed by fire the same year.

Until 1966, the Grand Loop Road cut right through the center of Norris Geyser Basin. Park officials moved the road to minimize the problems of human impact, traffic congestion, steam on the windshields of passing cars, and danger to pedestrians, who had to cross the highway to reach the geyser basin.

WALKING TOUR OF BACK BASIN

Just what Back Basin is "back" of is not obvious to present-day visitors, but the basin was in back of the museum before the Grand Loop Road was rerouted. NOTE: The Back Basin walkway may be accessible with assistance nearly to the southern corner of the basin (see map, page 231). As of 2012 the boardwalk from Emerald Spring to Cistern Spring has been made stairless, so that if the star geysers Steamboat or Echinus should rejuvenate, more people will see them.

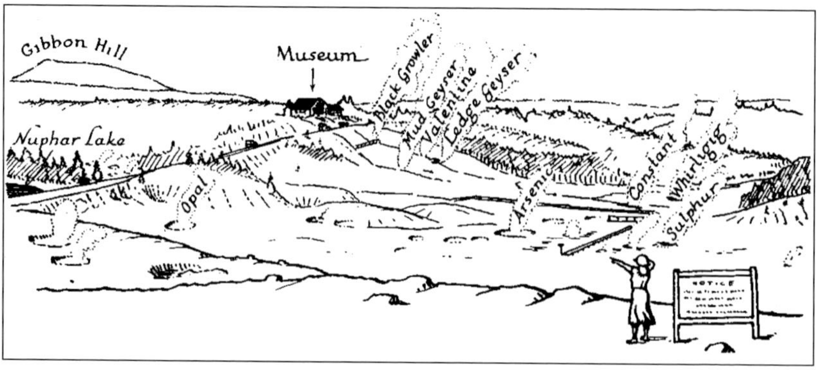

The Grand Loop Road cut between the Norris Museum and Porcelain Basin, as shown in this H.C. Bumpus sketch from 1935.

As you walk through Back Basin, you may wonder what has caused so many trees to fall and lie about helter-skelter, since they were not burned in the 1988 fires. Lodgepole pines have a very shallow root system, and when they grow very tall, as these have done, a strong wind can topple them easily. These trees are mostly about the same age and height; thus, winds have created a sort of domino effect among them. Park policy is to leave them lying unless they actually obstruct a path or road.

Turning south (left from the entrance walkway) near the museum, you first encounter **Emerald Spring [GEO.21]**. Emerald may bubble due to rising gases, even when its water is below the boiling point. At times it gets hot enough to actually boil, and then it becomes a muddy brown color and may erupt as high as 26 feet (8 m).

Emerald Spring is usually a beautiful shade of green, combining deep-blue water with a yellow sulfurous lining.

The next feature of interest is **Steamboat Geyser**, usually steaming or spouting up to 15 feet (3m) from behind a pile of colorfully stained rocks. But on occasion, Steamboat becomes the world's largest geyser. It has had an extremely erratic record of major eruptions, the first one noted in 1878. Since then its interval has ranged from a few days to 50 years! Eruptions were rare until the 1960s, when there were over one hundred of them. Three occurred in the 1970s and at least 40 in the 1980s. When Steamboat seems to be heating up, geyser watchers hope for more frequent eruptions, but they have been disappointed in recent years. Two eruptions occurred in 2002, three in 2003, and one in 2005.

Steamboat's major eruptions come with a tremendous roar and sometimes reach 380 feet (116 m), an almost unbelievable height three times that of Old Faithful. The water phase of these eruptions may last 3 to 20 minutes, fol-

A thrilling Steamboat Geyser eruption, May 23, 2005

lowed by as much as 12 hours of the steam phase. Minor eruptions from its two vents may go to 40 or 60 feet (12–18 m).

Bearing left after Steamboat's lower overlook you find **Echinus Geyser**, still an interesting geyser, but now infrequent and erratic. Ferdinand Hayden named it Echinus ("spine" in Greek) in 1878 for surrounding sinter-coated rhyolite rocks that resembled tiny spiny sea urchins (not so evident now). Its water is very acidic, unlike the alkaline water of Yellowstone's other large geysers.

Echinus became an interesting geyser in the 1970s; into 1998 its eruptions were both large and predictable, but since that time eruption patterns have become variable. The geyser has gone from complete dormancy to intervals of a few days to several months. To catch an eruption when you visit, ask at the museum for that day's pattern.

Photographers are inclined to be frustrated by Echinus; its prodigious amount of steam covers the sparkling water during most of the eruption. Remember to dry off your camera or eyeglass lenses immediately should they get wet in any geyser spray, because the silica in the water can leave permanent spots.

Near the upper viewing area for Echinus is **Black Pit Spring**, a very hot spring that fizzes and bubbles like oil in a frying pan.

Sparkling drops from Echinus Geyser's eruption may reach the excited spectators (1998 photo).

What Makes Norris Unique?

1. Extreme heat

Norris Geyser Basin is hot! The water in the springs is generally both hotter and more acidic than in the other geyser basins of Yellowstone. Here are some temperatures found in three different research drill holes:

- 401°F (205°C) in a hole drilled down 247 ft (75 m)
- 385°F (196°C) at 813 ft (248 m) deep
- 460°F (238°C) at 1088 ft (332 m) deep

2. Long history

Geoscientists infer from sinter cobbles found in glacial *moraines* that geothermal activity at Norris may have been continuous since 150,000 years ago.

3. No big formations and few predictable geysers

Although geyserite is deposited at Norris as at other geyser basins, Norris lacks the tall or grotesque formations you see in Upper Geyser Basin. Much of what looks like sinter at Norris is actually acid-leached volcanic rock, especially Lava Creek tuff. There are at least 70 geysers at Norris, but very few are predictable.

4. Change is the only constant

The whole area is so dynamic that changes in the hot springs occur constantly and rapidly. Some changes can be attributed to earthquake activity, but many are still puzzling to geologists and geochemists. Some of the variables they study here are temperature, chemical composition, amount of water and discharge, amount of sinter deposition, and acidity/alkalinity (*pH*).

5. Unique locale

Norris is uniquely situated at or near the intersection of three geologic features:

- the northwest rim of the Yellowstone Caldera
- the long Norris-Mammoth corridor, a zone of faults running north-south, where the earth's surface has subsided
- a seismically active fault zone that stretches east-west between Norris and Hebgen Lake.

6. Special springs

Some springs far out in the One Hundred Spring Plain (to be visited only with a ranger or other knowledgeable person) show truly unusual phenomena. Realgar Springs deposit red and orange material that may be a previously unknown form of *arsenic sulfide*. Large, circular Cinder Pool suspends on its surface tiny black hollow spheres, probably made of elemental sulfur colored by iron sulfide. And then Sulphur Dust Spring's bottom is covered with powdery, pale yellow, elemental sulfur.

7. Seasonal disturbance

One phenomenon scientists have researched is a seasonal disturbance that often occurs sometime between mid July and early autumn, particularly in Back Basin. For a week or two, many features at Norris go berserk: Emerald Spring becomes cloudy, Echinus Geyser turns unpredictable (even when routinely predictable), and Green Dragon Spring and Gray Lakes turn chocolate brown and boil furiously.

During the disturbances, geoscientists have noted an increase in the amount of water and gas discharged, increase in the turbidity of the water, large fluctuations in water temperatures, and decreased chloride and increased acidity in some springs. Occasionally, a small hydrothermal explosion creates a new thermal feature. Some geochemists now consider it likely that the Norris seasonal disturbance stems from the mixing of groundwater from two or more different underground zones having different chemical compositions.

Leaving Echinus, the walkway crosses the South Fork of Tantalus Creek for the first time and passes near several features that have erupted as geysers for short periods in the recent past. **Crater Spring** and **Arch Steam Vent** are to the right (north) and left (south) of the path, respectively. **Tantalus Geyser** (formerly Decker Geyser) is out in the sinter to the north.

In the case of Tantalus Geyser, the human history is more interesting than the thermal history. In the 1960s, Mrs. Hazel Decker was so determined to see Steamboat Geyser erupt that she spent 52 consecutive days in the area, sleeping in her car in the parking lot. Mrs. Decker was rewarded with about 10 eruptions of Steamboat. A nearby geyser that was named for her has been renamed Tantalus Geyser, but a small grove of trees out in the sinter is informally called Decker Island.

Tantalus Creek, the small creek that drains both Back Basin and Porcelain Basin, is named for a king in Greek mythology. He was doubly condemned: to stand up to his chin in water that retreated whenever he stooped to drink and to reach up for bunches of grapes that always evaded his grasp. (This myth is the source of our word *tantalize*.) The creek's water level and temperature rise and fall with basin-wide geyser eruptions.

A long stretch of the Back Basin walkway passes springs of different colors, shapes, sizes, and levels of activity, including sometimes yellow-green, sometimes superheated **Mystic Spring**. Just before you reach **Black Hermit's Caldron** (away from the trail's corner), you pass another example of a geyser whose name is better than its action, **Puff 'n Stuff Geyser**. The late Park Geologist Rick Hutchinson named it after a TV show of the early 1970s called *H. R. Pufnstuf*. The geyser gurgles below ground and sprays out some water but has never done much else.

Next is cavernous **Green Dragon Spring**, named for its usual color and its characteristic action, boiling vigorously and belching steam from three funnel-shaped vents. When the steam clears away, you can see greenish yellow crusts of sulfur and red deposits of iron on the cavern roof. Stretching away from this point are two very large hot springs called the **Gray Lakes**, whose waters are said to be in constant motion, caused by boiling springs on the bottom.

West of the Gray Lakes, not visible from the walkway but partially visible from the highway, are the **Hydrophane Springs**, whose color is reflected in its name and its steam. Hydrophane is a type of opal that becomes translucent when immersed in water.

Phillips Caldron, usually a pool of opaque water, honors Charles Phillips, a park ranger who was fascinated by geysers. Lamentably, while stationed for the winter at Old Faithful in 1927, he mistook poisonous water hemlock growing in warm thermal runoff for edible wild parsnip and died within a few hours of eating it.

West of the path, the **Muddy Sneaker Complex** (including one small geyser) got its name from park geologist Rick Hutchinson in 1971. It was originally a violent mud pot that sprang up suddenly in the trail. "Anybody who would walk in it or below it would get their shoes or sneakers muddy," according to Hutchinson. The path has since been moved uphill.

Very close to the path is **Blue Mud Steam Vent**, a deep round pot of vigorously boiling muddy water (in 2012), with edges lined with blue-gray mud.

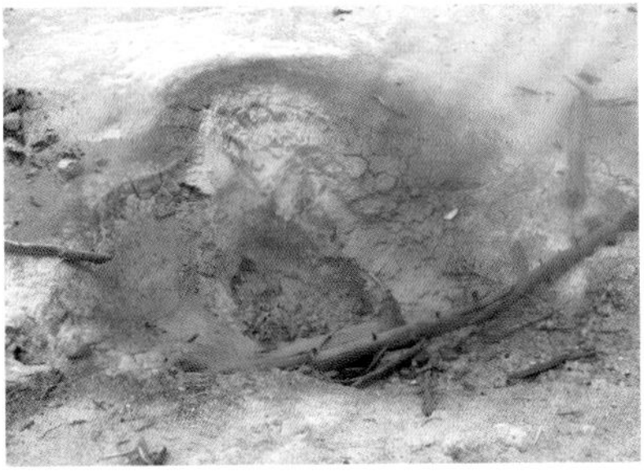

Blue Mud Steam Vent displays unusually colored mud and water.

Yellow Funnel Spring near the boardwalk corner deserves its name only part of the time. Sometimes you can't see the yellow-stained funnel for the opaque green, blue, or muddy water; sometimes it's merely a steam vent. **Son of Green Dragon** north of Yellow Funnel sometimes acts as a geyser.

This area of Back Basin, from Yellow Funnel Spring to Pearl Geyser, became so hot in July 2003, with soil temperatures near boiling and new fumaroles everywhere, that park officials closed the former straight boardwalk. In 2004 a new raised boardwalk loop was built to bypass the hottest area. On this loop you pass the small frequent spouter called **Orbicular Geyser** ("Orby"), numerous other spouting vents, and Porkchop Geyser.

In the 1980s, **Porkchop Geyser** was a porkchop-shaped perpetual spouter that formed a tall ice cone from its spray in the winter. Suddenly, on September 5, 1989, Porkchop exploded. A few lucky people were watching as chunks of geyserite were upended and debris thrown about in a true hydrothermal explosion. What remains is a steaming pool surrounded by jagged boulders.

Although very close to the side of Porkchop, **North** or **Second Eruptor**, with small eruptions from its deep vent, has a different temperature and water chemistry from Porkchop.

At the boardwalk corner is **Pearl Geyser**. Its almost translucent pearl-like deposits are now sometimes covered with mud. Pearl Geyser erupts up to 8 feet (2.4 m) high but is unpredictable. In late summer of 2012 Pearl's usually clear water was opalescent, and several pools and bubbling holes appeared across the boardwalk from it.

Bastille Geyser south of Pearl was born in 1992 on France's Bastille Day, July 14. It grew from a 2-inch (5 cm) hole to a 3-foot (1 m) crater in eight hours during a seasonal disturbance. It erupted up to 3 feet (1 m) high every four or five minutes when active, but it has stopped erupting and has filled in its vents with sinter. In late 2012 there were three large unnamed bubbling holes in a row here, one with a gold lining spurting water from deep below.

The next feature is **Vixen Geyser**, which may erupt from its red-stained crater for a few seconds every few minutes, except for its rare major eruptions up to 35 feet (11 m). Its much more usual eruptions spout no more than 10 feet

(3 m) high. Almost all Vixen's water drains back into its rectangular vent.

This geyser was named by a woman tourist who was splattered by an eruption in 1881 and exclaimed, "You vixen, you," according to tour guide George L. Henderson. In 1883, geologist Walter Weed wrote that according to Superintendent Norris, a geyserite cone displayed at the Centennial Exposition in Philadelphia in 1876 came from Vixen. That cone has apparently been lost.

On display now at the Smithsonian's National Museum of Natural History in Washington is a geyserite cone from Yellowstone measuring about 30 inches high by 18 inches diameter (75 by 45 cm). Labeled as collected in 1881 by Norris himself, this could not be the older cone. The provenance of the pictured cone is an unsolved mystery.

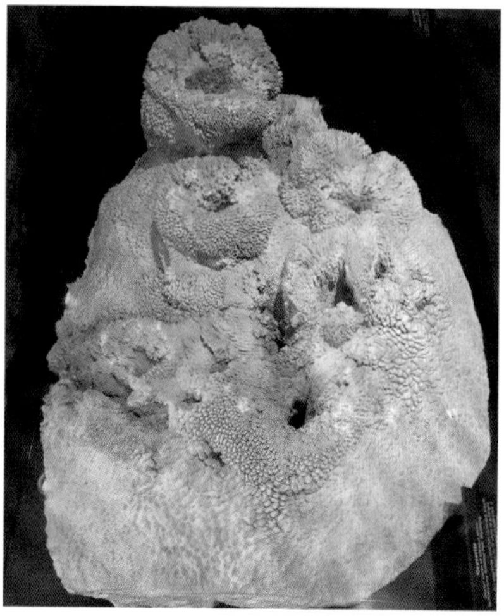

Geyserite cone donated by Supt. Norris to the Smithsonian (Foley, 2006)

After crossing Tantalus Creek, you must choose between going right (east toward Echinus via Cistern Spring) or straight ahead (north toward the museum via the shortest path).

East toward Echinus

Near the trail junction on the left are small **Corporal Geyser** and tiny **Dog Leg Spring** with two small vents. When one of these geysers erupts the other drains.

On the right is **Veteran Geyser**, which probably derived its name from the very old sinter deposits all around. Veteran's short eruptions may go out 40 feet (12 m) at an angle, but they occur in a long-term cyclic pattern of minutes to hours that is not yet fully deciphered.

At the boardwalk intersection is **Cistern Spring**. The remarkable colors in the runoff are unusual for Norris Basin—unless you are here during a seasonal disturbance when you may see only murky water. Cistern built its impressive terrace in the past few decades. Bacteria color the terraces canary yellow, orange, and brown when the pool is full. True to its name as a water reservoir, Cistern's water drains drastically when neighboring Steamboat Geyser has a major eruption; without the water, the bacteria die.

North toward the museum

If you turn back from Cistern and take up the loop trail again, or if you have continued straight on at the trail junction after crossing Tantalus Creek, you'll first encounter **Palpitator Spring**. Palpitator is actually a geyser and has small but extremely long eruptions of around three hours. It was named for steam pulsing below the ground that once produced uncannily rhythmic beats.

You will see perpetual spouting at the center of **Fearless Geyser** at your left (west) as the trail approaches **Monarch Geyser** on the right. Behind Monarch's crater is a devastated-looking hillside, showing that Monarch was a truly regal feature at one time, though it has not had a large eruption since 1913. Before that year it could rocket to a height of 200 feet (60 m), spewing out rocks and mud "with rumblings that shake the valley" (as an 1884 guidebook states). It then became so quiet that it's sometimes called Monarch Geyser Crater. However, proving that geysers can never be pronounced dead, it began having superheated boiling periods in 1993, with an occasional burst 20 feet (6 m) high. Some researchers believe there may be an underground connection between Monarch and Steamboat Geysers.

Partway up the small hill north of Monarch Geyser are **Mushroom Geyser** (named for its mushroom-shaped pedestal deposits, now gone) and Minute Geyser. **Minute Geyser** erupted at one-minute intervals as much as 40 feet (12 m) high until about 1902. Unfortunately located near the stagecoach loading dock, Minute Geyser's vent was blocked by a large boulder thrown in by vandals. This changed the action to another vent that spouts frequently. Minute Geyser has had occasional major eruptions in recent years.

As you continue through the woods, you might notice steam rising to the left (west). **Forgotten Fumarole** acted as a geyser from 2004 to 2008, erupting to 20–30 feet (6–9 m); **Rediscovered Geyser**, on a short path of its own, is usually a tiny perpetual spouter.

Bathtub Spring is on its own stretch of path between the main walkway and the museum. The spring usually looks just like an old-fashioned tub filled with yellow to light brown muddy water, sometimes spouting continuously. The massive buildup of geyserite is unusual for Norris features and was probably formed during alkaline water cycles within the hot spring, since not much sinter accumulates during acidic cycles.

WALKING TOURS OF PORCELAIN BASIN

Consult the Norris Geyser Basin map, page 231, for Porcelain Basin's walkways.

Porcelain Basin Overview

Approaching from the parking lot, turn right and pass through the museum breezeway to visit Porcelain Basin, or stop to visit the museum's geological exhibits. The far side of the breezeway affords a panoramic view of the basin and of Mt. Holmes about 10 miles (16 km) beyond.

The acres of geyserite and acid-leached lava here give the ground the texture and colors of fine pastel tableware. Porcelain Basin is aptly named, since geyserite is made of silica, and silica and alumina are major constituents of porcelain. In the varying light between dawn and dusk, pools of opalescent water reflect different shades of blue. The basin shows delicate tints of canary yellow, sulfurous yellow green, aqua, orange, rose, coral, white, tan, and gray. Minerals like iron oxides and arsenic sulfides are responsible for much of the staining. Bright lime-green algae love the acidity in some runoff channels, while yellow, orange, and brown microorganisms thrive where the water is neutral or alkaline.

The amount of water in Porcelain Basin's aquifer seems to vary greatly. The water supply was especially low in 1996, a summer when the two Norris museums and the campground happened to be closed as a government economy measure.

Porcelain Basin below Norris Museum

Porcelain Basin's eastern loop is partly wheelchair-accessible but steep in places. An extension of the eastern loop leads toward Nuphar Lake, Porcelain Springs, and Norris Campground. Because there are few signs pointing out the named features, this is the most difficult basin in the park in which to orient yourself. The western loop is about 0.5 mile long (0.8 km), the eastern loop a little less.

Porcelain Basin West Loop

You might begin your tour of Porcelain Basin by taking the stairs down to follow the western loop in a counterclockwise direction. This will bring you close to the greatest number of hydrothermal features.

First encountered as you bear right when the trail forks is **Black Growler Steam Vent**. One of the highest temperatures recorded at the surface of any feature in Yellowstone was in Black Growler's steam, once measured at 284°F (140°C).

North of Black Growler and a little farther from the walkway is Valentine Geyser, and even farther away (and harder to see when not erupting) is Dark Cavern Geyser. **Valentine Geyser** was called Alcove until one February 14 early in the 1900s, when the Norris hotel keeper watched as large amounts of rock, mud, water, and steam were blown out, forming a huge pit. It erupted quite regularly for some years to 75 or 100 feet (23–30 m), but is now irregular. This geyser has built a cone inside its alcove, the largest of any Norris geyser.

Dark Cavern Geyser usually erupts quite regularly once or twice an hour up to 20 feet (6 m) and sometimes higher and very forcefully. It seems to be connected both to Valentine and Ledge Geysers.

Ledge Geyser erupts from five vents, from which water jets out in the shape of the fingers and thumb of a hand. For its muddy eruptions, it was often called Mud Geyser in early years. Geyser expert T. Scott Bryan writes that water from the "thumb" projects at a steep angle and to a height of 125 feet (38 m), while producing an unmatched booming and roaring. But, like Steamboat Geyser in Back Basin, Ledge is totally unpredictable. It erupted once each in 2006 and 2007, and twice in 2008.

Between Ledge and Basin Geysers is now-calm **Jetsam Pool**; it has been known to erupt, but not for many years. The noisiest steam vent farther away from the boardwalk is **Guardian Geyser**.

One recent summer, **Basin Geyser**, the small, steaming pool located shortly before the trail junction, had yellow monkeyflowers growing in its alcove. Another year, the temperature of its water was posted as 202°F (94°C), a temperature that's above boiling at this altitude and much too hot for flowers.

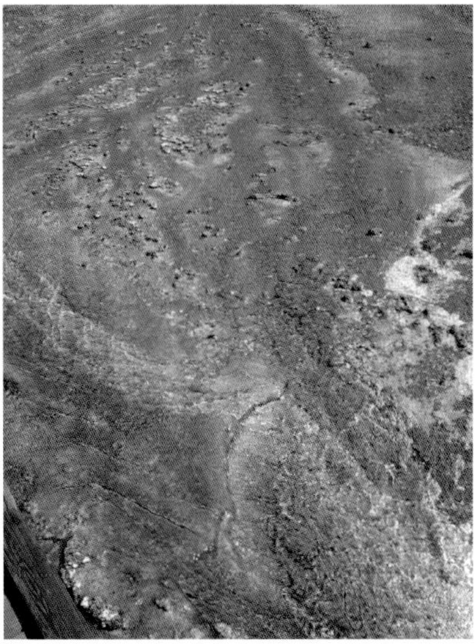

A bright green Cyanidiales alga

Continuing northwest

Out across the barren flats are at least eight geysers or perpetual spouters and many hot pools. The one with the most significant activity in the late twentieth century was **Fireball Geyser**, located 100 feet (30 m) or more from the walkway. Fireball's main jet angles to the right, while a lesser column shoots straight up. It erupts about every two hours.

Three geysers are near the walkway and on the right as you walk northwest. **Little Whirligig Geyser** sometimes sends up small, rapid bursts of water but is nearly dormant. **Constant Geyser** is farther from the walkway, making a triangle with the Whirligigs. Constant is not a perpetual spouter but does sometimes erupt for a few seconds several times an hour, sometimes to 30 feet (9 m). **Whirligig Geyser** (sometimes called Big Whirligig) is the third of this related threesome. The water of the bigger Whirligig swirls about in its crater during eruptions and a crack on the crater's far side emits a loud chugging sound. But Whirligig has recently been dormant.

Pinwheel Geyser, just east of the short spur of walkway, was a frequent performer until the ground settled some years ago, allowing runoff and sediment from above to cool and partially clog it. When this geyser is active, its runoff channel passes right across the crater of **Splutter Pot Geyser**, sometimes called the Washing Machine for its low-pitched belching water.

After passing below a tree-covered hillside, the walkway brings you to **Whale's Mouth Spring**, which rather

Crackling Lake takes its name from the sizzling gas bubbles in its water.

resembles an open mouth with teeth and is usually full of green water.

The jumble of high jagged rocks and fallen trees bordering the basin to the west appears on park maps as the **Ragged Hills**. These hills are full of rhyolite caverns that bears have used for hibernation. Smart bears! The ground there can be as much as 30°F (17°C) higher than the outside temperature.

Named in the 1960s for the popping sounds from many bubbles are large, hot, opalescent, blue-green **Crackling Lake** and its neighbor **Crackling Spring**, partway up the hill.

To your right as you mount the stairs from the basin is the **Milky Complex**, whose **Teal Blue Bubbler** will sometimes be spouting as you pass.

A few steps and a steep but shady path take you back to the start of this loop.

Porcelain Basin East Loop

From the stairs just below the museum, turn right (east) for the eastern loop around Porcelain Basin.

NOTE: The eastern loop is partly wheelchair-accessible if you go past Bathtub Spring and around the museum to avoid the stairs (see map).

First you'll see a solfatara full of steaming and bubbling fumaroles and spouters, lined in red, orange, or yellow and called **Vermilion Springs**. The variety in the colors here is due to different levels of acidity and different oxidation states of iron and sulfur.

Farthest from the walkway is **Locomotive Spring** (or Springs, since there are a red and a blue pool—though hard to see from the boardwalk), with occasional eruptions to 6 feet high (1.8 m).

Congress Pool next to the boardwalk became a geyser in 1891, after beginning life as a fumarole. The geyser was named for that year's Fifth International Geological Congress, and also (quipped its namer, geologist Arnold Hague) "because its earliest outbursts were powerful eruptions marked by periods of rest." *This* congress was held in Washington, D.C., but included a Yellowstone field trip. Congress promptly settled down to become a pool, a bubbling mud pot, or sometimes a weak steam vent.

There's more action on the hillside behind Congress Pool, where in 1929 an experimental drill hole went 265 feet (81 m) down. The enormous steam pressure had threatened to blow up the drilling rig. Despite being filled with cement, the **Carnegie II Drill Hole** (near the tree line) became a perpetual spouter many years later. The ground around it pulsates, threatening a future steam explosion.

Along the trail to the north toward the Norris campground is cool **Nuphar Lake**, which carries the botanical name for the yellow pond lily, yet harbors grasses and reeds. The lake is fed by rainwater and small thermal springs and has no outlet.

This section of boardwalk ends at the foot of **Porcelain Terrace**, where thermal activity is so intense and unpredictable that boardwalks have to be rebuilt frequently. After the 1959 Hebgen Lake earthquake, fractures formed on top of the terrace, and pools rich in sulfuric acid filled the fractures. This is causing the sinter to disintegrate and the hillside to crumble.

Porcelain Springs (beyond the end of the boardwalk) broke out on the west slope of Porcelain Terrace in 1971. As with most features at Norris, these springs change unpredictably from geysers to pools and back again. Sinter buildup—the most rapid in the park—has filled in some previously important springs in the basin below.

West of Basin Vista the opaque blue water of Sunday Geyser dominates the scene (2012).

Returning from Porcelain Terrace, if you bear right at the trail junction, you'll find a bench where you might rest a bit and admire the unusual and beautiful **basin vista★**. In the nearby collection of pools, each manages somehow to have a different color. The murky pools and stained sinter may be green, blue, aqua, yellow, yellow-green, reddish orange, mustard, or beige, due to different temperatures, chemical compositions, and degrees of turbidity of the water. The effect is like small jewels in the midst of desolation.

Before the intersection of walkways, you'll come to **Hurricane Vent**, above the path. Now usually just a deep hole in the hillside that emits a strong odor and sometimes splashes a bit of water, for a couple of years in the 1880s it played as a geyser that whirled the water about in its crater during eruptions. At other times it was a "prodigious steam vent whose violent gusts bear a striking resemblance to the driving blasts of a tempest," according to historian Hiram Chittenden.

Colloidal Pool is a large, shallow, funnel-shaped pool (or three or four smaller pools when the water level is low). In the past it has erupted muddy water as high as 30 feet (10 m). A colloid is a substance so fine grained that it is suspended indefinitely within another substance. In this case, silica and clay are suspended in water, as can be found in pools throughout Porcelain Basin.

The last interesting feature before the trail junction is the long narrow pool of **Sunday Geyser**, named in response to its large initial eruption on Sunday, July 12, 1964, but since then erupting rarely.

Turn left to return to the museum, Back Basin, or the parking lot. To the right, the path loops back along the basin's west side (see "Continuing northwest" on page 241).

VI. NORTHERN SECTION

From Livingston to the North Entrance

William Clark, of the 1803–6 Lewis and Clark expedition, passed the Great Bend of the Yellowstone at present-day Livingston on his return from the Pacific coast, thereby totally missing present park territory. But most visitors to the area later in the nineteenth and in the early twentieth centuries came this way, traveling upstream along the Yellowstone River.

The 54 miles (87 km) from Livingston to Gardiner traverse mountain-bound Paradise Valley, with its irrigated fields, horse and cattle ranches, ranchettes, and winter and summer recreation. The area abounds in both private campgrounds and public ones managed by U.S. and Montana agencies. Fishing is immensely popular in the Yellowstone River and its tributaries. Numerous hiking or horseback trails lead into the surrounding mountains and wilderness areas.

Livingston, Montana — **Airport: Mission Field**

Population: 7,050 — *6 mi. (9 km) E*

The town of Livingston, probably named for railroad director Johnston Livingston, was first settled in 1882, when the tracks of the Northern Pacific Railway reached this point along the Yellowstone River. Visitors to the new national park would change trains here for Cinnabar (and later for Gardiner, even closer to the park). Then they would connect with stagecoaches to take them through the North Entrance and on for the Grand Tour. Although passenger service has ceased, Livingston is still important as a railroad freight hub.

Livingston is a tourist, ranching, and art center with numerous nineteenth-century buildings listed on the National Register of Historic Places, including a classic railroad depot. The Park County Museum contains a wealth of memorabilia pertaining to Yellowstone Park and to the environs of Livingston. Two 1990s movies, *A River Runs through It* and *The Horse Whisperer*, were partially filmed in and around the town.

Livingston is also well-known for its wind. The town's location east of the Rocky Mountains and north of the Yellowstone Plateau assures that it gets more wind than any other Yellowstone gateway. It's a blessing when the wind is the

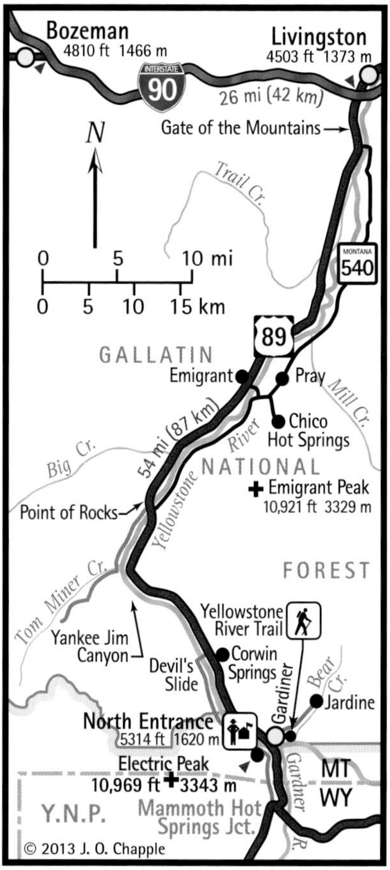

Approach to the North Entrance

winter chinook from the mountains, sometimes warm and dry enough in midwinter to melt all the snow.

From Livingston to the North Entrance

To drive to the park, take U.S. Highway 89 from the center of Livingston or from Interstate 90 just south of town. In about 3 miles (5 km), you pass through Rock Canyon, sometimes called Gate of the Mountains, cut by the Yellowstone River.

At the southern end of the canyon, look to the northwest to see cliffs with numerous layers of sedimentary rocks that tilt rather sharply. These roughly 400-million-year-old rocks of the Gallatin Range were tilted at about the same time the Beartooth uplift took place during formation of the Rocky Mountains. (See map on page 159 showing the extent of the Beartooth uplift.) The roadside exposures only hint at how complicated the deformation is. Soon after the completion of a road rebuilding project in the 1960s, blocks of this hillside slipped in a massive landslide that covered the road.

Nineteenth-century explorers dubbed this the First Canyon of the Yellowstone River. Farther upstream, explorers found three other canyons cut by the Yellowstone, each more spectacular than the one before. Second Canyon, located about 15 miles (24 km) north of the North Entrance, is now called Yankee Jim Canyon. Inside the park boundaries are Third, or Black Canyon, east of Gardiner (reached only by trail) and Fourth Canyon, the Grand Canyon of the Yellowstone.

Paradise Valley, so called since at least the 1880s, spreads out before you just as you emerge from the canyon. On your left (to the east) are the Snowy Mountains, one of several ranges that make up the Beartooth uplift. The highest peak visible from the valley is **Emigrant Peak** (10,921 ft / 3,329 m). To the west is the more rounded eastern edge of the **Gallatin Range**. Irrigation now helps overcome the low annual rainfall, making the valley hospitable to farming.

Ten or twelve miles (16–19 km) from Livingston, near Mill Creek, you begin to see effects of glaciers during the last ice age (the Pinedale), which was at its height about 25,000 years ago. Some areas are covered with large boulders dragged there by the glaciers. East of the highway and just south of Emigrant is a long terminal moraine, a mound of unsorted rocks and soil left when a major Yellowstone glacier dropped them, much as a conveyor belt would do.

The small settlement of Emigrant is about 23 miles (37 km) south of Livingston; at the stoplight a road leads eastward to the tiny town of Pray and to Chico Hot Springs. Chico, settled beginning in 1864, has a resort hotel established in 1900 that was sometimes used as a clinic in its first 50 years. You might enjoy a plunge in one of Chico's two public pools supplied with natural hot-spring water, or a meal in their gourmet restaurant.

Near Chico, at the mouth of Emigrant Gulch, the optimistically named Yellowstone City had 300 settlers in 1864 and could claim the title of easternmost town in Montana Territory. The settlers had all come as prospectors, so most moved on when the gold strike here petered out.

It may seem strange that Yellowstone City could have been the easternmost town, but Montana Territory was settled from west to east, unlike most U.S. states. The mining prospectors, who were the first white settlers, could most easily reach Montana's mineral-rich mountains from the southwest.

Mentioned frequently in histories of Yellowstone was the ranch settled in 1868 by the Bottler brothers, located about 3 miles (5 km) south of the present site of Emigrant. Sometimes travelers wrote of its cabin, built so poorly that the wind blew through it. Yet many others found it to be a welcome way station for food and company.

England's Earl of Dunraven came through in 1874 and reported from his camping spot: "evening was drawing on apace, and the scenery was being glorified with sunset effects. The level rays of the sun lit up most brilliantly the Eastern Mountains, striking full upon the sharp angular masses of limestone, bringing out in bold relief against the sky background the cruel jaggedness of their forms, which contrasted strongly with the smooth softness of the plain beneath, penetrating

Emigrant Peak is a prominent landmark in Paradise Valley.

and searching into the deep rifts and gorges, and defining in detail all the savage grandeur of the range."

About 7 miles (11 km) south of Emigrant, near a wide spot in the river, you'll find a welcome picnic and rest area. The long *mesa* to the east, **Hepburn Mesa**, is made up mostly of sediments, but it has a lava cap that has slowed erosion of the sediments below.

As you continue south, jagged formations to the west, called **Point of Rocks**, appear. You can take a century-old, rough dirt road from here southwest into the **Tom Miner Basin**, named for an early prospector and poacher. This scenic basin has ranches, a forest service campground, and trails into the Gallatin Range.

For Hikers and Mineral Collectors

You can follow a Gallatin National Forest trail into the mountains to find specimens of petrified wood like those preserved in Yellowstone. The petrified trees are located about a mile (1.5 km) from the end of Tom Miner Basin Road.

The specimens in Yellowstone Park are at the top of long and difficult trails up the western slopes of the Gallatin Range in the northwest corner. You're not allowed to collect them there. From this east side of the mountains, however, you may take home samples of petrified wood—but first ask for a free collection permit at the Forest Service Ranger Station in Gardiner. Also ask about recent bear sightings, since both black and grizzly bears live in the area.

On U.S. 89, you'll leave Paradise Valley and enter **Yankee Jim Canyon**. Here you also enter the **Gallatin National Forest**, which alternates with private land in checkerboard squares. Between here and the town of Gardiner are a Forest Service campground, a picnic area, and several river access points. Near the southern end of the 2.5-mile-long canyon are interpretive signs about cutthroat trout and about the historic use of the canyon as Indian trail, wagon route, railroad branch, and part of the 1912 to 1930 Yellowstone Trail.

To create Yankee Jim Canyon, the Yellowstone River has carved through volcanic rocks to the very old Precambrian basement rocks below. James ("Yankee Jim") George took over the road-building job from a southern-born prospector named Henderson and was able to blast enough rock to make the road through the canyon passable for wagons. From 1874 until about 1910 he exacted a toll from all who passed by. You can see the old road clearly across the river. In some places the old railway roadbed is also visible closer to the river.

The town of **Corwin Springs** used to have its own "plunge" or hot spring pool, using water piped from La Duke Hot Spring to the south. Near here a 5,000-year-old hearth was found on the Rigler Bluffs east of the river. Initially puzzled by the hearth's elevation and distance from the river, researchers concluded that the river must have been dammed by landslides and that Native American Indians must have camped along the edge of the resulting lake.

At Corwin Springs you may cross the bridge and continue to the park along a parallel dirt-and-gravel road. That road passes the historic sites of the towns of Electric, which had extensive coal mines with an aerial tramway, and Cinnabar, which was the first terminus of the Northern Pacific Park Branch Line. Cinnabar claimed to be the "capital of the United States" for a few days in 1903, because President Theodore Roosevelt had left his train and communications center there while he traveled through Yellowstone. A few months later, the railroad terminus was moved to Gardiner, and not long after, Cinnabar became a ghost town.

Heat over the Hot Spring

In the late 1980s, the Church Universal and Triumphant (CUT) began drilling into the La Duke Hot Spring aquifer in order to heat a spa and buildings. La Duke Hot Spring and the bottom of Devil's Slide are on the church's property. Since Yellowstone's geothermal systems may have some connections to underground systems outside the park, drawing off water as the controversial church had planned to do could have serious consequences for Mammoth Hot Springs.

The church's 12,000-acre (49 sq km) Royal Teton Ranch shared 5 miles (8 km) of border with the park. Potential harm to Yellowstone was averted when CUT agreed to cap its well. The U.S. Geological Survey studied the relationship between La Duke Hot Spring and those in Yellowstone, and all water use just north of the park is being closely monitored.

In 1999, the Forest Service purchased about 7,800 acres (32 sq km) of the ranch, acquiring its geothermal rights and adding to the lands now available for winter grazing by elk, bison, bighorn sheep, mule deer, and pronghorn.

On the main road, less than 2 miles (3 km) south of Corwin Springs, the La Duke Spring National Forest picnic area is an excellent place to get a good look at **Devil's Slide** on Cinnabar Mountain. The slide is not a landslide but is composed of tilted layers of sandstone and shale that have been stained with iron oxide. Early prospectors mistakenly thought the slide's red color was due to cinnabar, or mercuric sulfide.

To the left of the slide itself, what looks like a free-standing wall is an erosion-resistant *sill* of basalt, a layer of *igneous rock* squeezed while molten between layers of sedimentary rock and then cooled while below the surface. All of these layers formed horizontally but were turned up to their present positions by the same forces that caused the Beartooth uplift to the east.

Devil's Slide

South of the picnic area small La Duke Hot Spring boils out at the roadside edge of the Yellowstone River. Not far south of the spring the Yellowstone Park boundary now runs along the west bank of the Yellowstone River to the original, perfectly straight, northern boundary line. Land was added to the park here in 1932, when a New York City game preservation company bought and presented it to the U.S. government. The goal was to provide winter range for pronghorn. Trees and shrubs were planted on this land by the Civilian Conservation Corps as a nursery area to beautify the park.

In this area also you may notice exclosures west of the river constructed by the long-term Gardiner Basin Restoration Project. The aim is to return this area to pre-settlement grassland conditions, to benefit the pronghorn in particular.

Gardiner, Montana — **Gardiner Airport**

Population: 875 — *2 mi. (3.5 km) NW*

Gardiner had the reputation of a wide-open, freewheeling town when the park was new. There were 21 saloons in the 1880s. All sorts of undesirables tended to gravitate here and to nearby Mammoth Hot Springs.

Later, until train service ended in 1948, Gardiner was an outfitting station for horseback excursions into the park. The town still caters to hunters in the fall season and to park visitors year round. It's home to many people who work at park headquarters in Mammoth. Here also are warehouses and other adjuncts of the hotel and restaurant concessionaire Xanterra, and the headquarters of the Yellowstone Association.

A travertine quarry is located above town on a very old terrace not unlike those found at Mammoth Hot Springs. An old gold mine at Jardine, about 5 miles (8 km) northeast of Gardiner, reopened for a few years in the 1980s and '90s, but did not prove profitable.

The Yellowstone River Trail begins outside the park but soon enters park land and follows the Black Canyon for many miles. To reach the trailhead, take the Jardine Road where U.S. 89 turns south in Gardiner, before crossing the Yellowstone River. Turn in at the private Rocky Mountain Campground and ask for parking information at the store.

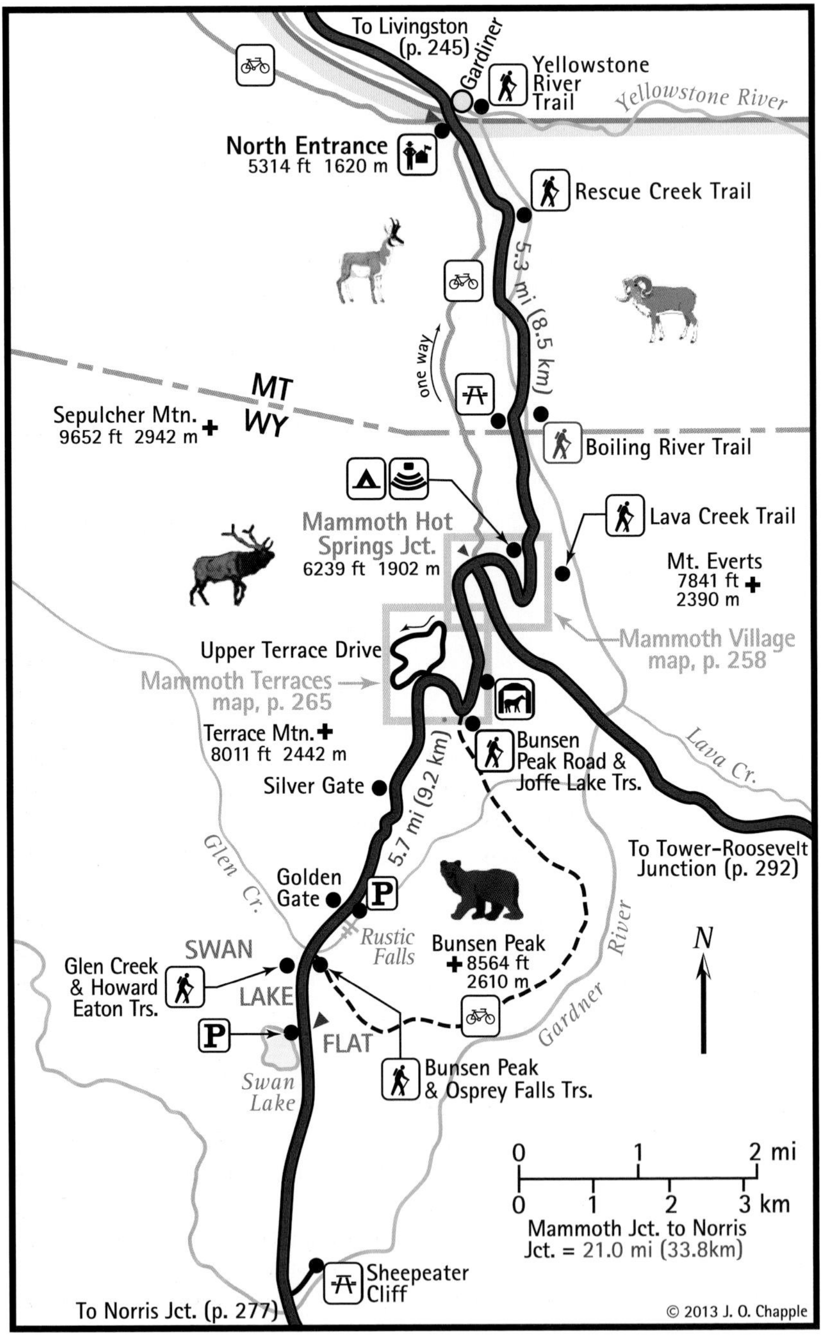
To Livingston
(p. 245)
Gardiner
Yellowstone
River
Trail
Yellowstone River
North Entrance
5314 ft 1620 m
Rescue Creek Trail
5.3 mi (8.5 km)
one way
MT
WY
Sepulcher Mtn.
9652 ft 2942 m
Boiling River Trail
Lava Creek Trail
Mammoth Hot
Springs Jct.
6239 ft 1902 m
Mt. Everts
7841 ft
2390 m
Mammoth Village
map, p. 258
Upper Terrace Drive
Mammoth Terraces
map, p. 265
Terrace Mtn.
8011 ft 2442 m
Bunsen
Peak Road &
Joffe Lake Trs.
Lava Cr.
Silver Gate
5.7 mi (9.2 km)
To Tower-Roosevelt
Junction (p. 292)
Glen Cr.
Golden
Gate
Rustic
Falls
Bunsen Peak
8564 ft
2610 m
River
N
SWAN
LAKE
FLAT
Glen Creek
& Howard
Eaton Trs.
Gardner
Swan
Lake
Bunsen Peak
& Osprey Falls Trs.
0 1 2 mi
0 1 2 3 km
Mammoth Jct. to Norris
Jct. = 21.0 mi (33.8km)
Sheepeater
Cliff
To Norris Jct. (p. 277)
© 2013 J. O. Chapple

North Entrance to Swan Lake Flat

From the North Entrance to Mammoth Hot Springs Junction

After you enter the park, you will follow the Gardner River through its canyon. You might spot mule deer, bison, and bighorn sheep in the canyon, particularly in winter; elk and pronghorn antelope are here year round.

This is the only entrance road that is kept plowed all winter long. It provides access to park headquarters in Mammoth Village. The road from Mammoth eastward is also kept plowed for winter access to the towns of Cooke City and Silver Gate, Montana (outside the Northeast Entrance).

It's only about 5 miles (8 km) from Gardiner to Mammoth, but the elevation gain from the North Entrance to Mammoth of nearly 1,000 feet (300 m) is enough to make a noticeable difference in the climate and vegetation.

Road Log

0.0/5.3 Yellowstone National Park boundary. The boundary runs along the north side of Park Street in the town of Gardiner. The road at the east end of town provides access for park personnel and passes National Park Service buildings and the concessionaire's warehouses. There the garage built for Yellowstone Park Transportation Company buses still carries the company's traditional bear symbol and the sign, "Y.P.T. Co. 1925."

The visitors' route now starts at the west end of Park Street, where you pass under the entry arch. The Park Service plans to modernize this entrance to Yellowstone, stressing its history while improving ambience, lighting, and traffic flow, in time for the NPS centennial celebration in 2016.

The **Yellowstone Association headquarters** and a small bookstore are located in a 1903 building by architect Reamer (designer of Old Faithful Inn). For over 60 years Hall's general store occupied the first floor and a large auditorium or dance hall the second. A display in the conference room compares Jackson's 1870s pictures with U.S.G.S. 1997 photos, such as the Golden Gate canyon before and after a road was built.

(4) North of the entrance arch are the covered tables of Arch Park. Beyond is the **Yellowstone Heritage and Research Center**, containing the park's archives and library, as well as the offices of the park historian and archaeologist.

The gravel road beyond the archives building, following the former Northern Pacific roadbed, is open to cars and bicycles. It continues for 5 miles (8 km) along the river in park territory and leads to Corwin Springs.

The **North Entrance Arch**, sometimes called the Roosevelt Arch, is just inside the boundary. Stagecoaches loaded passengers from the railroad station in Gardiner and passed through the arch to enter the park. President Theodore Roosevelt laid the cornerstone and dedicated the arch in April 1903. It's inscribed near the top with words from the Act of Congress that set aside this land "for the benefit and enjoyment of the people."

The North Entrance Arch was constructed from columnar basalt quarried near Gardiner.

According to research unearthed by Ruth Quinn for her book about architect Reamer, there is conflicting historical evidence as to whether he or Major Chittenden of the U.S. Army Corps of Engineers had the final say in the design of the arch.

0.1/5.2 (P) Sign about the Arch.

Some Plants and a Snake Near Gardiner

Since precipitation is low (about 12–13 in/30–33 cm per year) and the elevation lower than the rest of the park, the ecology here is different. As the road ascends to Mammoth Hot Springs, the vegetation changes from dry desert plants, such as Idaho fescue and the occasional prickly pear cactus, to higher elevation plants like Rocky Mountain juniper and rabbitbrush.

Big sagebrush (*Artemisia tridentata*) is common throughout the lower elevations. It's not related to the sage used as a kitchen herb (*Salvia officinalis*).

This is the only part of the park where rattlesnakes are occasionally seen. (See the Living Things chapter for more about plants and animals.)

Big sagebrush lives in lower elevations and throughout the western U.S.

0.5/4.8 North Entrance station. Stop here to pay the entrance fee (see the Travel Tips for fee information).

The road uphill to the west near the entrance station is open to cars only one-way from Mammoth to Gardiner—both ways for bicyclists. It was called the High Road when it and the present main route into the park were about equal in importance.

Near the entrance station, you might want to pull over and look around at the mountains.

0.9/4.4 **P** Large turnout area with interpretive signs about the wildlife and ecology of the Northern Range.

How the Mountains around You Got Their Names

From just inside the North Entrance gate, look toward the west to see glacier-carved and usually snow-capped **Electric Peak**, about 7 miles (11 km) away near the Montana/Wyoming state line. At 10,969 feet (3,343 m), it's the highest peak in the Gallatin Range and was believed to be the highest in the park until 1930s surveys showed Eagle Peak in the southeast corner to be 389 feet (112 m) higher (11,358 ft / 3,462 m).

Electric Peak got its name from a strange experience reported by members of the 1872 Hayden expedition. While attempting to climb this peak, the men heard crackling sounds, felt electric shocks, and found their hair standing on end. This experience has not recurred as far as is known, but electric storms are indeed common during the late afternoon.

The mountain to the southwest is **Sepulcher Mountain** (9,652 ft / 2,942 m). The name probably came from a tomblike formation in the rocks near its summit. Both Electric and Sepulcher are made of sedimentary rocks about 100 million years old.

Slumping down toward the road from Sepulcher's northeast side is an obvious area of hummocks left behind by major landslides. Geologists theorize that the underlying layer of shale on Sepulcher became water-saturated, allowing the volcanic rocks on top to slowly slide down.

To the southeast is a gradual slope to the top of 7,841-foot (2,390 m) **Mount Everts**. The mountain is named for Truman Everts, assessor of internal revenue of Montana Territory. But that's not why he's famous. In 1870, before there was a national park here, Everts was accidentally separated from the Washburn-Langford exploration party and lost for a total of 37 days during inclement autumn weather. Without food for much of that time, he somehow made his way from south of Yellowstone Lake to near Crescent Hill, about 12 miles (19 km) east of Mammoth. There, mountaineers Jack Baronett and George Pritchett found him unable to walk and barely alive. When the friend who had offered a $600 reward demanded that Everts pay it, he refused, saying he would have found his way out without help! He recovered from his ordeal and survived to father a child when he was almost 75.

1.2/4.1 **Rescue Creek Trailhead** and interpretive sign about migrating animals. This 8-mile-long (13 km) trail was part of the primitive nineteenth century "Turkey Pen Road" that miners used to reach Cooke City from Gardiner in the 1880s. Today's trail climbs about 1,200 feet (365 m) along the back of Mount Everts and then descends to rejoin the Grand Loop Road at Blacktail Deer Creek east of Mammoth.

Rescue Creek's name is the result of a misunderstanding from long ago. Ferdinand Hayden, leader of three 1870s expeditions through the park, thought that the mountain now called Mount Everts was where the lost Truman Everts had been found.

The field northeast of the footbridge had several uses in the early 1900s. Alfalfa and then wheat were planted on the flats near Gardiner. Part of the large field was used as a 1,000-yard (914 m) target range for the U.S. Cavalry in the years when they patrolled the park (1886 to 1918); the butts or trench in which the target crew operated still remains at the north end.

To the southeast is the northern shoulder of Mount Everts called **McMinn Bench**, where a man named Silas McMinn was allowed to mine coal from a tunnel he dug and sell it to the National Hotel at Mammoth in the late nineteenth century.

1.6/3.7 North end of **Gardner River Canyon** and bridge over the Gardner River.

P There are wide spots for parking on both sides of the road south of the bridge. On **Eagle Nest Rock**, just east (left) of the bridge, ospreys (not eagles) nested for at least 80 years, until an earth tremor dislodged the nest. Ospreys that rebuilt the nest were harassed by ravens at one time. Check the top of this sharp rock to see if the birds are back. Eagle Nest Rock, like most of the rock in the canyon, is made of marine deposits about 100 million years old.

Across the road from Eagle Nest Rock, look out in the river to see **Split Rock**, a large boulder that fell from above and split neatly down the middle. Now small plants grow out of the crack. In the 1880s, the road ran on the other side of the river. You can see a remnant of an early bridge, but it's mostly covered by landslide debris.

Gardiner or Gardner?

Why do we spell the names differently for a town and a river in the same vicinity? The river was named in the 1830s for Johnson Gardner, a rough and illiterate trapper. After 1870, the spelling on maps was Gardiner, probably the result of a mispronunciation. Since 1959, the official spelling for the river has eliminated the *i* to conform to earliest usage.

The post office at Gardiner, established in 1880, took its name from the stream. Sometimes mail consigned to the postmaster and unofficial mayor was addressed simply to "Jim on the Gardiner." The town officials have never seen fit to change that spelling.

Highway Robbery

Split Rock, in the middle of the Gardner River, has a story. On the night of July 4, 1887, two masked highwaymen hid behind the boulder, hoping to surprise the army quartermaster on his way to pay the troops. They mistakenly let the quartermaster's buggy go by and held up a stagecoach instead, robbing the passengers of $16 and an unusual coin with the head of Napoleon on it.

It was this coin that eventually gave them away. One of the robbers, William James, showed the coin to some companions about two months later. This led to the arrest and subsequent imprisonment of both robbers. Ironically, the owner of the coin was Judge John F. Lacey, who later, as a member of the U.S. House of Representatives, authored the act that brought law and order to Yellowstone.

2.0/3.3 Sliding Hill is an old name for the slope to the west, where keeping the road free after landslides has been a problem since the park was new. As recently as December 1999, a slide on the east side about 6 feet (2 m) deep and 40 feet long (12 m) closed the road for several days.

The river carries away the sediment as fast as it comes down, but in doing so, continually cuts away its own banks and often undercuts the road as well, especially during the spring runoff. A small lake (appropriately called Slide Lake) perches above this point; its seepage must contribute to the landslides.

High above you is an area that bighorn sheep use for lambing. The Park Service sometimes posts "Sheep management—area closed" signs to ensure that humans do not disturb the sheep.

2.2/2.9 **P** Sign indicates that at this spot you are very close to halfway between the equator and the North Pole, at the 45th parallel of latitude.

2.8/2.5 As the Gardner Canyon widens out, you come to a meadow where elk like to graze. Superintendent Norris started a garden here in 1879; later gardeners were the U.S. Cavalry and a Chinese man named Sam Wo. Park employees still call this land the Chinese Garden.

Bighorn rams pose on the cliffs in Gardner Canyon.

3.0/2.3 Bridge over the Gardner River.

(4) Forty-Fifth Parallel picnic area to the west.

P **(2)** Parking area and trail to **Boiling River** on the east, one of two places near park roads where regulations allow bathing in a river warmed by hot

Boiling River's intensely hot source spring

3.1/2.2 Montana/Wyoming state line. The boundary was inadvertently set approximately 1,200 feet (365 m) south of the 45th parallel, according to Yellowstone historian Aubrey Haines.

Local residents called this steep hill "Soap Hill" when the road grade was 15 percent. Below the hill in the 1870s was a short-lived establishment called McGuirk's Medicinal Springs, where Matthew McGuirk dammed Boiling River and charged rheumatic customers to "take the waters."

springs. Bathing directly in any hot spring is dangerous and is not allowed in the park at all. Boiling River is not at all suitable for very young children.

The trail leads about one-half mile (0.8 km) along the river to the hot spring area. The entire area is closed off until the water is low enough (usually in mid to late July) to make it safe for bathing.

Hot River is an older but unofficial name used by scientists for this spot. The river does not really boil; its temperature varies between 117 and 124°F (47–51°C) where the hot and cold waters mix. One other approved swimming area is described on page 50.

Special Caution: Be sure to keep your head out of the water entirely. The thermophilic amoeba *Naegleria fowleri*, if ingested through the mouth or nose, can cause a type of fatal encephalitis. The bacterium *Legionella pneumophila*, which causes Legionnaires' disease, is also present in some of these thermal waters. Although there have been no reports of these diseases in park personnel or visitors, it's wise to be careful.

A classic alluvial fan descends from the light-colored cliffs on Mt. Everts to the dark trees along the Gardner River.

Across the Gardner is a fine example of an alluvial fan, caused when flash floods from heavy rainfall makes a stream scour a canyon, carrying a torrent of debris. When the stream bursts out of its canyon, it spreads out, slows down, and drops the debris, creating a fan-shaped mound.

4.1/1.2 P **Lava Creek Trailhead** and interpretive sign explaining Mount Everts's late spring and summer mudslides.

To take the Lava Creek Trail, follow the orange blazes upstream to a bridge across the Gardner River. The trail continues to the mouth of Lava Creek and then ascends Lava Creek canyon to reach Undine Falls in about 4 miles (6.5 km). It joins the Blacktail Deer Trail in another 3 miles (4.5 km).

4.3/1.0 Side road leading east to employees' housing. Down this road is the elementary school for children of year-round park employees; junior high and high school students must go to Gardiner.

4.5/0.8 **Mammoth Campground** road to the west (right). This is the only campground in Yellowstone that's open all year. In summer it has 85 sites available on a first-come, first-served basis (four accessible sites); fewer sites are used in winter. The amphitheater, where ranger lectures are given each evening during the summer, is located near the campground's far end.

4.6/0.7 A 180-degree curve goes up a steep hill made of ancient travertine, revealed by the road cut here. The travertine of this **Cedar Terrace** was deposited many centuries ago.

5.2/0.1 The clinic, post office, and **National Park Service headquarters** for Yellowstone are housed in the buildings to the left of the median strip as you enter Mammoth Village, the Justice Center to the right. Facilities for visitors are farther on.

Near the clinic you might notice a small log cabin dating from 1895 and built as the mail carrier's cabin. It is still used as employee housing.

A left turn beyond the median strip brings you to parking for the visitor center.

5.3/0.0 Mammoth Hot Springs Junction. To the east is Tower Junction. (For the road log from Mammoth to Tower, see page 293.) The road south takes you past Mammoth's facilities and to the Mammoth Hot Springs terraces, then continues south to Norris Junction. To the north is the North Entrance.

FACILITIES AT MAMMOTH VILLAGE

P (3) **Albright Visitor Center**. An elevator at the rear of the visitor center may be used to reach a wheelchair-accessible restroom upstairs; other restrooms are under the porch at the front. The building's first floor houses a backcountry office, a ranger desk, a small bookstore, a small theater—showing a park orientation film, displays of park history, and paintings and photographs by Thomas Moran and W. H. Jackson. On the second floor are dioramas of Yellowstone's history and of the wildlife of the northern range, especially wolves.

This visitor center honors the memory of Horace M. Albright, park superintendent from 1919 to 1929. Albright played an important role in the establishment of the National Park Service and became its second director.

(2) Opposite the road to Tower Junction are the **Mammoth Hot Springs Hotel and Cabins**. Going south from the hotel toward the terraces, you'll find two eateries and a general store, with parking across the street. There's also a service station and a large restroom building.

Mammoth Hot Springs Hotel is open for summer and winter seasons. A succession of hotels was built on this same site, beginning with the National Hotel (1883–1936). The National Hotel's north wing, built in 1911–13, was incorporated into the present Mammoth Hotel, constructed in 1937. The newer parts of the hotel and the cabins behind it were designed by architect Reamer, who also created the unique United States map in the hotel's Map Room. It's made of 15 types of fine wood from nine countries and was carefully restored in 1997.

You'll find five picnic tables opposite the visitor center, two across the road from the store, and nine near Opal Terrace.

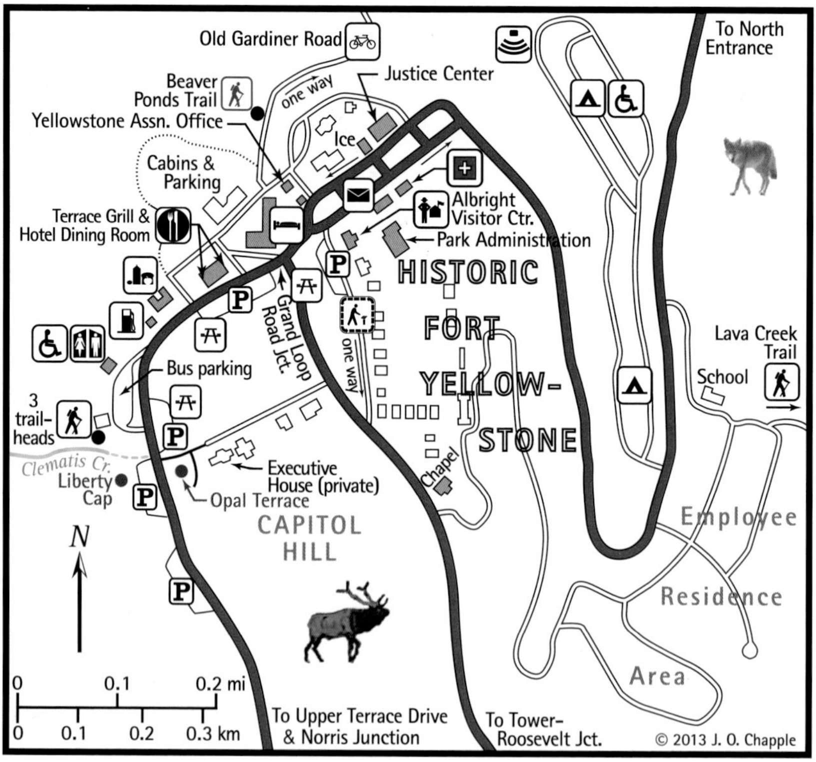

Mammoth Village

NOTE: Both this Mammoth Village map and the terraces map on page 265 have north at the top, so they differ slightly from some official NPS maps.

(8) Wheelchair-accessible restrooms are in the Mammoth Hotel lobby, the Terrace Grill, the visitor center, and south of the service station.

The flat grassy area in the center of Mammoth Village was used as a parade ground when the U.S. Cavalry was in charge of the park (1886–1918). Imagine the fine displays of horsemanship the soldiers put on for the guests at the hotel, despite fears that the hollow ground might cave in under the horses' hooves. There are still people alive who remember the years after the army left, when winter residents flooded the area for ice-skating.

A Plant Special to Mammoth

The resident elk herd at Mammoth helps keep the grass short.

Why are there cultivated green lawns at Mammoth, when this is supposed to be a natural and wild place? The U.S. Cavalry first created a bare parade ground at the base of the terraces but later brought in soil, seeded it with grass and clover, and installed an irrigation system. Perhaps the officers and other residents also wanted grass to help them feel at home while stationed here. This is the only place in Yellowstone where you'll see green lawns.

The large, closed store building bordering the open area along the road to Tower-Roosevelt was built in 1929 as the headquarters for Haynes Picture Shops. All the other buildings you see in this part of Mammoth, with one exception, are offices and workshops and housing for employees, since this is the center of administration and maintenance for the entire park.

The one public building found on the road toward Tower-Roosevelt is the **Yellowstone National Park Chapel**. Built in 1913 in the cruciform shape indicative of Episcopalian origin, the chapel has always been non-denominational and used for weddings as well as services. Times for Saturday mass and Sunday services are posted in front of the stone building.

The Y.N.P. Chapel was planned by year-round residents of Mammoth, including Judge John W. Meldrum, the U.S. Commissioner for the park who served from 1894 to 1935. It was built of native sandstone by a Billings construction company and furnished in oak.

Windows in the chapel vestibule.

The chapel vestibule is graced with painted and stained glass windows showing Old Faithful, the Lower Falls of the Yellowstone, and common flora and fauna of the area. These windows, made and given to the park by Miss Jessie Van Brunt, were installed at the front entrance in 1939.

Animals and Holes in the Ground

Mammoth is the year-round home of a herd of **elk** (also called by its Shawnee name *wapiti*, meaning white rump). These elk are not tame, so keep a safe distance away—the Park Service says 25 yards (23 m).

In early summer, you'll see mostly cows and calves grazing and resting in the shade. Sometimes they'll be on the terraces themselves, since there are fewer bugs there, and the white travertine reflects the heat away. In the autumn rutting season, the bull elk round up their harems and bugle to assert dominance. The males with small single-pronged antlers are yearlings.

Elk at Mammoth Hot Springs like to lie on the terraces even on hot summer days.

Watch your step if you're walking on the grass! Deep burrows dug by **Uinta ground squirrels** are everywhere. This rodent, which children love to watch, appears to be a cross between a red squirrel and a yellow-bellied marmot, both of which live elsewhere in the park. These squirrels stay underground for up to seven months of the year.

Another animal you may see at the outskirts of Mammoth is the **coyote**. Coyotes are smaller and slimmer than wolves and much less shy. In fact, there have been some incidents of coyotes biting humans in recent years after they were fed human food. **Special Caution**: Do not approach or feed any animals in the park.

While walking in front of the visitor center, you'll see three fenced holes in the ground that are much too wide and deep to be ground squirrel burrows. These are collapse features, where water has flowed through the travertine, weakened it, and dissolved it away until the ground above has caved in.

McCartney Cave

The hole, or collapse feature, farthest to the left as you look from the visitor center's front porch has historically been called McCartney Cave. In 1877, hotel and bathhouse proprietor James McCartney reportedly hid in this hole from Nez Perce for three days and later probably charged tourists to go down a ladder to its bottom. Here's how an 1898 guide to Yellowstone described the experience of entering the cave:

> About midway between the hotel and officers' quarters, surrounded by an iron railing, is McCartney Cave. The opening is about four feet in diameter, rather oblong in shape. By means of a ladder one can descend vertically some thirty feet, thence twenty feet on an incline to the bottom of the main chamber. The venturesome may, by means of a rope and light, continue explorations 100 feet further. Far beneath, in a subterranean chamber, water can be distinctly heard by the rope-supported explorer; but the hot vapors and gases constantly arising, stimulate an earnest desire to ascend to the surface....
>
> In the winter of 1881, there was a heavy fall of snow which drifted over many of the openings in the plateau. The following spring Mr. McCartney noticed a large pair of antlers protruding, apparently, from the ground; investigating, he discovered that an unfortunate elk had broken through the crust of snow, and falling into the cave, had died, suspended by his horns, in the opening.

Hiking and biking around Mammoth

In Mammoth you can take a historic walk, the Lower Terrace walk (both described below), or other short trails for hiking or biking.

Behind and to the north of the hotel is the start of the **Old Gardiner Road** or High Road (about 4 mi / 6 km long), which cars can only travel from south to north (from Mammoth to Gardiner). You can bicycle either way, but you'll avoid the long uphill grade if you start at Mammoth.

You can start the **Beaver Ponds Loop Trail** at the same point as the Old Gardiner Road. A slightly steeper way to begin the loop is at Clematis Creek (it's named for a flowering vine and pronounced KLEM-a-tus or klem-A-tus). Clematis Creek is located between Liberty Cap and the U.S. Commissioner's stone house.

Beaver Ponds

Although billed by the Park Service and several hiking books as a 5-mile (8 km) trail, to complete a loop from any point in Mammoth to Beaver Ponds requires a walk of at least 6 miles (9.5 km). The long-range views, birds, wildflowers, and the ponds themselves are delightfully worth the effort, as are the contrasts that you pass between the high desert and the moist forest microclimates. Beaver (*Castor canadensis*) are most active from dusk to dawn, so you're unlikely to see them in daytime, but you can see a dam they've built between the ponds. Incidentally, a 1996 parkwide aerial survey found about 50 active beaver lodges in the entire park.

Another trail reached from Clematis Creek is the **Howard Eaton Trail** to the upper terraces and beyond, accessed by crossing the creek before the Beaver Ponds Trail becomes steep. This trail segment leads you to Narrow Gauge Terrace (described on page 272). A recommended part of this trail is described on page 278.

Historic Fort Yellowstone

To get a feeling for army life here when the U.S. Cavalry was stationed at Fort Yellowstone from 1886 to 1918, take a ranger-guided tour or a short walk around the historic buildings described in "The Army Years" booklet available at the visitor center. This was not a stockaded fort as in Westerns but a permanent army post, of which there were many in nineteenth-century Montana and Wyoming Territories. Fort Yellowstone has been said to rival West Point for the quality of its architecture. Signs along the walk tell you about the buildings' use. Year-round park personnel currently occupy most buildings, so please respect their privacy.

The walk begins with **Albright Visitor Center**, the former Bachelor Officers' Quarters built in 1909. As with all the stone buildings, this one was constructed by Scottish stonemasons, who quarried the sandstone just down the hill near the Gardner River. The cavalry decided to build new facilities in stone after a devastating 1907 fire destroyed wooden stables and killed a number of horses. The last building in the first row was the **Guard House**, also used to admit park visitors, most of whom entered via the North Entrance.

The second and third rows included barracks, the post exchange, and stables, now used for offices and shops. Four small houses behind were noncommissioned officers' quarters and were dubbed **Soapsuds Row** when the wives took in laundry for extra money.

When the NPS took over administration of Yellowstone in 1916, approximately 200 soldiers were serving in the park. Of these, 22 stayed on as park rangers. Modern national park policies, philosophies, and even ranger uniforms evolved here.

LOWER TERRACES WALKING TOURS★

The Mammoth Terraces are constantly changing! You need to approach them closely to appreciate the variety of colors and the heat and power of the springs. Ask at the visitor center where to find the best hot spring activity. The tour has many steps, but it's worth the effort and covers a total of about 1 mile (1.6 km). A pamphlet about the terraces is available from the boxes near the parking areas. NOTE: Upper Terrace Drive has a wheelchair-accessible boardwalk (page 271).

Opal Terrace

Park at one of the several areas at the foot of the terraces. The easiest terrace to get to is **Opal Spring** and **Terrace**, the only formation east of the main road, inactive in recent years.

As you approach Opal Terrace, you may wonder why a large and beautiful house would have been built so close to an active terrace. Built in 1908, the house was designed by Robert Reamer in Frank Lloyd Wright's Prairie Style for Yellowstone Park Association President Harry W. Child. There was no spring here then, or if there was, it was tiny! Since 1926, Opal Spring deposited a foot or more (about 30 cm) of travertine each year it was active, but it has alternated between dormant and active since 1982. Nature now usually wins out in disputes over territory, but the NPS must also protect the house as a cultural site.

The runoff from Opal Spring—as with many of the springs above it—flows through underground channels, not on the surface. By injecting tracer dyes down a nearby sinkhole, scientists found that the hot-spring water reaches Boiling River in about two hours, flowing about 1.5 miles (2.5 km) below Mammoth.

We'll divide the remainder of the Lower Terrace area above the road into two walks, Parts I and II.

When it's active, Opal Terrace threatens to overwhelm Executive House (1996).

Lower Terrace Boardwalk, Part I

From 1992 to 2008 **Lower Hymen Terrace** (across Clematis Creek from the bus parking area) was delightfully active, but quite dry and white from 2008 to 2012. Next to the stone house here are trailheads for the Beaver Ponds, Howard Eaton, and Sepulcher Mountain Trails. Following the Howard Eaton Trail a short distance south after crossing the Clematis Creek bridge leads to Narrow Gauge Terrace, described on page 272.

Forty-five-foot-high (14 m) **Liberty Cap**, an extinct hot spring cone, is named for the conical hats given to emancipated Roman slaves, later worn during the French Revolution, and then depicted on early American coins. In 1874, the visiting British Earl of Dunraven looked at this formation and wrote: "Professor Hayden calls this the Liberty Cap; locally it goes by another name."

Liberty Cap, 1871, by W. H. Jackson

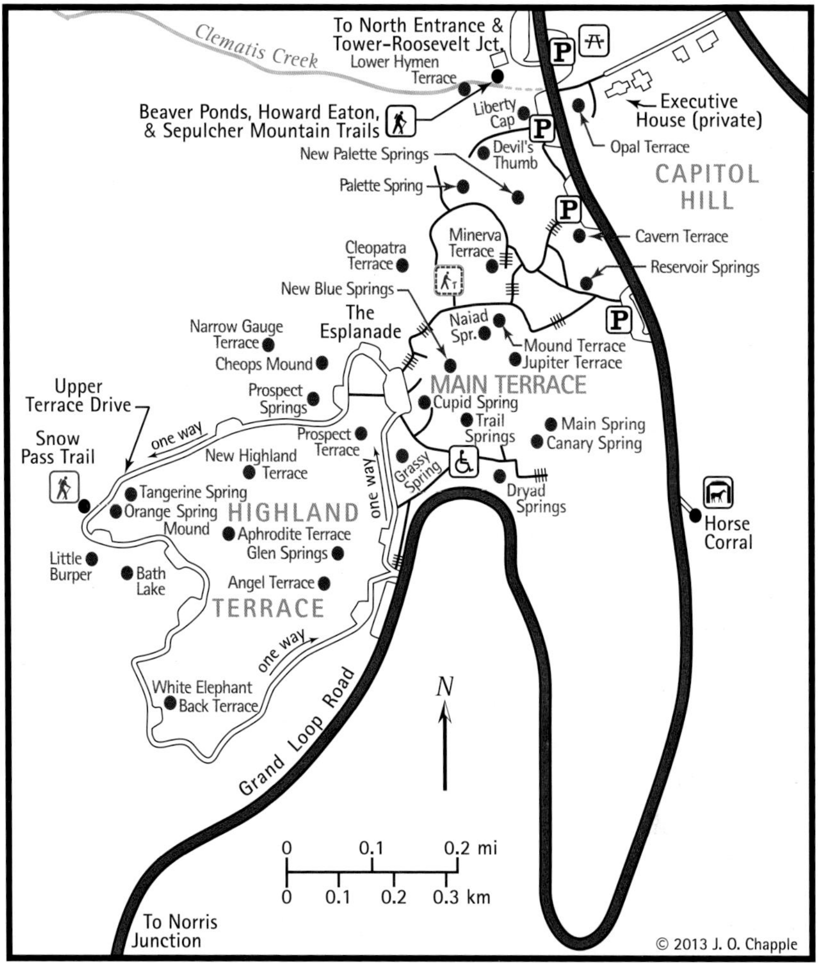

Mammoth Hot Springs Terraces

The spring that built Liberty Cap has been inactive at least since 1871. The formation is estimated to be about 2,500 years old. Travertine may have sealed the small orifice at the top or, when the cone reached a certain height, perhaps the water pressure was insufficient to lift the hot water to the top.

Another extinct cone to the left up the walkway is named **Devil's Thumb**. Not long ago a small boy commented as he passed, "Devil's Big Toe would be a better name!"

Adjacent to Devil's Thumb is **Palette Spring**. Active in recent years, this colorful spring has been so vigorously active since 2006 that part of the boardwalk had to be removed. Perhaps it will engulf Devil's Thumb in a decade or less.

As you observe Palette Spring's terrace building, note that behind where you now stand was **Hymen Terrace**, named for the Greek god of marriage, below on the north (right). Dormant since 1936, its upper section has crumbled to become unrecognizable as a terrace. The *Haynes Guide* for 1912 stated prophetically: "Hymen Terrace is growing fast; in fact, it is gravely feared that the openings may become choked from the abundance of depositing lime. If this should happen, it would be a matter of but a few days until the coloring would have disappeared, leaving the travertine rock bare and exposed to the destructive forces of the elements."

Palette Spring's array of colors (2012)

The next stairway south climbs to **Minerva Terrace**, named for the Roman goddess of wisdom and the arts. Minerva was very active and beautiful for most of the 1990s but sometimes inactive from late 1998 on. The boardwalk has to be changed whenever and wherever the terrace builds up too high. This boardwalk also goes past Mound and Jupiter Terraces, described in Part II.

At Mammoth's springs, particularly at Minerva Spring, enterprising early residents sold coated specimens to the tourists. Any item kept in this water was nicely coated in about four days or completely buried by calcium carbonate deposits in eleven days.

Lower Terrace Boardwalk, Part II

Part of Mound Terrace resembles a screaming Halloween ghost mask.

This hike starts from the next parking area south of Liberty Cap.

The same stairway mentioned at the end of Part I takes you past Jupiter and Mound Terraces, both deteriorating due to many years without new deposits. First comes **Cavern Terrace**, active into the 1970s, but now crumbling. At the first intersection you see a large collapse feature.

Climbing more stairs, you are below **Jupiter Terrace** and then **Mound Terrace**. Holes and crevices in Mound's travertine may remind you of faces and other images. Behind and above Mound Terrace is Naiad Spring, newly active in 2012. Naiads were the water spirits of classical mythology, known to weep copiously.

Many more steps will take you to **New Blue Springs**, more accessible from Upper Terrace Drive (see page 272). A very steeply descending asphalt path to the north passes under much-deteriorated Cleopatra Terrace.

The last parking area also takes you to many steps for a different access to **Jupiter Terrace**. Two large hot pools at the top of Jupiter used to discharge water here. Early tour guides always pointed out Pulpit Terrace, where stalactites had grown almost together around the edges of a semicircular pool into a pulpit-shaped formation. This feature has deteriorated and can no longer be seen. The southernmost mound of this complex of terraces bears the name **Marble Terrace.**

A Mountain Turning Itself Inside Out

In more than 140 years of recorded history, Mammoth's terraces have grown tremendously in height and width. In fact, the average yearly buildup of travertine in active areas is about 8 inches (20 cm) and can be as much as 2 feet (60 cm).

What Makes the Terraces?

The Mammoth area is underlain at depth by limestones, sediments consisting mostly of calcium carbonate **[GEO.24]**. Hot water dissolves the limestone from deep below Mammoth and carries it through cracks to the surface. As the water rises, the pressure confining it decreases, the water cools, and hot gas, mostly carbon dioxide, escapes. The water becomes supersaturated with calcium carbonate, which precipitates out on the surface as travertine.

The water in Mammoth's springs remains at about 163°F (73°C) year round. Where does all this hot water comes from? The heat comes from magma deep below the earth's surface, perhaps from the very large magma chamber under the Yellowstone Caldera or possibly from a separate magma source near Mammoth. The water all originated as rain or snow in different locations and travels to Mammoth along faults. Most comes from the Gallatin Range to the northwest, traveling deep underground and taking at least 60 but maybe even 10,000 years to arrive. A smaller amount travels north from Norris as shallow groundwater, and some is recycled local precipitation.

Why Are There No Geysers at Mammoth?

Two factors essential to create geysers are missing here: geysers require superheated water, and they need rock that can provide the required plumbing and buildup of pressure. Geyser-rich areas, such as Upper Geyser Basin, are underlain by rhyolite rocks of the Yellowstone Caldera that are rich in silica and provide the right conditions.

Colors and Patterns in the Terraces

Some of the bright colors in the runoff come from mineral deposits, but most come from microorganisms that thrive in hot water. These microorganisms begin to appear just a few days after a new spring is born.

The resident bacteria and algae help extract some of the carbon dioxide from the hot-spring water. Calcium carbonate is precipitated on top of the organisms, which in turn seek sunlight and begin to build up above the mineral deposits. Looking closely, you can find filamentous patterns in the formations, showing the results of this precipitation and growth.

Inactive terraces are white; long-inactive ones are various shades of gray. What makes the springs that build the terraces so unpredictable? The accumulating travertine tends to clog the plumbing, and varying water supply, chemistry, temperature, and frequent earthquakes may also contribute to the changes.

Some Facts and Figures about Mammoth Hot Springs

Every day at Mammoth an estimated 1.4 million gallons (5.3 million L) of water is discharged and about two tons of new travertine are deposited. However, Mammoth is not the world's largest set of active travertine terraces; a larger one, Pamukkale (ancient Hierapolis) in southwestern Turkey, covers several square kilometers, and there may be others.

Palette Spring's terracettes, including one shaped like a tall pulpit (2012)

Besides the large terraces, other types of travertine features at Mammoth are domes such as Liberty Cap, *fissure ridges* fed by water rising through cracks, and *terracettes*, semicircles of travertine at the edges of a hot spring pool.

In over a century of observation, geologists have concluded that the overall thermal activity has neither declined nor increased. Over time, some hot springs seal themselves and never reopen, others cease and resume, and new ones appear with no warning. Change is constant at Mammoth.

From Mammoth Junction to Norris Junction

In the 21 miles (34 km) between Mammoth and Norris Junctions there are no geysers to watch, but you'll find several other types of thermal feature as well as mountains of volcanic origin. Heading south on the Grand Loop Road, you'll pass Upper Terrace Drive's terraces, Obsidian Cliff, Clearwater Springs, Roaring Mountain, and tiny, sizzling Frying Pan Spring.

Road Log

NOTE: See the Mammoth Hot Springs Terraces map on page 265. Mammoth Village's facilities are described on page 257, map on page 258. Maps of Mammoth Junction to Swan Lake Flat and of Swan Lake Flat to Norris Junction are on pages 250 and 277, respectively.

0.0/21.0 Mammoth Hot Springs Junction. The road that passes the hotel, dining areas, general store, and service station takes you to the terraces and then on to Norris Junction and Norris Geyser Basin. The road that begins almost opposite the Mammoth Hot Springs Hotel goes east to Tower-Roosevelt Junction. Past the post office and administrative area is the road to the North Entrance.

0.3/20.7 **P** **(2)** Liberty Cap and Opal Terrace. (For walking tours of these and other lower terraces, see pages 263–67.)

The big hill across the road from the main terraces is **Capitol Hill**, composed of glacially transported gravel and once the center of authority in the park. In 1879, Superintendent Norris built his administration building (the "Blockhouse") on top of the hill and fortified it against possible Indian attack. It served as office and home for Norris and other civilian superintendents until it was torn down in 1909.

0.4/20.6 **P** Jupiter Terrace. This general area was the site of Camp Sheridan, the U.S. Army's first park headquarters, used from 1886 until 1897, by which time nearby Fort Yellowstone had supplanted it.

0.6/20.4 **P** Terrace Springs Trails parking area is the least convenient of the four places to park near the Lower Terraces and requires the most stair climbing.

In this area in the 1930s and '40s was a swimming pool that used hot-spring water. It was removed by the Park Service about 1950.

0.8/20.2 Side road to the **Mammoth Horse Corrals** at the east. Horses may be hired through the park concessionaire for escorted one-hour rides during the summer months. Arrangements can be made at Mammoth Hot Springs Hotel or at the corrals.

There was a lodge and campground in this valley many years ago, and an enclosure where bison were confined during the summer. This show herd assured early twentieth century tourists on the Grand Tour that they would see some of the then-rare beasts.

Also down this road near the corral office is the military cemetery, where soldiers and others who died at Mammoth were buried from 1888 to 1957. Many of the remains and gravestones were removed by the military in 1917 to Little Bighorn Battlefield National Monument (then called the Custer Battlefield). About 40 graves remain.

1.3/19.7 At the sharpest angle of the hairpin curve in the Grand Loop Road is the entrance to a side road to a service area with employee housing and a privately sponsored summer camp called the Youth Conservation Corps, for young people who do resource management and trail work.

From 1933 to 1941, this area housed the headquarters for the local Civilian Conservation Corps. The C.C.C. was a large project of President Franklin Roosevelt's New Deal, during which men aged 17 to 28 were recruited throughout the country to build and maintain roads, bridges, trails, and campgrounds, fight fires, and stock fish, while learning valuable skills and often supporting destitute families.

A steep hike on the former **Bunsen Peak Road** starts in the residential area here. To locate the trailhead, turn left at the Truck Route sign and watch for a closed-off road with a trail sign on your left. Please respect local residents and park as well out of the way as possible. An easier approach to this trail down to the Gardner Canyon and Osprey Falls starts near Rustic Falls, described at mile 4.8/16.2 on this stretch of the Grand Loop Road.

A short trail (really a road, used as a ski trail in winter) beginning at the end of the maintenance yard leads to little Joffe Lake, which has some small brook trout.

The hill between the residential area and Upper Terrace Drive has traditionally been called **Formation Hill**, since it leads to the main formation or terrace.

Centuries of Terrace Building

A descending series of travertine terraces passes through the Mammoth Hot Springs area from southwest to northeast, like huge stair steps. The oldest now-inactive terrace, Terrace Mountain, is the farthest to the southwest, about 2 miles southwest of Mammoth; while the younger and more active ones are parts of the upper and lower terraces. The most northeasterly feature in the series is Boiling River, 2.3 miles by road below and north of Mammoth.

- **Terrace Mountain** is the oldest and highest terrace. Its travertine deposits are about 375,000 years old.

• A thousand feet (300 m) below the summit of Terrace Mountain is much smaller **Pinyon Terrace**, about 10,000 years old. During its thousands of years of inactivity, its travertine has weathered into soil that supports plants and trees, but some collapse features remain.
• Next is **Highland Terrace**, crossed by Upper Terrace Drive. The named features of this upper terrace have been active only recently.
• **Main Terrace** is the flat-topped mound we look down on from Upper Terrace Drive. There the numerous springs and terraces have continued to be active on and off for the last few hundred years.
• The visitor center and many of Mammoth's other buildings are built on **Hotel Terrace** and its eastern edge, **Cedar Terrace**. The travertine of Hotel Terrace proves to be several thousand years old. Look across the terrace on a cold morning and you can see steam rising from two or more vapor vents. It is coming from hot water that flows underground toward the river from the active springs above.
• The hot spring runoff at **Boiling River** lines up neatly with this array of terraces. It has little terrace-building potential, because rain and river water dilute the dissolved calcium carbonate in the runoff. Some of the numerous smaller terraces are shown on the map, page 265.

1.8/19.2 Turnout for a good view of Canary Spring and its terrace and the whole Gardner River valley and mountains to the north.

2.0/19.0 Upper Terrace Drive (also called Mammoth Terrace Drive) begins here and leads one way to the right. See the map on page 265. No RVs, buses, or any other vehicles over 25 feet long are allowed on this road, because it's so narrow and winding.

If your vehicle is too large for the road, leave it in the large parking area at the turnoff.

The whole loop is 1.6 miles (2.6 km) long, short enough for a pleasant walk, but many people prefer to drive and stop for the sights. Whether walking or driving, you'll find several active springs, fine views of the valley below and the surrounding mountains, and a number of interesting formations.

Upper Terrace Drive★

There are two ways to access the first feature, Canary Spring, which has been quite active and beautiful in recent years.

To use the wheelchair-accessible boardwalks, you may park outside the turnoff for this drive or on the left immediately after entering the one-way road. Follow the gradually descending boardwalk to its lower stretch.

Alternatively, drive to the first wide parking spot on the right and take the boardwalks along the top of **Main Terrace**.

On this second route, a boardwalk spur passes **Cupid Spring** with its gracefully draping formations. Cupid's deposits have sealed off a feature called Cupid's Cave, named for the Roman god of love. In the early years of the park, tourists entered this cave, oblivious to the dangers of the carbon dioxide found in all such features.

To the right of the steps descending toward Canary is **Grassy Spring**, active since at least 2006 and building terracettes. The next feature, to the right of the boardwalk, is relatively new **Dryad Springs**, named for fairies in Greek mythology who lived within and guarded trees.

Approaching **Canary Spring**, you can see pools ringed with white hanging stalactites. When water pours from the spring to the scallop-edged terracettes below, microorganisms growing in the water create beautiful colored effects. After several years of large volumes of very hot water rapidly building terraces, Canary Spring began to slow in 2011.

No longer canary yellow, Canary Spring is creating a huge terrace (2012).

On Main Terrace, **Blue Spring** has been a prominent feature. Many steps lead to the terraces and road below, passing **New Blue Springs**, which was very hot and building terraces in recent years but quiet and white in 2012. To the left of the road is the gray and deteriorating mound of **Prospect Terrace**.

The next large parking area has an interpretive sign about Fort Yellowstone and an outstanding view of Mammoth and the entire region. This terrace rim was historically called **The Esplanade**.

The road turns sharply left at The Esplanade, where **Cheops Mound** and Narrow Gauge Terrace's travertine are crumbling on the right. The next small parking area is for **Prospect Springs**, which are now-dry pools and a foot-high (30 cm) cone that date from about 1935. Across the road from these springs are fenced-off deep holes that emit carbon dioxide and hydrogen sulfide.

Park across the road from New Highland Terrace to see the beautiful and very active lower section of **Narrow Gauge Terrace**. The old Narrow Gauge is a cracked fissure ridge named when it was thought to resemble a narrow-gauge railway roadbed. To reach the active springs, walk back down the road to a short trail through the trees to connect with the Howard Eaton Trail. Take the main trail a short distance to the north (right). The trail was relocated higher on the hill to accommodate the spreading runoff of Narrow Gauge. Covering some of the undisturbed pool is sometimes a delicate, thin crust of travertine, called calcite ice.

New Highland Terrace is known to have been active from at least 1928 and was truly spectacular from the late 1950s into the 1970s. The many dead trees on the sides and top of this formation attest to the sequence of active growth followed by inactivity. Trees grew for many years after the hot water ceased flowing; subsequently, further hot spring activity killed the trees. New activity has appeared at the top in the last year or two.

Orange Spring Mound (late 1990s)

On the inside of a sharp curve is **Orange Spring Mound**, composed of several cone-type formations grown together and a fissure ridge along its long axis, colored orange by bacterial mats. A jet at the top sometimes spouts to 3 or 4 feet (1 m). Recent activity from spouts at the roadside edge has necessitated moving the road farther away. One of Orange Spring Mound's often-active hot springs is named **Tangerine Spring**.

If you stop here, notice the little travertine cone across the road, called **Little Burper** for the tiny persistent bubbles it spouts when active. From a certain angle, its shape perfectly imitates that of Bunsen Peak in the distance.

You can start a pleasant round-trip hike of about 5 miles (8 km) here at Orange Spring Mound's parking area. The trail traverses parts of the Howard Eaton and Fawn Pass Trails, passing between Clagett Butte and Terrace Mountain to reach **Snow Pass** and little Summit Lake near it. To find the trail, turn your back on Orange Spring Mound and look up to the right. Pass the travertine flats of Pinyon Terrace, including some collapse features, where the gaseous carbon dioxide creates death traps for small birds.

In about 1 mile (1.5 km) you'll turn right at the intersection and begin a climb that totals about 700 feet (200 m). Stay left at the Clagett Butte Trail intersection, along a hillside that abounds in wildflowers. The top of the pass is a windy, grassy area. Summit Lake is a short distance farther in the trees.

There is little evidence now, but Snow Pass was the route of the original road from Mammoth around Terrace Mountain. One early guidebook described the Snow Pass road as so steep "that it would take a loaded wagon, drawn by four mules, a half day, allowing proper time to breathe the animals on the successive terraces. . . ." Not surprisingly, they called the Snow Pass road the "Hell Gate."

Continuing on Upper Terrace Drive

Beyond Orange Spring Mound, the road descends a steep hill. Below and to the right was Bath Lake, where early tourists bathed. It has dried out and refilled sporadically over the years; the bathhouse was removed about 60 years ago. Bath Lake has been dry since 1984. Nothing appears to grow where the water used to be.

Across the road from Bath Lake, a new spring broke out in 1978. Park Historian Lee Whittlesey christened it **Aphrodite Spring** for the Greek goddess of love and beauty, but it's now called Aphrodite Terrace—inactive for many years but showing a little color in 2012.

Many of the small evergreen trees

Rocky Mountain juniper tree

along Mammoth Terrace Drive are Rocky Mountain junipers. According to dendrologist John King, some of Mammoth's junipers are 1,500 years old, and one even dates from AD 300. Limber pine trees, their needles in sets of five, also grow along the drive.

Two more features along this twisting road are worth your attention: White Elephant Back Terrace and Angel Terrace. **White Elephant Back Terrace** is another fissure ridge, built up over centuries by sporadic seepage from the springs at its top. Solution caves, that is, depressions where runoff down the side has dissolved away the travertine, can be found along the northwest side of the "elephant." Here they're called **The Grottoes.**

Angel Terrace may have been named for its snowy whiteness or for the delicate microorganisms that sometimes live around it. Healthy trees grow on top of the tallest gray section, while dead trees provide witness to more recent activity. Elsewhere, the hot water and bacteria have created travertine stalactites and (where active) areas of yellow, orange, and salmon colors. High above and to the north of Angel, **Glen Springs** was active in 2012.

Features of historical interest on the Upper Terrace can now be seen only with a ranger. They include the River Styx, a partially underground hot stream, and solution caves such as the Stygian Caves or deep Devil's Kitchen, where tourists used to descend by ladder. They were allowed to enter the cave until someone realized that the carbon dioxide that had killed birds and small animals wasn't good for humans either! Enterprising Mammoth residents even offered refreshments from a "Devil's Kitchenette" just above the cave.

A sharp curve to the right brings you back to the Grand Loop Road.

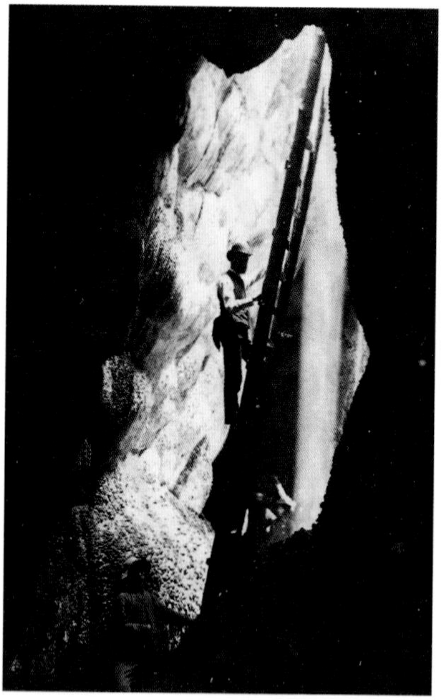

Descending into Devil's Kitchen, 1880s stereograph

Continuing on the Grand Loop Road

2.1/18.9 Turnout on the east for a warming and refueling hut for skiers and snowmobilers, built in the 1990s.

3.1/17.9 **P** Interpretive signs about the nearby "mosaic" burned area and 1988's North Fork fire, as well as a lovely view of Africa and Joffe Lakes and distant hills.

The lake below the road, called **Africa Lake** for its shape, was called "Beatty's Lake" for years, after a local truck driver named Roy Beatty lost control of his truck and drove it into the lake in 1931. Joffe Lake was named for Assistant Superintendent Joseph Joffe, who also helped prepare the *Haynes Guide* in the early twentieth century.

3.7/17.3 The Hoodoos (or Silver Gate) one-way road. Go slowly to find and take the very short, unmarked loop road to the west—a remnant of the 1899 stagecoach road. Park here to look closely at these unusual rocks.

The word hoodoo can mean something that brings bad luck, but in geology, it usually refers to standing sedimentary rocks eroded into sharp spires with bizarre shapes. Actually, the other official name for this place, **Silver Gate**, is more appropriate for this slope of Terrace Mountain, since the gray-white rocks did not erode in place. These huge, strangely shaped rocks are lying in an immense jumble that has slid from the slopes of Terrace Mountain to the west. The rock is predominantly travertine, like that at Mammoth Hot Springs but much older. Notice that the trees growing among the rocks are not very large, which suggests the landslide probably occurred in a recent century. (Also see pages 158–59 about hoodoos.)

4.4/16.6 Golden Gate at Kingman Pass (7,250 ft / 2,210 m). When you reach Kingman Pass, you've climbed more than

The Pillar of Hercules at Golden Gate, by F. J. Haynes.

1,000 feet (300 m) in the short distance from Mammoth. The name Golden Gate was used as early as the 1880s and stems from the sense you get here of passing through a gateway to the park.

The Golden Gate **[GEO.7]** is a canyon cut by Glen Creek through a large deposit of the Huckleberry Ridge tuff. This 2-million-year-old volcanic rock has been stained reddish yellow by iron oxide.

At the outer edge of the road is a column of rock known as the **Pillar of Hercules**, named by 1880s tour guide George Henderson, possibly after the Pillars of Hercules that guard the Strait of Gibraltar in Europe. It has been moved three times, once in 1889 to make room for the steamboat *Zillah* to pass on a horse-drawn truck on its way to Yellowstone Lake.

Near the top of the north slope of Bunsen Peak across the canyon is **Cathedral Rock**, named for its majestic spires at the time this road was built.

4.6/16.4 **P** Rustic Falls. A sign tells

Rustic Falls draws water from higher creeks and its own Glen Creek.

about the difficulties of building the Golden Gate road, which was designed by Lt. Daniel Kingman of the Corps of Engineers in the 1880s. Incidentally, Kingman also conceived of the figure eight pattern for the Grand Loop Road.

Rustic Falls on Glen Creek is only 47 feet high (14 m) but worth a stop, especially early in summer when the water level is high.

The canyon wall across Glen Creek is part of **Bunsen Peak**, named for the German physicist, chemist, and inventor, Robert Wilhelm Eberhard von Bunsen. Bunsen studied and theorized about the geysers of Iceland, as well as lending his name to the Bunsen burner used in laboratories. Bunsen Peak is a remnant of the 50-million-year-old Absaroka volcanics and is probably a volcanic neck, or feeder conduit, which survived because it was resistant to erosion.

4.8/16.2 Swan Lake Flat opens out before you as you exit Golden Gate canyon. The area through which the Gardner River meanders was historically called Gardners Hole—"hole" was the trappers' name for a wide valley. The Gardner River flows to the southeast behind the low hills west of Swan Lake, then makes a sharp turn to the northeast, and cuts through deep Sheepeater Canyon to join the Yellowstone River near Gardiner.

Just as you enter Swan Lake Flat is a large parking area for the **Bunsen Peak**, **Osprey Falls**, **Glen Creek**, and **Howard Eaton Trails**.

Until 1995, the road around Bunsen Peak was open to automobile traffic, but it's now available only for biking and hiking. The former road goes about 6 miles (10 km) around Bunsen Peak to end at a maintenance and residential area near Mammoth. After about 3 quite level miles (5 km) through sage flats, the old road begins the 800-foot (250 m) descent to the Mammoth area.

Hikers can climb Bunsen Peak either from the **Bunsen Peak Trail** near the

Electric Peak is the highest mountain seen from Swan Lake Flat.

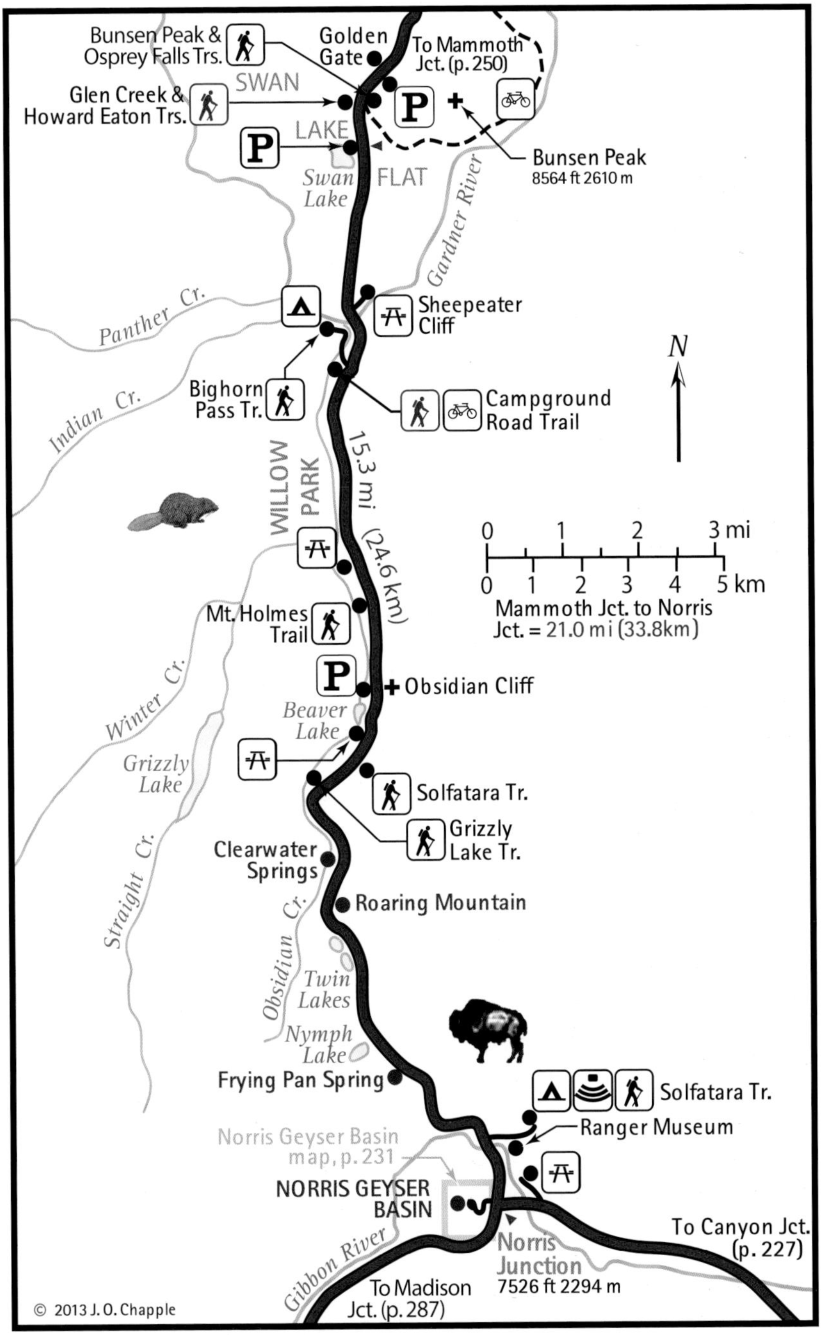

Bunsen Peak & Osprey Falls Trs.
Golden Gate
To Mammoth Jct. (p. 250)
Glen Creek & Howard Eaton Trs.
SWAN
LAKE
FLAT
Swan Lake
Bunsen Peak
8564 ft 2610 m
Gardner River
Panther Cr.
Sheepeater Cliff
N
Indian Cr.
Bighorn Pass Tr.
Campground Road Trail
WILLOW PARK
15.3 mi (24.6 km)
0 1 2 3 mi
0 1 2 3 4 5 km
Mammoth Jct. to Norris Jct. = 21.0 mi (33.8km)
Mt. Holmes Trail
Obsidian Cliff
Winter Cr.
Beaver Lake
Grizzly Lake
Solfatara Tr.
Grizzly Lake Tr.
Straight Cr.
Clearwater Springs
Roaring Mountain
Obsidian Cr.
Twin Lakes
Nymph Lake
Frying Pan Spring
Solfatara Tr.
Ranger Museum
Norris Geyser Basin map, p. 231
NORRIS GEYSER BASIN
To Canyon Jct. (p. 227)
Gibbon River
Norris Junction
7526 ft 2294 m
To Madison Jct. (p. 287)
© 2013 J. O. Chapple

Swan Lake Flat to Norris Junction

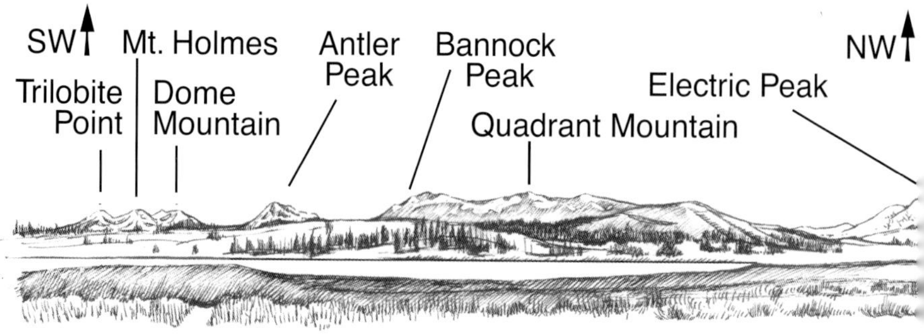

Swan Lake Flat Panorama

Starting to the east (left) and looking around clockwise, you'll see:

To the east and southeast are mountains of the **Washburn Range**, 9 to 12 miles (15–19 km) away.

To the south, the gently rolling terrain is part of the eroded Yellowstone Caldera.

Trilobite Point (10,011 ft / 3,051 m), a part of Mt. Holmes, the peak farthest to the left. It was named for ancient trilobite fossils found on the mountain.

Mt. Holmes, the second highest one in this panorama (10,336 ft / 3,150 m), with a fire lookout on top and snow near its top most of the year.

Dome Mountain with two peaks, the higher being 9,903 ft (3,018 m).

Antler Peak (10,063 ft / 3,067 m), looking very pointed, as elk antlers are.

Bannock Peak (10,332 ft / 3,149 m)—barely peeking out at Quadrant's left—named for the tribe who trekked annually through this part of the park to hunt buffalo to the northeast.

parking area or by taking the former road for about 3 miles (5 km), then climbing up from near the Osprey Falls Trailhead (see below). Either way, the elevation gain to the top is more than 1,300 feet (400 m).

For another hike starting here, take the road for about 3 miles (5 km), then descend about 800 feet (250 m) in about 1 mile (1.6 km) on the **Osprey Falls Trail** to the bottom of Sheepeater Canyon. Osprey Falls is a 150-foot (46 m) waterfall in a spectacular canyon not seen by many visitors. You can get a glimpse of the falls from the road.

The **Glen Creek Trail** goes west, starting across the main road from the parking area. It follows the former Snow Pass Road to join the long Fawn Pass and Sportsman Lake Trails, which cross the northwest corner of the park, or to meet the Sepulcher Loop Trail up Sepulcher Mountain.

For a delightful, easy 2-mile (3 km) hike, you can take the Glen Creek Trail for a few hundred yards (meters) until it joins the **Howard Eaton Trail**. Turn right for a gradual ascent to broad views of Swan Lake Flat and distant mountains to the south. Slightly farther

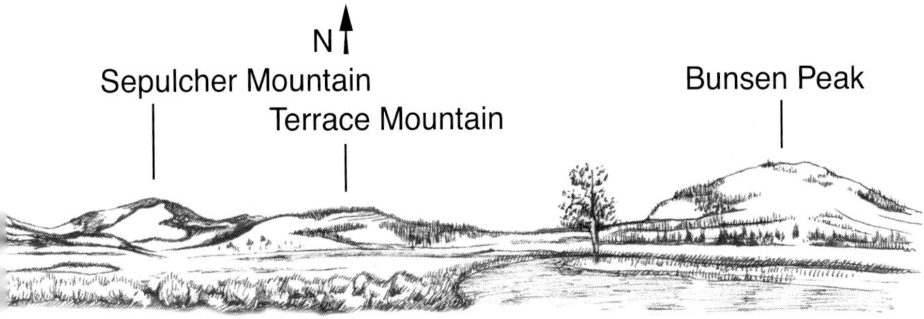

Quadrant Mountain (10,213 ft / 3,113 m), the flat-topped ridge in the middle of the view, named in 1878 by members of the Hayden Survey. Their topographer, Henry Gannett, wrote that "the summit, with the northern and western slopes, forms a curved surface, roughly resembling a segment of a sphere."

Unnamed nearby hills west of Swan Lake.

Electric Peak, near the park's northern boundary, about 4 miles (6.5 km) away. At 10,969 feet (3,343 m), it usually has snow—when it doesn't, a reddish area below its highest point is revealed.

Sepulcher Mountain (9,652 ft / 2,942 m) northwest of Mammoth, with a rounded top.

Terrace Mountain to the north of Swan Lake Flat, lower than the others (8,011 ft / 2,442 m) and topped by a travertine cliff.

Bunsen Peak (8,564 ft / 2,610 m) at the far right rear as you face the lake (northeast).

on, you reach a fine panoramic view toward the Mammoth area to the north.

Return from here or continue on the Howard Eaton Trail, following the path steeply down another 2 miles (3 km) to reach Mammoth through burned Douglas fir forest. According to ranger-interpreter Orville Bach Jr.'s hiking book *Exploring the Yellowstone Backcountry*, on this trail you'll find the greatest diversity of plant life of any short trail in the park. Bach also mentions the likelihood of black bears feeding on buffaloberries here in late summer.

5.7/15.3 **P** A short loop road (easy to spot by its lone tree) goes toward **Swan Lake** for a good place to stop and view the mountains of the southern Gallatin Range. Swan Lake is extremely shallow and has no fish. Over the years, it has sometimes been a nesting place for trumpeter and whistling swans and for ducks.

Geoscientists tell us that ice was almost a half mile (0.8 km) thick here during the last glaciation. At Swan Lake Flat, the ice would have piled up to over 9,500 feet (2,900 m) above sea level, completely covering some of the mountains in this area, including Bunsen Peak.

Some rock surfaces, even near the mountaintops, have small parallel grooves or glacial striations gouged out by small rocks trapped in the ice.

Swan Lake is located in a unique spot, a long narrow depression that geologists call a trough. From here, you can see mountains for almost 360 degrees around you.

8.0/13.0 (5) Side road to the northeast for Sheepeater Cliffs picnic area. To the left of the picnic area as you face the columnar basalt rocks is a natural amphitheater.

Cliffs like those above the picnic tables here extend north downstream along the Gardner River through Sheepeater Canyon. You can reach a trail into the canyon from the Osprey Falls branch of the Bunsen Peak Trail, which begins at mile 4.8/16.2. Fishermen have made another trail along the Gardner.

Superintendent Norris first applied the name **Sheepeater Cliffs** to the expanse of basalt cliffs farther down this canyon in 1879. The small Sheepeater tribe, related to the Shoshonis, were the only Native American Indians known to live in park territory. They had their own specialized mountain culture, subsisting mainly on bighorn sheep but also on small mammals, birds, fish, and native plants. In the Gardner canyon, Norris discovered remnants of shelters belonging to the Sheepeaters, who had been removed to nearby reservations before Yellowstone was established as a park.

Sheepeater Cliffs is a popular stop for children, who love to climb here and chase the marmots.

8.1/12.9 Gardner River crossing, sometimes called the Seven-Mile Bridge (it's about that far from the Mammoth area). At this point **Obsidian Creek** flows from the south and joins the **Gardner River**. **Panther** and **Indian Creeks** join the Gardner just west of here, creating a marshy area. Park fishing regulations allow children to fish with worms as bait on these four streams. The road follows Obsidian Creek for the next few miles south.

8.6/12.4 **Indian Creek Campground** is at the end of a half-mile (0.8 km) side road to the west. This is one of the park's first-come, first-served campgrounds, with 75 sites. It has vault toilets only and no showers. As you cross the creek, you'll pass a warming hut used by winter visitors.

Bighorn Pass Trail starts in the campground. This trail is 19 miles (30 km) long and goes all the way to U.S. Highway 191 near the park's west boundary.

1.5-mile (2.4 km) round trip trail for biking and hiking, called the **Superintendent's campground road**, follows Indian Creek south just after the creek crossing. It's a good place to see birds, elk, and moose. There's an isolated walk-in campsite at the end of the road.

Indian Creek was named in 1878, when Hayden expedition members noticed the travois marks left by the annual trek of the Bannock tribe.

9.9/11.1 Largest of several Willow Park turnouts for accessing Obsidian Creek. Yellowstone has some 20 varieties of willows. Since moose love willows, this is said to be a favorite spot for them, but a frequent visitor recently quipped, "They need to take down the signs so the moose will come back there!"

Beaver are known to live in Willow Park, but your chances of seeing one are not good, except at dawn or dusk.

Obsidian Creek here meanders along its gentle, clear-watered course through the wide meadow. It's uniformly 6 to 8 (2 m) feet wide or less and not very deep. This is another good fishing spot.

10.6/10.4 Moose Bogs. Large parking area with interpretive sign about moose and short trail to the creek. You can see both Mount Holmes and Dome Mountain from here.

11.0/10.0 (6) Apollinaris Spring picnic area on the west (not signed going south). Visit the spring across the road.

11.1/9.9 **Apollinaris Spring** on the east. Limited roadside parking, more in the picnic area. The travertine masonry steps from 1925 take you to a charming spot with a cold-water spring, named in the 1880s after a German spring water that is still being sold.

This water contains minute amounts of several chemicals and was thought by early park visitors to be healthful, but it does not comply with current standards for drinking water. In fact, officials recommend that you don't drink from any untreated spring, lake, or river in the park due to the danger of contracting *giardiasis* (pronounced gee-ar-DI-a-sis), an intestinal disease.

Tourists often drank Apollinaris Spring water in the early years of the park (1925).

11.4/9.6 🥾 **Mount Holmes Trailhead.** The summit of Mount Holmes is 10 miles (16 km) and 3,000 vertical feet (915 m) from this trailhead.

12.4/8.6 **P** Unmarked turnoff on west for Obsidian Cliff exhibit. **Obsidian Cliff** became a National Historic Landmark in 1996 for its importance as a prehistoric site. Obsidian is a black or dark-colored volcanic glass that commonly forms on the margins of

A Mountain of Glass

The vertical columns of pentagonal-shaped blocks of obsidian, rising some 250 feet above the road, present a glistening, mirror-like effect when illumined by the sun's rays. The greater part of this mineral glass is jet black and quite opaque with traces of similar formation variegated with streaks of red and yellow. The construction of the roadway along its base was accomplished in a novel manner and with considerable difficulty; blasting powder being ineffectual, great fires were built around the huge blocks of glass, which, when heated, were suddenly cooled by dashing water upon them, thus shattering the blocks into small fragments. This process made possible the construction of this really wonderful roadway, probably the only piece of glass road in the world.

—from the *Haynes Guide*, 1912

Obsidian Cliff and Beaver Lake as they appeared a century ago.

Don't be disappointed when you can't see your reflection in the rock of the cliff across the road! Not only are the purest bits of obsidian far from the road, but also the Obsidian Cliff that Haynes saw has probably changed, because many early visitors chopped off bits of the cliff as souvenirs and because moss and lichens have thrived on the rock, covering up much of its shine.

rhyolitic lava flows. Obsidian Cliff, composed largely of glass, is the western edge of a huge mass of lava that flowed and cooled here about 180,000 years ago, long after the last major Yellowstone caldera event (639,000 years ago).

Obsidian is hard and brittle and fractures with very sharp edges. As long as 8,800 years ago, Native American Indians obtained obsidian here and made extremely sharp and valuable cutting and piercing tools, which were traded extensively and have been found in archaeological digs as far away as Ohio.

The area away from the road is now closed to the public, but you can easily see some fine big specimens of obsidian right along the roadside south of the cliff. Other places in the park have outcrops of obsidian but are difficult to see.

The small gazebo that houses exhibits is itself worth looking at. It was built in 1931 from columns of quarried volcanic rock reassembled for this structure.

13.1/7.9 Beaver Lake. What lake? you may ask, since it's now largely a swampy meadow. Over many years, beavers have repeatedly dammed this lake. In fact, at one time a beaver dam said to be about 1,000 feet (300 m) long and the largest in the park stretched across the lake's northern end where the outlet is.

13.4/7.6 **(6)** Beaver Lake picnic area to the west. To the east a few yards up the small creek is a fumarole that gives off the rotten egg smell of hydrogen sulfide.

13.7/7.3 The road passes under an electric transmission line and Lemonade Creek at about this point. The upper stretches of the creek really are the color of lemonade or maybe limeade. In *Yellowstone Place Names*, Whittlesey quotes a story about stagecoach drivers who carried a "small bag of sugar along to treat their party to cold lemonade hardly distinguishable from the real article." In fact, not only is the clear green water warm and acidic, but it has recently been found to contain an arsenic-eating alga—and arsenic, of course.

13.8/7.2 Short road to the **Solfatara Trailhead** to the east. Sometimes closed due to bear activity, this trail follows a power line and the tourist road built in 1878, passing near Amphitheater Springs and Lake of the Woods. The trail continues about 6 miles (10 km) to the Norris Campground.

The hot spring area called **Amphitheater Springs** may have been named for its location in a sort of natural amphitheater or because boulders in the area look like seats carelessly arranged. Native American Indians passing through this area found vermilion (mercuric sulfide, a red pigment).

14.6/6.4 **Grizzly Lake Trailhead** and "Fire Weather" interpretive sign. The lake is a steep 2 miles (3 km) up the trail, which joins the Mount Holmes Trail in another 1.5 miles (2.4 km).

This is a heavily burned area where a 1976 fire left dead trees standing about. After 12 years, when the dead trees had dried out, the 1988 North Fork fire came this way, and a true firestorm resulted—a popular locale for photographers that summer.

15.5/5.5 **P** For about 0.3 mile (0.5 km)

Yellow monkeyflowers and microorganisms thrive below Clearwater Springs.

along the road, turnouts are available on the west side where **Clearwater Springs** are located along Obsidian Creek. The only sign here says "Unstable ground—boiling water" for a good reason: visitors have been burned in the hot springs.

15.7/5.3 Semi-Centennial Geyser (near the "Obsidian Creek" sign) is now a sometimes steaming, sometimes scummy pool drowned by Obsidian Creek. But in 1922, the year Yellowstone Park was 50 years old, it sprang to life with a huge explosion, hurling scalding water, mud, and rocks to an estimated 300 feet (90 m). The expelled material destroyed nearby roadbed and trees. A few weeks later the geyser had ceased to erupt at all. Semi-Centennial is the most northerly geyser in the park.

16.0/5.0 **P** **Roaring Mountain** and **Lemonade Lake**. You'll find it hard to hear any roaring now, and only on colder days do you see steam rising from the numerous vents, but the mountain was active and sometimes very loud in the park's first 50 years. The soil is still so acidic that little grows here. Lemonade Lake is greenish when it has water, but in summer it is usually dry. An interpretive sign explains how this and other park features change over time, especially as a result of earth tremors.

16.5/4.5 North Twin Lake has a lovely green color, particularly in morning sunlight. Its water may be too acidic for pond lilies.

16.9/4.1 South Twin Lake has a darker blue-green color, and pond lilies bloom near its shores. These lakes are twins only in being next to each other and separated by a small piece of land, being similar in size, and having no fish. They differ in acidity and color. North Twin Lake is very acidic (pH 3.5), since it receives most of its water from Roaring Mountain, perhaps via underground flow. South Twin Lake is fed by creeks and is much less acidic (pH 5.9). The northern

The Twin Lakes Problem

Various authorities have puzzled over and disagreed about which way Twin Lakes drain. The 1986 U.S.G.S. topographical map shows no inlet or outlet for North Twin Lake and only a south-flowing outlet for South Twin Lake.

One fact about drainage here has been established, however. This general area marks the *drainage divide*. North Twin Lake may have an underground outlet, which probably flows into the Gardner and Yellowstone Rivers. South Twin Lake and the creeks that rise to its south and east flow to the Gibbon and Madison Rivers.

lake is about 20 feet (6 m) higher than the southern one.

17.5/3.5 (P) **Bijah Spring** is a large hot spring west of the road. Parking is restricted to a wide area slightly north of it. No one has been able to decipher the spring's name, used since the 1880s, although it might be a corruption of *bijou*, "jewel" in French.

18.2/2.8 Nymph Lake was named in 1931 for *Nymphaea*, the botanical family of water lilies. Its water is too warm and acidic from nearby hot spring activity to support fish. It has deep holes and contains a great variety of microorganisms and plankton. This area for the next 0.2 mile was historically called Roadside Springs. In 2003 a new group of steaming vents appeared partway up the hill northwest of the lake.

18.4/2.6 (P) **Frying Pan Spring**, identified only by a parking space along the road and danger warnings. The unusual action of the springs on both sides of the road, reminiscent of hot grease sizzling in a pan, comes from rising gas bubbles passing through extremely porous and permeable rock and shallow water. The water is acidic enough (pH about 1.0) to eat through almost anything, but it's not extremely hot. There are other steaming springs and warm lakes nearby; the decomposing geyserite all around indicates old thermal activity.

18.6/2.4 Hazel Lake, named for its color by 1880s tour guide George Henderson.

19.4/1.6 (P) Norris Geyser Basin Overlook to the south. The overlook provides a view of the One Hundred Spring Plain, a thermal area at Norris Geyser Basin. You'll also see an extensive area that was burned in the 1988 North Fork fire.

20.2/0.8 **Norris Campground** side road to the east and the **Museum of the National Park Ranger** just a mile up the same road. The campground has more than 100 first-come, first-served sites, flush toilets, and a campfire circle where campers may attend evening ranger talks. The south end of the **Solfatara Trail** is in the C loop of the campground.

The ranger museum building has also been a soldier station and later a ranger station. Displays here relate to park rangers throughout the United States.

20.3/0.7 (P) Gibbon River bridge and a sign about the days when the U.S. Cavalry policed the park. To the southwest two different Norris Hotels have stood: one built in 1886 that burned down in 1887, and another that opened in 1901 but was abandoned after 1916, when stagecoach travel ended in the park.

21.0/0.0 Norris Junction. Norris Geyser Basin is on a short side road to the west (see description beginning on page 230), Madison Junction to the south, Canyon Junction to the east, and Mammoth Hot Springs Junction to the north.

From Norris Junction to Madison Junction

This short section (13.3 mi/21.4 km) of the Grand Loop Road follows the Gibbon River through its meadows and canyon. There's a good chance of seeing elk and buffalo on the way. Three thermal features to stop for are the Artists' Paintpots, Beryl Spring, and Terrace Spring near Madison.

Road Log

0.0/13.4 Norris Junction. Madison Junction is to the south, then southwest; Canyon Junction to the east; Norris Geyser Basin to the west; and Mammoth Hot Springs Junction to the north.

1.5/11.9 Northeast end of Elk Park. Mount Holmes dominates the northwestern horizon. Besides elk, watch for ducks, geese, and great blue herons on the meandering river.

2.5/10.9 P Gibbon River Rapids at the southwest end of Elk Park. Stop in the wide parking area to walk to the rapids. There's good fishing in this part of the Gibbon River, and even better fishing between the Gibbon Falls (at mile 8.6/4.7) and Madison Junction.

2.8/10.6 P Wide spot in the road for parking to see the (unsigned) **Chocolate Pots**. There's a colorful cone bubbling water from its top down below the road (very hard to see) and a large one across the river. These cones have built up from the bubbling mud squirting over their brims. The large amount of iron oxide in the water here creates the unusual bright orange-brown color that you see on the sides of the cones and on the river bottom. Bright orange and green bacteria and algae grow in the water that trickles down the sides.

3.3/10.1 **(9)** Picnic area west of the road. The terrain is very flat here near

This Chocolate Pot on the Gibbon River's bank nurtures unusual microorganisms.

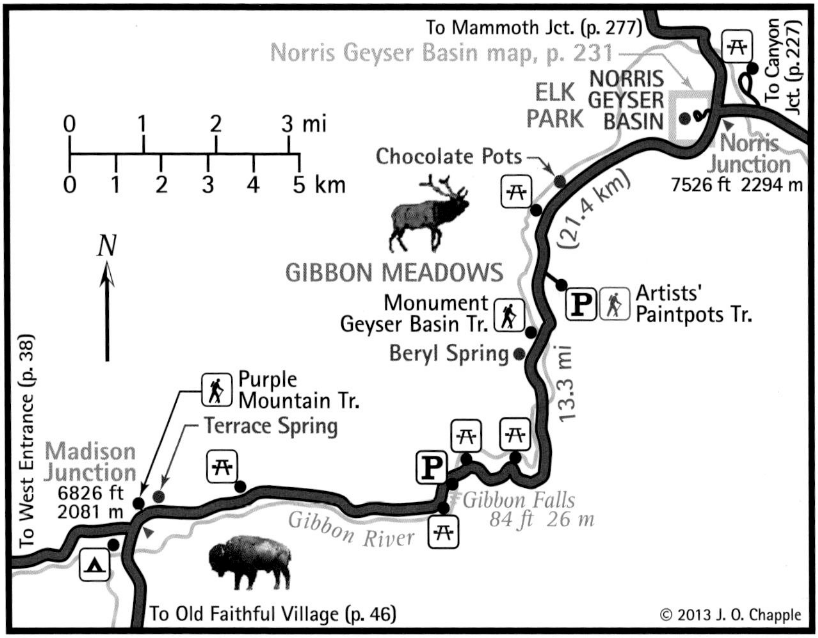

Norris Junction to Madison Junction

Gibbon Meadows, and the river twists and turns through numerous meanders before entering its canyon just to the south.

3.9/9.5 Side road to parking for **Artists' Paintpots**. The area is wheelchair-accessible only as far as the colorful features at the base of the hill. The gray and noisy paintpots are up a short but somewhat steep trail. The area's springs and their surroundings abound in colorful clays—orange, red, and pink. Green and yellow bacteria and algae line the runoff channels.

4.4/9.0 North end of **Gibbon Canyon** and a short side road along the river for fishing access. Tiny hot springs steam along the riverbank.

4.9/8.5 Gibbon River crossing and **Monument Geyser Basin Trailhead** parking area. A 700-foot (200 m) climb in about 1 mile (1.6 km) takes you to some tall and oddly shaped geyser cones, including the still slightly active Monument Geyser, also called Thermos Bottle Geyser, which is gradually sealing its own spout with sinter.

Blood Geyser, an iron-oxide-stained feature at Artists' Paintpots

5.0/8.4 Lone Tree Rock in the Gibbon River was pointed out to tourists in the stagecoach days. At least one lodgepole still grows out of a rock here, but maybe it's not the same tree.

5.3/8.1 **P** Parking for Beryl Spring on the south end of the bridge only. **Beryl Spring**, named for the blue-green gemstone, perpetually throws its superheated water 3 to 4 feet (1–1.2 m) into the air from the several bubbling spots in its pool.

One or more fumaroles hiss like steam engines behind Beryl, while along an old roadbed above it is a dormant paintpot and hot spring area. Both up- and downriver from Beryl are steaming hot springs, perhaps less active than in the past. Acid eats away at the bridge deck near Beryl.

According to Mary Bradshaw Richards's account, *Camping Out in the Yellowstone, 1882*, a "roarer" above the river poured forth a torrent of boiling water from a horizontal orifice, creating "frightful sounds, explosions of pent up water and steam, hissings, roarings, and earth shaking generally."

In the earliest years of the park, a very crude road paralleled the river and climbed the mesa south of here, bypassing Madison Junction.

6.1/7.3 Bridge crosses the Gibbon River. The original route to Madison Junction simply went down the middle of the river for a short distance.

High above the river to the west, the tall, pinkish gray cliffs are welded Lava Creek tuff **[GEO.9]**. It was blown out of the Yellowstone Caldera 639,000 years ago. The tuff is very thick here, because it is close to the caldera edge, and the tephra was not blown very far.

Rocks east of the river are lavas that filled in the caldera much later. To be more precise, they flowed out from far below 90,000 and 160,000 years ago, according to geochemists' analyses.

6.7/6.7 From about here to below Gibbon Falls, the original Grand Loop Road was replaced in 2010. The road formerly followed the river closely and included a dangerous curve, which rangers called Tanker Curve after a tanker truck overturned there in the 1970s. The new high road essentially follows the alignment of the historic 1878 road built by Superintendent Norris and passes two picnic areas with interesting names.

Crossing the Gibbon River in 1884, by F. J. Haynes.

Lacy ribbons of water fall over Gibbon Falls.

7.3/6.1 (3) Caldera Rim picnic area. The road closely follows the very edge between two distinctive areas: to the east and south the Yellowstone Caldera explosion created a huge cavity, not visible because lava filled it in. Look north to see the cliff composed of tephra from that caldera explosion.

8.2/5.2 (4) The name Iron Spring refers to a cold water spring half a mile above Gibbon Falls and west of the old road and river. The spring was obliterated by road building in the twentieth century. Stretching out west of that spring is an intriguingly named area, Secret Valley. In the 1949 *Haynes Guide*, Haynes wrote that Secret Valley "widens out above the road and is a fine grazing area for wild animals."

8.4/5.0 Gibbon River Bridge, which replaced the old bridge in 2010.

8.6/4.8 P Parking for **Gibbon Falls**. At 84 feet (26 m), Gibbon Falls is not one of the highest in Yellowstone, but it is remarkably wide. It's also a geologically significant spot where the river flows very near the northern edge of the Yellowstone Caldera **[GEO.11]**.

A walkway from this parking lot parallels the river for 0.2 mile (0.3 km), provides interesting interpretive signs, and affords excellent views from the brink to the entire breadth of the falls at the walkway's southern end.

9.1/4.3 (2) Side road to the large Gibbon Falls picnic area, which was left quite bleak by the 1988 North Fork fire.

9.8/3.6 In this area the road cut exposes a thick bed of tephra—Lava Creek tuff—deposited close to the Yellowstone Caldera edge.

11.1/2.3 This section of the Gibbon River shows the tendency of a river channel to meander through a nearly level valley.

11.9/1.5 (3) **Tuff Cliff** picnic area. A large section of the cliff fell as a result of the 1959 Hebgen Lake earthquake. Notice how a thick stand of lodgepole pines has grown back since the 1988 North Fork fire, making the cliff now hard to see.

12.6/0.8 Short road to parking for **Terrace Spring thermal area.**

A stroll of perhaps 0.3 mile (0.5 km) around this wheelchair-accessible boardwalk takes you past two pools, the higher and cooler one called **Bath Spring**. The night of the 1959 earthquake near Hebgen Lake, a couple was bathing here in the nude—until the spring drained completely! Very close to the road is **Terrace Spring** itself, a large hot lake.

Orange and brown bacterial mats

Algae now grow in Bath Spring (2008).

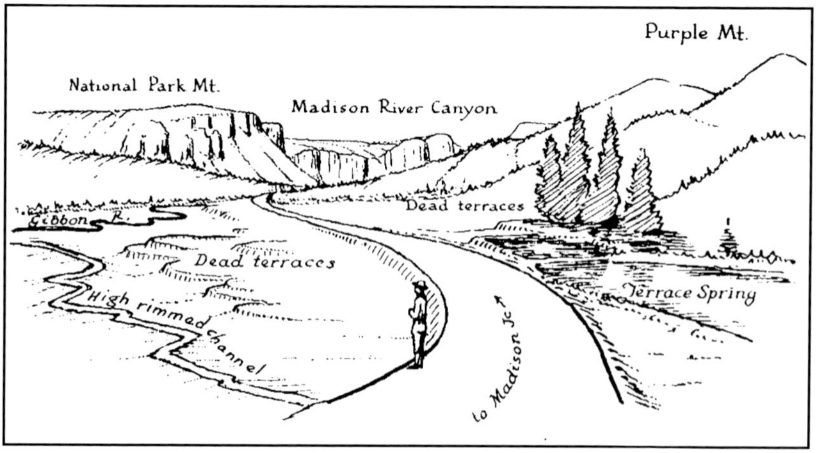

The Terrace Spring area looked like this to naturalist H. C. Bumpus in 1935.

Geology at Terrace Spring

The water at the north end of Terrace Spring appears to be boiling but has been measured at only 141°F (61°C). The bubbling is due to carbon dioxide gas bubbles expanding as they reach the surface of the water.

Terrace Spring is an unusual place in the park, in that the waters of the springs deposit both siliceous sinter and calcareous travertine. The deposits of sinter on the surface are to be expected, since the hot water comes up through rhyolite lava rich in silica. However, it's something of a mystery where the travertine comes from, since it has to come from rocks rich in calcium. The calcium and carbon dioxide could have risen up through cracks in the rock that extend from deeply buried older limestones through the rhyolite lavas.

line the edges of the springs and their runoff channels. Wildflowers grow in the steamy places—yellow monkeyflowers in some weeks of the summer and purple fringed gentians along with tall yellow sunflowers in other weeks.

13.2/0.2 **Purple Mountain Trail head**. This trail can take you about 1,600 feet up (490 m) in about 3 miles (5 km) to a spectacular view in all directions.

Purple Mountain was named for the color of the rock it's made of. The welded tuff (or volcanic ash fall) contains pink crystals of a variety of the mineral feldspar that here is rich in potassium, giving an overall purplish color to the rock.

13.4/0.0 Madison Junction. To the south is Old Faithful Village, to the west are the Madison Campground and the West Entrance, and to the northeast is Norris Junction.

For the road log from Madison Junction to the West Entrance, see page 43 and before. For Madison to Old Faithful Village, see page 47 and after.

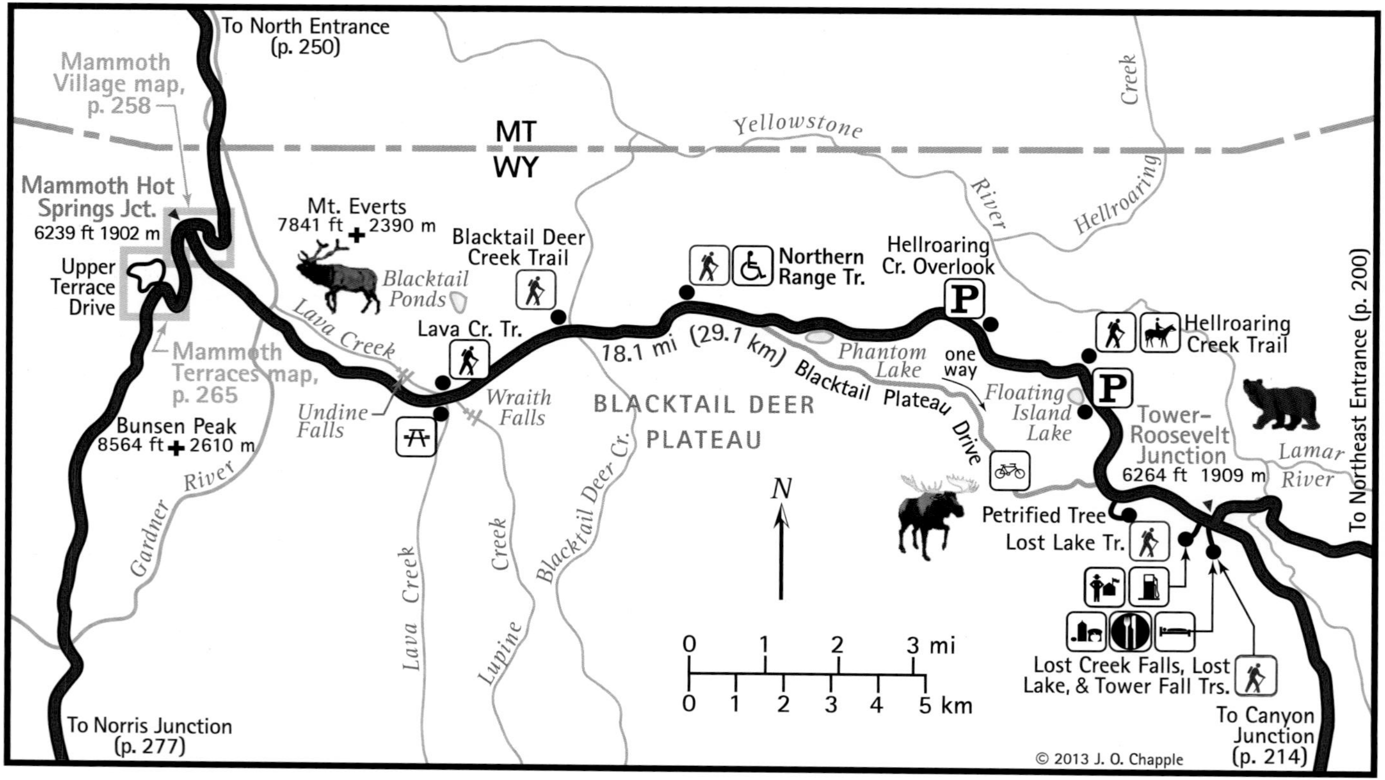

Mammoth Hot Springs Junction to Tower-Roosevelt Junction

From Mammoth Junction to Tower Junction

The road from Mammoth to Tower covers a distance of about 18 miles (29 km) and is kept open all year. It's the only four-season road in Yellowstone. As you pass this way, you'll encounter spectacular views of mountains near and far. You can stop to enjoy two pleasant waterfalls and the Forces of the Northern Range Trail or take a short side road to view the only petrified tree in the park reachable without a hard hike. Lava Creek has the only picnic area east of Mammoth Village on this stretch of road.

Road Log

0.0/18.1 Mammoth Hot Springs Junction. To the east is Tower-Roosevelt Junction. To the south are Mammoth Terraces and Norris Junction, to the north is the North Entrance at Gardiner, Montana. For facilities at Mammoth Village, see page 257.

0.1/18.0 **P** **(9)** Short road to the west for some residences owned by the federal government. It's okay to park along this road to visit Opal Terrace. The picnic tables and a large collapse feature are at the edge of the former U.S. Cavalry parade ground.

0.3/17.8 **P** Parking across the road from the **Yellowstone National Park Chapel** (described on page 259). Beyond the chapel, another street leads to residences and government buildings.

0.5/17.6 A runoff channel called Bluff Creek goes under the road from the terraces above.

1.1/17.0 At this point you're at the lowest elevation on the entire Grand Loop Road, 6,005 feet (1,830 m). Mount Everts is to the northeast.

1.7/16.4 Gardner River bridge, also called Sheepeater Canyon Bridge for the canyon from which the river emerges. When completed in 1939, this was the largest bridge in Wyoming, both in length (805 ft / 245 m) and height above the river (about 200 ft / 60 m high). Far below and to the northeast, Lava Creek and the Gardner River flow together.

You may be able to see the basalt columns that form some of the walls of the Sheepeater Canyon, but only in late afternoon light.

3.8/14.3 First view of Mammoth Hot Springs Terraces for those traveling west. Along the south edge of the road is a good example of a basalt flow with moderately developed columnar jointing (see "Lava Columns" on page 217). The cliffs above also look like columns.

A Quiet Geological Era Ends Violently

Sedimentation

Looking across the Gardner River at the cliff face of Mount Everts **[GEO.3]**, you can see sedimentary rocks whose ages span about the last 100 million years. The bulk of the rocks, from the level of the river to nearly the top of the cliff, were formed about 100 million years ago by the slow, gentle process of sediment deposition in fairly shallow seas, where the sandstones were probably ancient beaches. The shales were deposited when the water above them was quieter and deeper. As you drive along the base of the cliffs in the Gardner Canyon, you can look along the cliff face and distinguish the sandstones, because they form the cliffs' vertical portions. The shales (also called mudstones) erode more easily, forming the sloping parts.

These rocks formed toward the end of a long, quiet geological episode of slow sedimentation that lasted from about 515 million to about 80 million years ago.

Volcanism

At the crest of the cliff on the southern end of Mount Everts—best seen from east and south of Mammoth Hot Springs—is a thin layer of tephra that was deposited after being blown into the air 2.1 million years ago. This violent explosion was the Huckleberry Ridge Caldera event, the first of the three such major caldera-forming events. (There's more about Yellowstone volcanism in the Geological History chapter.)

A Sign of Violent Earth Movement

The photo (taken from a mile farther north) shows another sign of renewed geological activity on Mount Everts. In the left half you see where 100-million-year-old sediments are tilted down toward the north. These formerly flat-lying sediments were tilted, eroded to form a horizontal ground surface of exposed edges, and then covered with tephra. Geologists call this kind of intersection an angular unconformity. This shows the quiet period was ended by a regional tilting, followed by eruption of the Huckleberry Ridge Caldera.

The top of Mt. Everts shows an angular unconformity, formed where the uppermost horizontal volcanic deposits lie on top of tilted sedimentary layers.

4.0/14.1 P **Undine Falls** on Lava Creek. This triple waterfall has a total drop of over 100 feet (30 m). Geologist Arnold Hague named it in 1885. In classical mythology, undines were water spirits who could earn themselves a soul by marrying a mortal and bearing his child.

Like many falls in the park, Undine has an interesting geologic origin. About 700,000 years ago, the predecessor of Lava Creek was flowing through the valley to the east of the falls and gently eroding old shales that are about 100 million years old. A basalt lava flow then erupted and flowed down the valley, filling the low areas. Lava Creek is now flowing over the much harder basalt and has started to cut down through it.

At Undine Falls even the power of water cannot erode the lava very fast.

4.4/13.7 (5) Lava Creek picnic area, in a particularly delightful setting that used to hold a campground.

Lava Creek Trail can be accessed from the north side of the road by crossing the bridge over Lava Creek just east of the picnic area. The 4-mile-long (6.4 km) trail leads mostly downhill to end at Mammoth Hot Springs.

Lava Creek picnic area

5.0/13.1 **Trail to Wraith Falls** on Lupine Creek. If you're here in early to mid summer, take the time to traverse the half-mile (0.8 km) trail through the meadow to the falls, where you may see a profusion of wildflowers.

The falls itself drops over smooth rock about 90 feet (27 m), sometimes with only a trickle of water. One meaning

History of the Lava Creek Trail

From mile 1.7/16.4 to mile 4.4/13.7, the road follows Lava Creek. Across the creek to the north, you can catch glimpses of the old Bannock Indian Trail that became a road soon after mining began at Cooke City in the 1870s. The Bannock made an annual trip to hunt buffalo, traveling from their winter home in Idaho across what is now the northern part of Yellowstone to Wyoming east of park territory. They followed Lava Creek and continued eastward across Blacktail Deer Plateau.

When this became a miners' road, one freighter would handle a team of six to eight horses or mules unassisted. A snub block was usually dragged behind a rear wheel to keep the wagons from backing down inadvertently on the way up. On the steep descents, when the brakes could not hold back the wagons, they were either rough-locked by chaining or tying one or both of the rear wheels to keep them from turning, or else they were slowed by dragging a tree.

This part of the former Bannock trail is now the Lava Creek Trail.

of wraith, "a barely visible vaporous column," applies well to Wraith Falls.

6.2/11.9 **Blacktail Pond** (or Ponds) north of the road. In early summer, ducks and geese nest around the ponds (which at times of high water are one pond). If you walk in this vicinity, be careful of the boggy soil—locals call this area "shaky lakes"! The going may be difficult except late in the summer, when the area may be quite dry.

6.8/11.3 **Blacktail Deer Creek Trailhead** to the north. From here, you can hike to the Black Canyon of the Yellowstone River, which is about 4 miles (6.5 km) north, with a steep descent to reach the river.

If a less strenuous hike appeals to you, you might follow the trail for the first 3.5 miles (5.6 km), as far as **Hidden Falls** on Blacktail Deer Creek. The trail climbs to extended vistas in all directions and descends to the creek in the last half mile (0.8 km) to the place where the water falls over basalt columns. On a hot summer day, there's almost no shade until you reach the creek.

From the same trailhead, backcountry hikers join the Rescue Creek Trail toward Gardiner or skirt the north side of Blacktail Ponds to go west on the Lava Creek Trail.

Blacktail Deer Creek was called that by prospectors even before 1870. Blacktail is another name for mule deer, common in this part of the park year round.

Almost across the road from this trailhead, an unmaintained trail or old road goes south to a patrol cabin used by rangers. A restroom is provided.

8.0/10.1 The mountains visible to the west on clear days are part of the Gallatin Range, dominated by Electric Peak, the northernmost visible peak.

8.3/9.8 **Forces of the Northern Range Trail**. This pleasant easy walk of about one-half mile (0.8 km) passes attractive displays concerning ten aspects of nature in Yellowstone. This is a quiet place to stretch your legs or rest on the benches.

Across the road to the south is a service road with a wide parking area at its start. The outstandingly large glacial boulder on a short trail from the parking area has historically been called Frog

Rock for its crouching frog shape. If you get close you can imagine a frog's front leg and right eye and perhaps a tongue etched on the Boulder.

This service road is used by skiers in the winter to connect with Blacktail Plateau Drive about a mile to the east. Road planners throughout the park's history have always tried to keep the necessary reserves of road maintenance materials out of sight of the Grand Loop Road.

9.5/8.6 Beginning of **Blacktail Deer Plateau Drive**, a section of the former tourist road. This 7-mile (11 km) unpaved one-way road is closed at night, after storms, and all winter. The first road built through the area, it follows a tortuous route through the hillsides, climbing 500 feet (152 m) higher than the four-season main road.

If you take Blacktail Plateau Drive, you'll pass several fine stands of aspen trees and catch views of the surrounding mountains. In about 4.5 miles, the road descends steeply into a small canyon or gorge (The Cut). The nineteenth-century Bannock trail went through here, as did the 1870 Washburn-Langford exploration party. Devil's Cut was the name used by Superintendent Norris a few years later, shortened to The Cut by geologist Arnold Hague, who thought too many park features were named for the king of the underworld.

The hill immediately northeast of The Cut is Crescent Hill, where Truman Everts was found, lost and near death, after his 37-day ordeal in the wilderness. (See page 253 for the Everts story.)

Continuing on the Grand Loop Road

10.4/7.7 Phantom Lake is next to a low point on the road. The lake dries up by midsummer, which explains its name. Naturally, it has no fish.

11.7/6.4 Geode Creek crossing. A geode is a hollow, roughly spherical rock, with crystals lining its interior walls. There's no record of geodes being found right here.

All around you are stands of quaking aspen trees, notable for their white bark and their shivering leaves, which turn a brilliant yellow in the autumn.

13.0/5.1 Ⓟ **Hellroaring Creek overlook** turnout. A delightful 120-degree panoramic view of mountains, valleys, and streams is visible from here, as shown on the next two pages.

Fireweed changes to its fall colors under lodgepole snags.

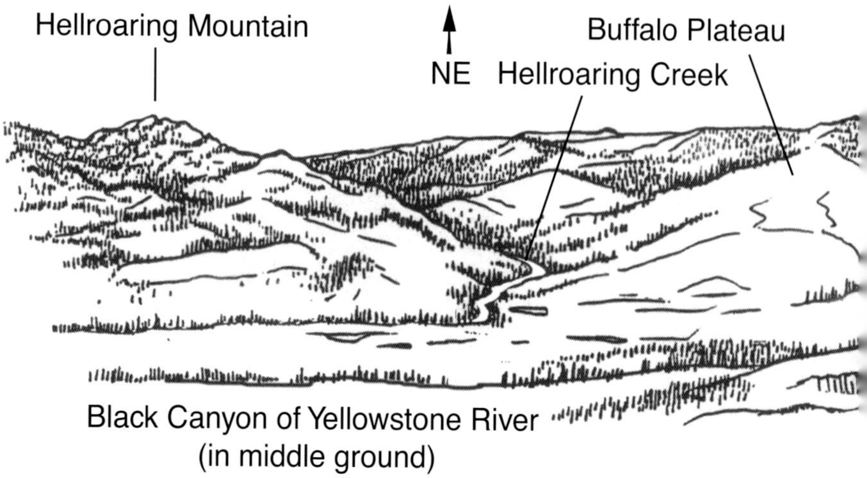

Hellroaring Creek Panorama

Left to right (north to northeast):

Hellroaring Mountain (8,359 ft / 2,548 m), whose conical peak is about 3.5 miles (5.6 km) to the north. The 1988 Hellroaring fire was started by an outfitter's camp stove igniting his tent. It burned thousands of acres of forest north and east of here, but of these, only spottily burned areas can be seen.

Hellroaring Creek flows south toward you between Hellroaring Mountain and Bull Mountain (far distance), turning west before joining the Yellowstone River. The creek got its name in 1867 when a prospector, who had gone ahead of his companions to hunt, reported: "It's a hell roarer."

Southeast of Hellroaring Mountain, notice the five or six **kettle ponds** ringed with deep green grass.

The **Black Canyon of the Yellowstone River** is so deep and narrow below here that you can only see the place where it must be.

14.5/3.6 Side road to **Hellroaring Creek Trailhead.** Horseback parties often head from here into the northernmost parts of the mountains in the Absaroka Primitive Area north of the park.

A short but strenuous hike goes to the Black Canyon. The trail descends 600 or 700 feet (about 200 m) in 1 mile (1.6 km) to a suspension bridge over the river. After crossing the bridge, you can follow the Yellowstone River Trail for a mile to Hellroaring Creek and then walk down the creek through sagebrush for about 1 more mile (1.6 km) to its confluence with the Yellowstone. According to Mark C. Marschall's *Yellowstone Trails,* the confluence is "a delightful spot" with "the cold clear rushing water of the creek, the deep surging river, a sandy beach and the sheer walls of the Black Canyon of the Yellowstone. Osprey nest in these cliffs and are frequently seen flying over the river looking for trout."

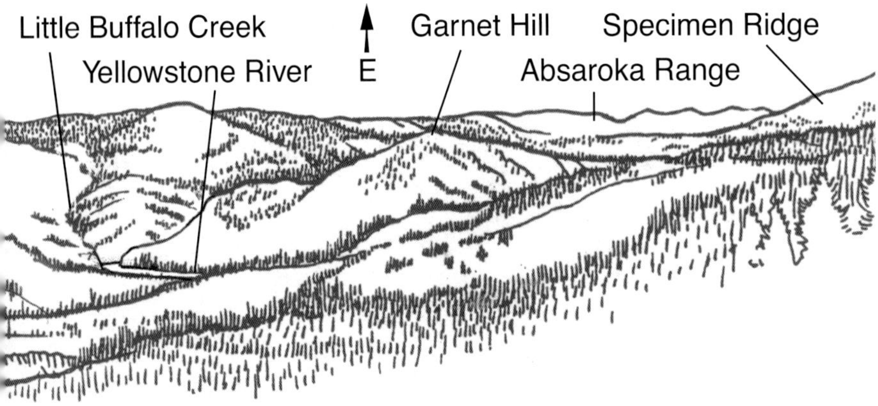

A vast expanse of treeless meadow rises gently to the north above the Yellowstone. It's part of the **Buffalo Plateau**, which stretches out of sight to the northeast.

Little Buffalo Creek flows out of the hills and into the Yellowstone River. When the light is right, you can see the Yellowstone River suspension bridge in this area.

Garnet Hill (7,060 ft / 2,152 m) is the nearby, partially forested low cone. The deep red silicate mineral called garnet has been found on Garnet Hill, but the examples found were not of gem quality.

The distant mountains to the right (east), nearly 30 miles (48 km) away, are part of the **Absaroka Range**.

Closer at the far right is **Specimen Ridge**, with alternating meadows and patches of trees.

15.0/3.1 **Floating Island Lake** earned its name many years ago when marshy rafts of vegetation and debris used to float on the lake. Neither beavers nor fish are found around here now, but you may see yellow-headed blackbirds, American coots (looking rather like dark gray ducks with white bill and red eyes), and other birds. In the drought years of the early twenty-first century, the lake has two or more grassy islands and has receded drastically from its shores, as you see from the "bathtub ring" at the far (west) side.

16.2/1.9 Elk Creek crossing. This immediate area was intensely burned in the 1988 Wolf Lake fire.

16.6/1.5 Eastern end of Blacktail Deer Plateau Drive (one way, do not enter here).

To the north, indicated by a Horse Crossing sign near the main road, is an area heavily used by riding parties from the Tower-Roosevelt corral. Down the hill is the historic site of Yancey's Hotel, where horseback and stagecoach parties from Roosevelt now come for cookouts.

16.7/1.4 Petrified Tree half-mile side road, not usable by large vehicles because it lacks turning space at the end.

It's sad to note that only one standing petrified tree remains of the many found on this hillside when the park was first explored. The surviving tree is protected by an iron cage, since souvenir hunters over the years have made off with all the others. Although the 1912 edition of the *Haynes Guide* refers to "two large stumps," editions from 1916 on include a picture of just one large standing stump. The remaining tree is (or was) a redwood, like those that grow today in California.

Lost Lake Trail goes south where the side road ends, following Yancey Creek for less than 1 mile (1.5 km) through waist-high wildflowers to quiet, lily-pad-covered Lost Lake. Near the lake, you may see moose or beaver, but reputedly no fish. Black bears are also seen frequently in this part of the park.

The trail continues another mile (1.6 km) to reach Roosevelt Lodge, passing the junction with the Lost Creek Falls Trail on the way. The last half mile (0.8 km) descends about 500 feet (150 m).

Curiously, **Lost Creek** does not flow out of Lost Lake, but originates near Prospect Peak in the Washburn Range and runs past the ranger station at Tower-Roosevelt Junction. Lost Lake's outlet stream is Yancey Creek.

About 1914 there were still two petrified trees.

16.9/1.2 "Winds of Change" interpretive sign explains the types of fires in the park in 1988.

17.9/0.2 Side road to **Tower Ranger Station**, where you can buy a fishing license or a backcountry use permit or ask questions about this part of the park.

The building nearest the main road,

now a private residence for park personnel, dates from 1907, when this was an outlying soldier station in a little-traveled part of the park.

18.0/0.1 Tower service station.

18.1/0.0 Tower-Roosevelt Junction. To the south on a short side road are Roosevelt Lodge and its cabins and a small general store (facilities described on page 215). East is the Northeast Entrance; south along the Grand Loop Road are Tower Fall, Dunraven Pass, and Canyon Junction; and west is Mammoth Hot Springs Junction.

NOTE: Construction on the Grand Loop Road between Tower-Roosevelt Junction and Chittenden Road may necessitate nighttime or total closure in 2013 and beyond. Check with Yellowstone authorities for details.

Geological Points of Interest in and near Yellowstone

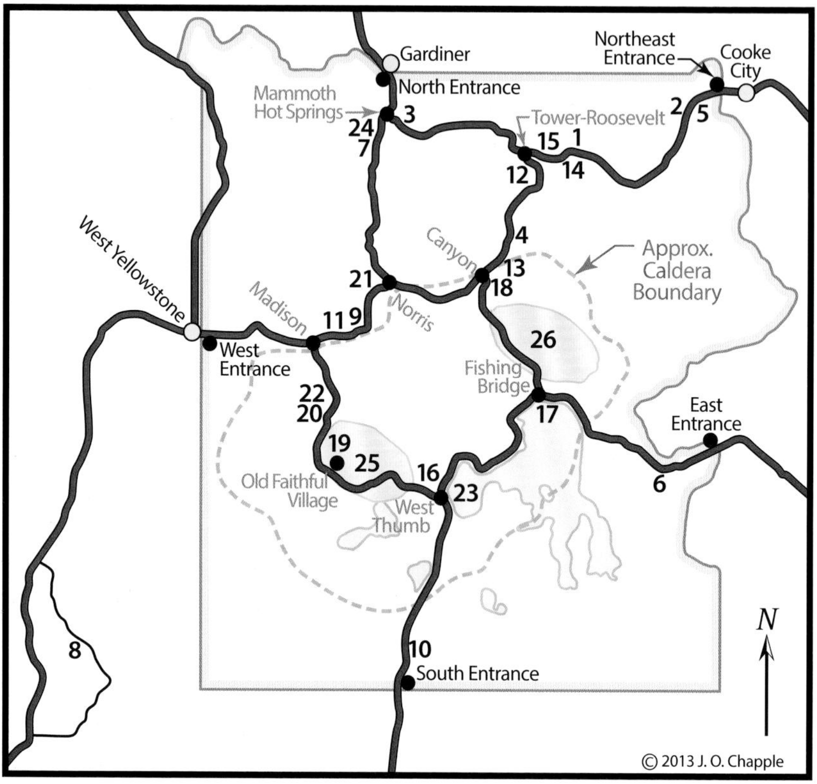

Page numbers after each geological point show where features are in the road logs.

1 Lamar Canyon, 209
2 Barronette Peak, 203
3 Mt. Everts, 294
4 Mt. Washburn, 221
5 Absaroka volcanics, 203
6 Sylvan Pass, 163
7 Golden Gate, 275
8 Mesa Falls, 115
9 Lava Creek tuff, 288
10 Lewis Canyon, 129
11 Caldera edge, 289
12 Basalt lava, 217
13 Glacial Boulder, 185
14 Glacial boulders (Lamar), 211
15 Kettle ponds, 211
16 Duck Lake, 112
17 Indian Pond, 167
18 Falls of the Yellowstone, 181
19 Old Faithful Geyser, 78
20 Grand Prismatic Spring, 64
21 Emerald Spring, 233
22 Fountain Paint Pot, 56
23 Thumb Paint Pots, 141
24 Mammoth Terraces, 267
25 Mallard Lake Dome, 68
26 Sour Creek Dome, 177

Natural and Human History

Geological History

THE STORIES IN YELLOWSTONE'S ROCKS

The greater Yellowstone area is a showcase for some of the world's best examples of spectacular geological features. Geology is more than just identifying rocks; it's about the evolution and structure of the earth beneath us. In this chapter we explain the 3-billion-year development of the region and speculate about future events. We also discuss some geological features you may find in the park. Numerals like [**GEO.1**] help you locate such places on the map.

Early geological history

The North American continent has existed for approximately 4.25 billion years, although it was not always so large. The oldest rocks in the vicinity of Yellowstone Park are about 3.5 billion years old and contain minerals that are about 4 billion years old. These rocks are accessible at the roadside on the Northeast Entrance Road in Lamar Canyon [**GEO.1**] and where U.S. Highway 212 crosses the Beartooth Pass outside the Northeast Entrance.

These very old rocks are *granites* and *gneisses*. They are coarse-grained rocks often containing mineral crystals one-half inch (1 cm) in diameter. They formed at depths in the earth of 5 to 10 miles (8–16 km) and at very high temperatures. Granites form by crystallizing, that is, solidifying, from molten rock. They appear as a uniform mixture of light and dark minerals. Gneisses form when existing rock is pressed and pulled by movements within the earth and is heated up but not melted. The rock is changed, or *metamorphosed*, and a new rock is formed. It contains different minerals and acquires an appearance of contorted light and dark bands of minerals. Since their formation deep below a high mountain range, the granites and gneisses have been uplifted to the surface and then eroded down. A new mountain range was formed about 2.5 billion years ago, then also uplifted to the surface and eroded down.

Not much is known about the Yellowstone region from the time of those ancient mountains until about 500 million years ago, a time gap of 2 billion years.

Along the Gallatin River Canyon north of the park and at a few places within the park, we can see sedimentary rock layers lying flat in a few cliff faces. Most *sedimentary rocks* are formed by transport of sediments, that is, rock or mineral particles, to low areas or shallow seas, where they are deposited. They are transported by wind, streams, ocean currents, or glaciers; then they become cemented together into solid rocks, compressed by thick layers of more sediment deposited on top.

***On the lower third of Barronette Peak's cliffs are alternating white and brown layers of sedimentary rocks that are about 350 million years old. The chocolate-colored rocks above these are part of the much younger Absaroka Range volcanics* [GEO.2].**

The flat-lying sedimentary layers in the park were deposited either in shallow seas or on land, depending upon sea level at the time. Two places to see cliffs of such rocks are at Barronette Peak near the Northeast Entrance **[GEO.2]** and at Mount Everts near Mammoth **[GEO.3]**. The sedimentary rocks in these places were deposited on top of the much older granites and gneisses between 515 and 80 million years ago. They are evidence that the ancient mountains described above had already been eroded away to form a level plain at or near sea level.

More Recent History

After an incredibly long time gap, 2 billion years, Yellowstone's turbulent years began. As many people now know, the continents move around on Earth's surface, fortunately at only a few inches (cm) per year, by a process that geoscientists call *plate tectonics*. Yellowstone Park is not immune to this process and, in fact, has been singled out for some special events.

The *plates* of plate tectonics are huge slabs that occupy the uppermost 60 miles (100 km) of the solid earth. They are obliged to slide around due to the uneven cooling and heating of Earth's interior. When Earth first formed 4.6 billion years ago, it was hot and almost entirely molten. It has been cooling down ever since, but not evenly, since radioactive elements deep in the earth keep adding some heat. The way the cooling takes place is illustrated in Figure 5. Parts of the interior rise, being hotter and less dense, while cooler portions sink. The plates move around and collide with one another. This is what caused the compression that formed the Rocky Mountains.

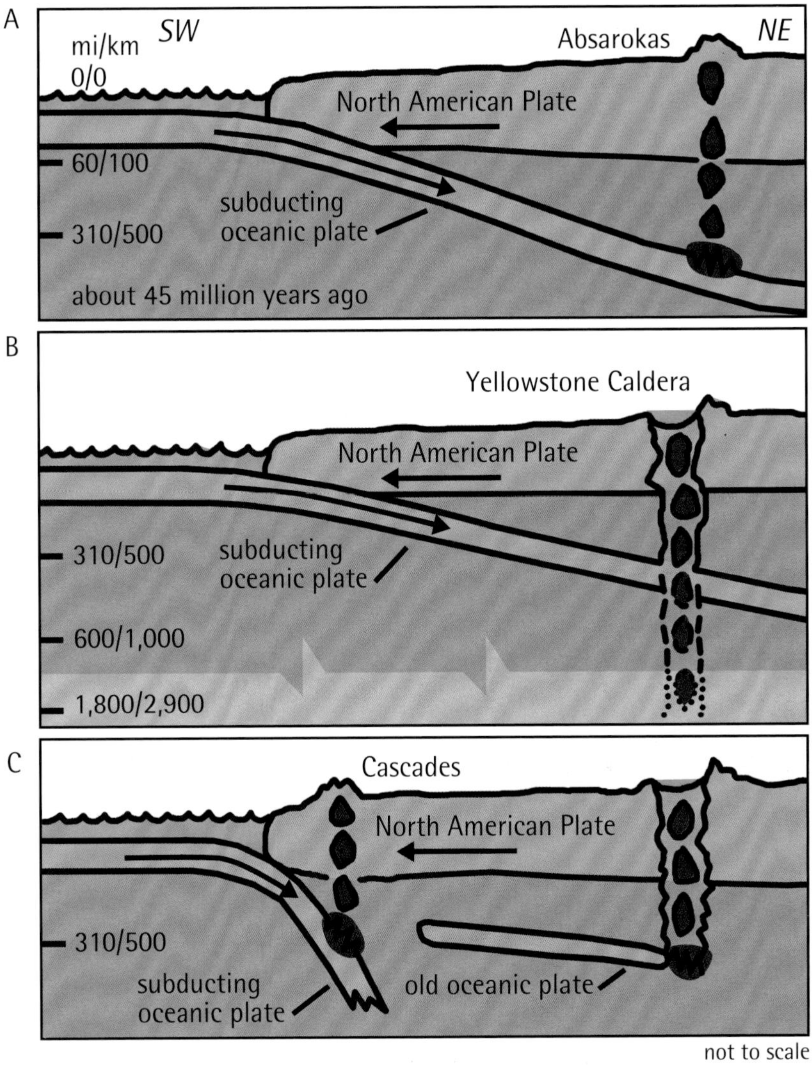

Figure 5. What's under Yellowstone: Moving plates, mantle plumes, and the Yellowstone hot spot.

The cross sections in Figure 5 are approximately southwest to northeast, from the coast of northern California to just east of Yellowstone Park, and reflect current geoscientists' thinking about what is now under the park. **A** shows the formation of the Absaroka Range about 45 million years ago. The oceanic plate is subducting in a northeastern direction under the overriding North American Plate. It has reached deep enough for melting to start and to form the *magmas* that rose and created the Absaroka volcanoes 53 to 44 million years ago. Most subducting plates dive into the earth at a very steep angle. It is one of the curious things about western geology that this oceanic plate went down at a very shallow, almost flat, angle. **B** illustrates the theory that the *Yellowstone hot spot* is caused by a mantle plume. Mantle plumes are thought to be formed very deep, perhaps 1,800 miles (2,900 km), under Earth's surface, in locations where there is hot rock. Because hot rock is more buoyant than cold rock, it rises like a column to the surface. A very distorted column containing a small percentage of melted rock extends down 310 miles (500 km), for which there is scientific evidence. This would be a very shallow plume. The dashed lines at the right in part **B** are drawn to 600 miles (1,000 km) deep, where there may be some evidence of melted rock, and the dotted lines are shown to 1,800 miles (2,900 km), where there is no evidence of a plume so far. Whether there is a shallow or a deep plume, it would have to punch through the descending subduction plate. The distorted column may be evidence of this collision. **C** illustrates another way that the Yellowstone hot spot could form. The shallowly dipping plate has broken off from a now steeply descending plate to the southwest—and is foundering in a not quite horizontal position to the northeast. Magma is being generated at the older plate's leading eastern edge, which is just under Yellowstone, while the Cascade Range is forming to the west. There is evidence for the positions of the subducting plates. Research is continuing.

—J.S.

The Rocky Mountains

Starting around 110 million years ago and lasting until about 40 million years ago, today's Rocky Mountains were formed. First, thick layers of sedimentary rock were pushed up and over one another, moving from west to east. Next, great blocks of granite and gneiss with sedimentary rock on top were also squeezed and pushed up. Most of this movement and mountain building took place outside the park. Almost entirely north and east of the park, the Beartooth Mountains arose about 60 million years ago, and the Absaroka volcanics (locations shown on the map on page 159) poured forth massive amounts of *lava* about 45 million years ago.

The Absarokas

During plate collisions, one plate sinks below another deeply into the earth (called subduction). This drags seafloor sediments and other near-surface rocks down to great depths, where they reach high temperatures and pressures. There they melt, forming magma. Since magma is less dense than the solid rock, it rises toward the surface. When magma reaches the surface, it forms a chain of volcanoes, such as the Absarokas. The Absaroka Range, which extends from Montana north of the park for approximately 100 miles (160 km) to the southeast into Wyoming, was formed about 45 million years ago when an oceanic plate from the west dove under the North American Plate. Most of the rocks in these mountains are either lava flows or the debris that resulted when the rocks were rapidly eroded to form mudslides. The outstanding example of these processes in the park is Mount Washburn **[GEO.4]**. The Northeast Entrance Road along Soda Butte Creek **[GEO.5]** and the East Entrance Road near Sylvan Pass **[GEO.6]** both pass through fine examples of these volcanic mountains.

The Yellowstone Caldera

The Yellowstone Caldera is the most recent of a long line of calderas that started forming around 14 million years ago far to the southwest in what is now the southwest corner of Idaho. A series of ever younger calderas are located to the northeast along the edges of the Snake River Plain.

A *caldera* is the collapse of a large land area after the emptying of a magma chamber in a massive volcanic explosion. Figure 6 shows the Yellowstone Caldera in particular, but similar events occur in the formation of all calderas. (A caldera is not exactly the same as a volcanic crater, which is a depression in the ground, usually circular in form, from which magma erupts.) The conditions for caldera formation require the concentration of heat and magma in a relatively small area near the surface.

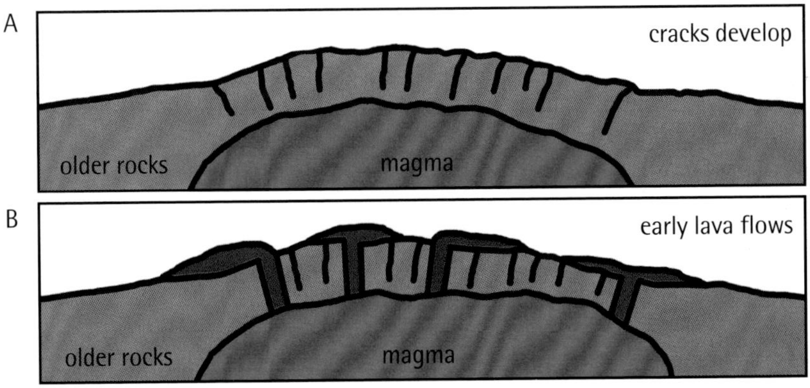

Figure 6. Cross sections showing evolution of the Yellowstone Caldera event cycle.

A shows rising magma (in red) forcing the overlying rocks to arch up. Cracks form in the arched rocks (in brown) and extend downward as the arching increases. In **B** cracks reach down to the magma chamber, and some molten rock (darker red) flows out on the ground surface as lava. This reduces the pressure, allowing steam to form from the water dissolved in the magma. **C** (next page) shows that after some time, accumulating steam and other gases build up tremendous forces and cause a gigantic explosion of tephra (pink), composed of magma, gases, and some older rock. The tephra is sent far and wide and high into the air. A space containing only gases remains

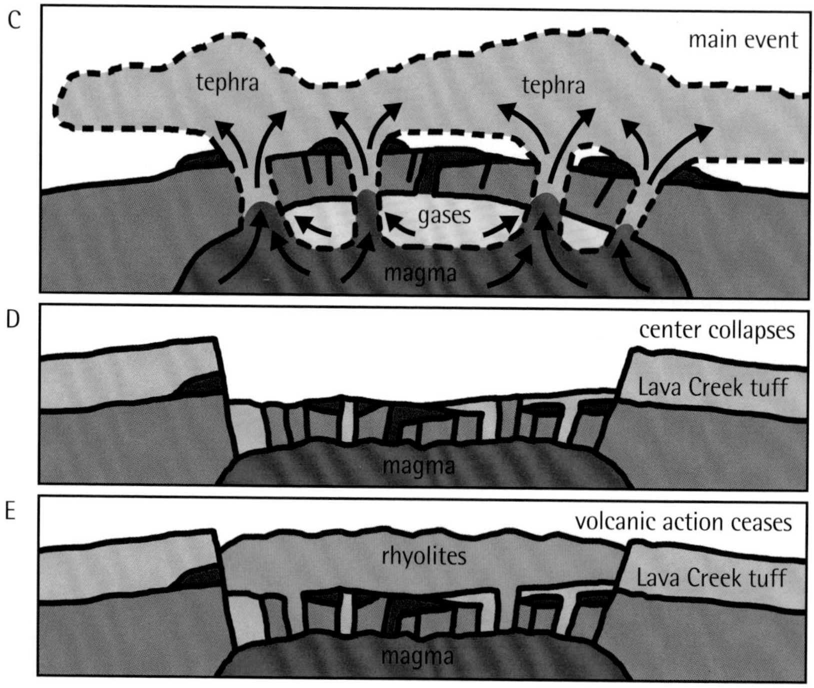

above the magma, leaving the rocks above unsupported. In **D** the *tephra* has fallen out of the air, forming both thick layers of Lava Creek tuff (pink) away from the explosive eruption and discontinuous layers and blocks of rock within the affected area. The overlying rocks have collapsed into the empty space, creating a large caldera many miles across. **E** shows how, after the main caldera-forming event, magma continues to rise through cracks to reach the caldera floor and make Yellowstone's high plateau of *rhyolite* lavas (orange).

—B.J.G./J.S.

In the Yellowstone area there have been three caldera events. Each time, a large magma chamber was formed, uplifting the land above. Cracks in the overlying rocks reached down to the magma, and some initial lava flowed out over the land (Figure 6B). The magma had a great deal of water dissolved in it, so after some time, as the cracks released some of the pressure, this water formed steam bubbles. Water as steam occupies a much larger volume than when it is dissolved in magma—about a thousand times as much—so suddenly the magma needed a much larger space. It is the same sort of violent process as when the water below a geyser overheats, the geyser erupts, and steam and water pour out. All this steam pressure in the magma caused a huge explosive eruption of *tephra*, rock fragments and molten globs that rushed out of the chamber and partially emptied it (Figure 6C). The unsupported roof of the magma chamber collapsed to create a caldera (Figure 6D). After the collapse, magma flowed out onto the caldera, partly filling it with rhyolite lava (Figure 6E).

Huckleberry Ridge Caldera Event. This first caldera formed about 2.1 million years ago. The ejected rock and steam spread up and out as a billowing incandescent cloud, probably traveling at 50 to 100 miles (80–160 km) per hour and being pushed by the material behind it. As it traveled and expanded, the cloud cooled and deposited tephra over the northern Rockies and the Great Plains. As far as Iowa, for example, the tephra was still as much as 3 inches (8 cm) thick. The total volume of erupted material was about 600 cubic miles (2500 cu km)! The explosion probably lasted for a period of days or weeks. An outcrop of this tephra can be seen in the park at Golden Gate **[GEO.7]** south of Mammoth Hot Springs, where it's called the Huckleberry Ridge *tuff.* In places, it's 550 feet (170 m) thick.

Outcrop of Huckleberry Ridge tuff along the road at Golden Gate [**GEO.7**].

Henrys Fork Caldera Event. The center of this caldera is just west of Yellowstone Park near Island Park, Idaho. This second major explosion happened 1.3 million years ago; the debris was again mostly tephra. This Mesa Falls tuff can be seen at Mesa Falls **[GEO.8]** west of the park boundary. The eruption was smaller than the previous one.

Yellowstone Caldera Event. The third and latest explosion was 639,000 years ago and the best understood. The earlier ones were similar but have been partly obscured by the later events. This one formed the present Yellowstone Caldera. Rocks and tephra blown out this time are called the Lava Creek tuff. You can see this tuff on the west side of the road just north of Gibbon Falls **[GEO.9]**, at Tuff Cliff near Madison Junction, and at the top of the Lewis River Canyon cliffs on the South Entrance Road **[GEO.10]**. This latest eruption, with tephra accumulations occasionally exceeding 1000 feet (300 m) in thickness, produced a volume of 240 cubic miles (1000 cu km) of tephra, which makes it intermediate in scale between the two previous caldera events.

In comparison with the impressive eruption at Mount St. Helens, Washington, in May 1980, the Yellowstone Caldera (or Lava Creek) eruption blew out about one thousand times more rock. The Mount St. Helens output of volcanic debris was about 0.25 cubic miles (1 cu km).

The elliptical caldera resulting from this last eruption is approximately 30 by 45 miles (48 by 72 km). A good place to see the northern edge of the caldera is along the east-west stretch of road that leads from Madison Junction to Gibbon Falls.

You may have noted that the intervals between the three caldera-forming events were 800,000 and 661,000 years, and the last caldera explosion was 639,000 years ago. We'll discuss below whether we are due for another soon.

Post-Caldera Lavas. After each of the cataclysmic caldera-forming eruptions, magma spilled out onto the caldera floor at intervals for several hundred thousand years as rhyolite flows (see "Rhyolite and the Plateau of Fire," page 49), filling much of the caldera. This explains why there is no deep hole or crater now visible in or near the Yellowstone Caldera.

It is difficult to get a sense of the Yellowstone Caldera when you're in the park. In fact, the existence of a caldera of this size was not proposed until the 1960s. After many years of geologic mapping, geoscientists realized the following: first, vast areas outside the oval-shaped area consisted of just one volcanic unit, the Lava Creek tuff, and it formed at just one time; second, most of the lavas within the oval area were younger than the Lava Creek tuff; and third, tephra seen in other states (as far away as Iowa) came from the Yellowstone area and has proven to be the same as the Lava Creek tuff.

A good place to get a feel for the enormous caldera event is along the Grand Loop Road in the vicinity of Gibbon Falls, south of Norris Junction. The 5 miles of highway between Madison Junction and Gibbon Falls parallel the caldera edge **[GEO.11]**. On the north side of the road, you can see a cliff whose upper part is Lava Creek tuff. This tuff was left when the caldera, which was on the south side here, slid down along a *fault* during its collapse (see Figure 6D). Over the past 639,000 years, the cliff has been eroded back a bit, but it still represents that rim fault.

If you now drive past Gibbon Falls and go north toward Norris, you have moved away from the caldera and its rim. Road cuts both north and south of the falls allow you access to very tall, nearly vertical walls of Lava Creek tuff, which is cream colored with hints of pink.

Basaltic Volcanism. A different type of volcanic rock encountered in the park is basalt. *Basalt* contains less *silica* than rhyolite and is black due to its high iron

A 1.3-million-year-old basalt lava flow near Calcite Springs extends across the middle of the photo. Vertical lines in the flow are shrinkage cracks outlining columns formed as the solidified basalt cooled [**GEO.12**].

content. It is much less viscous and flows out as sheets that sometimes spread for miles. Good examples can be seen near Tower Fall [**GEO.12**]. (There's a description of columnar jointing in basalt on page 217.) Basalt flows occurred before, during, and after all of the caldera-forming events, usually on the edges of the calderas themselves.

Most Recent History

More geological processes continue to leave their traces on Yellowstone.

Glaciers reshape the landscape

About 2 million years ago, at about the same time that the first caldera event in the Yellowstone region occurred, a worldwide climate change brought colder temperatures and, in some places, glaciers. Vast ice sheets covered much of Canada and spread south to the Ohio River. Elsewhere, glaciers also formed at high elevations, such as on the broad plateaus of the park, which average about 8,000 feet (2,400 m) above sea level.

We know that worldwide there were about 20 glaciations, or ice ages. Each glaciation lasted about 50,000 to 100,000 years, with shorter warm periods in between. The glaciers were at their worldwide maximum about 20,000 years ago, and have been retreating ever since, giving us the warm interglacial period we now enjoy.

Glaciers had several major effects on Yellowstone, and the last two glaciations left evidence all around. A small ice cap formed over Yellowstone, and almost the entire park was covered with ice. Often the ice was about one-half mile (800 m) thick, so that animals and plants were essentially nonexistent here. Although glaciers are solid ice, they flow slowly toward lower ground at rates of a few yards (meters) per year. The glaciers were major agents that modified the landscape drastically by transporting some rocks, digging and scraping away at others, and interacting with the park's thermal areas. Some examples of this activity follow.

The glaciers' ability to transport rocks is demonstrated in the area of the Yellowstone Canyon **[GEO.13]** and in the Lamar River Valley **[GEO.14]**. In both places, you see boulders as large as 10 feet (3 m) across that are clearly out of place. We know where they originated, because they match the 3.5- and 2.7-billion-year-old gneisses that form the Beartooths. These boulders are called *glacial erratics* (see picture), because they are many miles from the nearest outcrops of similar rocks.

Glacial erratics: The boulders, some as big as bison, in this Lamar Valley photo were carried by the glacier from the Beartooth Mountains and left behind when the glacier melted **[GEO.14]**.

The glaciers carried huge amounts of rock and soil along and dumped it at their downhill edges where they melted. These deposits (or *moraines*) can be seen in Paradise Valley along the Yellowstone River north of the park. Often large blocks of ice are left stranded in the moraines. When the ice melts, holes appear that sometimes fill with water. Look for these *kettle ponds* or kettle holes (pictured) mostly on the north side of the Northeast Entrance Road **[GEO.15]**. Streams of meltwater from the glaciers also carried away much of the debris and then deposited it farther downstream as outwash sediments.

This kettle pond was formed when a melting glacier left a large piece of ice along with mixed sand, gravel, and boulders. When that ice also melted, it left the hole that is now filled with water **[GEO.15]**.

The hot rocks underlying parts of Yellowstone had some unusual interactions with the glaciers. The glaciers dammed many streams by simply filling the stream valley with ice. Sometimes the lake that was formed behind the ice covered one of the many hot areas. Since water boils at a higher temperature when under pressure, the increased pressure from the lake caused the hot rocks below to *superheat* the surrounding groundwater. When the glaciers melted, the ice dam sometimes collapsed suddenly, letting the lake drain rapidly. The superheated hot water at depth, suddenly relieved of the high pressure, boiled in a flash and created a steam explosion that blew out much of the rock around it. Examples of this type of *explosion crater*, now filled with water, are Duck Lake near West Thumb Junction **[GEO.16]** and Indian Pond near Fishing Bridge Junction **[GEO.17]**.

Carving the Canyon

The magnificent Grand Canyon of the Yellowstone, with its steeply sloping sides, colorful rocks, and spectacular waterfalls, was carved after the latest caldera-forming explosion 639,000 years ago.

Before the caldera existed, the Yellowstone River had been eroding the Absaroka volcanic rocks north of the present canyon area. Then came the Yellowstone Caldera eruption. A lot of Lava Creek tuff blanketed the area, the caldera fell in, and rhyolites flowed out, nearly filling the caldera with lava. All the while the Yellowstone River continued to carve its steep-sided *V-shaped valley* through volcanic debris, the caldera rim, and the lava flows.

At the same time this was going on, glaciers were coming and going over Yellowstone. Knowing that during the last glaciation the whole area was buried in ice except for the tops of some of the highest peaks, we would expect that the canyon of the Yellowstone would have been filled with ice and would now be U-shaped with almost vertical walls and a flat, rounded bottom. But it is not.

A possible explanation consists of two parts. First, there has been geyser activity in this area for at least 480,000 years, and it existed during the glaciation. Either the valley was not completely filled with ice, or the glacial ice was not moving. Second, to the north a glacier flowing along the Lamar Valley blocked the Yellowstone River Valley, creating a dam and a lake that filled part of the Yellowstone Canyon. The canyon was then partly filled by lake sediments—until the Lamar Valley glacier retreated. The ice dam failed suddenly at one point during the retreat, causing a wall of water about 150 to 200 feet high (45 to 60 m) to flow north and west, rolling and carrying boulders along until they were dropped northwest of Gardiner, about 20 miles (32 km) downstream. There is evidence that this type of catastrophic flood occurred more than once.

After each flood event, the Yellowstone River redug its channel in the canyon and continued eroding to its present depth. Consequently, the Grand Canyon of the Yellowstone was cut mainly by the river, and all in about 150,000 years, a very short time geologically speaking.

The fast erosion was helped by local deep fractures that let water seep into the earth and be warmed by the still-hot rocks. The hot water rose toward the surface, and in addition to helping form the lake, reacted with some layers of the overlying rocks, breaking down and changing their minerals, weakening them. This process resulted in layers of weaker and stronger rocks and is still going on today. The river exploited this and cut down through the softer rocks very rapidly. The result is two splendid waterfalls, the Upper and Lower Falls of the Yellowstone **[GEO.18]**.

There are two falls because two layers of quite resistant, nearly half-million-year-old rhyolite protect weakened, easily eroded rocks below them. The Upper Falls has cut back through a layer of rhyolite and also a thermally weakened layer below it. The Lower Falls formed where a different rhyolite flow protects another weakened layer. Both falls will continue to erode the layers over the coming millennia.

Geysers, hot springs, fumaroles, and mud pots

Most visitors come to Yellowstone to see *geysers*. There are more geysers in Yellowstone than anywhere else in the world. What visitors also find, however, is a vast collection of places that spurt, hiss, boil, and bubble, sometimes with a nasty smell, often displaying a rainbow of colors, but always interesting.

What makes the different *hydrothermal* features do what they do? Basically, the great volume of groundwater is heated by very hot rocks quite near the surface at Yellowstone.

There is a very large amount of old groundwater, at least 60 but perhaps greater than 10,000 years old, just above the magma below Yellowstone. The source of this water may have been the glaciers that covered the area or rain and snow in the surrounding mountains, 12 to 45 miles (20 to 70 km) distant. Present-day rain and snowmelt seep down and mix with this old water, become warmed to the boiling point, boil into steam, expand greatly, and find a way to escape upward. Most of the features occur where faults are common, making it easy for the heated groundwater and steam to return to the surface.

Geysers such as Old Faithful **[GEO.19]** are one special kind of steam and hot water emitter. This kind needs a very steady supply of hot groundwater and special plumbing that includes a narrow *fissure* that goes deep into the ground and that has even narrower parts along the way. (For a more specific explanation of geysers, see "How Does a Geyser Work?" on page 88.)

Changes in the shape of a geyser's plumbing, its water supply, or water temperature can change the timing, height of eruption, or volume of water. The changes are normally due to blockage by precipitation of solids onto the fissure walls, minor earthquakes, or eruptions that are especially violent. Most geysers in Yellowstone erupt repetitively, but the intervals are not necessarily regular. Old Faithful Geyser is faithful in its timing, because the flow rate and temperature of the very hot water have been very constant.

The 1959 Hebgen Lake earthquake just outside the northwest corner of the park considerably altered conditions in Yellowstone. Some geysers changed their cycles, some stopped erupting, and dormant ones resumed eruptions. Smaller earthquakes affect Yellowstone's hydrothermal features every year.

In other places, where there is also a large supply of very hot groundwater near the surface, it rises to make a hot pool. These deceptively inviting pools have lovely colors, but their water is at or near the boiling point. Examples are Grand Prismatic Spring **[GEO.20]** in Midway Geyser Basin and Emerald Spring **[GEO. 21]** in Norris Geyser Basin.

How do the other hydrothermal features work? Steam vents, or *fumaroles*, are places where there's a steady flow of steam coming from a fissure in the ground. Fumarole activity is closely related to current precipitation and occurs where the old hot groundwater is not very near the surface. In these features a downward seepage of rainwater reaches hot rocks, the water boils, and the steam is vented through the fissure.

Fumarole activity sometimes leads to development of another feature where little water is present. The steam reacts chemically with the rocks and becomes very acidic, turning them into clays. When enough clays have been made, they tend to form a bowl-shaped soupy mass, a *mud pot*. The steam coming up through the clay will now make mud bubbles, sometimes more than 6 inches (15 cm) across. These are the delightful "blurping" bubbles that can be seen at several park localities, including Fountain Paint Pot **[GEO.22]** and sometimes at Thumb Paint Pots at West Thumb Geyser Basin **[GEO.23]**.

Mud pot near Imperial Geyser (Lower Geyser Basin).

Most of the rocks underlying the hot water and steam features in the park are silica-rich rhyolites. A major exception to this is the collection of terraced structures that have built up at Mammoth Hot Springs **[GEO.24]**. Before reaching the surface, hot water rising there encounters *limestone* rather than rhyolite. Limestone, composed of *calcium carbonate*, is sedimentary rock that was deposited in shallow seas and is mostly made up of the shells of marine organisms.

Groundwater arriving under the Mammoth area dissolves some of the limestone and brings it up to the surface, giving us another sort of *hot springs*. Here the water is under less pressure. It can no longer hold all the carbon dioxide in solution, and some of the gas bubbles escape, causing some of the dissolved calcium to deposit out, forming the terraces. This rock is a white or gray form of limestone called *travertine*.

The hot waters on Mammoth's terraces contain algae and bacteria that are orange, green, yellow, or brown and coat the travertine with color. This ever-changing palette is dependent upon the quantity and temperature of water at a particular spot. For more about the travertine terraces at Mammoth, see pages 267–68 and 270–71.

Two Unresolved Geological Questions

Among the many questions still to be answered about what exactly has happened and is happening even today in Yellowstone, two stand out.

I. What is the cause of the Yellowstone hot spot?

Geoscientists are studying two main possibilities for explaining how and why the Yellowstone hot spot formed and then migrated across the Snake River Plain to Yellowstone. Evidence for both theories is mainly based on interpretation of the chemical composition of the volcanic rocks at Yellowstone and on interpretation of magnetic data, gravity data, and earthquake waves that travel through the rocks below Yellowstone and the Snake River Plain.

Mantle Plumes. In this older theory, plumes are thought to come from hot areas at the top of Earth's metallic core, 1,800 miles (2,900 km) below the surface. The heated rocks are less dense than their neighbors and so rise as a column to the surface of the earth. Some of the rock melts on its way up. The idea is that as the North American plate traveled southwest over a stationary mantle plume, it left a trail of calderas that form the Snake River Plain. A possible Yellowstone hot spot plume is shown in Figure 5B (page 305). The figure shows the plume today at its current location under Yellowstone. About 17 million years ago, when present-day north-central Nevada was above the plume, large amounts of volcanics spilled out on the ground. Then, starting about 14 million years ago, the first of the calderas formed when southwest Idaho was above the plume. A deep mantle plume that stayed in one place while the North American Plate moved over it explains two things: how the trail of calderas formed, and how chemical elements from deep inside the earth reached the surface. How the plume punched its way through the subducting plate is not understood.

There are several difficulties with this idea. Analysis of earthquake waves identifies a plume of hot and partially melted rock below Yellowstone, but only in the uppermost 300 miles (500 km), not the full 1,800 miles (2,900 km) to Earth's core. The chemistry of the volcanics indicates that they come from very deep, although some geoscientists disagree about this. Another difficulty is that there is another track of calderas, called the Newberry volcanic chain, starting at the same place and time as the Yellowstone track but progressing northwesterly into Oregon. This direction contradicts the northeasterly trend of the Yellowstone track. The North American Plate cannot have been traveling in two very different directions at the same time.

A Fragmenting Subducting Plate. A newer theory is that the subducting oceanic plate tore apart and became fragmented. The edge of a sliver of the fragmented plate is illustrated in Figure 5C. In this theory, the subducting oceanic plate, instead of diving steeply deep within the earth, descended at a very shallow angle. As it did so it broke into several pieces. Magma formed at the leading edge of the largest sliver, creating the hot spot. This orphaned segment of the oceanic plate continued to move northeast under the overriding southeastward-moving North American Plate. In this theory, the "plume" is not formed in a stationary hot area deep in the mantle but is formed at a shallow depth by the movement of the plates themselves. This idea comes from interpretation and modeling of new seismic and other geophysical data recently gathered by the USArray, a transportable array of thousands of geophysical instruments comprising a dense grid covering the continental United States. Geoscientists are actively developing new interpretations with lots of variations. The new interpretations can explain the Yellowstone hot spot, the Newberry volcanic chain, and other features of the intermountain west such as the still-active basalt flows on the Snake River Plain more than 60 miles (100 km) southwest of Yellowstone. This theory does not explain how magma is generated at the front and along the sides of the fragments nor why the magma contains certain elements.

Both the mantle plume and the fragmenting plate theories have ardent adherents. This is an exciting time for geoscientists as they acquire new data, build new models, and confer with each other in attempts to explain the Yellowstone hot spot.

II. Are we due for another caldera eruption?

We saw above that the last caldera-forming eruption was 639,000 years ago, while the preceding two major eruptions were at intervals of 800,000 and 661,000 years. Time intervals between such major eruptions are not regular, but we are approaching the time when another massive explosion could occur. How likely is that—and should we be concerned? What evidence is there of the likelihood of a new caldera catastrophe?

The earth at Yellowstone is restless. Usually a thousand and frequently several thousand small earthquakes occur every year. Most of these are far too small to be felt but are recorded by the Yellowstone Volcano Observatory's (YVO) network of 26 seismic stations within or near the park. Earthquake swarms, several hundred earthquakes that occur within several days or weeks, are common. There have been at least 73 such swarms between 1983 and 2012. Most of these have occurred outside the caldera on the northwestern part of the park, some on the inside of the caldera on its northwest side, and a few inside the caldera on the southeast side under Yellowstone Lake.

Areas within the park also rise and fall, and the YVO has special recording stations for slow ground movements (changes in location, elevation, and tilt), geyser temperature, gas discharge, and water levels. In addition, historical data tells us that the Mallard Lake *dome* **[GEO.25]** just east of Old Faithful and the Sour Creek dome **[GEO.26]** east of Hayden Valley (see map on page 302) both rise (inflate) and then fall (deflate) in irregular cycles. In fact, the Sour Creek dome area rose a total of 36 inches (91 cm) between 1923 and 1984. It then fell somewhat for a decade but recently has been rising again; the Mallard Lake dome has moved similarly.

What does this heavy breathing and rumbling by the earth mean about possible eruptions? While the inflation of the domes could be due to rising magma, it's hard to explain the deflation without an eruption of lava, and there hasn't been such an eruption in the last 72,000 years.

Geoscientists have not detected magma close to the surface. Most think the inflation and deflation of the domes, as well as some of the mini-earthquakes, are due to movement of gases and hot water at depth, not to movement of magma. Some of the small earthquakes that are outside the caldera occur near the area of the large 1959 earthquake that formed Quake Lake (see page 36).

For these reasons geoscientists think that an explosive event that spews large amounts of tephra and forms another caldera is *not* likely in the near future.

While a large event involving hundreds of square miles is not of immediate concern, a commonly recurring acute hazard is a hydrothermal explosion such as the one that formed West Thumb Bay (see pages 138–39). Hydrothermal explosions are caused by hot subsurface waters that flash to steam, breaking the overlying rocks that confine them and ejecting the debris to form a crater. At least 26 such explosions have been documented in the more than 140-year historic record of Yellowstone National Park. Some have been preceded by no recognized warning signs; thus, one purpose of the monitoring program at Yellowstone is to identify warning signs of such explosions. Progress is being made.

—B.J.G./J.S.

Chronology

YELLOWSTONE SINCE 1800

This chronology juxtaposes events relating to Yellowstone Park and this region with relevant events from world and United States history. "A changing America has always had an impact upon Yellowstone. . . ." wrote historian Richard A. Bartlett. World events have likewise had their impact on the park.

EXPLORATION OF YELLOWSTONE

YEAR	IN THE YELLOWSTONE REGION	IN THE U.S. OR THE WORLD
1803	Lewis and Clark recruit the Corps of Discovery to explore Louisiana to the Pacific, missing the Yellowstone area by about 50 miles.	Pres. Thomas Jefferson buys Louisiana from France.
1806–8	John Colter leaves Lewis and Clark and explores Yellowstone area.	John Jacob Astor incorporates the American Fur Company (1808).
1826–40	Fur trappers and adventurers visit and tell about the wonders of the area, but are usually not believed.	About 60 million bison (buffalo) roam the Great Plains; Native Americans depend on them.

Jim Bridger (1804–1881), capable guide, fur trapper, and storyteller, explored the area as early as the 1820s.

YEAR	IN THE YELLOWSTONE REGION	IN THE U.S. OR THE WORLD
1832		Hot Springs in Arkansas is the first area set aside for national conservation (today a national park).

YEAR	IN THE YELLOWSTONE REGION	IN THE U.S. OR THE WORLD
1860	Capt. William F. Raynolds unsuccessfully tries to penetrate the mountains at the southeast corner of the future Yellowstone Park.	Abraham Lincoln is elected the 16th U.S. president.
1862		Homestead Act grants free land in the west to all settlers.
1863	Nez Perces are forced to sign a treaty saying they will vacate their land (then located in Idaho Territory).	President Lincoln signs a bill giving rights of way to the Central Pacific and Union Pacific Railroads and guaranteeing them money for laying track. Idaho Territory is organized.
1864	Gold is found at Last Chance Gulch (later Helena, MT).	Yosemite Valley in California becomes the nation's first scenic reservation, managed by the state. Montana Territory is formed out of Idaho Territory.
1865	Jesuit Father Kuppens visits Yellowstone area in the company of Blackfeet Indians.	Lewis Carroll publishes *Alice's Adventures in Wonderland.* Lincoln is assassinated.
1868		Wyoming Territory is organized.
1869	Charles W. Cook, David E. Folsom, and William Peterson successfully undertake and later write about their trip through the Yellowstone area.	Union Pacific and Central Pacific Railroads join at Promontory Point, Utah.
1870	Gold is found on Clarks Fork near present Northeast Entrance to Yellowstone. Gen. Henry D. Washburn leads a quasi-official exploration of the Yellowstone area, accompanied by other prominent westerners, such as Nathaniel P. Langford, Cornelius Hedges, and Truman Everts, and a military escort under Lt. Gustavus Doane.	Northern Pacific Railway begins laying track west from Minnesota.

Gen. Henry Dana Washburn (1832–1871) died before he could publish his expedition diary.

YEAR	IN THE YELLOWSTONE REGION	IN THE U.S. OR THE WORLD
1871	Dr. Ferdinand V. Hayden leads the first of three congressionally funded Yellowstone expeditions. A second summer expedition, led by army captains John W. Barlow and David P. Heap, also enters the area.	Chicago Fire on October 8th destroys 3.5 sq mi of the city, most 1870 census records, and Thomas J. Hine's negatives from the Barlow-Heap Yellowstone expedition.
1872	**Yellowstone National Park** is set aside by Congress. Nathaniel P. ("National Park") Langford is the unsalaried first superintendent. Second Hayden Survey traverses the new park.	Pres. Ulysses S. Grant signs the bill authorizing the Yellowstone reservation on March 1st.

YELLOWSTONE NATIONAL PARK HISTORY

The Act Setting Aside the Yellowstone Reservation

The U.S. Congress preserved this land for us and for all subsequent generations in language that reserved and withdrew the land "from settlement, occupancy, or sale" and assured that it be "dedicated and set apart as a public park or pleasuring-ground for the benefit and enjoyment of the people."

	IN THE YELLOWSTONE REGION	IN THE U.S. OR THE WORLD
1873	Capt. William A. Jones leads a U.S. Army Corps of Engineers party through the new Yellowstone.	Northern Pacific Railway's financial agent, Jay Cooke & Co., fails on September 18th; stock exchange collapses on Black Friday, the next day.
1876		Gen. George A. Custer, all his men, and many of the opposing Native American Indians are killed in the Battle of the Little Bighorn in south central Montana Territory.
1877	Pursued by General Howard's troops, Nez Perces cross the park, kill two, and frighten and wound other tourists.	

YEAR	IN THE YELLOWSTONE REGION	IN THE U.S. OR THE WORLD
1878	Supt. Philetus W. Norris hastily builds crude roads in anticipation of "Indian trouble." Members of the Bannock tribe cross the park but are killed and captured by Colonel Miles near Clarks Fork River, east of the park. Third Hayden Survey makes observations for the government.	John Wesley Powell writes *Report on the Lands of the Arid Region*, warning of the paucity of rainfall in the west.
1882	The Crow sell to the U.S. the small strip of their Montana reservation that lay in park territory. Crow, Bannock, and Shoshoni people are banned by treaty from entering Yellowstone.	German engineer Gottlieb Daimler invents a gasoline-powered internal combustion engine.
1883	Northern Pacific branch line reaches Cinnabar, MT; visitor numbers leap dramatically. The first large hotel takes in guests at Mammoth Hot Springs. Lt. Dan C. Kingman of the Corps of Engineers begins planning a loop system of roads. Hunting and fishing (except with hook and line) are disallowed.	Krakatoa volcano in Indonesia erupts, killing 36,000 people. Dust eruption creates brilliant sunsets around the world and lowers global temperatures for months afterward, but its caldera is only a fraction of the size of Yellowstone's.

Stagecoach tours started from the National Hotel at Mammoth Hot Springs (1915 photo, Haynes Studio).

YEAR	IN THE YELLOWSTONE REGION	IN THE U.S. OR THE WORLD
1884	Wyoming territorial law becomes the law of Yellowstone to help curb vandalism, poaching, and lawlessness. Frank J. Haynes opens a photo studio at Mammoth.	George Eastman devises a way to coat photographic paper in long rolls, an invention soon to replace the wet glass plate process used since the 1850s.
1886	The U.S. Cavalry arrives in the park in August to bring order.	
1886–87	First winter tour of the park, during which Haynes takes the first winter photographs of Yellowstone.	The Rockies and Great Plains experience one of the most severe winters in history, one that kills some 60 percent of range cattle.
1888		Dry film and the inexpensive Kodak camera ("You Press the Button, We Do the Rest") make amateur photography possible and then increasingly popular.
1889	Trout are first stocked in Yellowstone's so-called barren waters.	Montana becomes the 41st U.S. state.
1890	First Haynes guidebook appears: *Practical Guide to Yellowstone National Park*, by A. B. Guptill (Haynes uses name of his accountant).	The last major confrontation between Native Americans and the U.S. Army takes place at Wounded Knee, SD. Yosemite National Park is created by act of Congress. Idaho and Wyoming become U.S. states numbers 43 and 44.
1891	Hotels are completed at Lake, Fountain, and Canyon by the Yellowstone Park Association.	The National Forest Reserves Act authorizes the president to set aside forest lands; thus begins the national forest system.
1892	Initial Fort Yellowstone construction is completed. Roads are now complete in what later becomes the southern loop of the Grand Loop Road.	First U.S. motorcar is produced by Charles and Franklin Duryea in Springfield, MA.

YEAR	IN THE YELLOWSTONE REGION	IN THE U.S. OR THE WORLD
1894	The Lacey Act protects birds and animals and punishes crimes in the park; John W. Meldrum is appointed first U. S. Commissioner of Yellowstone to enforce the act and stays more than 40 years.	Strikes paralyze western railroads and other businesses.
1895	First attempt to save the buffalo from extinction by captive feeding and breeding at Alum Creek in Hayden Valley.	
1896		25 motorcars, the first for public sale, are produced by Duryea Motor Wagon Co.
1898	F. J. Haynes and an associate form the Monida & Yellowstone Stage Company to bring tourists through the West Entrance.	
1899	Haynes begins producing his postcards of the park.	
1900	Yellowstone has a few dozen bison (buffalo) left.	Bison are almost extinct in the U.S.
1901	Burlington Route (Chicago, Burlington & Quincy Railroad) reaches Cody, WY.	
1902	Henry G. Merry drives his Winton motorcar through the North Entrance, but cars remain illegal in the park.	
1903	Road from Cody to East Entrance and on to Fishing Bridge is completed. Pres. Theodore Roosevelt tours the park and dedicates an arch at the North Entrance. Later that year, Northern Pacific tracks reach Gardiner, MT.	Ford Motor Co. is incorporated and sells hundreds of Model As.
1904	Old Faithful Inn opens.	
1905	Dunraven Pass road is completed, linking the entire Grand Loop Road system.	National forests are placed under the jurisdiction of the Department of Agriculture, with Gifford Pinchot, a conservationist and multiple-use advocate, as chief.

YEAR	IN THE YELLOWSTONE REGION	IN THE U.S. OR THE WORLD
1907	The Union Pacific's Oregon Short Line reaches West Yellowstone.	
1911	Canyon Hotel is greatly enlarged and improved and opened to guests.	
1915	Motorcars are first admitted to Yellowstone on August 1st.	Ford produces more than 500,000 Model Ts in any color you want, as long as it's black.
1916	Yellowstone concessions are consolidated into three companies, for transportation, hotels, and permanent camps.	The National Park Service is created to manage 14 national parks and 21 national monuments; Stephen Mather becomes first director the next year.
1917	All passenger vehicles used in the park are now motorized.	U.S. enters World War I.

Stephen Mather (1867–1930), first director of the National Park Service, poses with an elk calf.

1918	U.S. Cavalry troops leave the park, except the few who stay on as rangers.	World War I ends; nearly 10 million people killed.
1920	First chief ranger, James McBride, is appointed.	
1921	Improved approach road to the South Entrance over Togwotee Pass is dedicated.	
1923	The Howard Eaton Trail, a 157-mile loop bridle trail, is dedicated.	Grasshoppers consume nearly everything green growing in Montana.

YEAR	IN THE YELLOWSTONE REGION	IN THE U.S. OR THE WORLD
1927	The Milwaukee Road carries rail passengers to Gallatin Gateway (near Bozeman, MT).	
1928	Several concession companies are bought out by Harry W. Childs and merged to become the long-lived Yellowstone Park Co. under William M. Nichols 8 years later.	
1929	Grand Teton National Park is created after much controversy over the possible expansion of Yellowstone Park.	U.S. stock market crashes, beginning a worldwide depression.
1930	First museums in Yellowstone are opened at Norris, Old Faithful, and Madison.	
1931	Fishing Bridge Museum opens.	
1933	The Yellowstone Library and Museum Association is formed (later the Yellowstone Association).	
1933–42	Civilian Conservation Corps serves Yellowstone.	The national C.C.C. builds bridges, fights fires, and helps pull the country out of depression.
1936	The Beartooth Highway to the Northeast Entrance from Red Lodge, MT, is opened.	

Automobiles could cross the Beartooth Plateau on the new highway—but with difficulty (1937 photo by F. W. Byerly).

YEAR	IN THE YELLOWSTONE REGION	IN THE U.S. OR THE WORLD
1937	Mammoth Hot Springs Hotel and cottages replace older hotel at the same site.	
1941		U.S. is attacked by Japan at Pearl Harbor and enters World War II.

YEAR	IN THE YELLOWSTONE REGION	IN THE U.S. OR THE WORLD
1942	Number of park visitors drops to below 200,000 from 582,000 in 1941. Many facilities are closed.	U.S. begins gas rationing and a 35 mph speed limit.
1945		World War II ends.
1948	Annual Yellowstone Park visitation tops 1 million for the first time.	
1956	National Park Service initiates Mission '66 to improve facilities in Yellowstone and other parks.	Congress authorizes construction of the Interstate Highway system, indirectly subsidizing road users and penalizing passenger rail service.
1957	A new Canyon Lodge and some cottages in Canyon Village are opened. Hatcheries close; fish stocking in park lakes and streams ceases.	
1959–70	Frank and John Craighead conduct first intensive research on grizzly bears in and around the park.	
1959	Earthquake on August 17th near Hebgen Lake (outside West Entrance) causes 28 deaths and great damage to property. Many Yellowstone hydrothermal features register changes as a result.	
1961	End of all rail service to park.	
1963	Snowmobiles travel to Old Faithful, beginning winter use of the park.	Leopold Report on wildlife management begins debate leading to major policy changes in all national parks.
1964		Congress passes Wilderness Act.
1965	Annual park visitation tops 2 million.	
1966	Goldfield Corporation purchases the Yellowstone Park Co.—soon purchased by General Host (1967).	Endangered Species Preservation Act results in listing of 78 rare and endangered species.
1970	New bear management policy put in place in the park.	
1972	Yellowstone celebrates 100 years.	

Black bears begging near the roads were a common sight before the 1970s.

YEAR	IN THE YELLOWSTONE REGION	IN THE U.S. OR THE WORLD
1973	In response to the Endangered Species Act, grizzly bears are declared threatened and (in 1975) gray wolves endangered (a more severe classification).	Arab oil embargo raises gas prices and encourages more economical car design.
1976	Yellowstone is designated a U.S. Biosphere Reserve in the country's bicentennial year.	
1978	World Heritage Site designation given to Yellowstone.	
1979	Congress purchases all park concession buildings from General Host for $19.9 million. TWA Services (later TW Recreational Services) takes over hotel and food concessions.	Oil crisis occurs again due to OPEC price increases and low U.S. imports.
1980		Mount St. Helens, WA, erupts on May 18th; the volume of volcanic debris expelled is only 1/1000th of that from the Yellowstone Caldera.
1983	Borah Peak earthquake in Idaho affects geysers, slowing Old Faithful's average interval.	
1988	Forest fires rage through Yellowstone with a destructive severity seen only once in centuries.	

The 1988 fires burned more than one-third of Yellowstone's territory.

YEAR	IN THE YELLOWSTONE REGION	IN THE U.S. OR THE WORLD
1992	Annual park visitation tops 3 million.	
1995	First wolves are introduced into Yellowstone from Canada.	World Heritage Committee adds Yellowstone to its World Heritage in Danger list.

A wolf being released in Yellowstone.

YEAR	IN THE YELLOWSTONE REGION	IN THE U.S. OR THE WORLD
1996	U.S. government stops the Canadian Noranda Minerals company from mining near Yellowstone's northeast corner. Amfac Parks and Resorts takes over as hotel, restaurant, and activities concessionaire.	Handheld digital cameras gain in popularity but may never replace film cameras entirely.
2001		September 11 terrorist attacks on New York and Washington drastically alter U.S. and worldwide transportation security procedures.
2002	Amfac changes its name to Xanterra Parks & Resorts.	
2003	Delaware North Parks Services replaces Hamilton Stores as the park's general store concessionaire.	

Dates in this chronology were mostly culled from U.S. history books and from both *The People's Chronology*, edited by James Trager, and the *New York Public Library Book of Chronologies*. For Yellowstone historical information, the author is particularly indebted to *Yellowstone, A Wilderness Besieged* by Richard A. Bartlett, Aubrey L. Haines's *The Yellowstone Story*, and the 1949 *Haynes Guide*.

Living Things

A YELLOWSTONE SAMPLER

No one thought in 1872 that such a relatively small tract of land in the vast western territories would actually become a preserve for bears, wolves, bison, and thousands of other common living things. But during the next century, these animals disappeared from most of the country, and Yellowstone became an island of wilderness within a sea of human settlement.

According to modern ecologists, the Yellowstone island is not large enough to adequately protect the unique resources found here. Several Yellowstone animals and birds have been listed as threatened or endangered under the 1973 Endangered Species Act. As of 2012, the Canada lynx remained on the list and Yellowstone grizzly bears were restored to the list in recognition of the diminishing supply of whitebark pine nuts essential to their diet. Court decisions removed gray wolves from the list in Montana, Idaho, and, most recently, Wyoming, though the latter is being contested. Removing federal protection allows hunting of wolves in Yellowstone's surrounding areas.

In this chapter, after pointing out some small living things that occur throughout the park (along with a couple of not-so-small rare snakes), we introduce you to some of the more common plants and animals living here, grouping them into three quite different *ecosystems*, or communities of organisms that function as a unit of nature.

Ecosystems are defined by the geology and soil types, the elevation, the latitude, and the amount of precipitation. The elevation in Yellowstone ranges from about 5,300 feet (1,615 m) to over 11,000 feet (3,350 m). For every 1,000-foot (300 m) increase in elevation, average daily temperatures are 3.5°F (about 2°C) lower, spring arrives about ten days later, and autumn about ten days earlier. The latitude here is about that of Bangor, Maine—between 44 and 45 degrees north. Precipitation varies greatly, and the snowpack at 9,000 feet (2,750 m) remains almost two months longer than at 7,000 feet (2,130 m). More rain falls on western mountainsides than in sheltered valleys east of the mountains.

Many of the plants and animals mentioned here occur in two or more of the ecosystems. Read about fish at the end of the chapter.

THE SMALLEST LIFE FORMS

Microorganisms

Microorganisms are living things that are ever-present yet individually invisible. Some are *extremophiles*, existing in extreme environments and often very colorful. Scientists are finding that microorganisms provide clues about life that may have existed earlier on Earth and about the possibility of life on other planets. The colorful filaments and microbial mats fascinate us for their beauty. Watch for them around many hot springs.

Lichens

As you follow trails throughout the park, you may notice crusty growth on a large boulder or an old tree trunk. This is probably a lichen, classified in the kingdom fungus but requiring algae to produce its food. An alga is an ancient form of life that can convert light to energy via photosynthesis, while a fungus obtains nourishment by breaking down organic matter (such as algae). The thousands of different species of lichen may be orange, red, yellow, green, gray, brown, or black. They can utilize water from fog and dew, and, along with the action of water and wind, they serve as one of the most important factors in turning rocks into soil. Lichens do not grow in the geyser basins—they cannot abide the sulfur dioxide.

Some forms of lichen commonly seen in Yellowstone are **old man's beard** (*Usnea longissima*), which hangs from tree branches in a dark green mass and can be a good source of vitamin C, and **wolf lichen** (*Letharia vulpina*), a bright yellow-green type found on sunny tree trunks and branches. In Douglas fir forests, such as near the Grand Canyon of the Yellowstone, you may see dark-brown **horsehair lichen** (*Bryoria* sp.) hanging from branches and looking like coarse, twisted hair.

Mosses and mushrooms

It takes an expert to differentiate some types of lichen from the mosses. Common sorts of **moss** form green mounds or mats and grow in moist places everywhere, and some lichens may look similar to them. Both mosses and lichens grow on other plants but derive their nutrients from air, water, and dust particles (that is, they are epiphytic, not parasitic).

In moist places throughout the park, you may see fungi, especially **mushrooms** of various shapes, colors, and sizes. Admire but do not pick them unless you're an expert. It's not against regulations to pick edible plants for immediate consumption, but at least six Yellowstone mushrooms are poisonous.

Insects, amphibians, and reptiles

Let's not talk about the biting horseflies and mosquitoes that torture hikers in early summer, nor about the moths that fly into the flame of your camp lantern, but only mention a few insects and larger creatures that are fun to see.

Those beautiful blue gossamer-winged insects hovering about the streams are **dragonflies** and their smaller relatives **damselflies**, both of the order *Odonata*, meaning toothed. Some dragonflies are also called darners for their resemblance to long, thin darning needles. They hold their two pairs of wings horizontally, while damselflies hold their wings above the body. They can eat as many as three hundred mosquitoes and other small insects a day. Look for reddish-gold dragonflies in drier parts of the park.

The **water strider** (*Gerris remigis*) is also called the Jesus bug for its ability to walk on water. Its extremely long back legs enable steering, allowing the bug to spread its body weight, while the middle pair of legs provides oar-like power.

Living in hot-spring waters is the **ephydrid fly** (*Ephydra bruesi*), whose larvae live on microorganisms. The adult flies you'll see swarming in shallow hot water may not eat at all.

Among the many types of butterflies, some conspicuous ones are the small blues like the **spring azure** (*Celastrina argiolus*), various shades of yellow ones called sulfurs (genus *Colias*), and the large yellow and black swallowtails of the family *Papilionidae*.

In August of dry years you may be surprised at the hordes of jumping short-horned **grasshoppers** (family *Acrididae* or *Locustidae*) in every field you pass. In a glacier north of Cooke City just outside the Northeast Entrance a great many grasshoppers have been preserved for some three hundred years.

Not a lot of **frogs** and **toads** live in Yellowstone, and those that live here seem to be diminishing in number. Most common is the 2- to 3-inch (5–7.5 cm) **Columbia spotted frog** (*Rana luteiventris*). These tiny animals are extremely sensitive to air and water pollution, and it has been discovered that they're falling prey to a parasite.

Small **garter snakes** (*Thamnophis elegans* or *sirtalis*) are fairly common but harmless. Along trails in the lower altitude river valleys, you have a slight chance of seeing a nonvenomous **bull snake** (*Pituophis* genera), which may be up to 7 feet (2 m) long, or a venomous **rattlesnake** (*Crotalus viridis viridis*)—up to 4 feet (1.2 m) long.

Three Yellowstone Ecosystems

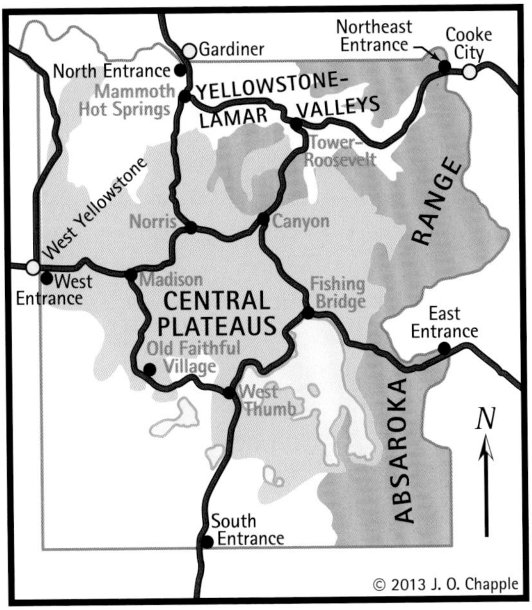

The map shows the extent of

- the forested community of the central plateaus
- the Yellowstone, Lamar, and Gardner River Valleys, and
- the Absaroka Range ecosystems.

Adapted with permission from Yellowstone Vegetation: Consequences of Environment and History in a Natural Setting *(1990), by Don G. Despain.*

I. THE FORESTED COMMUNITY OF THE CENTRAL PLATEAUS

You're likely to spend the majority of your Yellowstone visit in the central plateaus region, where most of the roads, the geyser basins, the Yellowstone Canyon, and the western and northern shores of Yellowstone Lake are found.

The undulating terrain, much of it within the Yellowstone Caldera, consists of rhyolitic lava and tephra, which weathers to a coarse, sandy soil, poor in nutrients and in ability to hold water. The altitude in the central plateaus varies from about 6,600 to 8,000 feet (2,000–2,440 m). Precipitation ranges from 20 to 40 inches (50–100 cm) per year.

This area includes excellent places to see water-loving birds and large animals—the Hayden and Pelican Valleys and along the shores of Yellowstone Lake. Here the soil is better but drainage is poor, creating marshy areas where trees don't do well. Grasses and sedges thrive here and create a nourishing habitat for wildlife.

Trees and shrubs of the forests and lakeshores

What you'll see most of in the central plateaus are trees, mile upon mile of **lodgepole pines** (*Pinus contorta*) with trunks close together, tall and straight, their needles growing only near the tops where they can reach sunlight. These trees got their name by serving as framework for Native American Indian dwellings.

Lodgepole needles always grow in twos and are stiff and twisted. The reddish-brown cones have short scales and a slender prickle. Some lodgepole cones (serotinous cones) can open and release seeds only in the intense heat of a fire.

Grouse whortleberry

Under stands of lodgepole you may find **grouse whortleberry** (*Vaccinium scoparium*) plants with tiny, fine leaves and white or pink hanging bells for flowers. The berries are a staple of the diet of bears, birds, and small mammals.

There are only eight species of evergreens and three of deciduous trees in the park. This is due to high altitude and poor soil, but also to the relatively short time that trees have had to become established since the end of the last ice age—about 10,000 years.

You'll see **Engelmann spruce** (*Picea engelmannii*) and **subalpine fir** (*Abies lasiocarpa*) along the drive from West Thumb Junction to Fishing Bridge Junction. These species would eventually dominate Yellowstone's forests if it weren't for the lodgepoles' superb adaptability to fire. Check the cones and needles to tell these spruce and fir trees apart. Spruce cones hang down from the branches. Their needles have sharp points but are relatively soft to the touch, occur singly on the branch, and are square in cross-section. To remember that, notice that the words spruce, sharp, soft, single, and square all start with *s*. If you crush spruce needles, they smell of camphor. Subalpine fir cones, on the other hand, sit upright on the branches, and the needles are flat and flexible.

Huckleberry

In late summer you are welcome to eat the edible berries on shrubs along the trails. Way out in front for flavor is the **huckleberry** (*Vaccinium membranaceum*) on its short bush.

Red raspberries (*Rubus idaeus*) can be found in some moist environments, as can **wild strawberries** (*Fragaria virginiana*) and **thimbleberries** (*Rubus parviflorus*), pictured on page 15.

Forest flowers

Here is a guide to some of the central plateaus' common wildflowers, arranged by color. Remember, it's against regulations to pick flowers.

Fireweed

PINK/RED/LAVENDER

Fireweed (*Epilobium angustifolium*) grows on its 4- or 5-foot (1.2–1.5 m) stem quickly after burns.

Indian paintbrush

The aptly named **paintbrush** or **Indian paintbrush** (genus *Castilleja*) is Wyoming's state flower. Its color is in the bracts, or specialized leaves from which the flowers arise, which may be red, white, orange, yellow, or pink. The roots of the paintbrush penetrate the roots of nearby plants and steal food from them parasitically.

Sticky geranium (*Geranium viscosissimum*) is common in damp meadows. It's a pink or rose-colored five-petaled flower with large, five- to seven-lobed leaves.

The **Everts thistle** (*Cirsium scariosum*) commemorates Truman Everts, the man who survived—in part by eating its roots—for 37 days when lost in Yellowstone in 1870. Peeled stems and roots are both edible.

Everts' thistle

Shooting star (*Dodecatheon pauciflorum*), like the houseplant cyclamen, has its petals flexed backwards and its dark, pollen-producing stamens projecting forward.

Shooting star

YELLOW

Yellow monkeyflower (*Mimulus guttatus*) thrives in the steamy atmosphere of hot spring basins, but the heat restricts it to 2 to 3 inches (5–7 cm) high there.

Monkeyflower

Isa Lake on the Continental Divide west of West Thumb has a splendid covering of **yellow** or **Rocky Mountain pond lilies** (*Nuphar polysepalum*), as do several ponds around Norris Junction. Native American Indians roasted the large seeds and ate them like popcorn, and the rootstocks are food for muskrats. Pond lilies are pictured on pages 43 and 108.

Yellow composite flowers are many and hard to distinguish. Two common ones that have distinctive leaves are **heartleaf arnica** (*Arnica cordifolia*) and **arrowleaf balsamroot** (*Balsamorhiza sagittata*).

Heartleaf arnica (left) & ***arrowleaf balsamroot*** (right)

Blue/Purple

Lupine (genus *Lupinus*) has long spikes of pealike flowers and many leaflets radiating out like fingers. It grows in moist soils, developing alkaloids that are poisonous to livestock late in the season.

Lupine with mountain dandelions

Harebell (*Campanula rotundifolia*), called Scotch bluebell in Scotland, has hanging bells almost an inch (2 cm) long.

Harebell

The official flower of Yellowstone is the **Western** or **Rocky Mountain fringed gentian** (*Gentianopsis detonsa*). It is often found near hot springs, especially in August.

Fringed gentian

Birds

More than three hundred different bird species have been sighted in Yellowstone. Here we name some birds with personality that are common to the central plateaus, first birds of the forest and then those of the lakeshore. Some of these species are also seen in the river valley and mountain pass ecosystems.

In the forests and along the rivers

You're in for a treat if you find an **American dipper** (*Cinclus mexicanus*—formerly called water ouzel) feeding on insects in cold mountain streams. Author Owen Wister observed in 1887 that "the spectacle of a little gray bird, like a fat catbird, skimming along the river like a bullet and suddenly dropping below the surface

Gray jay (left) *& Clark's nutcracker* (right)

where it was shallow, and walking along the bottom with its tail sticking out in the air, filled me with such elation that I forgot the geysers and watched him." This year-round resident sometimes sings like a canary.

In the case of the **gray jay** (*Perisoreus canadensis*) and the **Clark's nutcracker** (*Nucifraga columbiana*), it's the birds that are in for a treat. Whenever you sit down for a picnic, your meal will be of interest to one of these camp robbers.

The **mountain chickadee** (*Parus gambeli*) is heard more often than seen. It's a tiny, roly-poly, light-gray bird with a black head and white line over the eye. Its most common song goes *fee-bee-bee*, with the first note higher than the others; sometimes it will vary this and surprise you. The **black-capped chickadee** (*Parus atricapillus*) is also found here.

The male **mountain bluebird** (*Sialia currucoidus)* flashes by you wearing the most intense shade of sky blue imaginable, while his mate makes do with a bit of blue on her otherwise brown body. Bluebirds, a little smaller than robins, build their nests in snags.

A colony of **cliff swallows** (*Hirundo pyrrhonota*) once made their distinctive jug-shaped mud-and-stick nests under the eaves of the former Old Faithful Visitor Center. This small, square-tailed, buff-rumped swallow also nests on the back side of Soda Butte on the Northeast Entrance Road. Swallows live on insects they catch on the wing.

Common ravens (*Corvus corax*), purplish black, large relatives of the very common crow, show up in droves to feast on carrion. They can be over 2 feet (60 cm) long and have a large beak and an annoying croak. They're very intelligent birds that can mimic human speech and learn amazingly complex behaviors, such as opening the zippers on a backpack.

In and around the rivers and small lakes are many types of duck, perhaps the easiest to spot being the male **mallard** (*Anas platyrhynchos*), with his iridescent green head, white neck-ring, yellow beak, and blue on the wing feathers, while the female is mottled brown with orange beak and feet and some blue feathers.

Great blue heron & Sandhill crane

The **great blue heron** (*Ardea herodias*) likes to fish along the Madison and Firehole Rivers and near Fishing Bridge. Its blue-gray feathers include some stringy ones in the breast area. As long as 4 feet (1.2 m), the heron flies and often stands with its neck in an S shape.

The **sandhill crane** (*Grus canadensis*), although similar to the heron, flies with its neck outstretched. It is a duller shade of gray and a little smaller than the heron and has a red patch over the eye. It hunts rodents, insects, and seeds in the meadows and has a bugling call.

The most regal of all Yellowstone's birds is the **trumpeter swan** (*Cygnus buccinator*). Male cobs may be 5 feet (1.5 m) long with a wingspan of 7 feet (2 m); the female pens are a little smaller.

Trumpeter swan and cygnets

These snow-white swans with coal-black bills dabble (that is, go bottom up) for aquatic plants. Swans used to nest along the Madison River but now only at two lakes away from the roads. Their number in the park is down to ten residents, although migrating swans spend the winter here. Yet the Rocky Mountain population is stable, including at Red Rock Lakes National Wildlife Refuge in southwestern Montana, home to E. B. White's Louis, the remarkable mute swan in the children's book *The Trumpet of the Swan*.

Along the shores of Yellowstone Lake

Pelican colony

The **American white pelican** (*Pelecanus erythrorynchos*) can be 5 feet (1.5 m) long and have a wingspan of 9 feet (2.7 m). Park Service regulations protect the pelican's nesting place (the lake's Molly Islands) from approach by any watercraft.

A much smaller fish-eating bird is the **osprey** (*Pandion haliaetus*). Its body is black or brown above and white below, with a black patch under the crook of its wing and powerful talons for catching fish. One can see osprey nests on high pillars or tall pines in the Grand Canyon of the Yellowstone. The 2003 Frank Island fire destroyed many osprey nests.

The **California gull** (*Larus californicus*) nests on the islands of inland lakes, including Yellowstone Lake, and winters along the Pacific coast, turning from a brownish color when young to all white underneath and gray above as it matures.

The park has its share of **Canada geese** (*Branta canadensis*), which have become something of a pest around northern U.S. cities. This large goose is characterized by its black neck and white chin strap and its deep honking.

Small Mammals of the Forest

If something is flying over your head at dusk, it may be a **little brown bat** (*Myotis lucifugus*). Three to four inches (7–10 cm) long, this bat finds moths, mosquitoes, and other insects at night by echolocation. It hibernates for about half of the year.

Yellow-bellied marmots

On rocky slopes, near mountain passes, and at the Yellowstone Canyon, you'll see the much larger **yellow-bellied marmot** or **rockchuck** (*Marmota flaviventris*), whose low-slung body may be over 2 feet (0.7 m) long. The marmot digs burrows and spends much time underground but also loves to soak up the sun.

Nocturnal rodents are the common **deer mouse** (*Peromyscus maniculatus*) and the much larger **bushy-tailed woodrat** (*Neotoma cinerea*). This pack rat collects and hoards miscellaneous objects, especially shiny ones. Old Faithful Inn sets up mouse motels, since the concessionaire must follow the park policy of killing no wildlife.

The smallest rodent you're likely to see in wooded areas here is the **least chipmunk** (*Tamias minimus*), 7 to 8 inches (18–21 cm) long including the bushy tail it carries straight up as it runs. It's a gray to reddish-brown color with black and white stripes on both the back and face, and is known for stuffing its cheeks with seeds or berries.

The way to tell a **golden-mantled ground squirrel** (*Spermophilus lateralis*) from a chipmunk is to notice that the squirrel has stripes only on the body. This squirrel is some 4 inches (10 cm) longer than its chipmunk relative and may eat insects as well as vegetable matter.

Least chipmunk (left) *& Golden-mantled ground squirrel* (right)

Larger mammals

Ruminants are cud-chewing, hoofed mammals with an even number of toes. Four species are common in the central plateaus: mule deer, elk, moose, and bison. Bull elk and moose, as well as buck deer, have antlers and shed them every year, while both bull and cow bison have horns.

Mule deer & Elk

Mule deer (*Odocoileus hemionus*) are much smaller than elk and named for the size and shape of their ears; they are also called blacktail deer. Although their cousin, the **white-tailed deer** (*Odocoileus virginianus*), is the most numerous big game species in the United States, there are very few whitetails inside the park. Some live just north of Gardiner in Paradise Valley.

Rocky Mountain elk (*Cervus elaphus nelsoni*), dark brown with a light rump and tail, are of the same species as the red deer of Europe. A bull elk may be 5 feet (1.5 m) tall at the shoulder and more than 9 feet (2.7 m) long, weigh half a ton (450 kg), and carry a majestic rack of antlers several feet high. You can't tell a bull's age exactly by the number of points on his antlers, but if he has six (or even seven) points, he's a dominant male. As many as 25,000 elk have summered in the park, but the herds have been shrinking considerably in the twenty-first century. The northern Yellowstone elk herd now hovers around 4,000, a drop of over 75 percent since wolves were introduced in 1995. Mammoth Hot Springs and the Madison River still have their resident herds of elk, but they are now less commonly seen elsewhere.

The largest member of the deer family, **moose** (*Alces alces shirasi*)—confusingly called *elk* in Europe— are relatively rare in Yellowstone, probably fewer than one hundred, so seeing one is a treat. The 1988 fires caused a decline in moose population mostly due to the loss of the old-growth forest they depend upon in winter. Watch for an ungainly, large, dark brown animal—if it's a mature bull, it will have distinctive *palmate* antlers; that is, shaped like the palm and fingers of a hand. Both bulls and cows have

Moose

a dewlap of hanging skin under the throat. They eat willows and other plants that grow in shallow water all summer, but when snow is deep, they move high up to browse on fir trees.

The buffalo, more properly called the **bison** (*Bison bison*), symbolizes the wide open spaces of the American west. Ironically, the bison is also probably the most grievous case of man's wanton destruction of a natural resource in America's history. Not only did hunters nearly eradicate the bison during the last decades of the nineteenth century, but the slaughter was actually encouraged by the government to suppress the Native American Indians who depended upon them.

Bison herd in winter

Yellowstone's herd is sometimes called the only surviving wild population of bison. Though not fenced in, they are not genetically the same wild bison as when the park was new. The few bison left by 1900 were crossbred here with semi-domesticated animals from Texas and northern Montana in an early successful effort to undo damage to the environment. The restoration of the bison proved so successful, in fact, that by 1940 the park was giving them away to zoos.

The calm-looking bison can be every bit as cantankerous as a farmer's bull and can sprint faster than any Olympic runner. **The bison is the most dangerous animal in the park**; many people have been injured. Bison herds graze along the Madison and Firehole Rivers and in the Hayden and Lamar Valleys.

The Brucellosis Problem

The late 1990s saw a difficult problem arise between the agencies responsible for protecting bison and the ranchers who graze herds of cattle on private and public property all around Yellowstone. The basic problem is brucellosis, a disease that can cause a pregnant cow to abort her calf but does not cause abortion in bison. Montana ranchers fear the disease could be transmitted to their certified brucellosis-free cattle when infected bison migrate to winter feeding grounds outside the park.

Following the signing of an interagency agreement in 2000, the National Park Service and the Montana Department of Livestock sometimes haze bison back into the park from the north and west in winter; some are allowed to migrate north, some quarantined, and some relocated to Indian reservations.

Healthy calves are vaccinated, and winter bison hunts are held. These measures have been holding the Yellowstone herd to about 4,300. Factors complicating the story include the strong historical possibility that brucellosis was originally introduced into Yellowstone by infected cows brought in to supply milk for the early hotels and the fact that elk also carry brucellosis.

Bears

Grizzly bears were probably more common here than black bears in the nineteenth century. Recent estimates put the number of grizzlies in the Greater Yellowstone Ecosystem at about six hundred (with at least half of those in the park itself); black bears are not as closely watched, but now their number is similar or a little larger.

The so-called **black bear** (*Ursus americanus*) may be brown or cinnamon colored as well as black. To decide whether a bear you see at a distance is a black or a grizzly, try to observe its overall size. Adult black bears are usually about 3 feet (90 cm) in shoulder height and up to 5.5 feet (1.7 m) in overall length, weighing up to 250 pounds (114 kg). If you can see the face and ears clearly enough, observe their shape; black bears have a rather flat face in profile and pointed ears. Their claws are relatively short.

Black bear (left) *& Grizzly bear* (right)

In contrast, Yellowstone's **grizzly bears** (*Ursus arctos*) often have the grizzled or silver-tipped hair their name suggests but may have darker hair at certain times of the year. Grizzly boars (males) may weigh 700 pounds (318 kg) and sows 400 pounds (182 kg) and be 4.5 feet (1.4 m) in shoulder height and 6.5 feet (2 m) overall. Their most distinguishing features are a shoulder hump and extremely long claws, which help them dig roots but hinder them in climbing trees. Their sense of smell is incredible: the olfactory region in grizzly brains is about 250 times larger than that of humans.

You can't generalize about grizzlies, according to Dick Knight, former head of the Interagency Grizzly Bear Study Team, since each year they learn new tricks, and they are notoriously unpredictable.

Grizzlies eat a varied diet. When emerging from their winter dens, they find winter-killed carrion and newborn elk calves, supplemented with grasses and sedges. In early summer they fish in trout spawning streams, and throughout the summer, they eat various plants, small mammals, and insects, especially ants and army cutworm moths. In late summer and fall, they raid squirrels' middens full of whitebark pine nuts and feast on berries, when available. Black bears' diet is similar, except they do not dig for roots and tubers as the grizzlies do.

By mid November, the bears are hibernating in their winter dens. Although mating occurs in June and July, the fertilized egg is not implanted in the sow's uterus until after denning. This delayed implantation is a characteristic bears share with several of the park's smaller mammals, such as river otters and badgers. Grizzly cubs are born in the den in January or February and black bear cubs a month or two later. In the wild, bears live about 15 to 20 years.

Hikers should be aware that bears might be near the trails. Never approach a bear closer than 100 yards (90 m), do not hike alone, and make some noise as you go in order to let them know you're there. Bears don't like to be surprised! Human-bear encounters have increased in recent years, and backcountry hikers are advised to carry and know how to use bear spray. Overnight hikers must obtain a permit and follow the park regulations for making camp and securing food.

In and near Yellowstone Park in over 140 years there have been fourteen bear-caused fatalities (two of which cannot be confirmed). Sensational media publicity when a bear has killed a human makes it seem that there have been more.

Where Are All the Bears Now?

This is a question rangers must hear several times a day, since for at least 50 years, you were guaranteed the opportunity to see black bears along the roads and grizzly bears at the hotel garbage dumps. This situation led to lots of interaction between people and bears, and bears injured nearly 50 people each year.

In response to the problems with bears and concern about the possible extinction of the grizzly bear, the park changed its policies. The park expanded education about bear behavior, began using bear-resistant garbage cans, and strongly cautioned visitors against feeding bears or leaving unsecured food at their campsites. The most efficacious action, however, was to close all open-pit garbage dumps in or near the park. Bear Management Areas, closed to humans, also helped (see page 133). Yellowstone has learned to educate and manage the people rather than the bears.

As a result of these actions, a dramatic reduction of bear-human confrontations ensued. In recent years, there have been very few injuries, and very few bears have had to be relocated or killed.

So the answer to: "Where are all the bears?" is that they're still here and fending for themselves very nicely. You're less likely to see grizzlies than black bears near the roads in the summertime, since they often find their favorite foods at higher altitudes away from human populations. They're most likely to be living in roadless parts of the Hayden, upper Lamar, and Pelican Valleys. You'll see black bears somewhat more often, especially within a few miles of Tower-Roosevelt Junction, but also west to Mammoth Hot Springs and sometimes around Old Faithful and Madison.

II. THE VALLEYS OF THE LOWER YELLOWSTONE, LAMAR, AND GARDNER RIVERS

The northern valleys average a little lower and drier than the central plateaus overall, and the high desert ecology along the 5 miles of road between Gardiner and Mammoth is unique in the park, for precipitation there is sometimes as low as 11 inches (28 cm) in a year. In contrast, the Lamar Valley is a little higher and has about 30 inches (76 cm) of precipitation a year.

The ecology of these river valleys is also heavily influenced by glacial scouring, which has brought down volcanic and sedimentary soils from surrounding mountains. The soil holds water well and is high in plant nutrients. These are places where bison and elk thrive.

Valley Trees

Douglas fir (*Pseudotsuga menziesii*) is the evergreen you'll often see growing singly in the lee of big boulders (picture, page 211) along the road between Mammoth Hot Springs and the Northeast Entrance. Its scientific name means false hemlock, and it is not really a fir (genus *Abies*) at all. The needles grow around the branch, and the hanging female cones have little tridents between their scales. Old Douglas fir have very thick, deeply fissured bark that protects them from fires.

The **limber pine** (*Pinus flexilis*) has young branches so flexible they can be tied in knots without breaking. This pine grows at high altitudes, and its needles grow in bundles of five. Its cones are up to 8 inches (20 cm) long and green. The limber pine is common and very long-lived near Mammoth Hot Springs.

In the park, the shrub **Rocky Mountain juniper** (*Juniperus scopulorum*) grows only around Mammoth (pictured, page 274). Its scaly leaves look much like a cedar's, and its seed cones look like blue berries. Some junipers are lollipop-shaped, with bare trunks and bushy tops, a result of elk browsing on them in winter. There is an example of this tree that is more than 1,500 years old growing at Mammoth Hot Springs.

One of the three deciduous trees at home in northern Yellowstone is the **quaking aspen** (*Populus tremuloides*), which grows in sunny places on hillsides where there's abundant groundwater. Aspens are distinguished by white trunks and by leaves that quake or shiver in the slightest breeze due to flattened leafstalks. Fire does not destroy a stand of aspen, because the trees reproduce mainly by cloning from rhizomes, specialized horizontal root systems full of nutrients. One unexpected positive result of the 1988 fires was aspen's spreading into burned-over meadows, where thick vegetation had previously crowded out any aspen seedlings.

Aspens in autumn

Both of the area's other deciduous trees are types of cottonwood, the **narrowleaf cottonwood** (*Populus angustifolia*) and the **black cottonwood** or **balsam poplar** (*Populus balsamifera*). Look for cottonwoods along the Lamar River and at the confluence of the Lamar and Yellowstone Rivers. Black cottonwood have thick, furrowed, gray bark and trunks up to 3 feet (1 m) in diameter; the narrowleaf cottonwood is much smaller.

Valley shrubs and flowers

Many plants grow only in the park's lower elevations. For example, along all the rivers and some creeks are many species of **willow** (*Salix* spp.), which provide nutritious forage for elk, as do the stems, leaves, and bark of the aspen. The shrub **Rocky Mountain maple** (*Acer glabrum*) is found near Mammoth.

Yellow

Big sagebrush (*Artemisia tridentata*) is so common in most of the West as to be a symbol of the dry western plains. It's a gray-green shrub from 2 to 10 feet (60 cm–3 m) tall, bearing three-toothed leaves on many branches (see its picture on page 252).

A similar low bush found in the northern part of the park is **common rabbitbrush** (*Chrysothamnus nauseosus*). It's a rather nondescript plant with almost needlelike leaves covered with woolly white hairs, but in late August and September it bursts out with yellow flowers.

Two yellow flowers that resemble garden snapdragons are the **butter-and-eggs** (*Linaria vulgaris*) and **Dalmatian toadflax** (*Linaria dalmatica*). These are non-native plants introduced to Mammoth from Europe. Park managers are trying to control the spread of these and other exotics whenever possible.

Only in the high desert area between Gardiner and Mammoth will you see a cactus. It's the **plains prickly pear** (*Opuntia polycantha*), its fleshy stems covered with spines that are unpleasant to brush against. The roselike flowers are usually yellow but may be pink or purple on the outside if not fully opened. Pronghorn and elk will eat prickly pear in a hard winter.

Prickly pear

Blue/Purple

Larkspur (*Delphinium nelsoni* and other species) often grows where sagebrush is abundant. It's easy to recognize for the tubular spur that protrudes sideways from its deep purple blossom on a 1- to 2-foot (30–60 cm) stem. Larkspur is poisonous to cattle but not to sheep; elk avoid it until late summer.

Valley Birds

Yellow-headed blackbirds (*Xanthocephalus xanthocephalus*) are sometimes seen in the reeds at Floating Island Lake west of Tower Junction or beside some of that area's other ponds. The call of this blackbird is a loud "tseck."

On many shallow ponds in the area, you may see **American coots** (*Fulica americana*), which look rather like ducks but are actually a type of rail. Coots are slate gray with broad white bills, red eyes, lobed feet, and a habit of pumping their heads while swimming. When a flock of coots takes off, they seem to dance or skitter on the surface of the water.

You are very likely to see the distinctive **black-billed magpie** (*Pica pica*) between the North Entrance and Tower-Roosevelt Junction. Watch for a rather large black-and-white bird with an extremely long tail.

The **American kestrel** or **sparrow hawk** (*Falco sparverius*) is a medium-large bird with two black marks on its face, a buff-colored breast, gray wings, and a reddish-brown back with black flecks across it. The kestrel swoops out of the sky to pick up its prey but lives mainly on insects. Sitting on a high perch, a kestrel will wag its tail up and down repeatedly.

The **red-tailed hawk** (*Buteo jamaicensis*) is about twice as large as the kestrel and may be gray or brown on the upper body and lighter below, with chestnut red in the top of the tail. They have been known to soar for as long as 7 hours a day while hunting. There's a breeding population near Gardiner, and red-tailed hawks may be seen throughout northern Yellowstone.

The **golden eagle** (*Aquila chrysaetos*) may be more than a yard (1 m) long and have a 7-foot (2 m) wingspan. You may sometimes see them not far from the road in the Lamar Valley. Watch for a gracefully soaring, lustrous brown bird with golden-brown head and lighter-colored breast. The **bald eagle** (*Haliaeetus leucocephalusi)*, America's national bird, was listed as endangered in Yellowstone from 1978 to 2007, but this fish-eater with a wingspan up to 8 feet (2.4 m) can now be seen near lakes and rivers fairly often.

Small mammals of the river valleys

The **river otter** (*Lutra canadensis*) is a highly aquatic member of the weasel family. Three or four feet (1–1.2 m) long including its tail, it has lustrous, dark-brown fur and a broad, rather flat head. It feeds mostly on fish, amphibians, and insects. Otters dig dens in the riverbanks or use beaver and muskrat lodges. River otters can sometimes be seen playfully sliding down a steep bank into a stream in and around the Madison, Yellowstone, and Lamar Rivers, but they are crepuscular (active at dawn or dusk) or nocturnal.

A more common aquatic mammal in Yellowstone is the **muskrat** (*Ondatra zibethicus*), a rodent that grows up to 2 feet (60 cm) long and has thick, lustrous fur that is usually dark brown. Outside of national parks, its fur is responsible for a multi-million-dollar industry. You might see them eating aquatic plants in the still ponds of the Lamar Valley or around Obsidian Creek. Their cone-shaped lodges look like beaver lodges but are less substantial.

The wide lawns at Mammoth Hot Springs or the meadows near Roosevelt Lodge are full of the holes and burrows of **Uinta ground squirrels** (*Spermophilus armatus*). Ground squirrels are half the size of marmots (only about 1 ft / 30 cm long) and disappear underground for much of the year. In July or August, adults go into a sort of summer torpor called estivation, which may lead directly to hibernation, leaving them only about 90 days of activity.

Uinta ground squirrels

Larger mammals

The **pronghorn** (*Antilocapra americana*) is the smallest but by far the fleetest horned animal in Yellowstone. There's no point in chasing one. It can sprint up to 60 or 70 miles per hour (about 100 km/hr) and cruise at 30 to 40 mph (50–60 km/hr). In the world of animals, it's second only to the cheetah in sprinting speed and may be faster over longer distances. It's a very shy animal and will run at the slightest provocation.

The park herd lives between Mammoth Hot Springs and Cinnabar Mountain northwest of Gardiner. Fewer than three hundred have been counted in recent years, and the gradually diminishing herd poses a particularly difficult dilemma for the National Park Service. Since current wildlife management policy favors letting natural processes run their course, should the pronghorn be allowed to die out, with the possibility of having to face a costly reintroduction program in the future? Or should measures be taken to prevent this?

Pronghorn (historically called antelope)

Three members of the *Canidae* or dog family live in Yellowstone. By far the most numerous is the **coyote** (*Canis latrans*), whose population burgeoned over the many years when there were no competing wolves here. Look for a slim and crafty-looking animal with pointed nose and ears, weighing about 30 pounds (14 kg). It runs with its long, bushy, black-tipped tail between its legs. Coyotes are abundant enough in the northern valleys that you're almost sure to see one there, but they live throughout the park.

Coyote

After wolves were reintroduced they killed enough coyotes to reduce their population, but their number has recently rebounded. Coyotes eat mostly small rodents, stalking and pouncing on their prey, but can bring down a deer or elk when they hunt as a small pack, so the wolves must consider them competition.

Should you pronounce the coyote's name KI-yoat or ki-O-tee? Both are in the dictionaries—how you say it seems to depend upon how close you are to Spanish-speaking Mexico, where the name came from. Most residents of Wyoming and Montana say KI-yoat.

The smallest dog-like animal in Yellowstone is the **red fox** (*Vulpes vulpes*), which weighs about 10 to 12 pounds (4.5–5.5 kg). Some "red" foxes have white-tipped black hairs, giving them a silvery appearance.

A mature **gray wolf** (*Canis lupus irremotus*), also called a timber wolf, is likely to weigh two or three times as much as a coyote. It has a more massive body and a less pointed snout and ears. A wolf's tracks are the size of a large dog's, and its color may be anywhere from nearly white to black. You may see wolves along the Northeast Entrance Road, particularly early and late in the day.

Gray wolf

The Howl of the Wolf

For more than 60 years the howl of the wolf was silenced in Yellowstone. As settlers moved into the U.S. West, wolves killed their cattle and sheep, so killing wolves was everyone's civic duty. The government paid for wolf pelts; trappers baited buffalo carcasses with strychnine and turned in thousands of pelts. In Yellowstone, official policy condoned extermination of the wolf until 1926.

Finally things began to turn around for the wolves. After extensive debate and planning, 14 wolves were trapped in Alberta, Canada in midwinter 1995 and 17 in British Columbia in 1996. They were brought to the park, kept for a few weeks in specially constructed pens, and then released. A 1997 experimental release of ten young wolves from a northwestern Montana pack that had been preying on livestock was not as successful, since only two of them survived into adulthood. But most of the originally relocated wolves have thrived. They have dispersed into neighboring parts of the Greater Yellowstone Ecosystem and formed new packs. Early winter 2012–13 saw nine wolf packs in the park and 86 individual wolves, including some considered "border" wolves.

Wolves in Yellowstone's three-state area numbered over 1,700 in 2011, but state-managed hunting began that year in Montana and Idaho, and in 2012 it was permitted in Wyoming. The Yellowstone wolf population is declining, not only due to hunting but also to disease, wolf-on-wolf killings, and—since elk has been their primary prey—the lessening elk population (see page 342). Wolf project managers continue to watch Yellowstone's wolves closely, attaching radio collars to as many as possible. But in 2012 hunters killed seven collared wolves including the alpha animals, hindering research efforts.

Visitors still have opportunities to see wolves in the Lamar and Hayden Valleys, especially in winter, but they are harder to find than in the first years of this century. Seasoned wolf watchers continue to set up their spotting scopes and share their sightings with all who are interested.

Through the introduction of wolves to Yellowstone, the whole ecosystem is changing, from the grizzlies to the cougars, coyotes, and ravens who all profit directly from wolf kills, on down through the ecological pyramid. The wolves primarily prey upon elk. Now fewer elk graze on the aspen and willows, which in turn are increasing on the elk's northern range, creating more habitat for small animals and birds like warblers. The Yellowstone area is again becoming a remarkable example of what James Halfpenny, in *Yellowstone Wolves in the Wild*, calls a "trophic cascade"—profound effects spiraling down from the top to the bottom of the natural food chain.

III. MOUNTAIN PASSES

If you love flowers, then the mountain passes in and just outside of the park are places you must visit in July or early August. High passes within the park are Craig, Dunraven, and Sylvan, and outside are Beartooth, Dead Indian, Targhee, and Togwotee. All are deep in snow for eight to nine months each year, and yearly precipitation is about 40 to 50 inches (100–127 cm).

Evergreen trees

In this ecosystem lives one species that doesn't grow well at lower altitudes: the **whitebark pine** (*Pinus albicaulis*), which looks much like limber pine (page 346), but has much smaller cones that fall sooner. Its needles grow in groups of five or sometimes more. Mature trees have whitish bark and short purple cones with thick scales and sharp spines, but the trees may not produce cones until they're around one hundred years old. In late summer, when the cones fall and release their tasty and nourishing seeds, birds, squirrels, and bears enjoy the feast. Now healthy whitebark pine forests are being decimated by a global warming–related disease, blister rust, and by mountain pine beetles. Subalpine fir, Engelmann spruce, and lodgepole pine also grow around some of the mountain passes.

Mountain flowers

The very best places to get out of your car and enjoy the wildflowers center on Dunraven Pass—along the Chittenden Road at the north and along the Mount Washburn Trail beginning right at the pass. There and at other high places, you'll find many of the flowers already described and those listed below, as well as dozens of others.

Forget-me-not

White

White phlox (*Phlox multiflora*) is a low, mat-forming plant with small, snowy five-petaled flowers (see its picture on page 192). It appears in sunny places soon after the snow has melted.

Blue/Purple

The **forget-me-not** (*Myosotis alpestris*) is unforgettable due to its small and intense blue flowers with tiny yellow centers (or sometimes red or white centers).

Silky phacelia (*Phacelia sericea*) puts up a tall spike dense with purple flowers with long, protruding stamens, giving it a silky or feathery appearance. Insects are attracted by its strong, disagreeable odor.

Silky phacelia

Mountain mammals

Pika

Living in rock piles at high altitudes is a tiny relative of the rabbit family, the **pika** (*Ochotona princeps*), pronounced PEE-ka or PIE-ka. You may see it or hear its distinctive little "eek" in rocky places along the Yellowstone trails or at the Hoodoos (Silver Gate) near Mammoth. Pikas (also called rock rabbits or coneys) are usually less than 8 inches (20 cm) long, with round ears and no tails. They do not hibernate but survive the winters on the large stashes of hay they've carefully dried and stored during the summers.

The **bighorn sheep** (*Ovis canadensis*) has been prized historically by hunters for the wonderful curl of horn on the mature males, but hunting them is now strictly limited throughout the Rocky Mountains. Small herds of bighorn sheep roam around Mount Washburn and from Mount Everts north to Sheep Mountain outside the park. There are about two hundred bighorns in the park, sometimes causing traffic jams along the Dunraven Pass road.

Bighorn sheep

FISH AND FISHING

Fishing the Madison River

You may wonder, why is it okay to catch and eat fish in Yellowstone Park when we are forbidden to kill or capture all other animals, pick wildflowers, or even take away rocks? People began to question park policy toward fishing a few decades ago, and fishing practices began to change. The park now charges a fee for fishing licenses, which had always been free. As of the 2001 fishing season, all native sport fishing is catch and release only. See "Fishing" in the Travel Tips for current permit fees.

The number of anglers has dropped, but these anglers probably land more fish. Non-fishermen enjoy watching the fish feed, fight, and spawn at Fishing Bridge or leap up LeHardy's Rapids after spawning in the river. More important to the ecosystem, the bears and fish-eating birds, who were beginning to be deprived of a major element of their diet, now profit by the upsurge in the number of fish available.

There are about 20 species of fish in the Greater Yellowstone Ecosystem. The types of sport fish most common to Yellowstone's waters are native **cutthroat trout** (*Oncorhynchus clarki*) and four introduced species: **rainbow trout** (*Oncorhynchus mykiss*), **brown trout** (*Salmo trutta*, brought in 1890 from Scotland and Germany), **brook trout** (*Salvelinus fontinalis*), and **lake trout** (*Salvelinus namaycush*). Two less common native fish are **mountain whitefish** (*Prosopium williamsoni*) and **Montana grayling** (*Thymallus arcticus montanus*).

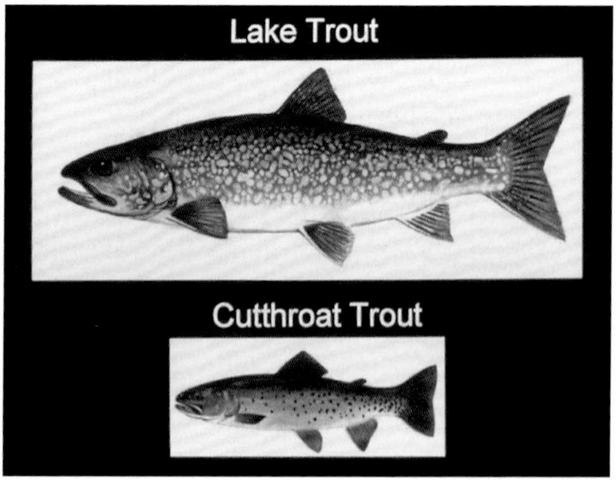

Fisheries in Trouble

Yellowstone's fisheries currently face four problems: predation by lake trout, tapeworms, whirling disease, and the New Zealand mud snail invasion.

Lake Trout

Although some larger lakes of southern Yellowstone were intentionally stocked with lake trout long ago, these large predator trout, illegally introduced into Yellowstone Lake in 1994, have caused a drastic reduction in the lake's cutthroat trout that may never be reversed. However, the combined NPS/Yellowstone Foundation aggressive efforts—gillnetting and electrofishing—had paid off by 2012: cutthroat numbers were rising, and more lake trout than ever were being removed. In addition, it is now known where they spawn. Meanwhile, anglers must kill all lake trout and either eat them or puncture the air bladder and dispose of the carcass in deep water.

Diseases and an invasion

The tapeworm (*Diphyllobothrium* sp. in larval stage) is a parasite that has been found here since before Yellowstone was a park. It is passed back and forth between the mammals and birds on land and the fish and crustaceans in water. Fortunately, tapeworms are harmless to man after the fish is cooked, although finding worms is unaesthetic. For reasons not yet understood, fish from Yellowstone Lake were found to have fewer tapeworms in the years after the 1988 fires. The large older cutthroat are the most likely to be infected, but no one is allowed to keep these according to present regulations.

Whirling disease is a relatively recent development. It's caused by a parasite (*Myxobolus cerebralis*) in another type of worm (the *Tubifex* worm) eaten by trout. Early this century biologists found the parasite in up to 20 percent of the lake's cutthroat trout and in 90 percent of Pelican Creek's, leading to closure of fishing in that creek. But in 2012 Yellowstone's supervisory fisheries biologist Todd Koel reported that all tested creeks other than Pelican Creek were free of whirling disease.

The New Zealand mud snail (*Potamopyrgus antipodarum*) reproduces so fast that it occupies habitat at an alarming rate. It can reach a density of 30,000 per square foot and could conceivably become a problem to the fish. It has been found in the Madison, lower Gibbon, Lewis, and Firehole Rivers, and near Gardiner.

TRAVEL TIPS

When you enter the park, you'll receive the official Yellowstone Park newspaper, *Yellowstone Today*, along with a map. The newspaper includes a half page or more of regulations and other useful information, including suggestions for your safety. In "A to Z Information" we provide some of these and add other tips to help you plan your trip.

For backcountry camping, bicycling, boating, and fishing, special regulations apply that are available in full at ranger stations and visitor centers. In advance of your visit, you may obtain information from National Park Service headquarters in Yellowstone (see the "Useful Contacts," page 361).

The chart of all Yellowstone facilities on page 364 tells you at a glance where gasoline, food, lodging, and other services are available within the park.

A TO Z INFORMATION

Accessibility. The National Park Service continues working to increase access to Yellowstone's facilities and outstanding features for visitors who use wheelchairs. The "Accessibility in Yellowstone" guide may be obtained at any visitor center in the park; by writing to Accessibility Coordinator, P.O. Box 168, Yellowstone National Park, WY 82190; calling (307) 344-2017; or visiting www.nps.gov/yell/planyourvisit/accessibility.htm.

Altitude sickness. Since Yellowstone's elevation averages about 8,000 feet (2,400 m) above sea level, visitors of any age may suffer from this condition. Minor symptoms, such as shortness of breath or loss of appetite, will usually disappear in a few days, but more serious problems, including nosebleeds, muscle pain, nausea, or rapid heartbeat, should be treated, especially if moving to a lower altitude does not seem to help. (*See also* "Medical services.")

Backcountry and backpacking. *See* "Camping" and the index for backcountry offices.

Bicycling. "Bicycling is permitted on established public roads, parking areas, and designated routes; it is prohibited on backcountry trails and boardwalks." Listed in a brochure available at visitor centers are the designated trails for bicycling. In this guidebook, they are indicated with a bicycle symbol. Please note that most park roads are far from ideal for bicycling, since they are narrow, winding, sometimes steep, and lacking bike lanes.

Boating. Permitted on park lakes (except for Sylvan, Eleanor, and Twin Lakes and Beach Springs Lagoon); motorized boating restricted to Yellowstone and Lewis Lakes. Personal watercraft are not allowed on any Yellowstone waters, nor boats exceeding 40 feet (12 m) in length or a noise level of 82 decibels (measured at 85 ft / 26 m from the vessel). A Coast Guard-approved life vest is required for each person boating.

Boating permits are required for all boats and float tubes. Permits can be obtained at any of the following locations: South Entrance, Lewis Lake Campground, Grant Village Backcountry Office, and Bridge Bay Ranger Station. In addition, Canyon, Old Faithful, and Mammoth visitor centers provide non-motorized permits, as do Bechler Ranger Station, West and Northeast entrance stations, and West Yellowstone Visitor Information Center. Boating fees for motorized vessels are $20 (annual) or $10 (7-day); for non-motorized vessels it's $10 (annual) or $5 (7-day).

Boats are not allowed on rivers and streams, except that hand-propelled vessels may use the channel between Lewis and Shoshone Lakes. Detailed regulations are given with permits. Only non-motorized boats are allowed in the most remote sections of the three so-called fingers of the lake: Flat Mountain Arm, South Arm, and Southeast Arm. This is primarily to protect the nesting pelicans, terns, and seagulls.

Cabins. *See* "Hotels and cabins."

Camping. Yellowstone has 11 campgrounds and one recreational vehicle park (see campgrounds chart on page 365). Sites in four campgrounds and the Fishing Bridge RV Park may be reserved in advance, but the other seven campgrounds are available on a first-come, first-served basis. Campground use fees range between $20.50 and $25; RVs, $45. In July and August, park campgrounds may be full by noon. No camping outside designated campgrounds is allowed, but Forest Service and private campgrounds are available along park approach roads.

For backcountry camping, you must obtain a free permit at a ranger station or visitor center no more than 48 hours before you set out. If you wish to reserve a backcountry campsite in advance, you must pay a $25 fee. The NPS publication *Backcountry Trip Planner* provides excellent backcountry information and advice. Write to the Backcountry Office, P.O. Box 168, Yellowstone National Park, WY 82190 or visit www.nps.gov/yell/planyourvisit/backcountryhiking.htm.

Collecting specimens. Removing any specimens from Yellowstone is illegal. Leave only footprints, take only pictures. Yellowstone and everything in it belongs to all the people.

Drinking water. It's safe in park villages and campgrounds. Stream and lake water must be boiled or filtered followed by iodine treatment. (Filtration kits are available in sporting goods stores.) This chemical treatment alone does not remove the diarrhea-causing parasite giardia found in park waters.

Driving. The speed limit throughout the park is **45 mph (72 km/h)**, less where posted. Watch for animals and pedestrians. "Wildlife jams" are common, particularly when a bear, bison, elk, or bighorn sheep is on or near the road. Some roads are full of potholes and most are quite narrow. See also "Road conditions."

Emergency telephone number. Call **911** for emergency medical, fire, or ranger response.

Entrance fees. The cost to enter the park: automobile $25, motorcycle $20, good for 7 days. An individual arriving on foot, on skis, or by bike pays $12 for the same period. The park keeps 80 percent of these fees for necessary projects. Various types of annual passes are available. Use your admission receipt to reenter Yellowstone and to enter Grand Teton National Park.

Fishing. Permitted in most Yellowstone streams and lakes, but a permit must be purchased and regulations followed. Permits are available at ranger stations, visitor centers, and Yellowstone General Stores. They cost $18 for 3 days, $25 for 7 days, or $40 for a year. Increases will help fund the 2011 Native Fish Conservation Plan. Anglers under 16 years of age may fish without a permit when supervised by an adult or obtain a free permit signed by an adult.

Pick up a copy of the fishing regulations from any visitor center, ranger station, or marina in the park, or from one of the sporting goods stores in gateway communities. You are responsible for following the regulations and being able to measure your fish and identify the different species. All native sport fish species now come under catch-and-release-only rules. If you'll be fishing in Montana, Wyoming, or Idaho waters outside park boundaries, you'll need to purchase a state fishing license. (See the last section in the Living Things chapter for more about fish and fishing.)

Flying private planes. Pilots who plan to fly to the Yellowstone area must be aware of the challenges of mountain flying: density altitude issues, short runways, downdrafts and mountain weather to watch out for, as well as personal limitations. Refer to the index for airports in the vicinity.

Geyser basin walks. Before you set out on a walk, especially one around the geyser basins, take a few precautions to make your visit enjoyable.

The sun at this elevation can be brutal, especially between 10 AM and 4 PM, so provide yourself with a hat, a long-sleeved shirt, and sunscreen lotion. Be prepared with rain gear for the rainstorms and even hail that can come up quickly in any mountain environment, especially during the late afternoons. Take your own drinking water; there is none along the walkways. Neither pets nor smoking are allowed in the geyser basins. The only restrooms near most routes through the geyser basins are in the parking lots.

Photographers and anyone who wears eyeglasses should know that the spray from geysers contains silica, which can damage glass. Wipe off lenses and eyeglasses immediately if they are dampened by spray.

Park regulations state: "You must stay on boardwalks and designated trails."

Be sure to watch small children vigilantly. Geyserite formations are extremely brittle and can easily break through, and even pools that do not look very hot may scald you!

Geyser websites. For descriptive and detailed geyser information: www.geyserstudy.org; for geyser eruption data: www.geysertimes.org; for details about major geysers and links to webcams and YouTube videos: www.yellowstone.net/geysers; for Old Faithful and other park webcams: www.nps.gov/yell/photosmultimedia/webcams.htm.

Hiking. Hiking in Yellowstone can mean anything from going a few hundred yards from your car to spending a week backpacking in the remotest backcountry. Parts of longer backcountry trails are included here when they're not difficult and are particularly interesting.

The chart of 56 Recommended Short Walks in Yellowstone, starting on page 366, may help you plan hikes according to what part of the park you are visiting and how much time you have. It shows the approximate distance and elevation change for each walk. Marked in the road logs and on the accompanying maps with the symbols or , these walks are recommended to anyone who wants to get away from the roads to see something fun, but especially for non-athletes, older people, and families with young children. Recommended trails are also listed in the index by name. The symbols and indicate that the Yellowstone Association has printed a self-guiding pamphlet, available both at a visitor center and at the start of the walk.

Most of these recommended walks involve round trips of less than 5 miles (8 km) and are not too steep. The chart does not include the very commonly found walks that lead less than one-half mile (0.8 km) from a road. These walks have no stream crossings by ford or wobbly log. Some popular backcountry hiking books are listed on page 369.

Horseback riding. Horses are available at Canyon, Mammoth, and Tower-Roosevelt for hire from the park concessionaire.

Horsepackers. For horsepacking trips, you must obtain a backcountry permit and follow NPS regulations.

Hotels and cabins. Accommodations usually fill up months in advance. Plan stays in more than one campground or lodging to facilitate seeing more and driving less. Employees of the concessionaire provide guided bus tours, some hotel tours, and evening talks. All hotels and cabins are reserved through Xanterra Parks & Resorts (see "Useful Contacts"). Dinner reservations are required at Grant Dining Room, Old Faithful Inn, and Lake Hotel. A chart of all facilities is on page 364.

Internet access. WiFi is available in certain locations within the park for a fee.

Medical services. Mammoth Hot Springs Village has a clinic open all year.

Open in summer only are the clinics at Old Faithful Village and Lake Village. Call **911** for emergency assistance.
Pets. "Pets must be leashed. They are prohibited on all trails, in the backcountry, and in hydrothermal basins. Pets are not allowed more than 100 feet from a road or parking area. Leaving a pet unattended and/or tied to an object is prohibited." Xanterra accommodations brochures add: "Pets are not allowed in the hotel rooms; however, dogs and cats are permitted in the cabin facilities if quiet and housebroken. Pets may not be left unattended." Consider seriously whether it might be best to leave your pet at home.
Picnic areas and restrooms. All picnic areas have tables and well-maintained restrooms, but many do not have water. The toilets, usually of the vault (outhouse) or chemical type, are indicated in this guide by the icon .
Ranger stations. Go to a ranger station for backcountry camping, boating, and fishing permits, or to report a problem. There are two kinds of rangers in Yellowstone, the law enforcement rangers and the ranger-interpreters who answer questions and present programs and hikes for visitors.
Religious services. Held in numerous park locations on Saturdays and Sundays; details are available at visitor centers.
Road conditions. Call (307) 344-2117 for information about park roads; 511 for road conditions in Montana or Wyoming.
Rock climbing. Rock climbing is dangerous and not recommended in Yellowstone. It is illegal in the Grand Canyon of the Yellowstone.
Swimming. There are no swimming pools in Yellowstone, and all bathing is prohibited "where water flows entirely from a hydrothermal spring or pool." You may swim in two places where river and hot spring water mix naturally: the Firehole River along Firehole Canyon Drive and the Boiling River in a part of the Gardner River near Mammoth Hot Springs.

River, stream, and lake water is very cold and may contain organisms dangerous to your health, so keep your head out of the water.
Telephones. A few public phones are located in visitor centers, lodgings, and restaurants. Service for cell phones is provided in some parts of the park, most reliably at Canyon, Grant, Mammoth, and Old Faithful, by some wireless companies. The NPS plans to add new communications towers in the near future.
Theft and vandalism. Both crimes have become more prevalent as the number of visitors has increased. Lock your car doors, and keep all valuables out of sight.
Winter visits. Only the road between the North and Northeast Entrances is plowed in winter. Other roads are groomed for snowmobile and snowcoach travel. Book your trip through the park concessionaire or through private snowcoach, snowmobile, and cross-country ski tour operators. See www.nps.gov/yell/planyourvisit/wintbusn.htm.

USEFUL CONTACTS

For easy access to all the websites in this section, visit www.yellowstonetreasures.com/linkfile.htm.

Yellowstone's supporting organizations

Geyser Observation and Study Association. GOSA is an organization of people who observe, record, and exchange information about geysers year round, including geysers elsewhere in the world. Visit their website at www.geyserstudy.org. For information about joining the organization and to subscribe to the bimonthly *Geyser Gazer Sput*, write: GOSA Press, c/o David Monteith, 10209 SE 216th St., Kent, WA 98031.

Greater Yellowstone Coalition. An umbrella organization of conservation groups. Members keep informed about many issues affecting the Yellowstone ecosystem. Based in Bozeman, the coalition has satellite offices in Cody, Jackson, and Idaho Falls. Mailing address: P.O. Box 1874, Bozeman, MT; phone: (800) 775-1834 or (406) 586-1593; website: www.greateryellowstone.org.

National Park Service headquarters at Mammoth Village provides information about the park. You can leave your name and address at (307) 344-2111 to have an NPS planning kit mailed to you; write to P.O. Box 168, Yellowstone National Park, WY 82190; phone (307) 344-7381; or visit www.nps.gov/yell.

National Parks Conservation Association. Founded in 1919, NPCA works to help the National Park Service fulfill its mission of preserving the natural and cultural resources of all national parks "for the enjoyment, education, and inspiration of this and future generations." Membership includes a subscription to their quarterly magazine. Their address is: 1300 Nineteenth Street N.W., Suite 300, Washington, DC 20036; phone: (800) 628-7275; website: www.npca.org.

Xanterra Parks & Resorts books in-park lodgings and sites at some campgrounds, as well as activities like tours, lake cruises, and horseback rides. Phone (866) 439-7375 or (307) 344-7311, or visit www.YellowstoneNationalParkLodges.com.

Yellowstone Association. A nonprofit organization that provides funding to the park in support of educational, historical, and scientific projects. One ongoing project is the Yellowstone Institute, through which adults and families may study wildlife, wildflowers, Yellowstone history, geology, ecology, and many other topics with experts in their fields, or participate in guided hikes and horseback trips.

A special facility at the Lamar Buffalo Ranch houses the classrooms, kitchen, and cabins for people attending Yellowstone Institute classes. To inquire about membership in the Yellowstone Association or for details about the classes, see any visitor center in the park; write The Yellowstone Association, P.O. Box 117, Yellowstone National Park, WY 82190; call (406) 848-2400; or visit www.YellowstoneAssociation.org.

Yellowstone Park Foundation. A nonprofit organization dedicated to raising money for projects that protect, preserve, and enhance the park, including the Wolf Restoration Project and the restoration of native cutthroat trout to Yellowstone. For further information, write The Yellowstone Park Foundation, 222 East Main Street, Suite 301, Bozeman, MT 59715; call (406) 586-6303; or visit www.ypf.org.

State recreation and tourism offices

Idaho Parks and Recreation Dept., P.O. Box 83720, Boise, ID 83720-0065; phone: (800) 635-7820 or (208) 334-4199; website: www.idahoparks.org.

Travel Montana, P.O. Box 200533, Helena, MT 59620; phone: (800) 847-4868 or (406) 841-2870; website: www.visitmt.com.

Wyoming Travel & Tourism, I-25 at College Dr., Cheyenne, WY 82002; phone: (800) 225-5996 or (307) 777-7777; website: wyomingtourism.org.

Chambers of Commerce

Big Sky: P.O. Box 160100, Big Sky, MT 59716; phone: (406) 995-3000 or (800) 943-4111; website: www.bigskychamber.com.

Billings: P.O. Box 31177, Billings, MT 59107; phone: (406) 252-4016 or (800) 735-2635; website: www.billingscvb.visitmt.com.

Bozeman: 2000 Commerce Way, Bozeman, MT 59715; phone: (406) 586-5421 or (800) 228-4224; website: www.bozemanchamber.com.

Cody: 836 Sheridan Ave., Cody, WY 82414; phone: (307) 587-2777 or (800) 393-2639; website: www.codychamber.org.

Cooke City & Silver Gate: 231 West Main or P.O. Box 1071, Cooke City, MT 59020; phone: (406) 838-2495; website: www.cookecitychamber.org.

Dubois: 616 W. Ramshorn St. or P.O. Box 632, Dubois, WY 82513; phone: (307) 455-2556 or (888) 518-0502; website: www.duboiswyoming.org.

East Yellowstone/Wapiti Valley, WY: phone: (307) 587-9595; website: www.yellowstone-lodging.com.

Gardiner: P.O. Box 81, Gardiner, MT 59030; phone: (406) 848-7971; website: www.gardinerchamber.com.

Idaho Falls: 630 West Broadway or P.O. Box 50498, Idaho Falls, ID 83405; phone: (208) 523-1010 or (866) 365-6943; website: www.idahofallschamber.com.

Island Park: P.O. Box 83, Island Park, ID 83429; phone: (208) 558-7755; website: www.islandparkchamber.org; or East Idaho Visitor Info, phone: (800) 847-4843.

Jackson Hole: P.O. Box 550, Jackson, WY 83001; phone: (307) 733-3316; website: www.jacksonholechamber.com.

Livingston: 303 E. Park St., Livingston, MT 59047; phone: (406) 222-0850;

website: www.livingston-chamber.com.

Red Lodge: 601 N. Broadway or P.O. Box 988, Red Lodge, MT 59068; phone: (406) 446-1718 or (888) 281-0625; website: www.redlodge.com.

West Yellowstone: 30 Yellowstone Ave. or P.O. Box 458, West Yellowstone, MT 59758; phone: (406) 646-7701; website: www.destinationyellowstone.com.

U.S. Forest Service headquarters

Six national forests either border Yellowstone Park or are very nearby. The Forest Service website is www.fs.fed.us. Ranger districts are listed here with phone numbers under their respective national forests if they are near the Yellowstone approach roads.

Beaverhead-Deerlodge N.F., phone: (406) 683-3900; Madison Ranger District, phone: (406) 682-4253.

Bridger-Teton N.F., phone: (307) 739-5500.

Caribou-Targhee N.F., phone: (208) 524-7500; Ashton Ranger District (for Mesa Falls Scenic Area), phone: (208) 652-7442.

Custer N.F., phone: (406) 657-6200; Beartooth Ranger District, phone: (406) 446-2103.

Gallatin N.F., phone: (406) 587-6701; Bozeman Ranger District, phone: (406) 522-2520; Gardiner Ranger District, phone: (406) 848-7375; Hebgen Lake/Earthquake Lake areas, phone: (406) 823-6961; Livingston District, phone: (406) 222-1892.

Shoshone N.F., phone: (307) 527-6241; Clarks Fork and Wapiti Ranger Districts, phone: (307) 527-6921.

METRIC CONVERSIONS

Yellowstone National Park speed limit: 45 mph (72 kph)

1 meter = 3.28 feet
1 kilometer = 0.6214 (about 5/8) mile
1 foot = 0.3048 meter
1 yard = 0.9144 meter
1 mile = 1.6093 kilometers

To convert temperatures:
From degrees Fahrenheit: subtract 32, multiply by 5, divide by 9 = degrees Celsius
From degrees Celsius: multiply by 9, divide by 5, add 32 = degrees Fahrenheit

FACILITIES IN YELLOWSTONE

Village or Junction	ATM	Auto Services[a]	Boat Ramp	Cafeteria / Restaurants[b]	General Stores	Gift Shops	Groceries / Fishing Supplies[c]	Laundry (Self-Service)[d]	Lodging: Cabins & Hotels	Medical Clinic	Post Office	Ranger Station[e]	Showers (Public)	Visitor Center[f]
Bridge Bay			x				x					x		
Canyon Village	2x	x		4x	2x	x	x	x	x		x	x	x	x
Fishing Bridge	x	x		x	x		x	x					x	x
Grant Village	x	x	x	3x	x	x	2x	x	x		x	x	x	x
Lake Village	x			4x	x	2x	x	x	x	x	x			
Mammoth Hot Springs	2x	x		2x	x	x	x		x	x	x	x	x	x
Old Faithful Village	3x	2x		7x	2x	3x	2x	x	x	x	x	x	2x	x
Tower-Roosevelt		x		x	x	x	2x		x			x	x	

a) Mammoth, Old Faithful Lower Station, and Tower Junctions have gasoline only; other stations also have repair services and diesel fuel.
b) These restaurants require dinner reservations: Grant Village, Lake Hotel, Old Faithful Inn.
c) Bridge Bay has a mini-store only.
d) The only public laundry at Old Faithful is in the Snow Lodge.
e) Mammoth has the backcountry and law enforcement ranger headquarters.
f) Visitor centers open at 8 AM and close between 6 and 8 PM; inquire locally for seasonal closing time. Madison, Norris, and West Thumb Junctions have small info/book centers only.

CAMPGROUNDS IN YELLOWSTONE

Village or Junction	Number of Sites	2012 Fees ($)	Elevation (in feet)	Features
Bridge Bay[1, 2]	432	20.50	7,800	A, F, DS, G
Canyon[3, 6]	273	25	7,900	A, F, S/L, DS, G
Fishing Bridge[3, 4]	346	45	7,800	F, S/L, DS, G
Grant Village[3, 5]	430	25	7,800	A, F, S/L, DS, G
Madison[5]	278	20.50	6,800	A, F, DS, G
Indian Creek[6]	75	12	7,300	A, V
Lewis Lake[1]	85	12	7,800	V
Mammoth[6]	85	14	6,200	A, F, G, S
Norris[5]	>100	14	7,500	A, F, G
Pebble Creek[6]	27	12	6,900	V
Slough Creek[6]	23	12	6,250	V
Tower Fall[3, 7]	31	12	6,600	V

NOTES:

This information was valid in 2012 and is presented so that readers may compare the campgrounds. All are open between late June and Labor Day—only Mammoth Campground is open in winter—but contact Xanterra Parks & Resorts or the NPS for exact dates and current fees. For contact information, see "Useful Contacts" in the Travel Tips chapter.

The first five campgrounds in the list are operated by Xanterra Parks & Resorts, and you may reserve their sites in advance. The remaining seven campgrounds are operated by the National Park Service, with sites available on a first-come, first-served basis. It is a good idea to arrive at the campground of your choice by 10 AM to be sure to obtain a site. For RV sites, inquire about length and availability.

1) Popular with boaters and fishermen, who get going early.
2) Few trees in the campground, except in the loops farthest from the entrance; some large sites.
3) Areas where you're most likely to see bears early in the season.
4) For hard-sided vehicles only.
5) Most convenient to the geyser basins.
6) Ideal locations for backcountry hikers.
7) Sites are small and close together.

Key to Features:

- A Accessible sites available
- S/L Pay showers/Laundry nearby
- F Flush toilets
- V Vault toilets
- DS Dump station
- G Generators OK 8 AM to 8 PM

56 RECOMMENDED SHORT WALKS IN YELLOWSTONE

Walk Symbols: 🚲 Biking allowed ♿ Wheelchair-accessible

Name and Type of Walk	Round Trip or Loop Distance	Elevation Change	Map Page
NORTHWEST CORNER (U.S. 191)			
Part of Fan Creek Trail	4 mi (6.4 km)	150 ft (45 m)	30
WEST ENTRANCE TO MADISON JCT.			
Two Ribbons Nature Trail ♿	0.75 mi (1.2 km)	Level	38
Harlequin Lake	0.5 mi (0.8 km)	100 ft (30 m)	38
MADISON TO OLD FAITHFUL			
Sentinel Meadow Trail (extension of Fountain Flats Dr.)	4.4 mi (7 km)	120 ft (36 m)	46
Fountain Paint Pot Loop (partly ♿)	0.5 mi (0.8 km)	50 ft (15 m)	46
Midway Geyser Basin Loop ♿	0.6 mi (1 km)	50 ft (15 m)	46
Mystic Falls	3.5 mi (5.6 km)	100 ft (30 m)	46
Black Sand Basin ♿	1 mi (1.6 km)	Level	46
OLD FAITHFUL VILLAGE			
Part of Mallard Lake Trail	0.5 mi (0.8 km)	50 ft (15 m)	74
Geyser Hill and Beyond	3.5 mi (5.6 km)	50 ft (15 m)	83
Observation Point	0.5 mi (0.8 km)	150 ft (45 m)	83
Extension to Biscuit Basin	1.6 mi (2.6 km)	50 ft (15 m)	83
Castle & Daisy Geysers ♿ 🚲	2.4 mi (3.9 km)	Almost level	83
Extension to Black Sand Pool	1 mi (1.6 km)	100 ft (30 m)	83
OLD FAITHFUL TO WEST THUMB			
Lone Star Geyser 🚲	5 mi (8 km)	Level	104
SOUTH ENTRANCE TO WEST THUMB			
Moose Falls	2 mi (3.2 km)	100 ft (30 m)	128
Riddle Lake	4.5 mi (7.2 km)	Level	128
WEST THUMB TO FISHING BRIDGE			
Yellowstone Lake Overlook Loop	2 mi (3.2 km)	400 ft (120 m)	138
West Thumb Geyser Basin ♿	0.5 mi (0.8 km)	Almost level	138
Natural Bridge 🚲	3 mi (5 km)	60 ft (18 m)	138
Lakeshore at Lake Village to Fishing Bridge	2 mi (3.2 km)	Level	149

Name and Type of Walk	Round Trip or Loop Distance	Elevation Change	Map Page
East Entrance to Fishing Bridge			
Storm Point Nature Trail	2 mi (3.2 km)	Almost level	162
Pelican Creek Nature Trail	1 mi (1.6 km)	Level	162
Fishing Bridge to Canyon			
Mud Volcano Loop (partly ♿)	1 mi (1.6 km)	150 ft (45 m)	172
Canyon Area			
Uncle Tom's Trail	1 mi (1.6 km)	300 ft (90 m)	179
Clear Lake	2 mi (3.2 km)	100 ft (30 m)	179
Crystal Falls	0.5 mi (0.8 km)	Almost level	179
Grand View	1 mi (1.6 km)	Level	179
Part of 7-Mile Hole Trail (Silver Cord Cascade overlook)	2.5 mi (4 km)	Level	179
Red Rock Point (close to Lower Falls)	1 mi (1.6 km)	500 ft (150 m)	179
Brink of (Lower) Falls	1 mi (1.6 km)	600 ft (180 m)	179
Northeast Entrance to Tower			
Part of Pebble Creek Trail (geologic formation)	0.5 mi (0.8 km)	Level	200
Trout Lake	1 mi (1.6 km)	200 ft (60 m)	200
Part of Lamar Valley Trail (historic remnants)	1.6 mi (2.6 km)	Almost level	200
Part of Slough Creek Trail	4 mi (6.4 km)	400 ft (120 m)	200
Part of Specimen Ridge Trail	3 mi (5 km)	150 ft (45 m)	200
Tower-Roosevelt to Canyon			
Roosevelt Lodge: Lost Creek Falls	0.6 mi (1 km)	150 ft (45 m)	214
Part of Mt. Washburn Trail (wildflowers)	1 mi (1.6 km)	200 ft (60 m)	214
Cascade Lake	4.4 mi (7.1 km)	Almost level	214
Canyon Jct. to Norris Jct.			
Little Gibbon Falls	2 mi (3.2 km)	100 ft (30 m)	227
Ice Lake ♿	0.6 mi (1 km)	Level	227

Name and Type of Walk	Round Trip or Loop Distance	Elevation Change	Map Page
NORRIS GEYSER BASIN			
Back Basin Loop (partly ♿)	1.5 mi (2.4 km)	70 ft (21 m)	231
Porcelain Basin West Loop	0.5 mi (0.8 km)	100 ft (30 m)	231
Porcelain Basin East Loop (partly ♿)	0.5 mi (0.8 km)	70 ft (21 m)	231
NORTH ENTRANCE TO MAMMOTH			
Boiling River	1 mi (1.6 km)	Level	250
MAMMOTH HOT SPRINGS			
Beaver Ponds Loop	6 mi (9.6 km)	500 ft (150 m)	258
Lower Terrace Boardwalk, Part I	0.5 mi (0.8 km)	100 ft (30 m)	265
MAMMOTH JCT. TO NORRIS JCT.			
Upper Terrace Drive (partly ♿)	1.6 mi (2.6 km)	150 ft (45 m)	265
Snow Pass	5 mi (8 km)	700 ft (210 m)	265
Part of the Howard Eaton Trail (above Mammoth)	2 mi (3.2 km)	150 ft (45 m)	277
Indian Creek Campground: Superintendent's Road 🚲	1.5 mi (2.4 km)	Level	277
NORRIS JCT. TO MADISON JCT.			
Artists' Paintpots	1.5 mi (2.4 km)	100 ft (30 m)	287
MAMMOTH JCT. TO TOWER JCT.			
Wraith Falls	1 mi (1.6 km)	Level	292
Hidden Falls on Blacktail Deer Creek	7 mi (11 km)	580 ft (175 m)	292
Forces of the Northern Range Trail ♿	0.6 mi (1 km)	Level	292
Part of Lost Lake Trail	1.8 mi (3 km)	Almost level	292

YELLOWSTONE BOOKS AND MAPS

SUGGESTED READING

Geology

Fritz, William J. and Robert C. Thomas. *Roadside Geology of Yellowstone Country,* 2nd ed. Missoula, MT: Mountain Press Publishing, 2011.

Good, John M., and Kenneth L. Pierce. *Interpreting the Landscapes of Grand Teton and Yellowstone National Parks*, 2nd rev. ed. Moose, WY: Grand Teton Natural History Association, 1998.

Hendrix, Marc C. *Geology Underfoot in Yellowstone Country*. Missoula, MT: Mountain Press Publishing, 2011.

Smith, Robert B., and Lee J. Siegel. *Windows into the Earth: The Geologic Story of Yellowstone & Grand Teton National Parks*. London: Oxford University Press, 2000.

Hiking and Backcountry Camping

Adkison, Ron. *Exploring Beyond Yellowstone*. Berkeley, CA: Wilderness Press, 1996.

Bach, Orville, Jr. *Exploring the Yellowstone Backcountry: A Guide to the Hiking Trails of Yellowstone with Additional Sections on Canoeing, Bicycling, and Cross-Country Skiing*, 3rd ed. San Francisco: Sierra Club Books, 1998.

Evans, Lisa Gollin. *An Outdoor Family Guide to Yellowstone & Grand Teton National Parks*, 2nd ed. Seattle: Mountaineers Books, 2006.

Marschall, Mark C. and Joy Sellers Marschall. *Yellowstone Trails: A Hiking Guide*, 6th ed. Yellowstone National Park, WY: The Yellowstone Association, 2008.

Schneider, Bill. *Hiking Yellowstone National Park*, 3rd ed. Guilford, CT: FalconGuides, 2012.

Schreier, Carl. *Hiking Yellowstone Trails*. Moose, WY: Homestead Pub., 1997.

History

Bartlett, Richard A. *Yellowstone: A Wilderness Besieged*. Tucson, AZ: University of Arizona Press, 1985.

Bonney, Orrin H. and Lorraine Bonney. *Battle Drums & Geysers*. Vol. 2, *Discovery & Exploration of Yellowstone: Doane's Journal*. Houston: Bonney, 1970.

Haines, Aubrey L. *The Yellowstone Story*, 2nd rev. ed., 2 vols. Boulder, CO: University Press of Colorado, 1996.

———. *Yellowstone Place Names: Mirrors of History*. Niwot, CO: University Press of Colorado, 1996.

Watry, Elizabeth A. *Women in Wonderland: Lives, Legends, and Legacies of Yellowstone National Park*. Helena, MT: Riverbend Publishing, 2012.

Whittlesey, Lee H. *Death in Yellowstone*. Boulder, CO: Roberts Rinehart Publishers, 1995.

———. *Yellowstone Place Names*, 2nd rev. ed. Gardiner, MT: Wonderland Publishing, 2006.

Living Things

Brock, Thomas D. *Life at High Temperatures*. Yellowstone National Park, WY: Yellowstone Association for Natural Science, History & Education, 1994.

Halfpenny, James C. *Yellowstone Wolves in the Wild*. Helena, MT: Riverbend Publishing, 2003.

———. *Yellowstone Bears in the Wild*. Helena, MT: Riverbend Publishing, 2012.

Herrero, Stephen. *Bear Attacks: Their Causes & Avoidance*, Rev. ed. New York: Lyons Press, 2002.

McEneaney, Terry. *Birds of Yellowstone*. Boulder, CO: Roberts Rinehart Publishers, 1989.

Parks, Richard. *Fishing Yellowstone National Park*, 3rd ed. Guilford, CT: Lyons Press, 2007.

Phillips, H. Wayne. *Central Rocky Mountain Wildflowers: Including Yellowstone and Grand Teton National Parks*, 2nd ed. Guilford, CT: FalconGuides, 2012.

Phillips, Michael K., and Douglas W. Smith. *The Wolves of Yellowstone*. Stillwater, MN: Voyageur Press, 1996.

Schullery, Paul. *The Bears of Yellowstone*, 3rd ed. Worland, WY: High Plains Publishing Co., 1992.

Scott, Douglas M., and A. Suvi. *Wildlife of Yellowstone and Grand Teton National Parks*. Salt Lake City: Wheelwright Press, 2008.

Sheehan, Kathy B., David J. Patterson, Brett Leigh Dicks, and Joan M. Henson. *Seen and Unseen: Discovering the Microbes of Yellowstone*. Guilford, CT: FalconGuides, 2005.

Smith, Douglas W. and Gary Ferguson. *Decade of the Wolf: Returning the Wild to Yellowstone*, 2nd ed. Guilford, CT: Lyons Press, 2012.

Varley, John D., and Paul Schullery. *Yellowstone Fishes: Ecology, History, & Angling in the Park*. Mechanicsburg, PA: Stackpole Books, 1998.

Wilkinson, Todd. Photographer: Michael H. Francis. *Watching Yellowstone & Grand Teton Wildlife*. Helena, MT: Riverbend Publishing, 2004.

Maps

Christiansen, Robert L. Geologic Map of the Yellowstone Plateau Area. Plate 1 in "Geology of Yellowstone National Park—The Quaternary and Pliocene Yellowstone Plateau Volcanic Field of Wyoming, Idaho, and Montana." U.S.G.S. Professional Paper 729-G. Reston, VA: U.S. Geological Survey, 2001.

National Geographic Trails Illustrated Maps. Evergreen, CO: Trails Illustrated; four Yellowstone quadrants based on U.S.G.S. 15-minute topographic maps, revised 2008; excellent references for all but backcountry hiking.

U.S.G.S. 7-1/2-minute topographic maps of all of Yellowstone Park, available at some Yellowstone visitor centers, at bookstores and outfitting stores, or from: U.S. Geological Survey, Map Distribution, Building 41, Box 25286, Federal Center, Denver, CO 80225; strongly recommended for backcountry hiking.

Photography

Dance, Doug. *Once Around the Sun in Yellowstone*. Winnipeg, MB: Doug Dance Nature Photography, 2005.

Meagher, Mary and Douglas B. Houston. *Yellowstone and the Biology of Time: Photographs Across a Century*. Norman, OK: University of Oklahoma Press, 1998.

Whittlesey, Lee H., comp. *A Yellowstone Album: A Photographic Celebration of the First National Park*. Boulder, CO: Roberts Rinehart Publishers, 1997.

Specialized Guides

Bryan, T. Scott. *The Geysers of Yellowstone*, 4th ed. Boulder, CO: University Press of Colorado, 2008.

Eversman, Sharon and Mary Carr. *Yellowstone Ecology: A Road Guide*. Missoula, MT: Mountain Press Publishing, 1992.

Rubinstein, Paul, Lee H. Whittlesey, and Mike Stevens. *The Guide to Yellowstone Waterfalls and Their Discovery*. Englewood, CO: Westcliffe Publishers, Inc., 2000.

Wuerthner, George. *Yellowstone: A Visitor's Companion*. Mechanicsburg, PA: Stackpole Books, 1992.

SOME REFERENCES USED IN RESEARCHING THIS BOOK

Bargar, Keith E. *Geology and Thermal History of Mammoth Hot Springs, Yellowstone National Park, Wyoming*. Washington, DC: U.S. Geological Survey Bulletin 1444, 1978.

Blevins, Winfred. *Roadside History of Yellowstone Park*. Missoula, MT: Mountain Press Publishing, 1989.

Chittenden, Hiram M. *The Yellowstone National Park: Historical and Descriptive.* Cincinnati, Ohio: Robert Clarke Company, 1895.

Christiansen, Robert L. "Geology of Yellowstone National Park—The Quaternary and Pliocene Yellowstone Plateau Volcanic Field of Wyoming, Idaho, and Montana." U.S.G.S. Professional Paper 729-G. Reston, VA: U.S. Geological Survey, 2001.

Despain, Don G. *Yellowstone Vegetation: Consequences of Environment and History in a Natural Setting.* Boulder, CO: Roberts Rinehart Publishers, 1990.

Dunraven, Earl of. *The Great Divide: Travels in the Upper Yellowstone in the Summer of 1874.* London: Chatto and Windus, 1876.

The Geyser Gazer Sput. Palmdale, CA: The Geyser Observation and Study Association. Issued bimonthly; Web site: www.geyserstudy.org.

Haynes, F. Jay and Jack E. Haynes. *Haynes Guides* (published annually, 1890–1966). St. Paul, MN: F. Jay Haynes; St. Paul, MN: Haynes Picture Shops, Inc.; and Bozeman, MT: Haynes Studios, Inc.

Keefer, William R. *The Geologic Story of Yellowstone National Park.* Washington, DC: U.S. Geological Survey Bulletin 1347, 1971.

Kershaw, Linda et al. *Plants of the Rocky Mountains.* Edmonton, Canada: Lone Pine Publishing, 1998.

Marler, George D. *Inventory of Thermal Features of the Firehole River Geyser Basins and Other Selected Areas of Yellowstone National Park*, 1973. USGS GD 73-018. Microfiche. Photocopy by The Geyser Observation and Study Association, ed. Lynn Stephens.

Morgan, Lisa A., ed. "Integrated Geoscience Studies in the Greater Yellowstone Area—Volcanic, Tectonic, and Hydrothermal Processes in the Yellowstone Geoecosystem." Washington, DC: U.S.G.S. Professional Paper 1717, 2007.

Paperiello, Rocco. *Report on the Norris Geyser Basin for 1984.* Available from The Geyser Observation and Study Association.

Parsons, Willard H. *Field Guide: Middle Rockies and Yellowstone.* Dubuque, Iowa: Kendall/Hunt Publishing Co., 1978.

Quinn, Ruth. *Weaver of Dreams: The Life and Architecture of Robert C. Reamer.* Gardiner, MT: Leslie & Ruth Quinn, Publishers, 2004.

White, Donald E. et al. "The Geology and Remarkable Thermal Activity of Norris Geyser Basin, YNP, WY." U.S. Geological Survey Professional Paper 1456, 1988.

Whittlesey, Lee H. *Wonderland Nomenclature: A History of the Place Names of Yellowstone National Park.* Helena, MT: Montana Historical Society Press, 1988. Microfiche.

Yellowstone Science. Yellowstone National Park, WY: Yellowstone Center for Resources. Issued periodically.

Yellowstone Today. Yellowstone National Park, WY: Division of Interpretation, National Park Service. Issued quarterly.

GLOSSARY

NOTE: Terms in **boldface** are defined in this glossary. Consult the index for terms not covered here that may be defined in the text.

algae. Aquatic non-vascular plants or plant-like organisms, now included in the Eukarya group.

alum. Potassium aluminum sulfate, a chemical used in medicine to contract blood vessels or tissues.

Archaea. One of the three main groups of organism, distinct from **Eukarya** and **Bacteria**. Archaea are single-celled, and their cells lack nuclei. Their membranes differ from all other organisms.

arsenic sulfide. One of the poisonous compounds of the grayish-white element arsenic.

bacteria. Single-celled microorganisms varying in shape, metabolism, and ability to move.

basalt. A type of volcanic rock or **lava** that is relatively low in **silica**, allowing it, when molten, to flow easily; it is high in iron, which turns it black.

butte. A medium-sized, isolated, flat-topped, and steep-sided hill in an arid region.

calcium carbonate. The chemical compound found in shells and some bones; used as a gastric antacid.

caldera. A large circular or elliptical crater or depression formed by the collapse of a large land area after the emptying of a **magma** chamber in a massive volcanic explosion.

carbon dioxide. An odorless, colorless gas; an excessive amount replacing oxygen in the air can suffocate animals.

cirque. A steep-sided natural amphitheater gouged out by glacial ice on the side of a mountain.

cone-type geyser. A **geyser** that erupts in a steady column of hot water from a narrow vent. The water cools, precipitates **hydrous silicon dioxide**, and forms a cone. Compare with **fountain-type geyser**.

Continental Divide. A highland of North America, separating water that eventually flows into the Pacific Ocean from that which flows into the Gulf of Mexico.

crinoid. A type of ancient ocean plant with a cup-shaped body and a slender stem, related to today's starfish and sea urchins and helpful in dating fossils. Also called a sea lily.

dike. A thin tabular sheet of igneous rock that cuts across preexisting rocks, squeezing into those rocks when molten, then cooling and solidifying below ground. Compare with **sill**.

dome. In geology, an uplifted area, circular in outline. Also called resurgent dome.

drainage divide. The boundary between two areas that contribute water to a stream or lake.

Eukarya. Single- or multi-celled organisms whose cells contain a distinct membrane-bound nucleus.

exchange of function. Underground connection among **geysers** or **hot springs** so that the activity of one affects the behavior of the other. Examples are found at Fountain Paint Pot and Upper Geyser Basin.

exclosure. An area fenced off by botanists to exclude all large browsing animals and then compare the enclosed area with its surroundings.

explosion crater. A feature found in volcanic terrains. A sudden pressure drop causes hot water to flash into steam and blast a hole in Earth's surface.

extremophile. A living being that can live and reproduce in extreme environments, such as very acidic and very hot ones.

fault. A fracture in rock where the two sides have moved past each other.

fissure. A crack in rock along which there is a distinct separation.

fissure ridge. A linear mound built where hot water has risen through a **fissure** and deposited **travertine** along its centerline.

fountain-type geyser. A **geyser** that erupts from a broad pool, usually in a series of bursts. Compare with **cone-type geyser**.

fumarole. A vent from which steam and other gases are emitted; in **hydrothermal areas** they form where there is insufficient water to form a **geyser** or **hot spring**.

geyser. A **hot spring** that throws forth jets of water and steam intermittently.

geyser eggs; geyserite eggs. Small round, oval, or scallop-shaped bits of **travertine** or **geyserite** that accumulate around a **geyser**, either lying loosely in a pool of water or sometimes cemented to the ground.

geyserite. The white or pale gray brittle rock precipitated from the water thrown up by a **geyser** or at the edges of a **hot spring**. Also called **hydrous silicon dioxide**, siliceous sinter, or **silica**.

giardia. A microscopic parasite found in natural waters contaminated by feces from infected humans or animals. Its outer shell protects it and makes it tolerant to chlorine disinfection.

glacial erratic. A boulder carried by a glacier and deposited, often many miles from where the glacier plucked it from the bedrock.

glacial horn. A steep spire- or pyramid-shaped peak formed by glacial erosion in three or more **cirques** surrounding a mountain.

glass. In geology, rock that formed when **magma** cooled too quickly for crystals to form.

gneiss. A **metamorphic rock** having alternating light and dark colored bands.

granite. A coarse-grained **igneous rock** that crystallized at depth from **magma**, containing a large amount of **silica**.

granite-gneiss. A **metamorphic rock** formed from preexisting **granite**.

hoodoo. An often odd-shaped column formed by uneven erosion of horizontally layered rock.

hot spring. A source or pool of water at higher than human body temperature (98°F / 37°C).

hydrogen sulfide. The poisonous gas with the smell of rotten eggs given off by the water in many **hydrothermal areas**.

hydrothermal system or area. An area where very hot water underground, in combination with a system of fractures, creates **hot springs** and related features.

hydrothermal explosion crater. *See* **explosion crater**.

hydrous silicon dioxide. A chemical compound of **silica** and oxygen that contains water; chemical name for **sinter** or **geyserite**.

hyperthermophile. A kind of **extremophile** microorganism that lives in environments above 176°F (80°C).

igneous intrusion. **Igneous rock** that was injected as **magma** into older rock.

igneous rock. Rock that has solidified from **magma**, having cooled either slowly deep within Earth or quickly on Earth's surface.

iron oxide. Several chemical compounds containing iron and oxygen in different proportions that can color rocks shades of yellow, red, or black.

iron sulfide. The compound of iron and sulfur that can color rocks black.

kettle pond. A pond formed in a depression caused by the ground collapsing when a buried block of glacial ice melted. Also called kettle hole.

lava. Molten rock that has risen from below and flowed out on Earth's surface.

limestone. A **sedimentary rock** composed mainly of **calcium carbonate**.

magma. Liquid or molten rock, including any dissolved gases and crystals, found deep within Earth.

meander. The winding, snakelike turning course of a river that flows very slowly over nearly level terrain.

mesa. An isolated flat-topped mountain, usually more extensive than a **butte** but less extensive than a plateau.

metamorphic rock. A type of rock formed from preexisting rock by natural processes such as heat and pressure, without melting the preexisting rock.

moraine. A pile of rock debris carried and then left behind by a melting glacier.

mud pot. A bowl-shaped area where steam rises in bubbles through rock that has been chemically changed into clay.

obsidian. A form of **rhyolite lava**, usually black, that cooled so quickly upon contact with air that crystals did not have time to form.

paint pot. A **mud pot** colored by **iron oxide** and other oxides.

perpetual spouter. A **hot spring** that erupts continuously, as opposed to a **geyser**, whose eruptions occur between periods of quiet.

petrify, petrification. A process whereby wood is turned to stone (fossilized) by the infiltration of water containing **silica** or **calcium carbonate**, which replaces the woody material.

pH. An indication of the acidity or alkalinity of a solution; a value of 7 represents neutrality. Lower numbers show greater acidity and higher numbers show greater alkalinity. The symbol comes from German *Potenz* ("power"), and H, the symbol for hydrogen.

pitchstone. An old name for **obsidian**, so-called because of its resemblance to hardened pitch.

plate tectonics. The widely accepted theory that large slabs (tectonic plates) of Earth's outer layer move about on top of the weaker layer below.

Precambrian. The oldest geologic age for rocks on Earth, from the time Earth was formed some 4.6 billion years ago until 542 million years ago.

rhyolite. A type of volcanic rock or **lava** that is relatively high in **silica** content; it is viscous (like asphalt or molasses), so flows slowly.

sedimentary rock. Rock formed from the weathered products of preexisting rocks that have been transported, deposited, and cemented.

serotinous cone. A type of evergreen cone that opens and releases its seeds only in the intense heat of a fire, ensuring that forests of pines such as lodgepole replace themselves quickly.

shale. A very fine-grained, clay-rich **sedimentary rock** that breaks into thin sheets.

silica. The chemical compound made of oxygen and silicon, the first and second most abundant elements in Earth's crust.

siliceous. Adjectival form of **silica**.

sill. A layer of igneous material that squeezed between and parallel to the layering of preexisting rock while it was molten, and then cooled below the surface. Compare with **dike**.

sinter. *See* **hydrous silicon dioxide**.

snag. Standing, dead, and often limbless trees left after an intense fire or drowned by flooding.

solfatara. An area with many **fumaroles**. The word comes from the first known solfatara near Naples, Italy, where a volcanic crater exhales **hydrogen sulfide**, sulfur dioxide, and steam.

steam explosion. *See* **explosion crater**.

superheated. Existing at a temperature above the boiling point.

talus. A steep slope made of loose rock debris eroded from a cliff, or the rock debris itself. Also called scree.

tephra. Any material, regardless of size, shape, or origin, ejected during an explosive volcanic eruption.

terracette. A semicircular formation of **travertine** built up at the edge of a gradually rising **hot spring** pool, as at Mammoth Hot Springs.

thermal area. *See* **hydrothermal area**.

thermophilic. Thriving in extremely hot water.

till. A mixture of debris of all sizes from clay to boulders, left by glacial ice.

timberline. The upper limit at which fully erect trees grow; the number varies with latitude.

travertine. **Limestone (calcium carbonate)** precipitated from **hot spring** waters.

tree line. Term used by botanists to mean the upper limit of growth for all trees.

tuff. Hardened **tephra** that has fallen to earth after a volcanic explosion. Bottom layers of tuff become welded into dense rock due to heat and pressure.

valley shape. In earth science, U-shapes are created by the scraping and scooping-out action of glacial ice; V-shapes are eroded through rock by rivers.

wapiti. Meaning white rump in the Shawnee language, this has become another word for elk.

Yellowstone hot spot. The center of volcanic activity that has progressed in a northeasterly direction for 17 million years from near where the corner of Oregon and Idaho meets the Nevada border.

INDEX

Page numbers in *italics* indicate pictures; the letter *m* after a page number indicates a map.

I

N

O

X

Y

PICTURE CREDITS

The publisher wishes to thank the following photographers and institutions for the use of illustrations in the fourth edition, which appear courtesy of them:

Linton Brown, p. 98; **Bruce Chase**, p. 233b; **Colorado Historical Society**, pp. 42a (WHJ-32952), 68 (WHJ-503), 141 (WHJ-4351); **Duncan Foley**, p. 238 (© 2006); **Haynes Foundation Collection, Montana Historical Society**, pp. 42b, 55, 71, 157, 187, 208, 275, 288, 326; **Leslie Kilduff**, pp. 11, 33, 52, 58, 60, 77a, 77b, 92a, 93, 95, 99, 100, 142, 181, 217, 228a, 252a, 252b, 259, 260, 261, 264a, 280, 286, 289, 297, 347; **Barbara Lasseter**, p. 106; **Graham Meech**, pp. 56, 92b; **Record Group 79, National Archives and Records Administration, Yellowstone National Park**, pp. 84b, 205, 264b, 300, 319, 320, 322, 325; **U.S. Department of the Interior, National Park Service, Yellowstone National Park**, pp. 37, 64, 136, 163, 170, 212, 282, 327, 328, 329, 338a, 339a, 339b, 339c, 340a, 341a, 342c, 344a, 344b, 349, 350a, 350b, 351; **Courtesy National Park Service, Yellowstone National Park**, pp. 148 (YELL 319), 274b (YELL 343), 281 (YELL 28782-2); **NPS Photo**, pp. 353b, 353c, 354b; **Michael Newcomb**, pp. 85, 94b; **Jens Paape**, pp. 49, 75, 175.

Front cover photo of Old Faithful Geyser, **Don Forsyth**. Frontispiece of Giant Geyser, May 31, 2007, **Pat Snyder**. Back cover photo of Firehole River at Upper Geyser Basin, **Albrecht Hofmann**.

All remaining photos were taken by **Bruno Giletti**, except those on pages 73, 81, 237, 243, 256a, 266a, 268, and 272, which were taken by the author.

The wildflower paintings by **Mary Vaux Walcott** on pages 334, 335, 336, 337, 348, 352, and 353 are published here with the permission of the Smithsonian Institution from Walcott's 1925 four-volume book, *North American Wildflowers*.

Four panoramas, pp. 150–51, 222–23, 278–79, and 298–99, were drawn for *Yellowstone Treasures* by **Nathan Welch**.

Sketches on pp. 177, 232, and 290 were created by **Hermon Carey Bumpus** for his 1930s Yellowstone booklets, "Trailside Notes."

Scanning work was done by **Bengt Dellby**, **Tom Monego**, and **Christy Welch**, and new photos were prepared for the fourth edition with assistance from **William Leidenthal**.

ABOUT THE AUTHOR

Author at Midway Geyser Basin bridge.

Montana native Janet Chapple has been savoring the atmosphere of Yellowstone Park since she was a child, when her father worked at Old Faithful Inn. On her many visits since then, she has combined intensive personal observation with research into the work of park experts, as well as reading widely and attending Yellowstone Institute courses. Her enthusiasm has inspired many others to accompany her on her trips. In connection with her long career as a professional cellist and teacher, Janet edited and helped write a booklet on music practice. She lives in Oakland, California, with her husband, Bruno Giletti, professor emeritus of geological sciences at Brown University. Bruno contributed to most of the geological explanations and drew the original geological diagrams for this guidebook.

Please tell us if you find errors or want to contribute information that should be added to the next edition. The author's e-mail address can be found on the book's companion website, www.yellowstonetreasures.com, where you can also order *Yellowstone Treasures*.

~

There's a place upon this good green earth
Like nowhere else you've ever seen,
Where misty mountains soar above, majestic and serene.
Clear and gentle waters flow, past grazing elk and buffalo
Like a picture from the past, inside a dream.

But sleeping restless deep below the summer sun and winter snow
There lies a secret waiting to be told,
And with a shudder and a rumble wakes,
As pulses race and timber shakes,
Like it did as mighty ages rolled. . . .

From *The Jewel*, © 2007 Ray Doyle (Doyle Well Music BMI). Used with permission.